Children's Safeguards Review

by Roger Kent

for The Scottish Office

SOCIAL WORK SERVICES INSPECTORATE FOR SCOTLAND
1997

social work services INSPECTORATE

Purpose and responsibilities

Our purpose is to work with others to continually improve social work services so that:

- they genuinely meet people's needs; and
- the public has confidence in them.

Corporate member of Plain English Campaign. 27
Committed to clearer communication.

The Social Work Services Inspectorate
James Craig Walk
Edinburgh
EH1 3BA

011 495864 5

Contents

Living away from home in schools, children's homes or foster homes requires the child to be safe - to be in a Safe Haven. Such places should be seen as anchorages. You drop anchor to be secure but you can weigh it and move, or stay as long as you need. You can shelter from a storm or plan a period with a definite purpose. You are protected from adverse influences but other people from the shore will always have access to you to see that you are alright and your ship must be part of the harbour community. We must strive to ensure our Havens are truly safe.

Introduction

In July 1996 I was asked to report to the Minister of State at the Scottish Office on the arrangements for protecting children who are cared for away from home in Scotland. I had to look at the measures taken for the protection of such children and assess whether the safeguards that are in place are the most effective that can realistically be designed to protect them from abuse and other harm.

Having accepted the task I then realised I had some misgivings about the title. There are children who have left their natural parents - their natural home - in circumstances that mean there is no prospect of them growing up there. For them, if all has gone well and the substitute arrangements have worked, but have stopped short of adoption, the place where they now are, be that foster home or in some circumstances children's home, is their home. Another kind of home.

Sir William Utting was asked to conduct a similar Review for children in England and Wales. There are some significant differences between Scotland and England and Wales including the definition of a child, the presence of a Children's Hearing System and Reporters, the legal framework, and the fact that there has been a new Children Act in force south of the border for some years while ours was not fully implemented until April 1st 1997. So where he has had to consider the effects of the Children Act 1989, I have tried to complete my report so that it follows hard on the heels of the full implementation of the Children (Scotland) Act 1995. Although our contexts are different I have kept in close touch with Sir William whose report will be published shortly. I have been fortunate enough to have had the services of Mrs Mary Thomas and Mrs Marion Boyle and the three of us have been accommodated in the Scottish Office premises housing the Social Work Services Group and the Social Work Services Inspectorate. The Scottish Office funded the team and also paid for work I commissioned from Mrs Meg Lindsay at the Centre for Residential Child Care at Jordanhill, Dr Andrew Kendrick at Dundee University, and the National Institute for Social Work. Government financial support also enabled me to ask for discrete pieces of work from two consultants, Jan Burnell of the Centre for Strategy and Communication and Mike Laxton of Phase Three Consultancy, the former of whom was particularly valuable. I am grateful for the resources put at my disposal and also for the hard work put in by those who have helped me.

The methodology I adopted was to meet a number of people, to analyse a number of inspection reports, to invite written evidence and to call for a Literature Review. In the end I, or my small team, met 120 people or groups of people and visited a range of establishments in different parts of Scotland. The Centre for Residential Child Care considered 200 reports from Local Authority Social Work Department and other Inspectors, looking for their relevance to the protection of children in special boarding schools and children's homes; their work will be published shortly. Dundee University's Review of the relevant literature is appended, summarised and is widely used in the main body of the report. I have gathered much information and have been given many views - the interpretation put upon what I have heard is my own. The responsibility for what is said in this report lies with me.

I have been tempted to broaden the scope of what I have been asked to do but I am sure I should in the main confine myself to the comparatively narrow issues of physical and sexual abuse of children and young people who are not with their family. It is quite clear the Government commissioned the two Reviews following the spate of episodes of abuse that have come to light in recent years. Whilst the major and widely reported scandals have, to date, come from England and Wales, it has to be recognised that there are, today, men in prison in Scotland for abusing children in residential care, boarding schools and foster homes - and abusing the trust placed in them when given the privilege to care for other people's children. However, "harm" is clearly within my terms of reference and I have not ignored it.

I was also tempted to widen the remit in order to look at the whole of residential and foster care practice. There has been a plethora of reports in the last decade but still one feels that Social Work is misunderstood - or does not explain itself adequately - and that residential child care is not seen in the positive constructive light it should be with the status that the children deserve. More pride in the job and less apology would make the residential world safer for the children to live in. Pride follows recognition and being valued.

Much of the headline hitting, and headline deserving, activity that led to Ministers calling for an audit of measures to protect children stems from adults telling us about yesterday. 30 year olds are now able to reveal what happened to them 20 years earlier. It has contaminated us all. Some people who have worked in children's homes are now hesitant to admit it. It is now less likely for young people to experience the abuse which is being revealed from the comparatively recent past. In my view the steps taken have significantly improved the protection of children. More openness has made it somewhat easier for children and others to speak up. Equally, complacency is clearly dangerous and the need for vigilance is imperative. The effect on children who are abused is life-long. It is important to note that many of the incidents of abuse, the preponderance by some accounts, are precipitated by other children. This emphasises the need to create a climate in which abuse of any kind is not tolerated. There are still occurrences of abuse in the population this report is concerned with.

There are more than 10,000 children and young people being cared for away from home in Scotland. About half of them are in boarding schools be they special or be they fee paying. Approximately one-quarter are in foster care and slightly less in residential care. There are children in hospital and children in penal establishments. There are a significant number in school hostels and some young people under 18 in the armed forces. Each one is important and each one deserves, and is entitled, to be safe and to feel safe in the company of adults put there to care, nurture, tend or teach him or her. We have a responsibility for vigilance.

This report seeks to set out and discuss the dangers that exist, the action taken in the last decade, the present safeguards, and possible new safeguards and to make recommendations. Whatever changes are recommended and made, we must remember that some essential things cannot be regulated. They include the motivation of Local Authorities and other providers of services, the attitudes of all who work with and care for children and young people, and the supportive involvement of friends and relatives.

I must emphasise that we run some risk of tilting the balance that exists between the innocence of our children and protecting their safety. The abuse of children is abhorrent; they are entitled to the protection of adults and it should be expected. So too are they entitled to loving care. If child protection is the driving force rather than child care we may create a safe climate that is also a sterile climate. I have been saddened to hear of quite recent incidents of physical and sexual abuse. I have also been troubled to find that some carers in homes, schools, or foster homes are now frightened to put an arm around any child.

Roger Kent

CHAPTER 1

Definitions and Descriptions Used in this Report

1.1 "Child"

The UN Convention on the Rights of the Child, ratified by the UK in December 1991, defines "child" as every person under the age of 18.

Scots Law is less consistent about young people aged 16 to 18.

In the eyes of the Social Work (Scotland) Act 1968, anyone under 16 was a "child". In certain circumstances, such as where a child was subject to a supervision requirement, provisions under the Act could be extended to people up to 18 years of age.

The Child Protection Guidelines prepared and followed by Local Authorities often stated that there was no requirement to follow them after the child reached the age of 16.

Schools are normally considered to have some responsibility for pupils aged between 16 and 18, but no distinction is made in the penal system between under 18s and under 21s.

The Children (Scotland) Act 1995, Section 93 defines a "child" as "(i) a child who has not attained the age of 16 years: (ii) a child over 16 who has not attained the age of 18 and in respect of whom a supervision requirement is in force; (iii) a child whose case has been referred to a children's hearing by virtue of section 33 of this Act"

For the purposes of this report a child or a young person living away from home will be someone under the age of 18.

1.2 "Children living away from home"

This includes children living for at least part of the year in:

- Foster homes, as children looked after and accommodated by the Local Authority
- Residential care homes, as children looked after and accommodated by the Local Authority
- Secure accommodation, as children looked after and accommodated by the Local Authority
- Penal Establishments. There are young offenders under the age of 18 and there are some children under 16 in remand centres or young offenders institutions
- Supported accommodation, usually after residential or foster care
- Residential (boarding) schools. This includes not only schools which are registered under the Social Work (Scotland) Act 1968 or the Children (Scotland) Act, but also all schools registered under the Education (Scotland) Act 1980 which are providing residential accommodation (i.e. not only special boarding schools such as Harmeny or Camphill Schools, but also "mainstream" independent boarding schools such as Fettes College or Dollar Academy). Some children in residential schools return home at the weekends, so stay there only from Monday to Thursday nights; five day repeating care is enough to allow them to meet the criterion of "living away from home"

- Hospitals, or other residential accommodation provided by health authorities and trusts
- School hostels provided by local education authorities for children who come from remote areas and attend secondary school too far from their homes for them to be able to return there each evening. Most of the children are able to return home every weekend, so stay there only from Monday to Thursday nights; this is 5 day repeating care, as for some children in residential schools
- the Armed Forces, which recruit young people under the age of 17 for initial training.

There are other circumstances under which children may stay away from home for at the most a number of weeks. These may include school exchanges or holidays abroad, or other activities such as language courses or outward bound training connected with their education. Children may take part in cultural activities on a national or regional basis, such as orchestral or theatrical events. They may compete in sporting tournaments. They may come to Scotland to be away from the troubles in Northern Ireland, or Bosnia. They may go on camps organised by youth groups such as the Scouts or Guides, or the Army Cadets. There is work to be done to ensure the safety of children who are **staying** away from home for reasons like these, but I have not included them because I believe that it is the task of this Review to concern itself primarily with children **living** away from home, as described above.

1.3 Child Abuse

The Joint Steering Group for Child Protection in Scotland[1] says:

> *"Children may be in need of protection where their basic needs are not being met, in a manner appropriate to their stage of development; and* ***they will be at risk*** *through avoidable acts of commission or omission on the part of their parent(s), sibling(s) or other relative(s), or carer (i.e. the person(s) while not a parent who has actual custody of a child)."*

For a set of events or circumstances to qualify as abusive, three elements must be taken into account:

> *"Whether there is demonstrable damage or harm to a child or a prediction of harm to the child;*
>
> *whether the injury/state of the child must have been avoidable through action by parents or carers responsible for that child;*
>
> ***whether the potential harm or future risk is linked to the action or inaction of the parent or other carer.*** *This would also apply where it was not possible to establish the identity of the perpetrator."*

The Joint Steering Group formulated five categories of child abuse, while recognising that there is often overlap between the categories. While they refer to being under the age of 16, they make it clear that *"in certain circumstances, such as children with special needs (mental or physical disability) or children subject to supervision requirements, the upper age limit may be extended to 18."* The categories are:-

1.3.1 Physical Injury

> *"Actual or attempted physical injury to a child under the age of 16 where there is definite knowledge, or reasonable suspicion, that the injury was inflicted or knowingly not prevented."*

1.3.2 Sexual Abuse

> *"Any child below the age of 16 may be deemed to have been sexually abused when any person(s), by design or neglect, exploits the child, directly or indirectly, in any activity intended to lead to the sexual arousal or other forms of gratification of that person or*

1 Child Protection In Scotland - Management Information: Report by a Steering Group (Scottish Office 1992)

any other person(s) including organised networks. This definition holds whether or not there has been genital contact and whether or not the child is said to have initiated the behaviour."

1.3.3 Non-organic Failure to Thrive

"Children who significantly fail to reach normal growth and developmental milestones (i.e. physical growth, weight, motor, social and intellectual development) where physical and genetic reasons have been medically eliminated and a diagnosis of failure to thrive has been established."

1.3.4 Emotional Abuse

"Failure to provide for the child's basic emotional needs such as to have a severe effect on the behaviour and development of the child."

1.3.5 Physical Neglect

"This occurs when a child's essential needs are not met and this is likely to cause impairment to physical health and development. Such needs include food, clothing, cleanliness, shelter and warmth. A lack of appropriate care results in persistent or severe exposure, through negligence, to circumstances which endanger the child."

Lists of indicators of abuse are valuable as reference for those who are wondering whether a child is being abused. They are usually to be found in the Child Protection Guidelines for each area.

1.4 Safety

It is one of Skinner's 8 fundamental principles for underpinning residential child care that "*Young people should feel safe and secure in any residential home or school*", and I would want to be able to apply this to all children living away from home.

It is a sad fact that it is easier to obtain clear definitions of abuse than of safety. Yet an atmosphere of safety is essential to allow children to develop their potential as human beings, quite apart from allowing them to recover from any damage that may have been caused by their past experiences. Children who feel safe are more confident, assured and hopeful, with a positive attitude to life and a feeling of self-possession. They are able to trust others.

The Skinner report put it well:

"The Importance of Feeling Safe"
This principle is a fundamental one. If young people and children do not feel safe and secure then the task of meeting their emotional, developmental and other needs can hardly be begun.

Admission to care - perhaps particularly residential care - is inevitably a lonely and frightening experience. To cope with it young people and children need support and care and they need confidence that they are not at risk of attack or victimisation by other children, staff or visitors. Indeed their needs are so great that they will sometimes even accept abuse if they can also get some comfort. Pre-requisites of good residential child care therefore include provision that homes are staffed and managed in such a way that residents are safe and feel safe. Staff should be carefully selected and supervised so that the likelihood of abuse is minimised... Where appropriate staff should be trained in the physical management of children and young people with physical disabilities to allow them to carry out care routines and programmes in ways which inspire feelings of safety".[2]

There should be an atmosphere without violence, aggression, tension and alienation. Limits are set to what is acceptable behaviour and what is not. You should never do anything in a care setting that you would not do elsewhere.

2 Skinner Angus, for the Social Work Services Inspectorate for Scotland (1993): Another Kind of Home: A Review of Residential Care (Edinburgh, HMSO)

CHAPTER 2

Dangers Faced by Children Living Away from Home

2.1 Introduction

The dangers listed and described in this chapter are the ones which seem to me to be of most importance to children living away from home. I have tried to describe them separately in order to get some kind of clarity about the types of things we are trying to protect children from. Issues such as physical injury, sexual abuse and bullying can all affect young people whether they are living in a fee paying boarding school or a small children's home or indeed, in prison. When protecting children, we have to be ready to think the unthinkable. The "things that couldn't happen here" may do so; the apparently best, most sensitive and caring member of staff may be an abuser; there may be a sub-culture we never would have suspected.

The general public is rightly very concerned about abuse of young people by adults. That is only part of the problem. Abuse of young people by young people needs wider discussion and clearer policies and practices among all who provide care for children and young people living away from home.

We must always remember, however, that we have not really safeguarded children if we have only protected them from one type of abuse in order for them to fall prey to another.

2.2 Physical Injury

We have moved a long way during this century in what we are not prepared to tolerate happening to children. In Scotland the use of the tawse or belt in schools continued until the late 70s. The cane was still being used to discipline children in some Children's Homes and approved schools in the 1960s, although in 1946 the Curtis Committee was writing about caning and birching that "*Whatever there is to be said for this form of punishment in the case of boys with a happy home and full confidence in life, it may, in our opinion, be disastrous for the child with an unhappy background.*[3]" It would now be unthinkable for either of these to be used; the Skinner report says clearly: "*No young person regardless of age should be subjected to any form of physical punishment, or the threat of physical punishment. No young person or child should be hit or smacked.*"

If a foster carer is shown to have smacked a child in care, that may be enough to ensure that they do not foster again. If a member of staff in a residential child care unit hits a child, that may be enough to ruin their career.

There are recent cases in residential care of children's limbs being broken while they are being restrained by staff. There is clear evidence of children striking other children and causing injury but the records are neither kept nor collated in such a way as to establish the quantity or the trends.

2.3 Sexual Abuse

One of the features of recent years has been the growing concern over children and young people being sexually abused when in the public care. Often these cases are brought to light only because ten or more years after leaving care young men and women speak up about what happened to them in the school, the children's unit, or in foster care. The way in which these

3 Curtis, Myra (1946) Report of the Care of Children Committee, (London HMSO)

things emerge leaves a lingering fear that there must be many more cases that we never hear about, where either adults abused as children in care never do tell anybody about it, or where children and young people being abused in care now are suffering in secret. There have been instances involving children living away from home in settings other than "in care".

Children may be abused by parents, relatives or other trusted figures at home, by staff in school, by neighbours, sports coaches or friends' parents, by carers, nurses, Social Workers or teachers, by other children and young people, and, rarely, by strangers. 'Stranger danger' is less important than the general public believes: a recent study[4] of abusers found that only 10% of them were strangers to the child they abused.

Homosexuality and paedophilia are not synonymous. Although some paedophiles may prefer a particular type and age of child, it is often the case that an adult who abuses children below the age of puberty may not care whether they are male or female. The normal adult homosexual male is horrified by the activities of those who abuse children.

Professor Waterhouse told me that in her research with child sexual abusers the men gave the impression that there was a difference for them between social parenting and biological parenting: the abuse of a step-daughter was perceived by perpetrators as not as serious or grave an offence as the abuse of your own daughter. Their sense of boundaries was less clearly defined in social parenting. This has implications for institutional care where there are no biological links, and where she believes there should be more emphasis in training on responsibility to children and how you define the boundaries.

Sexual abuse is secretive. There are no obvious outward signs such as black eyes or broken bones, and even where it is suspected it may be impossible to obtain medical evidence. The child is probably the only witness to the offence, and abusers go to great lengths to ensure that children keep the secret to themselves. If the abuser is in a position of authority and the child has been abused before, it may be very hard for the child to disclose; if they do, they may not be believed. Scots Law requires corroboration in criminal cases where the standard of proof that is applied is "beyond reasonable doubt" and abuse is a very private affair. In a criminal case it may be impossible to prove child sexual abuse without an admission of guilt by the abuser or firm corroborative evidence. Child protection proceedings are governed by civil law and decisions are made on the balance of probabilities.

Sexual abusers often choose to target the most vulnerable children, the natural victims. They may look for children with a need for affection that they can exploit, seeming to offer love while seeking their own gratification. Or children who have been abused before, and who expect little better out of life, believing either that this is how things are, or that this is what they themselves deserve. Or those who, having been abused, know no other way of expressing affection with another person, or getting attention from them. Or children with a disability who are used to adults cleaning them, changing them, generally doing things to them without asking their permission first. Or children who cannot communicate well, and who do not in any case have a clear sense of what is or is not normal behaviour. Or children with low self-esteem, who are unable to believe that there is anybody who might want to protect them from abuse.

These children will often be living away from home, in foster care, residential care, boarding schools and occasionally hospitals. Those who abuse them could be members of staff or people in a position of authority and trust, or could be other children and young people.

Two sets of evidence quoted in "Childhood Matters"[5] suggest that in the general population, one-third of all sexual abusers of children are aged under twenty. There is some evidence[6] that children and young people in care are more at risk of being sexually abused by their peers than by adults. In a recent survey by The Centre for Residential Child Care[7], 66% of units providing residential child care for looked after children in Scotland were caring for young people whom they knew to have been sexually abused, and 33% of the units were caring for young people

4 Waterhouse, L, Dobash, RP & Carnie J, (1994), Child Sexual Abusers, (Edinburgh, Scottish Office Central Research Unit)

5 Williams of Mostyn (1996) Childhood Matters: Report of the National Commission of Inquiry into the Prevention of Child Abuse, (London, the Stationery Office)

6 Spencer JW & Knudsen DD (1992) Out of Home Maltreatment - An Analysis of Risk in Various Settings for Children in *Children and Youth Services Review* Vol. 14 No.6

7 Lindsay, Meg (1997) The Tip of the Iceberg - Sexual Abuse in the Context of Residential Child Care (Glasgow, The Centre for Residential Child Care)

whom they knew to have abused others. In all, 90% of the establishments caring for known abusers were also caring for children known to have been abused. The Church of Scotland's Board of Social Responsibility believes that peer abuse is the most significant risk to children and young people in care.

2.4 Bullying

Valuable work has been done to reduce bullying over the last few years. It has been taken more seriously as a danger to children, and programmes are being instituted in many schools to stop it. The Rector of one fee-paying boarding school told me the incidence of bullying had plummeted following more training and a better approach by senior pupils.

Bullying can be physical, or it can be verbal and emotional. Verbal bullying can be specific to a particular child, or it may take the form of a racist or sexist taunt applied to a particular child. Intimidation does not require actual physical contact.

Children who are living away from home may be at particular risk of bullying unless adults are vigilant. A study of boarding schools in one English County showed that rates of bullying as reported by children varied greatly from school to school.[8] It is most usually the vulnerable children who are picked on by others. This may also be the case for children who attend day school and return to a residential child care unit each evening. If they are being bullied at school and at home they have no place where they can feel safe. Residential care staff have a duty to ensure that they are alert to the possibility of bullying, and that they deal effectively with it. Children and young people who are bored are more likely to bully others, and there is unfortunately a lot of boredom in children's homes. Bullying is one of the main reasons why children run away.

Children are often safer when they are placed closer to their own homes. Children from different cultures may be singled out for bullying. In the 1970s, English children whose parents were based at the Benbecula artillery range were beaten up in the school hostel in Inverness when there were football internationals; a girl was recently given a bad time in a secure unit for being the only child from Tayside; in a Young Offenders Institution in the West, young people from Edinburgh are threatened ; black children may be at risk if they are the only ones in a unit. Cross-cultural placements have their dangers.

Young people in care have given evidence about staff watching but not intervening when one young person was hitting another. They have also reported that there are some members of staff who themselves bully residents.

2.5 Emotional Abuse

It is important always to try and provide the best possible care for children who are looked after away from home. However, professional carers are not able to provide the unconditional love which is available to children in the best families. Staff have lives of their own. They may move on or away, they may marry, have children of their own, be promoted to other jobs. It may seem to children that nothing lasts, not even friendships. Others will be moved away out of the care home into new placements and the child may fear never to see a particular friend again. There can be some mitigation for these problems, but there is no solution.

What must be done, however, is to avoid abusing the child by failing to provide for many of his or her basic emotional needs. As discussed later, we must be careful not to provide a sterile environment without warmth or touch. Young people want and need respect from those who care for them. They also want to be appreciated for the person they are. If they are always being run down and criticised, if they are never allowed to follow their own interests without being made to feel awkward, if they are generally made to feel unwanted, ugly, awful, boring, or a nuisance, how can they grow and develop?

8 Roger Morgan Chief Inspector, Oxfordshire CC (1993) School Life: Pupils' Views On Boarding (London HMSO)

2.6 Restraint

Physical restraint may at times be necessary in residential units. To quote the Skinner report again:

> *"The concept of physical restraint involves securing the child's body so that it is not a danger to himself or to others. Physical restraint may be necessary in dangerous situations where there is serious risk to the child or young person's safety, or the safety of others. It may also be necessary in some situations which seriously threaten the stability of the group and the running of the home - this includes serious damage to property. Powerful and threatening young people can push other children into highly disruptive behaviour and should not be allowed to do so."*

Young Scots in care talk of restraint being used in circumstances that they do not consider to be as serious as this, and in ways that seem to them to be dangerous.

Restraint is a difficult and emotive topic. There are concerns about the methods of restraint used, and experts seem unable to agree as to what are the most effective and least damaging. It is agreed that training is essential, yet there are still staff in residential child care who have not yet been trained; it is also agreed that staff need to have their training refreshed every year, or their skills will deteriorate.

Although the Skinner Report recommended that a working group should produce Guidance on sanctions and control, nothing has yet emerged, and until it does Local Authorities are making the best decisions they can in the circumstances. This leads to various different methods of restraint being used, amid arguments about the merits and demerits of each. I was impressed by the document on Care and Control in Residential Child Care produced by the former Lothian Region, because it seemed to be essentially practical, it concentrated on avoiding and defusing violent situations while recognising that restraint may be needed, and it emphasised the importance of training and of keeping proper records.

At a recent international conference four young people in care were chosen by others to state their wish to improve the quality of residential care; one girl said that she wished never again to see anyone being restrained. Young people in residential care have told me they feel they are physically at risk from the way in which the adults caring for them use restraint. They also said they find it disturbing to see others being restrained. Carpet burns were thought of as fairly commonplace, but examples were also quoted of more serious harm: broken noses or limbs.

Young people suspect that advantage may be taken of their helplessness when they are being restrained, so that they may be sexually harassed. They feel very exposed. This is particularly difficult for children who have in the past been sexually abused, for whom the restraint may stir up appalling memories.

Why do we need so much restraint in children's homes? We do not train foster carers in it because they usually do not see the need for it. It may be that children in foster care are younger, or easier to care for. Or it may be that there is something about group living that encourages emotions to spiral out of control. We do know that violence to staff is a major issue. The "powerful and threatening young people" to whom Skinner refers can cause real injuries, and staff are sometimes quite frightened. However, a balance should be struck between the protection of staff and the safeguarding of young people. Safeguarding must be the predominant consideration.

Young people also may fear the violence of other residents, and recognise the need for physical intervention by staff to protect them; without it, they might feel very unsafe. Restraint may also be needed to stop a child running away if by so doing they will put themselves at serious risk. The difficulty with physical restraint is getting the balance between the abusive use of it, and the negligent failure to use it in circumstances which demand it. This is all the more reason why Scottish Office Guidance should be in place.

2.7 Exclusion from School

The Skinner report was very clear on the issue of education:

> *"Young people and children should be actively encouraged in all aspects of their education, vocational training or employment and offered career guidance. Their individual educational needs should be identified and met."*

The education of children in residential child care is still not being taken seriously enough. Some units work hard with the children and the schools to ensure that they attend regularly, but far too many refuse to go to school, or are excluded.

Children who do not attend school are at risk of several types of harm. There is firstly the damage that is done to their future because they are not receiving proper education; this can be of particular importance to a child who has been in care and may have to go into the world without family support. There is the question of what the child is doing during school hours: children who are excluded from or avoiding school may be involved in socially unacceptable, even criminal, activities. There is also the effect on the residential care unit of children not attending school: valuable staff time will have to be used to support the non-attenders during the day, and it is often found that those who do not have a structured day expect to be awake and active until quite late at night.

2.8 Racial Issues

Racist remarks about residents must never be permitted by staff.

Sometimes children who are seen to be different are picked on. Just as the only Catholic may be given a bad time in a group of Protestants, the only black or Asian child in a children's unit can be made very unhappy by the other residents. Therefore, although in some ways things are easier for children from ethnic minorities in Scotland than in England, for they do not appear to be disproportionately represented in care here, the few who are in care are less likely to find safety in numbers.

Adults may believe that the best thing to do is to treat all children from ethnic minorities just like the white children, without realising that there are customs which should be considered, and given a place in the home. Staff and managers need to find out whether a particular child needs a special diet, a place that can be a focus for prayer, help with a hairstyle, pictures, books and music, or anything else that reinforces their sense of self. Staff should enlist the help of a local cultural, social or religious group that can give them increased understanding. It is hard for most children to have to live away from home; it is particularly hard for a child to fit in when so many things express a completely different culture.

Where a child's background is mixed-race, the issues are more complex and there is a risk that staff may make judgements about the importance of the child's heritage without noting what matters most to the child.

2.9 Drugs and Alcohol

Children and young people may have a drug habit when they come into care, or they may develop one while in care. It has been suggested in oral evidence that a young person coming into an adolescent unit for the first time will feel very isolated to begin with; if they see that the quickest way to make friends is through copying the drug taking of more settled residents, this will be a tempting option.

Because drug-taking is an illegal activity, it allows the exciting feeling of opposing authority, of having a daring lifestyle rather than a nondescript one. It offers an escape for a time from a difficult and unrewarding life.

It puts young people at risk from contact with dealers who operate outwith the law, and possibly from harmful effects from the drugs. They may be a danger to others around them while they are under the influence of drugs - as they might be were they high on alcohol. They may need to steal, or to prostitute themselves, in order to pay for drugs. If they inject, they risk serious infection.

Alcohol is a more socially acceptable drug that is used every week by 27% of all 15-year-olds in Scotland. Only two-fifths of Scottish secondary school pupils aged 12 - 15 told a recent survey that they never drink it.[9] It makes under-age drinkers feel grown-up, and they boast of hangovers as older people do. It is a major cause of unwanted teen-age pregnancies, it leads to violence and other forms of crime. It is a factor in most personal crimes including child abuse, and including abuse of children living away from home.

Young people need information about the effects of alcohol, and to learn how to use it safely. It is difficult to teach safe social drinking in a residential unit, but at the least staff should model appropriate behaviour: it is not good enough to tell children that they should not drink, and then to come in boasting about the size of your hangover.

2.10 Exploitation

In some places there are people who hang around children's homes, hoping to make use of the young people in some way. These may include drug pushers, who would like either to sell their product to the children, or to use them also in pushing. They may include pimps, who are hoping that the young women and men may be unprotected enough to be used as prostitutes, earning good money for the pimp. There may be others who wish to involve the young people in apparently simpler forms of criminal activity, such as theft or housebreaking. Some may just see the young people as possible sexual partners for themselves.

Residential care staff often have to be permanently on the watch for these exploitative figures, and some otherwise normal-looking buildings have had to have lights installed so that at night it is safe for the young residents to come back to the place where they live.

2.11 Running Away

> *"Young people and children may run away from a home for different reasons. They are less likely to run from a home when they feel safe and secure."*[10]

The Skinner report suggested that the causes of a child's absconding should be discovered not only by looking at the behaviour and emotional state of the child, but also at whether there were deficiencies of any sort in the establishment in which the child is placed. This attitude is supported by recent research: *"In particular there needs to be awareness that frequent running away by several young people from a single home may indicate abuse or other failings in the management or practice in the Home"* [11].

Most children who run away from children's homes have previously run away from their own homes, but the frequency increases when they are taken into care. If staff know that this is how particular children handle their problems, it may be important to tackle that by talking about it directly with them when they come into care, to find out why they need to run away. They may be able to help them find another way to handle problems. They can certainly explain that their carers are concerned for them, and point out some of the dangers involved in running away.

Children who run away can put themselves in a variety of dangers. They are subjected to the rigours of the Scottish climate, often in winter. They are likely to eat badly, to find it hard to keep clean, and to become ill. They may spend time with people who will lead them astray, or exploit them in some way. They may have their possessions stolen, be beaten up or sexually abused. They may seek to support themselves, or to provide themselves with a roof over their heads, through crime or prostitution. They may turn to alcohol or drugs for comfort. Their feelings about themselves and about their life will lurch further downhill.

9 Goddard, Eileen (1996) Teenage Drinking in 1994 (London, HMSO)

10 Skinner 3.8.28

11 Payne, M (1995) Understanding Going Missing - Issues for Social Work and Social Services, (British Journal of Social Work, Vol. 25 No. 3

They may find it very hard to bring themselves to return to the place they left, even if the place they are now in is appalling.

2.12 Self Harm

Self harm and self mutilation are sometimes dismissed as "attention-seeking behaviour", which must apparently be ignored once any physical wounds have been treated. Yet self harm is an extreme form of response to a situation, and should always be taken seriously. Adults who cut themselves when they were children may carry all their lives the wounds they made on their arms or stomach.

The reasons why a child is attacking him- or her-self should always be sought and wherever possible remedial action should be taken. The anti-bullying programme in the Young Offenders Institution/Remand Centre wing of Cardiff prison caused serious attempts of suicide to fall from 23 attempts in 1992 to 8 attempts in 1994, and there was an 80% reduction in acts of self harm[12]. If the reasons for the suicide attempts or the self harm had simply been attention-seeking, these reductions would not have occurred.

Some self harm may be a desperate bid for attention. If children need attention and care so much that they are prepared to seek it in such a damaging way, staff should find ways of giving it, and then of gradually helping them to learn more acceptable ways of gaining attention.

2.13 Prostitution

Little research has been done in Scotland into the involvement of children in care in prostitution, although some English studies have recently shown under-16s of both sexes going out from residential care units to work as prostitutes. Young people who have a low self-image, who have been sexually abused and who believe that what someone else does to their body does not matter, are more likely to do this than others, particularly if their parents have put them forward for the use of other men. It may depend on the ethos among the children and young people within a home, but it seems that the same mechanism applies in relation to prostitution as to drugs: a lonely and isolated young person who is new to a unit may choose to follow the activities of the young leaders there.

Young people in care can get paper rounds or Saturday jobs, but if they need more money to pay for a drug habit, or finance themselves when they run away, prostitution may appear superficially to be an easy option. Risks to them run from HIV through all the sexually transmitted diseases, and include physical violence from partners or from pimps. They are opened up to adult situations and adult emotions before they have developed enough skills to deal with them, and when they are still having to deal with many other emotional problems. They are likely to be the ones to come into trouble with the law, not the adults who are knowingly having sex with minors.

It can be extremely difficult for residential staff to deal with a problem such as prostitution when it has started before the young person came into care, and may indeed be the reason for their arrival. Skilled and proactive help is needed for this small group of young people, and specialist advice and consultancy should be made available.

2.14 Poor Practice in Care Establishments

Many of the most vulnerable young Scots are being cared for in residential child care units. For some the system works well, and they are kept safe while they are given a chance to get on their feet in preparation for adult life or for returning to their families. The experience that others have is less positive, and it may be caused by bad practice.

Some line managers express despondency about residential child care, and some care staff seem to lack pride in the job they do. This springs in part from the bad publicity that the service has

12 Tattam D (1995) Bullying in Prisons, (Young Minds Newsletter, Issue 22pp 18-19)

received, but it is counter-productive. If you regard something as by its nature second-rate, it will become so. There will be no motivation for those who manage it, work in it or live in it to improve it. We fight in the right way for the things we believe in, so that they may become even better. Commitment to residential care and belief in it is crucial to successful management. Any body - including any Local Authority - which does not believe in its value should not be providing it.

Bad practice within units is shown by such things as a stressful atmosphere, and a lack of friendliness and openness between staff and residents. Bullying, threatening behaviour and verbal abuse may be tolerated. The emphasis is on what children and staff are doing wrong, not on what they are doing right. Staff may not spend time in a positive way with residents, who are left alone for much of the time. The residents are bored, and disaffected. There is no clarity of purpose. Nobody really sees the point in being there, except that there was nowhere else to go. There may be plans for each child, but nobody really believes in them. It is hard to believe in a service when there is no body of knowledge, no skill, no effectiveness.

Units change over time. Staff who were previously able and capable can be so adversely affected by low morale, depression, exhaustion or burn-out that they cease caring properly for children. They may feel that they are having no support in caring for extremely difficult young people, that their career is completely stuck, and that nobody respects what they do. Equally the culture, care and morale of a depressed Home can be turned around. With good leadership, empowered staff and strong engagement with the children, a Home in great difficulties can still become a great Home and a good place to live and work.

We should not tolerate within residential child care any Home where the ethos permits children to be out until 3a.m., where they expect to be able to climb out of the window if staff watch the doors, where they involve themselves in burglary and prostitution. Under such circumstances it would be better to close down the unit, on the basis that it has gone too far. Children have rights, but those rights include the right to be protected, and there are times when adults have to be able to take firm and decisive action in order to do that. The way that the English and Welsh Children Act has been interpreted has meant that in some cases the duty of caring staff to protect children has been made secondary to the children's wishes. I would not go so far as to echo in its entirety - although I support much of it - the view of a journalist who recently said:

> *"This evasion of adult duty reflects a muddle over the status of children. Instead of getting adults to discharge their duties towards children properly - by adequately training all residential care workers for example - the Government empower children through the Children Act to resist that adult world through children's rights. But rights belong to adults. Children have needs. Children's rights provide adults with an excuse to move away yet further from proper standards of parenting and care".13*

Children do have rights - but we must remember that they are young, and may often want the wrong things, and that the right to be protected from harm and danger is the premier right. They have to know where the walls are.

As the Skinner report said, *"Physical and emotional security are the basis for healthy growth and development and residential care must provide this before anything else can be achieved"*. Children need continuity of care in an environment which is predictable and consistent, where the staff work well as a team for the good of the residents, and have in general good relationships with one another and with the young people. They genuinely like young people and feel personally involved and responsible. Children like and respect them, and consider their approval important. There is clarity of purpose.

Rules and procedures for the running of establishments are valuable in the right context, but if the professional ethos is not as it should be rules and procedures will rarely help and may become counter-productive. Rules and procedures can be used by defensive agencies to protect their good name at the expense of the child, and this should never be allowed to happen. They must always remember that their primary objective is to care for the child.

13 Melanie Phillips, the Observer 16 March 1997

2.15 Poor Practice by Field Staff

The professional ethos is essential to the practice of Social Work, and what has been said above about rules and procedures for establishments bears repeating in this context also. It is important to be clear about how often a child should be visited by a Field Social Worker, because many children and young people are not being seen often enough, particularly if the Social Worker believes that their placement is secure. Frequent visits are not likely to be helpful to the child unless the Social Worker is engaged with him or her, and able to listen as well as talk. It may initially be difficult for the Field Social Worker to structure a visit if it has no purpose other than to see the child. It is, however, a very positive message for the child if the only purpose is to see him or her.

Visits might be abandoned on the grounds either that the home or school was too far away from the office base, or that the key worker at the unit would undertake the work of the child's Social Worker. Some Social Workers do not engage sufficiently in face to face work, playing down or neglecting this area of their skills. Reviews are too frequently cancelled, sending a message to the child that they are of little importance to their Social Worker, or to the Department.

2.16 Misuse of Foster Carers

Foster carers are often called upon to care for very difficult children, sometimes with inadequate knowledge about them. If children have been seriously damaged sexually, physically or emotionally by their parents, they may expect their substitute parents to behave in the same way towards them. This can cause them to act in bizarre ways which may seem impossible to handle. They may trash their rooms, refuse to be touched, scream if offered ice-cream, act in a sexually provocative manner, shock the neighbours with their vocabulary, defecate in the corner, or simply sit without moving or reacting to anything. Sometimes they may challenge the continued existence of the foster family as a group.

It goes without saying that foster carers must have been carefully vetted. They need to be carefully chosen for a particular child because they have the strengths and skills to cope with him or her. They need to have been given the quality of training which will allow them to find ways round apparently impossible obstacles. They must know as much as possible about the child, so that they can more easily face up to the problems which cause the behaviour, and offer help. They must be supported by their own Social Worker, and by the Social Worker for the child, with other professionals involved as necessary.

Too many foster carers say that they are being asked to care for children:

- in an age range that they do not find congenial
- without proper Social Work support
- without being listened to for their knowledge about the child
- with inadequate information
- without support from other therapists, either because they are not called in or because therapists do not understand the importance of working with the foster carers
- without help in interactions with difficult parents
- for too long after they have said they have had enough.

In these circumstances, there is a risk that the foster carers will reject the child, that they will resign and be lost as a resource, that their family will start to disintegrate, or that stress will cause one of them to abuse the child being fostered.

According to Professor Triseliotis, only 25% of foster carers continue fostering for more than 10 years. Some leave because of changes in their own lives, but many leave because they are tired and disillusioned. There is a risk that the resource may trickle away if not properly supported.

2.17 Thinking SCRO Checks are Enough

It is important to safeguard children by ensuring that those who have relevant convictions do not work in residential child care. It is currently possible for Local Authorities and certain other bodies to check with the Scottish Criminal Records Office (SCRO) to discover whether particular individuals have criminal records which show them to be unsuitable to work unsupervised with children. SCRO checks are very valuable, but they have limitations. They show the **convictions** that people have, but only a small proportion of those who actually come to the attention of the police for sexual offences are eventually convicted. The abusers who have been caught have often abused many children previously. Many adults working with children and offending against them never come to the attention of their employers; even if they do, they may still not be reported to the police. Offences committed abroad are unlikely to be uncovered, nor are some committed in the Armed Forces.

It must be remembered that Frank Beck, the abusers in North Wales, Peter Harley of Dumfries and many others had no criminal convictions when appointed to their responsible posts in residential child care. If too much reliance is placed on SCRO checks, other important barriers may not be put in place. There is real risk that employers may derive a false sense of security if they do not understand there is much more to do than looking for convictions.

2.18 Being Lost by the System

The Bridge Child Care Consultancy Report into Gloucestershire Social Services Department's records following the West case showed that between 1970 and 1994 they had lost track of many young people who had been in care. In checking almost 3,000 files, the Consultancy found that the records on nearly 400 young people were missing, and that the whereabouts of 97 young people were not recorded, or were simply recorded as 'unknown' when they left care. There was a lack of detailed information on individual files, making it hard to understand why young people ran away or went missing. The Bridge managed to find most of the missing people but at the end of the study four young women had still not been traced.[14]

Ordinary families may lose their children: they may run away just as children in care run away. It is estimated that approximately 100,000 children and young people go missing in the UK every year.[15] However, we owe it to the children who are looked after by Local Authorities on behalf of us all to ensure that we do not lose them. They have to know that somebody cares what happens to them. The concern in Gloucestershire was that more young people might have fallen victim to the Wests. There are many, lesser, dangers which lie in wait for those who go missing. Children in England can run away but go to a refuge which is safer than the streets.

2.19 Internet

All boarding schools have computers and so do most Children's Homes. Children living away from home have access to computers, frequently without supervision. Some of the material accessible through the Internet is outrageous in the extreme and children should not be exposed to it any more than they should be exposed to pornographic or extremely violent videos and magazines. There are "lock-out" arrangements to prevent access to inappropriate files but they are of no use unless people know how to use them. Being separated from your parents should not mean that adults responsible for your care try any less hard to protect you.

14 Community Care 14 - 20 November 1996

15 Abrahams, C. And Mungall, R. (1992) Runaways: Exploding The Myth, (London, NCH.)
Payne, M. (1995) Understanding Going Missing - Issues For Social Work And Social Services, (British Journal of Social Work, Vol 25 no 3.)

2.20 Not Enough to Do

The time of children in boarding schools tends to be structured, with activities filling most of the week and little spare time. In contrast a few young secondary school children in Local Authority school hostels have no staff in charge of their activities and little planned for them at weekends when they cannot go home. The latter are far more at risk than the former. Children who have nothing specific to do, and no caring, interested adults around, are more likely to drift into the wrong activities with the wrong people out of sheer boredom.

It is neither kind nor sensible to offer little structured activity to children living away from home. Children need the disciplined school week, the activities after school and at weekends, so that their free time is precious and well spent. Research by the NSPCC showed that children were more likely to bully others when they were bored. Children and young people who are sitting about in residential units with nothing to do are more likely to erupt into destructive emotions than those who are interested and involved in something positive.

As the Skinner report says:

> *"Staff must be able to provide some structure to the activities of the weekends and holidays. If resources do not allow them to do this then the growth of boredom, frustration and anger amongst the young people and children should come as no surprise."*

2.21 Very Sterile Care Climate

A positive result of heightened awareness of the dangers of sexual abuse for looked after children, and of the large numbers who have suffered abuse at some time in their lives, has been that agencies and their staff have become more careful about the ways in which they use touch, and handle issues of affection, sex and sexuality. Children and young people can feel safer because their needs for some distance are recognised. There is a negative side to this, however, if staff become so wary of touch and of emotion, and so defensive about them, that they create a sterile care climate.

Young people who have been abused need to learn that there is good touch as well as bad touch, and that they can relax with the former, knowing that they are safe from the latter. If all touch is taboo, they will not learn the difference.

Some schools or child care agencies are so aware of the danger of malicious allegations, or of allegations arising from misunderstandings, that they deny children the physical and emotional support they need for this reason too.

When bad news comes from home, or there has been an off day at school, or a bout of depression has followed influenza, staff must be able to offer appropriate comfort. There must also be a place for the spontaneous expression of joy and delight. The key to providing this safely lies in staff knowledge and understanding of the resident, in staff support of one another, and in the open use in the unit of 'safe caring' practices.

We cannot replace in a residential unit or school the same warmth and love which should be found in families. However it is essential that we provide the necessary warmth, affection and comfort for children's healthy development if we are not further to damage emotionally children and young people who have usually had a raw deal from life.

2.22 Wrong Placement

During this Review I was concerned by examples of older teenagers having to share a room with quite young children. I was concerned that Homes designed for 10 children are from time to time having to put up extra beds in order to be able to care for 12. I was concerned by what is called "hot-bedding", when for example a child who goes home for the weekend may have their bed and the room containing their personal belongings occupied while they are away.

16 Burgner, Tom (1996) Moving Forward: Review of the Regulation and Inspection of Social Services (London, HMSO)

17 The Centre for Residential Child Care (1995) Checklist Of Information To Be Obtained When Placing Children In Out Of Authority Residential Establishments In Scotland (Glasgow, The Centre for Residential Child Care)

There must be vacancies available, and therefore some degree of choice, when children need a care placement, or they may be wrongly placed, or left in a placement long after it has ceased to be useful for them. Statistics for 1995 show an occupancy rate for children's homes of 94%, leaving little lee-way for choice. Tom Burgner recommended a national data base for vacancies[16]. The Centre for Residential Child Care keeps such a data base for Scotland, but Social Workers seldom consult it before they place a child. The Centre also publishes a booklet to help Social Workers to know what to look for in choosing a placement for a child, but finds it is little used[17]. Oral evidence suggests that they are often so desperate to find a place - any place - that they are unable or unwilling to check whether the unit which has a vacancy will meet the child's needs.

As has been shown, a significant proportion of residential care units have placed in them both children who have been abused, and children who abuse others. Abusers are more likely to target vulnerable children with low self-esteem, and the abused are at risk because of this. Vulnerable young people have to live with fear in the unit, when they should be able to feel secure and safe. Staff have to spend too much time trying to ensure the safety of all their charges rather than on positive activities.

It is interesting to note that the English and Welsh Guidance for the 1989 Act says "*admissions should take careful account of the suitability of the Home and its current staff and residents, to the needs of the child to be placed. For example it would be inappropriate to place a sexually abused child in a Home accommodating children who are themselves abusers*". Sadly this is an unrealistic aspiration: it would currently be impossible to ensure that sexually abused children were always placed away from young abusers; even were enough placements available, we would not necessarily know the full history of all children when they come into the establishment, and some are, of course, both abusers and abused.

Foster care places are even harder to obtain, and increasing numbers of children under 12 are being placed in children's homes, although the Skinner report strongly recommended that this should only happen in exceptional circumstances[18].

Children are more at risk from foster carers if they remain with them after the carers have asked that they should move on. The National Foster Care Association has told me that there is evidence that under these circumstances they are more likely to be physically, or even sexually, abused.

2.23 Multiple Placements

> "... *stability and continuity are not only essential for good care but they are the necessary conditions for a child to grow up well*"[19]

Research has highlighted the disruption to children and young people caused by multiple placements and changes in educational provision.[20] A recent study by Barnardo's of 145 children placed in their Scottish projects showed that they averaged 3.7 moves before reaching the current project, while 31 had experienced more than 5 moves, and one child of primary school age had moved 40 times.[21] It is difficult and disruptive for children to leave their own homes and come into care, and most of them feel rejected. The problem is compounded for them when they perceive that they are rejected again by foster carers or professional carers.

Most moves made by children from one placement to another are part of a positive plan for their care. Others arise from a breakdown or problem with the placement. Sometimes children who are not causing any difficulties are moved from placements where they are happy; this is most likely to happen if one of their peers abuses them, and the abuser is seen as being 'hard to place'; some children may not speak about abuse for fear of being moved. There may be a need for a co-ordinator or arbitrator who is not involved directly as a Social Worker for either child, and can make detached decisions.

Some children may be difficult to care for, but if they are we do them no service by letting them

18 Skinner Angus (1993) op. cit.
19 Kahan, B. (1994) Growing Up In Groups, (London, HMSO)
20 Several studies quoted in Literature Review
21 Community Care 12-18 December 1996

believe that they and their problems are too hard to handle. That gives them a sense of being out of control. They may feel they have a destructive power which they can exploit, and suffer for, elsewhere. Any failed placement requires calm and clear thinking, and a better assessment of the child to ensure that as far as possible this does not happen again.

Although a fostering placement will be the preferred choice for most children and young people, some will require and benefit from a placement in a residential unit, and for them it will be the placement of choice. The recognition of this fact in appropriate circumstances helps to avoid repeated failures in fostering for those concerned.

When children feel safe, happy and well cared for, they do not want to leave, unless perhaps to return to their families.

2.24 Not Healing the Damage

Many children come into care because of the severe damage that has been caused to them in their families or in the community. For some it may be enough to be in a safe place, with love and care to allow them time to heal. The foster carers or the residential care workers may have the skills to help them to heal. Others need some kind of therapy, yet often this is not being offered to them, sometimes because nobody has thought to do so, sometimes because there is nobody available with the relevant skills, or because the financial cost would be too high for the agency's budget. Some may be inappropriately placed in a unit which is unable to do more than offer them a roof over their heads and food.

Some children recover well from sexual, physical or emotional abuse. Others may have their future life critically harmed by it, and may find it difficult to make healthy relationships or to deal with a normal life. They may later have to spend time receiving treatment for mental illnesses. A few will themselves become abusers.

It is clear from the work done by, for example, the Halt Project that young sexual abusers can, if treated before they are adult, learn different ways of behaving. It is also clear that young abusers who are not stopped may become more dependent on their abuse, and increasingly dangerous to children as they become older. It is generally agreed that it is much harder to stop the sexually abusive behaviour of adults than that of children.

There is a need for external professional oversight of care therapies and practices. Some, such as that operated under Frank Beck, bear little resemblance to the needs of individual children. Others might be appropriate in a given situation, but the staff are not competent to implement them. There are theories, such as Therapeutic Crisis Intervention (TCI), CALM or Control and Restraint General Services for controlling situations, which start out well, in which the staff are trained, but the practice of which may deteriorate over time. External managers must ensure that practice is always suitable for the task and that staff training is updated and reinforced when necessary.

When children are in care, we have the time to heal their hurts. We must ensure that enough staff and foster carers have the necessary skills, and that therapeutic help for children with deep-seated problems can be obtained when it will be most effective.

2.25 Recruiting Inadequate Staff

It is just as essential to try to avoid recruiting the slipshod carer as it is to try to avoid recruiting the possible abuser. Slipshod carers are the people for whom residential child care is just a job, and who will never really involve themselves closely with the young people; they may not even like them. They will do the minimum to get by on each shift, and are often happier interacting with other staff in the office than engaging with the residents.

They may not see the point in being clear about practice within the unit, and about safe caring. They are unlikely to notice when a colleague, or a child, is behaving slightly oddly. They will attend training, but it will make no difference to what they do day by day. The children will lack respect for them, and have no motivation to behave well for them, so they may have to use sanctions such as restraint more than their colleagues do. They may have a negative effect on the whole atmosphere of the establishment.

2.26 Compounding disadvantage

We have to be sure that by taking a child into care we are improving that person's lot. If there is real physical danger at home then almost any placement is safer, but we have a duty to provide care of the highest standard possible, striving to help the child overcome any disadvantage; we should expect the young person to be well equipped for the future when leaving care. It is a fact that we may start with damaged material - all the more reason to try harder. It is a fact that children who have been in care are over-represented in the ranks of the homeless, those with poor school achievement, those in prison and those who grow to be dependent on welfare. These are harmful consequences of being in care which we must do all in our power to eliminate. The work of carers is so important they should be seen as undertaking one of the most valuable tasks in society.

2.27 Insurance Companies

There have recently been increasing numbers of claims for compensation by adults who as children were abused in care. Typically, Local Authorities are covered by insurance companies, to which they turn when such claims are justified and must be met. This compensation could pay for the treatment which some young adults need to help them deal with lasting trauma. However, insurance companies have attempted in some parts of the United Kingdom to dictate the responses of Local Authorities to allegations and to complaints. In one area for example, the insurance company forbade the Authority to give young people access to their records; it is suspected that they also wanted to stop publication of a report on the abuse, and to suppress information in order to avoid claims for compensation.

This is a clear case of financial considerations causing damage to children. Anything which makes it harder for children to speak out must be a danger to them and the law should be altered to reduce the power of the insurance companies.

2.28 Outdoor Pursuits

Children who participate in contact sports, such as football or rugby, or who go rock climbing, hill walking or cycling put themselves at some risk of injury, even of death. There are many important issues involved, but these are more than adequately dealt with by the Scottish Sports Council and the governing bodies of the different sports. I do not consider it to be appropriate for this Review to duplicate their work, but I would expect adults who supervise sport and outdoor pursuits to be properly trained and to follow the guidelines for the activity concerned.

2.29 Domestic Accidents

Every home has its hazards - stair rods, bars of soap, faulty irons - and it is the task of the adult to protect the child from them until they are of an age to learn to protect themselves. Children must, however, be helped to grow up, and to learn to do safely for themselves tasks which have an element of danger attached. The boiling kettle may serve as an example of this because it is essential for children to learn once they are old enough how to make a hot drink without scalding themselves; adults who care about them do not keep them away from kettles but teach them how to use them safely.

It is part of caring to prepare children for life on their own once they leave the parental or foster home, or the residential unit or school.

2.30 Trips Abroad

Trips abroad for groups of young people have been organised by schools or youth organisations for many years, and many have built up a body of good practice about them. Usually parents are able to see their children leave home without too much concern for their safety. Children often stay on an exchange basis with families, travelling to the foreign country in groups. They travel together for holidays. The children are usually accompanied by teachers or team leaders, and sometimes by the teachers' or team leaders' husbands and wives and perhaps a parent or two. If the group is from a state or other well run school, parents waiting at home can be sure that the teachers have been properly chosen and vetted, and that police checks for convictions have been made. They may have this assurance about team leaders. They are unlikely to have it about the teachers' husbands and wives, nor about the accompanying parents. The increase in travel options may make exchanges more popular but there is a great deal that is hit and miss. If it is an exchange, neither the Scottish parents nor the host families abroad are likely to have been checked and vetted.

The murder of an English child on a school trip to France in 1996 must have brought many parents face to face with their worst fears. However, there are in most group arrangements for children circumstances which protect them: they are usually not highly vulnerable children; they keep in contact with their parents; they have the protection of the adults in the group; they have the protection of their friends.

CHAPTER 3

The Background

3.1 The background to this report is an appalling catalogue of offences against children that has resulted in a large number of inquiries, a great deal of publicity and a lot of harm. Since 1990 England has seen the pin-down régime in Staffordshire, the abuse in Leicestershire and the unfolding of events in Hackney, Islington, Cheshire, Liverpool and elsewhere. In Wales, staff in Children's Homes have gone to prison in both the north and the south.

In Scotland we have to face up to the fact that, while perhaps we find smaller numbers and less anxiety about organised abuse, we have since 1990 seen a houseparent in an Edinburgh special boarding school, a nurse in a Glasgow children's hospital, a Lothian residential worker, two foster carers in Tayside, a residential worker in Perth, an officer in charge in Dumfries, another in Strathclyde, and a teacher from a special boarding school in the old Highland region go to prison for abusing children in their care. Former residential care staff are currently awaiting trial in Edinburgh.

Many of the offences were committed several years before, but not all. We have seen in England and Wales large numbers of adults come forward telling of abuse in the 70s, and we in Scotland have the same experience but not yet to the same degree. We have not much experience of young people telling of things that happened last week, although I have reason to believe that if we had a Scottish Consultancy Index that recorded the names of employees, volunteers or foster carers who had been dismissed, resigned, moved to other work or left in circumstances which suggested the welfare of children might have been put at risk, it would have received about 50 names in the last three years. This would have covered risk of both sexual and physical abuse. We can not be confident that if we are being told little this is because little is amiss. Abuse brings emotional upset as well as physical pain and it is not easy for someone to disclose or to pick someone to disclose to. Sadly the pattern with large scale abuse is for one person to say something and for the police then to interview lots of others who were in the same place at a similar time and to uncover more. On the other side of the coin so much is now surfacing from the past that there is fear that compensation may attract people to exaggerate or invent.

3.2 It would seem that the larger size of the older establishments and the fact that staff lived in contributed to a lot of the problem. For reasons other than protection of children both these features have decreased. We have largely broken away from the old 100-strong approved school and staff no longer want to live in. Although the number of children looked after has fallen in recent years and the number in residential care has fallen even more dramatically, the children involved present more challenging behaviour and more serious problems. Looking after them presents an ever-growing challenge for both foster carers and residential workers.

Efforts have been made to increase the number of foster placements and we have consciously striven to reduce the overall number of children in care. It is highly likely that we have reached a plateau with foster placements and I do not expect the number available to increase. Although well-trained and well-chosen foster carers provide the best placements for most looked after children, it is now time to rethink the proportion of the "looked after" population who can realistically be fostered, not only in terms of numbers but in terms of the particular children and their individual needs. A good experience of group care is better than going to the wrong foster home, and infinitely preferable to going to a succession of foster homes.

Some people would argue that we have gone too far in avoiding taking some children into care. The issues are complex.

We have tried to improve the quality of residential child care by making the units smaller. We have had some success in this since the Skinner Report was published, for numbers of large children's homes without education (over 20 residents) are half what they were at that time. What we have signally failed to do is lift the status of the staff, giving both grown-ups and children a sense of pride in their children's home and the feeling that they both are there because that is the right place for them to be. Talk of "warehousing children" because the right opportunity, thought to be fostering, is not available, denigrates the value of the residential home and devalues the child. It is insulting to the children looked after in residential care. If we are in any instances merely warehousing then the practice must stop, and this is the watershed when things must change, the dramatic steps must be taken to achieve that change. Tinkering around in these circumstances is not enough.

Putting the adolescent who does not want a substitute family with foster parents is not fair to either, nor is placing a teenager with foster parents who want a toddler. Residential child care should, in the words of others, be a positive choice - the intensive care unit of child care, not just a place to store the child while the Social Worker works with the family. Where it is not good for children, we must improve it. Managers must accept responsibility for the care that is provided. When people are ill, doctors and nurses try to keep them at home and treat them there. If they have to go somewhere for treatment, they try to return them home quickly. What they do not do is to send them to a hospital where the staff are less well trained than those in the GP's surgery, or indeed entirely untrained. Why do we act as we do when children need treatment in residential care?

3.3 Meantime in England, I understand, the school population of the emotionally and behaviourally disturbed children is up and in Scotland there is no shortage of demand for the better special boarding schools.

In the Scottish fee-paying boarding schools the overall numbers are down and would be down further were it not for the high proportion of boarders from overseas. Out of all the abuse that has been uncovered the fee-paying sector appears to suffer less. The images from bygone days seem to have gone and although some will question the motives for sending children away to school, presumably the level of parental interest is a factor.

3.4 In England there has been a considerable growth in the number of places for young people in privately run children's homes and there has been the introduction of private fostering agencies. Neither of these developments have been mirrored in Scotland. The role of the NSPCC in England has changed but they are a very powerful force in a very different way and are asked to do a lot of investigations and to provide independent visitors to residential units. In Scotland the old RSSPCC has changed its name to Children 1st and retrenched and has dropped out of investigative work.

Training for residential staff has lurched around for decades. After the war as training became available it was concentrated on the Field Social Workers. Some time later separate training in residential child care was introduced but dropped in the 80s in an effort to match the residential qualifications to those of Field work. The effort was probably commendable but has not yet worked. With the wisdom of hindsight it might have been better to put the front line horse before the social work cart but we have ended up with a largely untrained workforce in residential and foster care; the small amount of training that does happen is based on a social work model which is not always appropriate to the task.

CHAPTER 4

Initiatives Taken in the Last Decade

4.1 Quite apart from style and emphasis a great deal of positive deliberate action has taken place in the last 10 years which affects the security of children and young people living away from home. Right across the living away sector the big dormitory has gone. Some boarding schools, particularly schools for children with special educational needs, still favour bedrooms with several occupants but a new pattern has evolved without directive or command.

As part of the implementation of Community Care it became a requirement from April 1991 for all Local Authorities to establish Inspection Units at 'arms length' from the management of Social Work Departments. While this was initially introduced for adult residential services, by the summer of 1991 the scrutiny of children's residential services was added. The duty to carry out two annual inspections of each children's home was placed on the 12 Regional and Islands Authorities. This development brought a constructive focus upon practice in children's residential care. It led to the revision of registration guidelines, and to the production of standards against which inspections take place.

4.2 Not the least of the definite initiatives which have been taken is the Skinner Report, Another Kind of Home[22]. This was first published in 1992 and reprinted in 1994. The report was universally well received and is still referred to and is still to be seen at hand in many establishments. It had a positive impact on residential child care. However, many have suggested recently that the original impetus has been lost: posts have been frozen, officers in charge have less involvement in admission decisions, emergency admissions are increasing and there are fewer qualified staff applying for jobs.

The report was called for by the Secretary of State for Scotland who accepted all its recommendations. It has a different focus from this document but is very relevant to protection and safety and in a sense impinges on my remit. It calls for high quality care; in my deliberations it is a major theme that the better the care the safer the child.

4.2.1 Skinner sets out 8 fundamental principles which merit restating:

- ***Individuality and Development***
  Young people and children in residential care have the right to be treated as individuals who have their own unique relationships, experiences, strengths, needs and futures, irrespective of the needs of other residents. They should be prepared for adulthood and supported until they are fully independent.

- ***Right and Responsibilities***
  Young people, children and their parents should be given a clear statement of their rights and responsibilities. They should have a confidential means of making complaints. They should be involved in decisions affecting them and in the running of the home. Their rights should be consistently respected.

- ***Good Basic Care***
  Young people and children in residential care with or without education, should be given a high standard of personal care. They should be offered new, varied and positive experiences of life and should be included in the wider community.

22 Skinner, Angus (1992) op. cit.

- ***Education***
  Young people and children should be actively encouraged in all aspects of their education, vocational training or employment and offered career guidance. Their individual educational needs should be identified and met.

- ***Health***
  Young people's and children's health needs should be carefully identified and met; they should be encouraged to avoid health risks and to develop a healthy life-style.

- ***Partnerships with Parents***
  Young people and children in residential homes and schools should be cared for in ways which maximise opportunities for parents' continued involvement, and for care to be provided in the context of a partnership with parents, wherever this is in the interests of the child.

- ***Child Centred Collaboration***
  Young people and children should be able to rely on a high quality of inter-disciplinary teamwork amongst the adults providing for their care, education and health needs.

- ***A Feeling of Safety***
  Young people and children should feel safe and secure in any residential home or school.

These 8 principles are now enshrined in the Children (Scotland) Act 1995 but many providers of residential care for children and young people have been using them increasingly since 1992. They will be found to underlie much of what is written in this Review, particularly when I consider the dangers and harm that children may face, or the safeguards that will protect them from danger and harm.

4.2.2 Amongst the 66 recommendations of the Skinner Report some are quite explicit in terms of their impact on safety.

Recommendation 2 calls for young people and children to have the opportunity to express their views as to the type of placement they would prefer. Going to somewhere that they approve of is likely to contribute to the child's feeling of safety. Recommendation 3 urges the recognition that residential placement is a positive option. This is highly desirable but sadly is still not the way a significant number of people see things. Recommendation 4 proposes that children under 12 should only exceptionally be put in residential care. There has been a drop in numbers since 1992, but there are still as many under 12s in residential care as there were in 1989.

Recommendation 7 stipulates that Local Authorities and other agencies should develop standards and guidance for evaluating residential child care within the framework of Skinner's 8 principles. The standards should be applied by both managers and local inspection units to ensure a consistently good quality of residential child care provision. There has been talk since the publication of the Skinner report of the creation of national standards with local variation but at the present time no such document exists.

Recommendation 9 dwells upon locks to bedroom doors but also stipulates that young people and children should be able to make and receive telephone calls in private. This has been given considerable emphasis and by and large seems to have been fairly well implemented. Recommendation 10 dwells on building design and this has a place in the general scheme of protection.

Recommendation 11 calls upon the SWSI to issue practice guidance on providing residential care for young people and children who have been abused and those who abuse others. This has been taken forward by publication of guidance through The Centre for Residential Child Care.[23]

23 Lindsay, Meg (1995) Guidance for Residential Workers Caring for Young People Who Have Been Sexually Abused And Those Who Abuse Others (Glasgow, The Centre for Residential Child Care)

Recommendation 12 calls for more in-service training and that in particular it should include racial awareness training. Not much of this takes place but it should and there are concerns that children from ethnic minorities may be less likely to articulate their concern or anxiety.

Recommendation 16 looks to agencies preparing statements of rights and responsibilities taking into account Skinner's 8 principles. It also suggests that a document outlining them be given to each young person or child before admission to a home. The response to this has been quite good and most agencies have a leaflet that incorporates this. However I have some misgivings as to whether such leaflets ever actually mean anything to the child and more thought needs to be given to how they can become more reader-friendly. It would make sense to ask Who Cares? whether a group of their members would take on drafting a leaflet as a project.

Recommendation 18 says that all complaints, allegations or suspicions of physical or sexual abuse of young people or children in residential care should always be referred to managers or appointed agents outwith the home and its management. A record should be kept of any allegations made. There is room for this to be tightened up.

Recommendation 19 looks to young people and children being involved in the way their home is run and I have been pleased to discover that some Homes have residents' meetings, which may be minuted, at which residents can express their views as a group, knowing that what they say will have at least some influence on the management of the Home. This recommendation also suggests that Local Authorities should consider instituting local procedural rights for young people and their parents and that no review should be postponed without consulting them. Sadly I found the practice of cancelling reviews at short notice still to be prevalent and a source of considerable irritation to young people.

Recommendation 20 invites Local Authorities to support the development of Who Cares? and for the Scottish Office to continue to fund this body. This has taken place and it is clear that Who Cares? is an important ingredient in the network to protect the well-being of children who are in care.

Recommendation 26 suggests that budgets should always be sufficient to provide structured week-end and holiday activities. Alas, these are easy budgets to cut quickly. The fact is that boredom will contribute to a lack of safety and cutting them proves to be a false economy.

Recommendation 30 is concerned with the registration of any child in a residential education establishment for whom a Local Authority has responsibility. There remains some confusion about which boarding schools should be registered under Section 34 or 35 of the Children Scotland Act.

Recommendation 31 looks for liaison arrangements to ensure that the health needs of children in care are identified and met. The close relationship between Local Authorities and health boards in the care of the elderly does not seem to be mirrored as far as the care of children is concerned.

Recommendation 32 covers smoking. Clearly smoking is a health hazard and causes harm. Skinner's report wanted more action in helping young people to avoid smoking and helping staff not to smoke in front of children. I do not believe that this call has been responded to but I have to recognise that smoking is of major importance in the lives of some young people and that staff would have great difficulty in imposing an out and out ban.

Recommendation 34 is concerned with training on sexuality and suggests that all residential child care staff should have some training in this area. Some strides have been made and I am aware of some training but I think there is still a distinct lack of understanding on the part of many untrained residential staff about adolescent development and what is experimentation and what is abuse.

Recommendation 35 was also about in-service training but is looking to equip staff for working with young people who are experimenting with alcohol, drugs or solvents. Local Authorities were asked to prepare practice guidance for care staff and it would clearly be very important for newcomers to the work. It has to be said that quite a lot of residential child care staff will have grown to be fairly experienced and may themselves know rather more than people in management or in training.

Recommendation 36 stresses the importance of being able to arrange a confidential discussion between parent and child or between parent and a member of staff. Recommendation 38 suggests the formation of local and national organisations for parents of young people and children in care. There is little evidence of anything actually happening on this front.

Recommendation 39 invites Local Authorities to consider joint training initiatives for education and social work and other disciplines to collaborate in providing good residential child care. Work done recently has concentrated on community care. There is room for much more joint training amongst those who work with children and young people and I would suggest the inclusion of youth leaders as well as teachers and other staff in boarding schools.

Recommendation 40 makes it quite clear that people receiving allegations, or who are suspicious themselves, about the possible abuse of young people or children living away from home need to inform the police without hesitation.

Recommendation 41 considers sanctions and control. The SWSI convened a working group to issue Guidance on sanctions and control, and practice Guidance from the work of this group is about to be published through The Centre for Residential Child Care. The recommendation is quite explicit that after the Guidance has been issued Local Authority inspection units should review at least annually the adherence by each home to the Guidance and should involve young people and children in this review. Given what I have been told by the young people themselves about their grave concerns over what they perceive to be an excessive use of restraint it seems very important that this matter should be progressed.

Recommendation 43 invites Local Authorities and inspection units routinely to gather information on absconding rates from residential homes and schools and to investigate patterns, causes and solutions based on the recommendations of a previous absconding working party. Until this year there was little evidence of anything happening in this Field, but a Scottish Office working party is now preparing proposals. It is intended that new reporting arrangements should be piloted later this year, and that in 1998 a new scheme will be introduced that will help to quantify and analyse the episodes of children absconding or going missing. Absconding will frequently reflect something else and it seems very important to get to grips with it.

Recommendation 44 suggests the review of the future needs for secure accommodation. This review has taken place and the recommendations have been accepted.

Recommendation 45 is about salaries and conditions of service for residential child care staff. It suggests that salaries should be improved and this has taken place. Whether it has taken place to an adequate degree is open to some doubt.

Recommendation 46 asks the Scottish Office itself to consider the applicability in Scotland of the recommendations of the Warner enquiry which had yet to report at that time. It suggested that appropriate guidance should be issued from the centre but this has not yet taken place.

Recommendations 47 and 48 are about the targets for the levels of training and qualification for residential child care staff. Significant inroads have been made into the target which calls for more senior residential child care staff to hold a diploma in social work. Less progress has occurred on the level of qualification for staff who are not unit managers or team leaders.

Recommendations 50 and 51 refer to new entrants. It calls for there to be two weeks induction training and for new staff with no previous experience to be appointed initially on a probationary basis. There has been some progress but it does not seem that all staff are getting two weeks training and in practice the development has been patchy. Few Local Authorities appoint people on a probationary basis although this is common practice in the voluntary sector. I will suggest that this matter be brought to employers' attention once again.

Recommendation 53 points to the difficulty in getting practice placements for students in residential child care. There has been little change in this situation and practice placements are still problematic.

Recommendation 55 sought funding for the establishment of a Centre for consultancy and development in residential child care. This has taken place and the impact of the Centre for Residential Child Care has been significant.

Recommendation 56 is about supervision of staff. In the same way that induction training has developed in a rather patchy way, there is no common pattern showing that supervision has taken root across the whole field. There are good examples (especially in the voluntary sector) but generally there is some way to go.

Recommendation 64 calls for agencies to extend their work on quality assurance and for SWSI to monitor the development of quality assurance in residential child care between 1992 - 1996. Skinner suggested the Inspectorate should undertake a national inspection of residential child care in 1996. This was postponed because of local government reorganisation. Since then the work to develop the Children Scotland Act has meant that the inspection has not been able to attract the right amount of time. The work that I have done in reporting on safeguards should not be allowed to be seen to compensate for the absence of this national inspection.

Recommendation 65 suggests that Local Authority inspection procedures should always include interviews with young people and with children and their parents. Generally this is now taking place.

4.3 The Skinner Report was straddled by two English reports - the Utting Report "Children in the Public Care" and the Warner Report "Choosing with Care"[24]. The former came out in 1991 and the latter in 1992. There was also a report by Baroness Howe at this time[25].

4.4 Like Skinner, Utting was writing at a time when there had been a retrenchment of residential child care and when it was necessary to restate its value. Both wanted to stress there has to be a positive choice for residential child care and both expected the service to be primarily about adolescents. In 1997 it remains necessary to publicly reaffirm the continued need and worth of residential child care, but also to question whether there may not now be a need to increase it. We have not eliminated under 12s from the children's home population and may run the risk of not meeting their needs properly because we do not plan for them.

From a protection standpoint Utting advised an extension of the role of the independent visitor for children with disabilities and for all children in residential care. He did this because of his desire to encourage *"a culture which encourages and supports staff in listening to children, taking on their distress and acting to resolve it"*. He did not want to rely on a child's ability to understand a complaints procedure, to know how to use it and be prepared to do so; he wanted there to be someone for the child to talk to before deciding on the course of action. He also wanted an independent adjudicator to handle any intractable dispute between a child and the care authority and suggested the Local Authority associations might establish something.

Sir William Utting also called for guidance to be offered on constructive methods of control. He suggested managers set clear, personal personnel objectives for staff and for employers to address the issue of raising the status and morale of residential child care staff. He set similar training targets to Skinner.

24 Utting, W (1991) Children in the Public Care: A Review of Residential Child Care (London, HMSO)
Warner, N (1992) Choosing with Care: The Report of the Committee of Inquiry into the Selection, Development and Management of Staff in Children's Homes (London, HMSO)

25 Howe, E (1992) The Quality of Care: Report of the Residential Staff's Inquiry (London, Local Government Management Board)

4.5 The Howe Report was produced by a working party chaired by Lady Howe, and made recommendations about improving "The Quality of Care" for both adults and children. Among these were better support for staff, with better training (often through NVQ, National Vocational Qualifications, of which the Scottish equivalent is SVQ) and supervision; improved career development opportunities; improved relationships between Field Social Workers and residential staff; responsibility to be devolved to unit managers, who should receive systematic management training; and that external managers should be experienced in, and knowledgeable about, residential care.

4.6 The Warner Committee was established in February 1992 following the conviction of Frank Beck at Leicester Crown Court and had to examine the selection and recruitment methods and criteria for staff working in children's homes and to examine issues relevant to the protection of children in such homes. The report reflects the English scene in many ways, such as a burgeoning private sector which we do not have here in Scotland, but it had powerful and important things to say about selection and appointment of staff which are applicable anywhere. The Chief Social Work Inspector in Scotland anticipated the Warner recommendations and advised there should be appropriate guidance.

Warner gives trenchant advice on supervision and appraisal. In Scotland I believe the quality of supervision has gone up and I have found good examples. Regular appraisal is a tool in industry, central government (where the Scottish Office appraisal scheme has been running for 25 years) and business, but it has yet to bed itself down in Local Authorities let alone social work or residential child care. This may be in part due to anxiety by managers about the reactions of the unions or about performance related pay.

Warner complains that a lot of the training strategy, which should be providing practical training for the majority of residential child care staff, actually qualifies a few of them through the Diploma in Social Work to leave the service. However, it is now claimed that the specific residential child care initiative in England that followed Utting and Warner shows an 80% retention rate of staff qualified by the Diploma in Social Work.

Warner also stresses the need to have easy access to psychiatrists, psychotherapists and psychologists saying that he thinks 70% of children in homes are there because of emotional and behavioural difficulties and about one-third have been sexually abused.

4.6.1 He lists his concerns as:

- *An increasing number of difficult children to care for in homes.*
- *Low esteem of homes and staff and consequent staff morale and recruitment problems.*
- *A lack of sustained attention to children's residential care by employers and senior management in social services departments.*
- *Non-existent or inadequate arrangements for staff appraisal and supervision in many places, and other poor management practices.*
- *Deficient and sometimes unsafe employment practices, with a need for a more systematic and rigorous approach to the recruitment, selection and appointment of staff.*
- *Inadequate knowledge and training to enable staff to cope with the children in their care.*
- *A shortage of specialist support services from the National Health Service for the children and staff in homes and deficiencies in the educational service provided for children in residential care.*
- *Inadequate definition of policy and standards at the national level; and an absence of adequate joint planning arrangements at the local level.*

4.6.2 That was a report commissioned in England about the state of affairs in England. Five years later it paints a fairly clear picture of our own scene in Scotland here today. Utting, the year before Warner, had pressed for personal personnel objectives. Warner went much further and urged personal development contracts linked to the English and Welsh NVQs. He urged induction training for all new staff and management training for all new heads of homes. He wanted a wider range of selection techniques and a review of the application of equal opportunities policies. He wanted a probationary period that was monitored and a designated appointing officer to oversee appointments and systems used to appoint. In Scotland we have made progress in the last 10 years over job descriptions, statements of functions and objectives, and application forms designed specifically for children's homes. We have not done so well with person specifications but there is evidence they are being used. We lack the personal development contracts and the wider range of selection techniques. One Scottish Local Authority was part of a post-Warner consortium drawing on the expertise of a firm of recruitment consultants and seeking to improve selection for residential child care. This lay dormant for 2 years but there are now signs of a resurgence.

4.6.3 Warner made recommendations on recruitment, selection and appointment many of which have been heeded, both north and south of the border, but also on training, supervision and appraisal which have not received as much attention. Had the recommendations been implemented there would now be fortnightly supervision of all staff, annual appraisal of staff performance with written documentation of shortcomings and training needs, and a personal development contract between individual staff and their employers. He also made a recommendation that there should be a new professional qualification for the sector.

4.6.4 Warner concluded that his committee were only too aware that various reports had been published on children's residential care without producing the necessary change and improvement nationally. He called for a Development Action Group in England and Wales which would be a pro-active standing body independent of the Government but reporting to the Secretary of State. It would be the sort of body that could not be neutered, it would be interventionist and a goad for change. It would act as a public watchdog ensuring improvements take place, and also as a development agent to facilitate the change process. He envisaged something with a very high profile. He did not get the dynamic superbody offering national leadership he wanted, but his advice was heeded in some part by the creation of the Support Force for Children in Residential Care headed up by Adrianne Jones and funded by central government.

4.7 In June 1995 the Support Force published a Code of Practice for the employment of residential child care workers[26]. This document is, quite simply, excellent. It covers preparing the ground, selecting staff, checking and monitoring, introducing new staff, staff development, staff support and management. It offers check lists, action steps and model forms and worked examples. It would be relatively simple to produce a tartan version that took account of any differences in the Scottish position, and well worth the small amount of work involved.

4.8 In England and Wales the publication of the Utting Report led to the creation of the Residential Child Care Initiative which was a response to widespread concern about children in public care. This set out to increase the number of staff qualified by the Diploma in Social Work and in the first year 139 students enrolled with central government funding. The Initiative was time-limited and there were four intakes for each of the four years with a total of 432 students all told.

In Scotland the Skinner Report led to changes in the funding of part of the overall training strategy with some Local Authority funding being top-sliced and being redistributed with a bias towards child care. The aim was to increase the proportion of residential care staff with a Diploma in Social Work and also to increase the proportion of staff with SVQ Level 3 (HNC) in social care. The targets were, in the first group 20% by 1995 and 30% by 1997 and in the second group 40% by 1995 and 60% by 1997. Most importantly there was another target that by 1994 100% of newly appointed staff should have had two or more weeks induction in their first three

26 Support Force for Children's Residential Care chaired by Adrianne Jones (1995) Code of Practice for the Employment of Residential Child Care Workers (London, Department of Health)

months of work. The figures for 1995 show that 16.4% of the workforce in residential child care homes were trained to SVQ level 3 (HNC) or above, while in 1989 - before the advent of SVQs - the percentage was 10.75%. One is reminded of Zeno's paradox; no matter how fast Achilles runs he can't overtake the tortoise given a head start.

4.9 Local Government reorganisation in April 1996 led to an increase in the number of Local Authorities responsible for providing, purchasing and regulating child care from 12 to 32. This has led to increased difficulties in the provision and purchasing of services for the much smaller Authorities, including the closure of units; there are particular problems where a relatively large unit is located within the boundary of a small Authority. A total of 27 Inspection Units are in operation. There is now even more scope for variations in standards between Authorities, and in the way in which Regulations are implemented. Foster carers in some areas no longer have access to other Social Workers skilled in foster care work if their own link worker is unavailable, because some new Authorities are too small to have dedicated teams. They find that increasingly foster carers have children placed with them by more than one Local Authority, and that this can lead to problems.

CHAPTER 5

The Literature Review

Preamble

I have chosen to pick up points that seem to me of particular interest to the rest of my report rather than to summarise Andrew Kendrick's Literature Review. A summary of a Literature Review is by nature a condensation of a condensation. Such a work is bound to be subjective. I have therefore taken positive action by bringing to readers' attention those things which have a direct bearing on my report.

Perhaps this chapter should be treated like a menu, an indication of the more satisfying fare that is available through the Literature Review. References have deliberately not been given, because it is intended that the interested reader will go from this chapter to the relevant part of the Literature Review to follow something up. There may be generalisations here, and there may be conflicting information from different pieces of research. It simply indicates that information is available, that more details can be found in the Literature Review which will indicate the books and articles where the real meat is to be found.

The language of this chapter is usually my own, but it is influenced by the language of the original sources, and jargon, American English and rather out-dated terms all appear from time to time.

One of the obvious things about the Literature Review is the way in which it has shown up those areas where little research has yet been done. There are clear lessons to be learnt from this.

In looking at the literature, it is important to remember that we belong to a comparatively small country, but one which has its own legal system and its own way of doing things. Research which has been carried out in other countries may be obviously applicable to Scotland; on the other hand, it may not. Research work done elsewhere can enlighten and alert, and we can learn from it, but we should not believe that what has happened elsewhere is necessarily true of Scotland.

For anybody interested in the safeguarding of children, the Literature Review is in many ways an exciting document. It will make you think about issues which have been in the back of your mind until now. This chapter should act as an indicator of the value you will find in it.

Contents of the Literature Review

5.1 Introduction

The starting point of the Literature Review are Articles 19 and 20 in the UN Convention on the Rights of the Child, relating to protecting the child. Following this is the concern in the Warner Report that *"there have been so many inquiries whose findings seem to have gone largely unheeded by the service as a whole"*. Four years later cases of widespread abuse continue to hit the headlines and it is possible for Doran and Brannan to write *"the lack of research and the piecemeal implementation of recommendations following a number of inquiries leaves one feeling that professionals have not addressed their 'responsibility' for the abuse and protection of children"*.

Abuse of children living away from home is a matter of serious concern around the world, and the literature reflects this.

One of the issues in the Literature Review is what constitutes good or at least acceptable residential child care. Since this is part of a whole complex of issues there are no hard and fast boundaries in terms of the literature and research which could be included in the Review. So some of the decisions made as to what was included were determined to a large degree by feasibility given its wide ranging scope and the limited timescale for carrying it out.

5.2 Definitions of Abuse in Out-of-Home Care

A crucial problem concerns the point at which acts are defined as abuse, given that there is no absolute definition.

It may be helpful to define abuse in out-of-home care as being of three types:

- physical and sexual abuse
- program abuse
- system abuse

Physical and sexual abuse is like abuse in family situations but is perpetrated by the professional carer or foster carer.

Program abuse occurs when a unit's programmes are " *below normally accepted standards; have extreme or unfair policies; or rely on harsh, inhumane, or unusual techniques to teach or guide children*". Among these would be the "Pin-down" regime in Staffordshire, and Frank Beck's "Regression Therapy".

Many authors try to define "system abuse". Hard to define, it may be the opposite of what Barbara Kahan is talking about when she says *".... stability and continuity are not only essential for good care but they are the necessary conditions for a child to grow up well"*. Children are damaged by a system stretched beyond its limits and incapable of guaranteeing their safety, where disruption is caused by multiple placements and changes in educational provision. Keeping the child in an inappropriate environment when more appropriate facilities are available may be a further form of abuse.

A situation would be considered harmful if it:

- endangers the protection, security and/or safety of the child
- prevents the child from obtaining basic care and satisfying physical and emotional needs
- places obstacles in the way of a child's development or restricts developmental opportunities for the child
- prevents the child from participating in the special care and treatment needed for adequate developmental progress.

A recent UK definition says that system abuse occurs when:

- children's needs are not recognised or understood and therefore not considered separately from those of adults

- services are unavailable

- services permit unskilled and unsafe environments

- services for children with emotional and behavioural disorders allow organisations to avoid or shift responsibilities

- there are intrusive procedures or practices which undermine children or their families.

5.3 Abuse in Residential Care

There is a debate as to whether all residential institutions, being harmful, should be closed as quickly as possible or whether, although ideally children should be cared for by their families, residential institutions are necessary and the goal is to reduce the possibilities of abuse so as to create the most supportive environment.

There is a history of concern in the US about children in institutional care that goes back over 20 years. Currently concern has shifted to other issues in child protective services.

In the UK, the abuse of children living away from home has only recently been addressed. There has been little in the way of systematic research and responses to the problem have typically been in reaction to inquiries into high profile cases.

The general lack of clarity about what constitutes institutional abuse forms a major barrier to detecting and measuring the extent of the problem. A number of US studies report on abuse in residential care, including "institutional abuse" (or system abuse), or inappropriate treatment. In one study inappropriate treatment was the most common mistreatment alleged and confirmed; the author suggested that it would be most effectively addressed by appropriate supervision, consultation and training.

In the UK there is a lack of information on the extent of abuse and neglect of children in residential establishments. Several major inquiries have highlighted that the problem of abusive programmes is more widespread than had previously been recognised.

A 1992 study in the UK identified 84 severe cases of alleged abuse in residential or educational settings; 42% of the children had been placed because of previous abuse. Types of abuse were:

- sexual abuse - 69
- physical abuse - 16
- emotional abuse - 4
- inappropriate restraint - 6
- other forms - 9

The perpetrator was:

- a peer (half the cases)
- staff member (43%)
- a sibling (the rest)

81% of abusers were male.

ChildLine said that callers who said they were in residential placements were most likely to report bullying and violence from other residents as their main problems; however, 25 children in England and Wales alleged current sexual abuse, in 9 cases from male residents, in 8 cases from male staff and for most of the remainder on home visits.

In a 1996 survey of organised sexual abuse it was believed that agencies tended to report only a small proportion of the cases known to them, largely the high profile ones. Their definition of institutional abuse was *"a case in which an adult used the institutional framework of an organisation for children to recruit children for sexual abuse"*. Of the 211 cases reported, there were 45 cases of "institutional abuse" of which 16 were in residential institutions.

In a study of 67 children in special residential schools, it was found that one-fifth had experienced some form of suspected or confirmed abuse, either physical or sexual. Most of this research focused on physical abuse, sexual abuse and neglect. Two cases of programme abuse in the UK - Pindown in Staffordshire and "regressive therapy" in Leicestershire - have been the subject of major inquiries.

5.3.1 Boarding Schools

Little research has been carried out in boarding schools.

In 1960s research based on the writings of some 12,000 children in 66 boarding schools in England and Wales, sexual abuse of boys by staff was mentioned by over three-quarters of the boys.

Research in relation to the ChildLine Boarding School Line found over one-third of the calls related to bullying and sexual abuse. Thirty four cases were classified as sexual harassment (3.5%); most were reported by girls and in 21 cases male teachers were the perpetrators. Sexual abuse was reported in 155 calls with just over half the calls from boys. The overwhelming majority of allegations were against staff: in 12 cases the headmaster or housemaster, in 97 cases a teacher, with more than one teacher involved in a few cases. In one-quarter of the cases, the callers indicated that the same person was abusing others.

5.5% of the calls involved physical abuse, the third largest problem for boys.

5.3.2 Hospitals

There is little literature on child abuse in hospitals. In US research on the rates of abuse in different care settings, the rate in "hospitals/other facilities" was the second lowest. Sexual abuse was most frequent, followed by physical abuse and neglect.

In the UK the literature is very limited. In an overview of the changes in the care of children in hospital there is no mention of either abuse or child protection.

In the 1991 case of Beverley Allitt, the Clothier Report found the hospital's recruitment procedures at fault, and problems with both staffing levels and management skills. It identified only two cases of nurses attacking child patients, one in the US, one in Canada[27].

The Allitt case was linked to Münchhausen Syndrome by Proxy, in which factitious injury or manifestation of illness is inflicted on others. In nearly all cases it is mothers who inflict it on their own children, but between 1975 and 1993 at least 14 criminal trials occurred with a connection with the syndrome; only four of these led to convictions. The motivators included the needs for recognition and for power and control. In some cases, the perpetrators had a previous history of self harm or suspicious behaviour; it was suggested that attention to the background of nurses at the point of selection was essential, as were ongoing supervision and appraisal.

27 The lack of literature is surprising. There are other examples

A registered nurse convicted of indecent assault on two 13 year old boys and sentenced to two years in prison was found guilty by his Association of professional misconduct, but allowed to remain on the register to practice.

The Royal College of Nursing has prepared guidance for nurses and their managers *"in the light of recent cases where children have been harmed by nurses and other health staff caring for them"*.

5.3.3 Penal Institutions

Abuse of young people by staff in penal establishments is the least well documented of all. The Howard League for Penal Reform Commission of Inquiry into Violence in Penal Institutions for Teenagers looked at this, with a focus on the use of physical control and restraint.

5.3.4 Factors in Abuse in Residential Settings

Institutions may be damaging because:

- they function as a closed system with their own policies and procedures
- work in institutions brings out the worst in child care workers (often overworked and underpaid, they have little say in decision making)
- staff are poorly trained and inadequately screened
- staff may be tired, alienated and burnt-out, with increasingly negative attitudes towards children
- child to adult ratios may be too high
- there may be stressors such as staff lay-offs and movement of groups of children to new living areas
- staff may not be seeing progress in the child and so have no job satisfaction.

5.3.5 Targeting of Residential Care by Paedophiles

Paedophiles are shown to be attracted to work in schools and other child care institutions, including health care facilities. This may be because of the vulnerability of children in institutions, which in itself may be partly because of earlier sexual abuse the children have suffered in their own families.

Research has identified the ways in which paedophiles target their victims, and their strategies for getting access to them. They are often attracted to children with low self-esteem.

There are two principal archetypes of institutional abusers:

- the charismatic caring professional, usually part of the leadership
- the isolated but dutiful staff member, perhaps overhelpful, who frequently does things outside normal duties.

Sexual abuse may come from grooming and exploiting particular children over time, or it may come from an "impulsive and isolated act".

There are notes on institutional abuse in the context of sex rings.

5.4 Abuse in Foster Care

The literature on the abuse and neglect of children in foster care placements is scarce. Material from the US tends to be more systematic than that available in Britain.

One American study found that all the perpetrators in the sexual abuse cases were male, but in the neglect cases most were female. The carers in abusing families were likely to be childless, or single, or to have been fostering for a long time. Another study found foster siblings involved in physical abuse, neglect and sexual abuse. (Other studies have found that sexual abuse by non-parental adolescent care givers is more common than that by older non-parental care givers.) Low remuneration led to a shortage of foster homes and to less good parents being licensed, so that when disturbed children were placed with them without adequate support there was tension and abuse. However, other studies found it hard to correlate maltreatment and foster home characteristics.

UK evidence tends to be anecdotal. It is hard to tell the incidence of abuse from the studies. In the case of both physical and sexual abuse, the abuser is most usually the foster father, although foster brothers are involved in sexual abuse. Physical abuse may be a greater problem in foster than in residential care.

A study looking at allegations found that just over 1/5th of the cases were substantiated, and in a further 1/5th of cases investigators could not determine whether or not abuse has occurred.

There is a larger literature on the problem of foster carers dealing with allegations than on the incidence of abuse by foster carers. As a result of surveys, there are recommendations as to what Authorities should do when allegations are made.

Foster carers tend not to be prepared for the possibility of allegations. Many were not given enough information about the child's sexual history, and after allegations the lack of information continued.

In different studies, there is some disagreement as to whether there is more danger of abuse in residential or foster care. There is evidence from the US and Canada that abuse is more prevalent in foster care than in the general population. Some allegations of abuse may be accounted for by greater demands of good parenting being made of foster carers.

Various studies have discussed the difficulties and problems involved in fostering sexually abused children. The incidence of sexualised behaviour is high, and may be directed towards another child in the family. This may increase the likelihood of further sexual abuse.

A US study found that younger children abused in foster homes were likely to have been abused previously; this is not as likely for older victims. Perpetrators may be able to identify and exploit children who have been sexually abused.

Stress can be a factor in abuse; fostering children who have been sexually abused is extremely stressful. Maltreatment in foster care appears to exacerbate problems in the children. Regular reviews to assess levels of stress are important. Foster carers for severely troubled children need additional supports and resources.

5.5 Responding to the Abuse of Children Living Away from Home

The monitoring and investigative elements of abuse often have an ad hoc quality. It may be hard for people involved in care to define something as abuse or neglect because this requires action to be taken. Institutions may be reluctant to report incidents of abuse because they fear damaging their reputation or they believe it could not happen in their unit. Difficulties of disclosure may be increased for the child victim in cases in which the alleged offender is a professional. Some workers may react to allegations about a colleague by denial.

Acquittals, if the issue does get to court, also have serious implications for the agency.

Factors that affect willingness to report abuse include:

- people do not recognise when incidents or circumstances are damaging
- people are afraid to speak up
- institutions protect themselves
- there is excessive respect for the professional.

Specialised investigative procedures for institutional abuse are rare, though recommended. In the UK there is a lack of formalised written procedures and policies for dealing with allegations. Investigations of allegations or suspicions should include an independent element.

It is important that the victim is supported by a professional worker through any court process.

Because of lack of knowledge, staff in child protection fail to recognise incidents involving use of restraint or medication as abusive.

Reducing the potential for conflict of interest in decision making should be a major concern.

The response to allegations of abuse is often the removal of the victim. This was shown in a US study in which confirmed reports of abuse also resulted in closure of the institution in one-third of cases.

There needs to be a corporate, co-ordinated approach to inquiries. The investigation should lead to clear written formal agreements.

A model for an institutional abuse review team is put forward.

Where things go wrong there is a tendency to look at the issue as a staff problem, rather than as a matter of protecting children. Where there are thorough checks and monitoring systems in child care, the worst abuses may be prevented from happening.

Action that should be taken to protect and support the child after allegations have been made is suggested. Action that should also be taken in relation to the alleged abuser, other staff, other parts of the organisation and the community at large are put forward. After a review of a particular case, the service as a whole may need to be evaluated.

5.6 Mandatory Reporting, Sex Offender Registers and Community Notification

In the US, it has been found that individual workers have had trouble whether they have reported or not reported maltreatment; some have been demoted or fired for reporting, leading to 4 States now passing legislation to protect employees who report in good faith. It is noted that those who do report need active support.

By 1966 all US States except one had enacted mandatory reporting legislation. Originally, mandatory reporting laws concerned the duties of physicians to report physical injuries with the focus on custody and protection and not on action against the perpetrator. Now all States require mental health professionals (including Social Workers) to report suspected abuse and an increasing number of States require reporting by any person. More types of abuse are included. The number of child abuse reports increased 500-fold between 1963 and 1992 but without a comparable increase in resources, and Child Protective Services dominate child welfare, with in one area 90% of children reported as not receiving a service. There is a high rate of unsubstantiated reports, but also substantial under-reporting by mandated reporters. The need for education and training in relation to mandatory reporting is noted.

Since 1980 each Canadian province and territory has had its own mandatory reporting legislation, relating to all persons who believe on reasonable grounds that the child is, may be or has been in need of protection. In some areas there is an explicit duty on professionals. There are few clear penalties for failure to report.

In Australia all States and Territories except two have legislation, but they differ in the types of professionals who must report, and in the types of maltreatment to be reported.

In Ireland now there is pressure for the introduction of mandatory reporting of child abuse by all those with responsibility for the care of children. Those who report in good faith would have legal indemnity.

The UK does not have mandatory reporting laws and "*only Local Authorities, Social Workers, health and social service board Social Workers (in Northern Ireland) and police have a duty to report suspicions that a child is in need of care and protection*".

In the United States the "Jacob Wetterling Act" requires States to enact a registration system for child sex offenders by 1997. They must register with law enforcement agencies who can disseminate information about them. However, although registration laws are intended to address high recidivism rates, these are relatively low. In some areas police lack the time, personnel and money to pursue violators of the Act.

There is tension between the protection of children, and the rights of individuals.

Registration affects only a small proportion of sex offenders, those who are convicted: public notification provides people with a false sense of security. There is a danger that the stigmatising effect of notification may make sex offenders more likely to reoffend.

In Australia, the Parliament of Victoria has recommended that the Victoria police establish and maintain a sex offender register, involving life long registration of adult offenders and requiring adolescent offenders to register for 5 years (summary offences) or until they are 20 years of age (indictable offences).

In June 1996, the Home Office in England published a consultation paper on proposals which included:

- stronger supervision of convicted sex offenders following release from custody
- requiring sex offenders to notify the police of their address
- prohibiting sex offenders from employment involving access to children.

5.7 Racism and Abuse

There are particular problems for black children who are looked after by the Local Authority because mainstream services often do not meet their needs. It has been found that black children are more likely to flourish when they are living with black foster carers, who can give them an important understanding of, and confidence in, themselves as black young people.

Black children are severely disproportionately represented in care in England, and enter care twice as quickly as white children. Less preventative work is done with their families, less effort made not to admit them to care.

There is little information on the experience of black children in care. However, there are examples of racist practice and racist abuse in institutional care of all kinds, sometimes unchecked by staff and even in some cases used by them.

One study suggests that the Children Act 1989 "*takes into account, for the first time, the multi-ethnic and multi-cultural nature of our society*" by making it a duty to consider the racial origin, ethnicity and linguistic background of the child[28].

28 This is picked up in the Children (Scotland) Act 1995

Examples are given of good practice and of how improved standards might promote equality in residential settings.

5.8 Abuse of Children With Disabilities

Although the particular vulnerability of children with disabilities has been highlighted, there has been little systematic investigation of factors leading to their maltreatment. But:

- children with disabilities are over-represented in samples of abused children
- many such children and families have high risk characteristics.

The abuse is more complex because there are two linkages:

- abuse may be implicated in the creation of disability
- children with disability may be targeted for abuse.

Child abuse can give rise to medical problems, developmental problems and psychological problems.

Children with disabilities are more likely to spend time in residential and specialist facilities; this increases the likelihood of abuse.

Identifying abuse is much more difficult where the child has a physical or learning disability; problem behaviour is too often accepted as normal for people with mental handicaps. The child may have difficulty with communication both because of disability and because when we deny children sexuality, we tend also to limit their vocabulary.

People with disabilities saw these as contributory factors to abuse:

- physical and social isolation
- lack of choice
- lack of physical and psychological resources to defend oneself
- physical immobility
- the ability to "switch off" one's body at will (because of the frequent intrusive behaviour displayed by adults)

Institutions also put pressures on children not to tell.

Sex education programmes have a vital part to play in protecting children.

There is a gross lack of therapeutic work with children with disabilities who have been abused, although therapy is found to be effective, in different ways for both boys and girls.

The criminal justice system fails to make sensible arrangements to meet the needs of children with disabilities as witnesses.

5.9 Runaways and Child Prostitution

5.9.1 Runaways

Approximately 100,000 children and young people go missing in the UK every year - a substantial proportion from residential care homes. They are likely to have experienced serious difficulties in their lives. Running away increases vulnerability. Those who abscond and return could be away for anything from a few hours to a week or more. Most of the young people from residential care had started running away before they went into care.

Reasons for running away could include:

- problems at home or in care, including verbal, physical and sexual abuse
- rejection
- school problems
- feeling that being taken into care was outside their control
- negative experiences of the care system
- not wanting to be in care
- poor relationships with staff
- peer pressure
- bullying
- seeking excitement
- feeling powerless or hopeless.

Research in the US has shown a much higher rate of earlier childhood sexual abuse among runaways than among the general population.

A significant proportion of runaways come from a small number of care homes. Frequent running away by young people from a single home may indicate abuse or other failings in the home.

Runaways face considerable risks. They may:

- become the victims of crime, including assault
- take to crime, drug and alcohol abuse and prostitution, to survive.

When they return to the unit, they need support to reintegrate and to resolve the difficulties which led them to run.

5.9.2 Child Prostitution

There has been until recently very little research on child prostitution in the UK, but a clear link is made between residential care and prostitution. "Fitting in" with the group in a unit is one factor predisposing to it.

Prostitution is for many a survival strategy for life on the streets as children and young people are denied an adequate income by any other means. There is a link between early sexual abuse and prostitution which may not be direct, but happens because sexual abuse leads to running away which then leads to prostitution.

The police use the criminal justice system to respond to young people who are involved in prostitution by prosecuting them, when the law should be recognising the need to protect young people from sexual abuse and exploitation.

Very few child care workers have developed an understanding of the behaviour of adolescent prostitutes or of appropriate long term interventions.

5.10 Bullying, Peer Abuse and Self-harm

5.10.1 Bullying

Group living is problematical because the interactions of emotionally disturbed young people may make treatment more difficult.

There has been an increase in literature about bullying recently but so far there is limited research on bullying in institutions. Studies of young offenders have shown that a high proportion of them are involved in bullying as either bullies or victims, often with staff condoning bullying. Although one study found actual violence between young prisoners to be rare, a recent survey in two adult male prisons and two young offender institutions found high levels of victimisation.

The authors of this find bullying too loose a concept and want to define victimisation in terms of assault, threats of violence, verbal abuse, cell theft, robbery and social exclusion. Another recent study found high levels of violence in a young offender establishment.

The Social Services Inspectorate in Northern Ireland found significant levels of bullying and peer child abuse in residential care. The Social Services Inspectorate in England identified incidents of peer abuse which did not appear to have been investigated in accordance with guidance. Bullying is a source of considerable distress to young people.

Bullying in Secure Units occurs at a lower level than within the prison system. A study of one Secure Unit in Scotland showed how close supervision by staff seemed to limit bullying.

Bullying in boarding schools is less sadistic and violent than in the past, but the ChildLine Boarding School Line found that bullying was the most common problem, referred to in 1/5th of calls.

When an institution creates an atmosphere in which young people feel valued and safe, there is less likelihood of violence and bullying.

Co-ordinated strategies on bullying, the "whole person approach", are seen as helpful.

Over the first two years of an anti-bullying programme in the Cardiff Prison youth wing, serious attempts of suicide fell from 23 attempts to 8, and there was an 80% reduction in acts of self harm.

Staff vigilance and open discussion are deterrents against bullying because both bullies and bullied know that staff will deal with it. There needs to be open discussion about bullying and a clear statement of its unacceptability.

"Whole school" policies on bullying are recommended for boarding schools.

5.10.2 Peer Abuse

There is increasing evidence of the problem of the sexual abuse of children by other residents. However, most staff interviewed during inspections in England were unaware of the Children Act Guidance[29] that it is inappropriate to place a sexually abused child in a home accommodating children who are themselves abusers. Although this should be avoided, it can never be entirely prevented - for example, a young person's history of sexual abuse or abusing may not emerge until after placement.

The problems of controlling sexual behaviour may arise primarily from the "fusion of sex and aggression".

Residential child care staff find sexual behaviour and sexuality difficult to handle. Reasons are given why sexual abuse induces such anxiety among residential staff.

In one study approximately 1/3rd of the peer abusers had a previous known history of abuse. However, in some residential establishments, abusive histories are not acknowledged and the young abusers develop a "cover story" which can interfere with treatment. There is a need for more specialist residential treatment facilities for young abusers. They should not be placed in foster care with younger children. In this area of work foster carers must receive special training and support.

Where young abusers have to be placed in the same unit as the abused, there must be:

- careful assessment of the risks
- agreed protection plans
- appropriate levels of surveillance.

29 This is not in the Guidance to the Children (Scotland) Act 1995

Work will also require to be undertaken to enable the abuser to accept responsibility for behaviour and to learn more appropriate ways of relating to others.

There is often no departmental guidance to residential staff; placement decisions are made without:

- considering the need to activate child protection procedures
- making Social Workers and key workers of abused and vulnerable children party to the placement decision
- giving them relevant information about the abuser's history
- adequate information at the right time
- risk assessments
- ongoing monitoring of risk
- proper staff training.

Staff must model good, respectful, balanced relationships and help young people to develop self respect, and to be clear and firm about what they want and do not want. Healthy and open attitudes to sex are vital, with information about what is considered acceptable behaviour. There should be written policies available in social services departments and residential establishments about sexual relationships for young people in care.

5.10.3 Self Harm

Suicide and self-harm in penal institutions are of continuing concern. Self harm is widespread throughout the prison system; most of those involved are young and it includes 2/3rds of all female prisoners. Most self harm and suicide attempts were a response to pressures within the prison system and to bullying. There appear to be 3 groups of prison suicides: the psychiatrically ill, life or long sentence prisoners, and those who lack the inner resources to help them to cope with hours of unfilled time in prison. The latter group tend to be younger than the others. The Prison Service has had some success with the "listener" scheme where prisoners were supported and trained by the Samaritans to befriend others.

A high proportion of all the young people who attempt suicide are in residential care.

Self harm in secure accommodation tends not to be a response to bullying but related to a past history of abuse. The main response to it involves:

- constant observation
- counselling
- referral to specialist agencies.

Self destructive behaviour is a factor in the breakdown of residential placements and in making secure care placements. Of the 74 young people in Secure Care in Scotland on a date in 1994, 62 were considered to be a risk to themselves.

Causes of death of children who died in all types of care in Scotland since 1989 include drug overdoses, solvent and drug-related deaths, road traffic accidents where the child had taken a risk, hangings and murder.

It is suggested that staff should not view self harm as an indication of a failing placement but rather that these problems should be faced in a systematic and planned way. Appropriate referral to the general practitioner, in the first instance, and to a consultant is essential.

If the significance of the environment in prison is recognised in self-harm and suicide, then prevention strategies may take on a broader and more supportive approach. For many, this may take the form of contact, activity and time spent listening.

There is a need for residential staff to have information about preventing drug and solvent abuse, to be properly trained, to have counselling skills but also access to specialist counselling services. Drug related issues should be discussed with children and young people. Staff should be aware of their responsibilities as role models, and be constantly vigilant.

Although Heads of Secure Units in Scotland said that half the young people in secure accommodation were having problems with drug, alcohol or substance abuse, only one unit had a written policy on the management of such problems, and only 3 of the 7 units felt their staff were trained to cope with behaviour arising from the misuse of substances. Since 1993, 2 young people in secure care have died as a direct result of such abuse. In one Young Offenders Institution, three-quarters of the prisoners used drugs, many of them doing so every day.

5.11 Controls, Sanctions and Physical Restraint

Setting limits and defining boundaries are important and should be carried out as positively as possible. Residential units should only have those rules and limits which are absolutely necessary, and children need to understand what the limits are for, and how and for what reasons they will be applied.

> *"Ill-considered and inappropriate discipline can increase the psychological damage already experienced by children in residential care"*
>
> *"... effectively controlled institutions and successful staff are characterised by the sparing use of sanctions".*

Sanctions must be clearly defined and wherever possible will be both immediate and consistent. They must be achievable as it is pointless to make threats which cannot be carried out. Sanctions and punishments must be appropriate to each child and young person and must be relevant to the problem.

The Literature Review lists sanctions which should not be used. Skinner found that a number of them were being used in residential establishments.

Residential staff should only take action to restrain a child as a very last resort, but 80% of young people in a NAYPIC survey complained of unnecessary forcible restraint. This has been found by other studies. However, there is a high incidence of violence against residential child care staff.

The issue of physical restraint has been taboo in many agencies but the lack of practical guidance and training is damaging. The most important parts of a policy on restraint relate to avoiding, de-escalating and debriefing after violence. Policy needs to be linked closely to training and management; if it is not clear and specific:

- staff will lack confidence
- young people will be unclear how difficult behaviour will be responded to
- inappropriate or hidden restraint techniques will be used
- restraint may not occur when it should do.

Criteria for selection of a method of physical restraint should be considered from the perspectives of young people, staff, managers in the agency and general issues. These are listed.

Rigorous published research on the safety of different approaches is not available. Four approaches have been used as the basis of restraint systems:

- the immobilisation of the subject by the use of weight or strength
- the restriction of movement of the long bones by some form of hold or lock
- maintaining the subject in an off-balanced position
- the use of pain compliance.

The techniques used in restraint must be effective, safe, ethical and appropriate to the specific setting. Certain techniques which should not be used are listed[30] but it is noted that injuries are also caused by the involvement of excessive numbers of staff or by failure to co-ordinate intervention. Training needs to be updated regularly.

Staff should be aware of the child or young person's fears or phobias and of their state of mind, including whether they are under the influence of alcohol, drugs, solvents, etc.

5.12 A Safe and Secure Environment

> *"Physical and emotional security are the basis for healthy growth and development and residential care must provide this before anything else can be achieved".*

Positive factors which provide security are:

- continuity of care and experience
- an environment which is predictable and consistent
- the continued involvement of parents, representatives of involved agencies and the community
- clarity about staff responsibilities
- clarity about expectations
- proper orientation of new staff
- continuing training for staff
- proper supervision
- freedom from abuse and neglect
- promoting children's rights
- care and treatment that promote growth.

A number of areas were identified to reduce the risk of abuse. These included:

- challenging exclusiveness and secrecy in relationships
- discouraging staff from taking children home
- sharing responsibility for trips and outings
- monitoring of links between staff and young people
- guidelines about privacy boundaries
- guidelines on sexual issues
- open communication about sexuality.

One study stresses the individual responsibility of the child care worker to protect a positive climate for children and the action the worker can take for their own development, and in the face of abuse by others.

There are three forces with potential to stop institutional maltreatment or prevent it. These are: *the child* - through self-reporting, ombudsman, advocacy; *the staff* - through selection, training, support; *the community* - through involvement, review.

Children may disclose abuse, but they need to be believed by adults.

Almost all Local Authorities now have arrangements for children to make complaints outside the line management of the home. Children's ability to complain may be limited by a lack of user-friendly information. Staff and children are dissatisfied with complaints procedures because some are unclear about the outcome of complaints, while others are not confident that views will be taken seriously or that they would be supported during investigations. Some children fear reprisals from people who have power over them.

30 They include the use of pain compliance

Children in care and their parents are not necessarily all given information about complaints procedures. Children may be concerned that there might be recriminations or disapproval if they complain or they fear their views would not be taken seriously. Children with foster carers or home on trial should be covered by the same procedures as children in residential care. Two main purposes for complaints procedures exist: resolving complaints and improving services. Both England and Scotland now have statutory complaints procedures. Social Work managers may set up difficulties which hinder complaints. There needs to be a culture which makes it easy for children to complain. There are positive effects to reacting positively.

Details are given of a project on alternative approaches to detecting and reporting possible maltreatment.

All residential units for children should now have arrangements for private telephone calls, but not all do. The ChildLine telephone line is much used by children in care and has had since 1992 a special line for children in care. Telephone helplines are one of a number of different protective strategies from which children can pick those they find most helpful.

An internal programme audit where each child is periodically interviewed confidentially and asked whether anybody has ever treated him or her improperly reveals an average of 18 complaints out of 500 interviews annually.

Children and young people should be consulted about the standard and provision of services. A Scottish example of good practice in consultation over the development of child care services is given. Consultation is part of the new statutory Children's Services Plans.

The idea of children's rights makes young people the most important part of residential services; this means continually questioning attitudes, practice and behaviour. An increasing number of Local Authorities have established Children's Rights Officer posts, some in partnership with voluntary child care organisations. Children's Rights Officers provide independent advocacy, support and representation to young people. Most have regular and frequent contact with young people and offer advice and information to help resolve difficulties. There are other types of advocacy posts.

In the US, federal standards say that every child *"should have an identifiable advocate"*.

Norway has an ombudsman for children as an independent spokesperson, a national defender and a public conscience arouser on their behalf. The Swedish children's ombudsman is employed by a voluntary organisation and works outside the State administration. Jerusalem has a Children's Council to function as an informed advocate and lobby on behalf of the children and has appointed an ombudsman. New Zealand has a Commissioner for Children. Costa Rica appointed the Defensor de la Infancia and later gave the initiative full legal status. In Australia there have been calls for a children's commission but only South Australia has set up a Government agency to speak and act on behalf of children. It is now suggested that priority be given to establishing in the UK a children's commissioner who could promote a charter for children *"bringing together all issues concerned with children for which public services are responsible"*.

Information is given about organisations which bring together young people in residential and foster care for collective action and mutual support.

5.12.1 Recruitment, Selection And Assessment

Many Inquiries into abuse in residential care highlighted inadequacies in recruitment practice. Reports on recent practice in England show that there are still problems.

The Warner Report made specific recommendations for selection and recruitment methods for staff working in children's homes. The Support Force for Children's Residential Care put these into practical form for Authorities to follow. The Literature Review gives key points from both; because my report discusses them elsewhere, I do not intend to include much about them in this chapter.

A 1993 report covers some of the recruitment changes in Social Work and Social Services Departments following the Warner Report.

Information is given about screening devices developed in the United States which try to identify sexual offenders or conversely the right kind of staff for young people's units.

Details are given of checks on criminal records in each part of the United Kingdom and of proposals for the future.

A 1994 report felt that the Warner analysis of criminal records checks was slim and missed the chance for a wider debate. It was concerned:

- about the way records are interpreted as a pointer to future behaviour
- that decisions are often made on "common sense" only
- that there is wide variation in interpretation and decision-making.

Other sources may be used for vetting and in addition superannuation information can be checked against the person's CV and qualifications can be verified through CCETSW's registry, or for SVQs the Scottish Qualifications Agency.

Recently, the National Commission of Inquiry into the Prevention of Child Abuse recommended a fully integrated, automated register accessible to employers and voluntary organisations.

In 1993 the Gulbenkian Foundation said that more work needed to be done on effective vetting procedures. A 1991 study found many professionals sceptical of screening strategies.

The essential elements of a foster care assessment process are put forward, but while there is common agreement over the qualities that are needed for good foster parents, there is frustration over how to determine which foster carers possess them. Assessment depends heavily on self-reporting and people do not always tell the truth.

One organisation changed its assessment method because of an instance of sexual abuse by foster carers. They brought into the process more information giving and openness on the part of Social Workers, about the children, most of whom were known to have been sexually abused, and about the need to investigate and assess as to whether the applicant's family was a safe one. They would ask referees whether they had any reason to believe that the applicants would abuse a child, and contact any former spouses of applicants. Family interviews look at issues such as sex and sexuality, power relationships, and attitudes to secrets, feelings, norms and taboos.

A number of training programmes for foster carers on child sexual abuse have been described in the literature. It is seen as important that foster fathers are included in preparation and training about abuse and its effect on the victim, and that other children in the foster family are prepared if they are to receive into the family a sexually abused child who might affect their lives.

Perpetrators do not have characteristics which allow them to be easily distinguished from others. It is unlikely that selection and assessment will ever be able to screen out all abusers. It is therefore essential that Social Workers and management should be alert to the possibility that sexual abuse could still occur within foster care or residential care.

5.12.2 Support for Carers and Staff

Staff supervision in most homes is irregular and excludes some temporary staff. It represents an opportunity to raise concerns about particular children or the actions of another member of staff. It needs to be sensitive to staff expressing their own need for help and their own dependency.

Commitment to supervision may help an agency to recruit suitably qualified and experienced staff to senior and manager posts.

The importance and necessity of training has been consistently highlighted in the literature; *"training of staff in institutions is a major factor in preventing and correcting institution abuse".* Training is essential to good child care practice and ultimately to the safety of children.

It can:

- ensure the practice does not stagnate
- prevent poor practice becoming the norm
- bring new ideas and practices into children's homes.

Staff find it hard to raise their concerns about professional issues, but must be helped to raise them outside their line management structure in the confidence that genuine complaints will not have repercussions.

Staff teams need support from specialists in other agencies to help them to cope with abused, disturbed and violent young people. There is also a need for staff care schemes such as stress counselling.

Foster carers also need emotional and practical support to avoid "burn-out" and stress-related abuse.

"An important safeguard for children's homes ought to be the new independent inspection and registration arrangements". Line managements should monitor homes through the effective collection and use of information. A national definition of standards will provide a more rational framework for registration and inspection.

The work of establishments should regularly be reviewed. Reviews should incorporate feedback from residents as well as from others associated with it: the views of official or informal visitors, parents and the wider community are all valuable. Children in foster care also need a rich social network. A balance needs to be struck between the positive use of external visiting and subjecting homes to endless visits from strangers.

While all Authorities have guidance on the vetting and surveillance of visitors, there are still problems with the security of buildings.

5.13 Conclusion

Children in the care of the state have often experienced abuse and neglect in their own home environment; the least they should expect is safety from abuse when in care.

> *"If a society damns its institutions as reflecting its evil and uncaring self and therefore doesn't provide them with enough resources, it becomes a self-fulfilling prophecy that under-funded institutions will attract individuals who are less well trained and less motivated, less caring and less responsible, and less healthy, thereby providing an increasingly fertile ground for all kinds of abuse". (Siskind, 1986, p.28)*

CHAPTER 6

The Existing Safeguards

There is no perfect way to ensure that children living away from home are protected from all dangers. There is, however, much that can be done to ensure that as many safeguards as possible are in place. The duty of care is on the provider - the governing body, the Local Authority or other agency - to ensure that children are protected.

In relation to those who wish them harm, to paedophiles for example, it may be helpful to think in terms of barriers. We cannot have an impenetrable wall, but the more barriers that are in place, the harder it is for the paedophile to cross them, the greater the protection for children and young people. Ideally, when there are enough barriers, the difficulty created for paedophiles is so great that they are deterred from working in this area. However, if paedophiles are deterred from entering one part of the system we have to be alert to the possibility they will target another area - for instance move from children's homes to foster care or special boarding schools. The word in Liverpool is that children's units are no longer good for paedophiles to work in and that they are talking about moving in to work with children with disabilities as being easier for them. Unless we are universal in our thoroughness, they will always find somewhere they can operate.

Constant vigilance and regular reviewing of the situation are essential. There must be strong bulwarks and bastions in place to protect vulnerable children and young people.

6.1 Recruitment Policy and Selection For Residential Child Care

6.1.1 General

The first essential is to ensure as far as possible through efficient and rigorous recruitment practices that the right people are chosen to work in residential child care, the wrong deterred or rejected. If you select enough of the right people they themselves may help weed out some of the wrong people. If you are responsible for care you are also responsible for selecting the right staff. It should be a thought-provoking business and it requires time and resources.

The least we should be able to do is to ensure that we do not employ people with convictions for offences against children, indecent behaviour or other crimes that indicate that they may be a danger to children. We should seek to avoid employing people who might in future do something that would lead to conviction. However, we must be careful to ensure that the task of appointing staff is about getting the best candidate into post. While remembering that some of the worst abusers have been charismatic figures, we must be aware that you can have charismatic figures for good as well as for evil.

Some Social Work Departments use their own personnel staff for recruitment, while others use a central personnel or manpower services function in the Local Authority. A close link with the social work function is essential. Some central personnel staff do not understand as clearly as those who have their base in social work just what it is that makes child care work special, and meriting particular attention; most of them, however, do work closely with managers of child care services, and understand their concerns. It is important to see that selection policy is a line management responsibility and that the custodian of recruitment standards is the Head of Social Work. If central personnel staff also have responsibility for the appointment of teachers, they will have some experience of the need for safeguards in this field too. Staff involved in vetting candidates for work in residential child care should themselves have been thoroughly vetted.

Much work has been done over recent years on safeguarding children through better employment practices, most notably by the working party under Norman Warner which resulted in the report Choosing With Care[31]. Most Local Authorities and other bodies which provide residential child care in Scotland either have in place or are developing policies based on its recommendations. Some disagree with Warner about psychometric testing and probationary appointments, and these are discussed below.

After the Warner Report was published, the Support Force was set up under the chairmanship of Adrianne Jones to produce a Code of Practice on recruitment, based on its recommendations.[32] This gives a step-by-step guide to recruitment that is down-to-earth and easy to follow. It was produced for England and Wales, but the differences between their system and the Scottish system are minimal, and a Scottish version could easily follow from the published Code. Some Scottish bodies are already using it, making the slight adjustments that are necessary themselves. A Scottish version should be published as soon as possible and should be followed by all bodies which recruit staff for residential child care. Both the Warner Report and the Support Force Code of Practice are essential safeguards.

I highlight below recruitment issues which seem to me of particular importance, or where there is some degree of controversy. It must always be remembered that there is something special about work with children who are not living with their own parents, and that work practices, including recruitment and personnel practices, need to be special if children are to be protected. Every time you cut a corner on recruitment, you come unstuck. Where there is a clash of interests, the rights of the children must come first.

6.1.2 Advertising posts

The Warner Report says:

> *"A feature of children's homes where disturbing episodes have occurred has often been a reluctance to fill vacancies from a wide field of competition".*

Views have been expressed in oral evidence about the ease or difficulty with which new care staff for residential child care establishments may be found in different areas of Scotland. Some find that through advertisements they are able now to obtain staff with the Diploma in Social Work, others say that they can always come up with staff locally, others say that it is extremely difficult to attract a good calibre of staff to this type of work. Unless it is a question of redeploying staff who will otherwise be made redundant, all posts should be externally advertised, and posts of heads of home should be advertised in the national press. Some employers take a cynical approach, believing there will only ever be a handful of applicants and then not of a very high calibre. Raising the status and profile of the "care industry" - because it is not yet a professional group - would improve the overall position.

6.1.3 Application Form

Concern about equal opportunities has led to demands that application forms should be brief, and should not demand information which might be used wrongly to discriminate against an applicant on the grounds of for example age, disability, sex or race. It has recently been suggested by the Convention of Scottish Local Authorities that Local Authorities should not seek "*Personal data including forenames and former names, marital status, nationality and ethnic origin*" on application forms. This may make sense for many types of local government work, but it needs modification for residential child care.

The Warner Report recommends that employers should use an application form specifically designed for work in residential child care and should collect information relevant to the post on

31 Warner, N (1992) op cit

32 The Support Force for Children's Residential Care (1995) op cit

offer. This is quite right. The form should always ask for information on an applicant's full name, including where relevant any maiden name, and any change of name since the age of 18. All changes of address in the preceding three years, age and date of birth and a full employment history must be there. Without full personal details, it is hard to make the necessary police and other checks on the chosen candidate.

Application forms are an essential basis for interviewing. The employment history needs to be full, and any gaps in it must be investigated with referees and at the interview stage, to ensure that there is nothing which might suggest that the candidate is not a suitable person to work with children and young people.

There is without doubt a conflict of interests between the rights of children living away from home and those of adults seeking work, but the rights of the adults must give way before the greater rights (and needs) of the child. I have found that staff in residential units have been ready to acknowledge the special importance attached to this, indeed would welcome the enhanced status coming from working in a job where special steps have to be taken.

6.1.4 References

References must be obtained prior to interview for all on the short list. In this again, best practice in residential child care dictates that the COSLA Code of Practice should not be followed. There should be at least two of them, on headed paper and from someone in authority, and one should be from the last social work employer, to see how the applicant's strengths were perceived in a similar environment, and to check that there was no untoward reason why they left when they did. It should be made clear on the application form that this will be done. In requesting references, the employer should state that they are kept confidential, and are never supplied to the candidates, and that nobody is ever told they are appointed "subject to references". At this point referees should be sent a full job description and person specification, and practical questions should be asked on a pro-forma to ensure that the recruiting body elicits the information it needs on all candidates. The Support Force Code of Practice provides sensible suggestions for these, of which possibly the most important question is whether the referee would employ the candidate again.

References have fallen into disrepute in some areas, on the basis that they are not always reliable, but if they are taken with other vetting procedures they are an important safeguard because they are a valuable source of information about candidates. They give the referees the chance to express any doubts they may have about the candidates as members of staff working with children. On this issue I am not in agreement with the Support Force Code of Practice, which suggests that referees should be asked whether the reference may be shared with the candidate. The reason why it is essential to reassure the referees that references are confidential, is that they should feel safe to be honest about the candidates, without fear of any later reactions from them about what was written. References must then be read with some care. Some leave questions hanging in the air, and it is important, if there are any concerns about what is not being said, that the person in charge of recruitment to a particular post makes contact by telephone with the referee. References by telephone are also needed to clarify gaps left in the employment information provided by the candidate on the application form. The prospective employer must keep clear notes of the call and share this information with the interview panel as part of the reference. If there is proper appraisal and supervision the shortcomings of a member of staff will have been made known to him or her and a reference should not come as a surprise. Some employers may believe it is good practice to share a reference with the person subject to it, but it is not the responsibility of the interviewer to share it. In a less than perfect world it is better to leave the door open for a referee to make an adverse comment in confidence. I have a greater anxiety: an unscrupulous employer may overemphasise the virtues of an applicant in order to move him or her away.

Both the prospective employer and the referee need to bear in mind that they owe a duty of care to looked after children; if the applicant had appeared in the past to be a risk in any way to children and young people, the referee would be negligent if he or she did not make every effort to alert the prospective employer.

Most people giving oral evidence generally agreed that references should be read by the interview panel before the final interview with the candidate, although there was one view expressed that it was better for the panel to decide on a chosen candidate at interview without having seen any references, and then to check that the references for the chosen candidate were in order. This came from a belief that the panel should make up their own minds about the candidate without being influenced by the references, and should use these later only to confirm their decision. I believe this begs a number of questions, and that references should be circulated by the person in charge of the interviews to the interview panel before they see the candidates. At the risk of offending equal opportunities sensitivities I believe careful reading of references should dictate some of the questions.

Social workers recruiting foster carers expect to interview referees as part of the vetting process. Although this is currently not done for recruitment to jobs in residential child care, it should be done with at least one referee. The telephone could be used if they live at too great a distance, but it would be more effective to use a professional colleague in the relevant part of the country for this task.

A reference is not a testimonial. A testimonial is usually non-specific, a warm endorsement from a former employer 'to whom it may concern' that the person concerned did a good job and is thoroughly recommended. Testimonials, being general, are not helpful for child care posts. What is needed are references which are specific to the particular job. In addition, testimonials are not a sufficient safeguard as the system is open to misuse.

6.1.5 Interviews and a Multi Method Approach

It is not adequate to choose a member of staff for residential child care on the basis of only one interview lasting up to 30 minutes, although this may be enough for some other types of post. It has been suggested to me in oral evidence that in parts of the country where it is hard to find applicants to work in residential child care, too rigorous a recruitment process may deter candidates. I am sure that if staff are inadequately vetted, we risk having too many people in the service who are not suited for the extremely arduous task of child care, and allowing those who might be a real risk to children and young people to slip through the net. Staff who are adequately vetted feel that it gives recognition to the gravity and importance of the work they do. People can be prepared for the experience of objective selection techniques and even unsuccessful candidates can benefit from the process.

You can do many things to weed out risky staff at interview, but you cannot guarantee to do so. However, at least by ensuring the appointment of some good staff you are more likely to be able to weed out the risky ones later on. I therefore strongly support the Support Force Code's guide using a mixture of assessment methods in selection. It says:

> *"The formal selection process may include different mixtures of the following:*
>
> *written exercises*
> *oral presentations*
> *group exercises*
> *psychometric testing*[33]
> *individual interviews".*

It gives examples of selection exercises. It also suggests visits to the home, to give the candidates the chance to decide whether they wish to proceed, and to involve children and young people in selection.

33 See below about psychometric testing

It is clear that a combination of procedures should be used in selection. Selection exercises should be used alongside full and sensitive interviewing to allow the selection panel to see more aspects of the candidates than might emerge in a interview alone. They can look at strengths and weaknesses, at attitudes and qualities. It is important to explore candidates' attitudes to sexuality, and their ability to discuss sensitive issues. This will probably show whether they will be able to talk in a helpful and positive way with children who are trying to sort out their own thoughts and feelings - or whether they are prepared to learn how to do this. It may offer a way of discovering that a candidate's attitudes to children are such that he or she might be a danger to them.

It is also helpful to look at the candidate's understanding of child development. A recent Scottish study of child sexual abusers found that it was a striking feature of them that they had no sense of paternal responsibility for the children; they believed it was up to the children to protect themselves, and they never saw themselves as having the responsibility to protect children. Candidates should be asked whose responsibility it is to stop certain things from happening.

Attitudes to power and authority could also usefully be explored. Abuse is frequently an issue of power.

Young people from the children's unit in question should if possible be involved in the recruitment process, after due preparation. It should be made clear to the candidates and to them that they have no right of decision-making, but that their views will be taken into account. They may be sensitive to undercurrents which adults will ignore, and may be able to alert the interviewers to something which should be investigated at another stage in the vetting process. At the very least, they are likely to see whether a candidate is capable of communicating with young people.

In recruiting care staff, we have much to learn from the recruitment of foster carers about thoroughness, and individual agencies should compare their own systems. The sharing of best practice, through a communication focal point, might be something The Centre for Residential Child Care could look at.

6.1.6 Psychometric and other forms of testing

The Warner Report proposed that aptitude and personality tests should be evaluated to see what could appropriately be used in the selection of staff for children's homes. The Support Force suggested that Psychometric Testing might be used, but with caution. At the time it was written there were no tests specifically designed for residential child care workers, or as a means of screening out potential paedophiles.

Management and Personnel staff who gave evidence were divided on the value of Psychometric Testing, with some agreement that it could indicate which candidate had good managerial potential. Some of them were able to indicate that aptitude tests for child care workers are being developed now. A Care Assessment Consortium of seven Local Authorities, one of which was Scottish, was formed two years ago, working with Saville and Holdsworth, a firm which specialises in recruitment, to see how councils could improve their recruitment to residential child care posts. An objective selection technique, the theory runs, means trying to fit the person to the role, so you have to pinpoint what the successful characteristics of the people you need are. I am impressed by what I have seen of this work. There is a simple approach to selection:

- Diagnosis. Through a thorough in-depth study of the job, you develop an understanding of its nature and can prepare a job analysis. You establish the skills needed, the personality characteristics, the motives, the abilities and the attitudes which lead to a real likelihood of someone being able to do the job successfully (and ideally in a superior way). You do this by identifying the competencies which are sets of related behaviours arising from underlying aspects of the individual which are determinants of job success. 'Underlying aspects of the individual' includes knowledge, skills personality, values and motives. As they are focused on what people actually do, competency based approaches have the potential to offer a clear and integrated set of dimensions against which performance can be described and measures. Work to derive competencies has been done by the Consortium for residential child care (specifically Heads of Homes and Residential Social Workers).

- The assessment process. For a competency based interview you have to go through the candidate's track record with them competency by competency, in an absolutely explicit and open way to see how far they demonstrate each. The interview guide offers a list of suggested questions. The interview can be the sole methodology used, but this can be subject to bias, and objectivity is increased by the assessment centre or multi-method approach. With this you use a number of different techniques which can include tests, questionnaires giving insight into personality, group exercises and role play. You can for example gain various evidence to suggest how far an individual has a particular quality such as resilience. Such structured interview guides have been prepared for jobs in residential child care and a training programme and relevant materials have been designed for line/Human Resource managers who will be the interviewers.

- Development. This is ongoing as part of performance management, to identify performance gaps and close them, through using very good performance measures on the job and day to day supervision to ensure that the people you select do a better job. You could improve a worker's resilience, for example.

- Monitoring. You check on the validation processes and technique, by tracking performance using performance measures. You look to see the correlation between the results of assessment process and the effectiveness on the job - you review the pertinence of the competencies to the performance on the job and whether they need to be updated as a result of the monitoring. You check how well the individual performs, comparing that with how his or her potential was seen at the beginning, to see whether the techniques being used are those which produced the best results.

The introduction of this most promising system, which has gone ahead in a few areas, has been halted in others by local government reorganisation.

Saville and Holdsworth have also looked at the possibility of validating Psychometric Testing as a tool for the exclusion of paedophiles. Their conclusion is that psychometric testing should not be used alone in the selection procedure but that it could be usefully used as part of a selection procedure. However, it is clear in my view that any research would depend on a number of paedophiles slipping past the process, then being found out, so that the process can be modified and tested again, and this would take two decades at least. It is not, in my opinion, a feasible option at the present time. However quite a small investment could enable work to be undertaken pulling together some of those who work with convicted offenders to describe their characteristics. This might enable clinical psychologists to offer advice that contributed to the selection process.

6.1.7 Criminal Record Checks

It is essential that Criminal Record Checks are carried out on all who are chosen for work in residential child care and who will have substantial unsupervised access to children. In Scotland, this responsibility is efficiently handled by the Scottish Criminal Records Office, (SCRO), which can check conviction information relatively quickly. If a person has worked in England, however, there is no national body as yet, and checks must be made with relevant police forces; this takes much longer. Police checks are unlikely to be able to uncover some offences committed while a person served in the Armed Forces. If someone has lived and worked elsewhere in Europe, it is unusual for checks to be made. It may be possible for someone coming from abroad to bring a certificate showing that they have no previous convictions, but prospective employers are not able to be certain that they are genuine. In a few cases Interpol can do checks, but this depends on the situation in each particular country, and on other factors; it is not a normal part of Interpol's duties.

Local Authorities in Scotland can make direct contact with the SCRO, having received the signed permission of the person they wish to appoint and themselves signing a form of indemnity. A few independent providers of residential child care are in direct contact with SCRO on their own behalf, but most have to approach them through the Local Authority. We do not have in Scotland the equivalent of the Voluntary Organisations Consultancy Service which makes recruitment checks on behalf of certain voluntary bodies in England and Wales. I would expect the current system's problems of access for independent bodies to be sorted out in the light of the Cullen Inquiry and of this Review.

In order to ensure the accuracy of the information given to the SCRO, the employer should insist on seeing proof of the applicant's name and birth date.

Until now, it has only been possible to obtain information about convictions and pending cases. It must be borne in mind that a comparatively low proportion of those who commit sexual offences against children are reported to the police, and a low proportion, about 5%, of these are convicted. The Police Act 1997 would bring the Scottish position in line with that of England and Wales, where certain other types of factual information can be provided that might indicate a person's unsuitability for work with children.

'Hard', or factual information is one thing. There is also 'soft' information in the Intelligence legitimately collected by the Police or others that would help us to be aware as to which people might be a danger to children. One of the problems with Thomas Hamilton was that, although there was 'soft' information about him in the files of a number of organisations, it was not enough to allow tough action to be taken. We need to find legitimate ways of accessing 'soft' information. Under the Police Act 1997, the applicant for a post working with under-18s will request through the employing body an Enhanced Criminal Record Certificate which will give not only details of convictions but also any information the Chief Officer of the appropriate police force considers might be relevant for the job in question. This is likely to be in place during 1998, and will give useful additional safeguards.

No person should be allowed "substantial unsupervised access" to children living away from home unless police checks have been carried out. Taxi drivers, for example, may be put in this position when taking pupils from residential schools home at weekends, or when taking children from children's homes or foster carers to and from school daily; they should be checked, unless a vetted escort is used.

6.1.8 Other checks - Education

The General Teaching Council is a useful model for a possible register of social services staff. All teachers in Scottish Local Authority schools must be registered with it.

All applicants for registration must complete an application form, which contains a section where offences must be detailed. Half of the form goes to the SCRO, where they match the information to what they have on computer; the Council also checks their names with relevant police forces outside Scotland. If there is an offence, the GTC must take a view as to whether it is relevant to the applicant's suitability to teach. If the applicant is suitable, they pay an initial £15, then £10 per year, to cover all the expenses of the council.

Teaching is a notifiable occupation. In addition to the initial police checks, the police will inform the Registrar at the GTC if a teacher commits an offence later in his or her career - as long as it is clear to the investigating officer that he/she is a teacher.

The GTC receives information from schools if there is inappropriate behaviour which might show a teacher to be unsuitable. The Registrar can decide to take no action, or to issue a warning, but otherwise the issue goes to the Investigating Committee, which acts as a screening body and can decide whether there is a case to answer. A teacher removed from the Register can seek restoration later, but there is no right of appeal within the GTC: any appeal must be to the Court of Session. Local Authorities have been asked to tell the GTC if a school or an authority forces a resignation for any teacher.

While from most points of view the GTC is efficient, it has two drawbacks. The first is that student teachers are checked for convictions not before they do their teaching practice, but at the end of their training; by this time they will have already had access to children in the classroom. The second is that independent schools are free to use teachers who are not GTC-registered; this must be a matter for concern, for although the schools tend to use registered teachers it is a loophole which allows people found to be unsuitable to continue to teach.

Two lists can be consulted to check whether there are any doubts about teachers. "List 1R", collated by the Scottish Office, shows teachers who have been struck off, or students who were stopped in training and therefore had registration refused or withdrawn. The English equivalent is "List 99", but whereas List 99 also shows other people in work connected with schools, janitors for example, who have been found to be unsuitable, List 1R does not.

6.1.9 Other checks - Social Work

The Department of Health collates the Consultancy Service Index for England and Wales. This lists people who have been dismissed or have resigned from work in the child care field in circumstances which suggest the welfare or safety of children has been put at risk; it also contains the names of people who have been notified to the Department by the police following convictions for offences against children or which suggest that the person involved might be a risk to children. This can be consulted by potential employers. There is currently no equivalent list in Scotland, although there is an informal arrangement under which Directors of Social Work may contact colleagues by letter to suggest that if they thought of appointing a certain individual to a post, they should perhaps make contact for a discussion of concerns first. All involved have long recognised the inadequacies of this system, including the lack of protection for the individuals named, and it led to an agreement that Social Work Departments should always insist that applicants for posts give the Director of their current or last Local Authority post as a referee. An additional safeguard would be some form of Consultancy Index which could include the necessary protection for the individual. It would be acceptable to the Civil Rights lobby for it to use as its standard of proof "the balance of probability" rather than "beyond all reasonable doubt".

Video libraries seek evidence of identity before renting out a film. Civil Servants must have positive vetting before they are allowed to look after confidential information. Do we not have a greater need of identity checks and positive vetting for adults who are to look after our children?

The Right Hon. John Bowis MP, when a Minister of State for Health, spoke enthusiastically at the launch of a vetting agency run by a much respected retired police Chief Superintendent. It offered a full vetting service on a private basis to all employers of residential child care staff, but unfortunately at a time of financial stringency most Local Authorities and other bodies found it too expensive to use.

6.1.10 Probationary Appointments

The Warner Report and the Skinner Report recommended that probationary periods of 12 months should be standard practice for all new appointments to children's homes. Managers in many Local Authorities have told me that they believe these are a bar to recruitment. On the other hand the chief executive of one large national provider of residential care expressed the view that on the contrary he has found that a high calibre of staff is attracted to an organisation which seems to express high standards by its use of the probationary period. If all child care employing bodies use the probationary period, then staff will not be tempted by organisations which do not.

The probationary period is an important safeguard for children. It is not always going to be clear at the interview stage that a person is unsuitable for work in residential child care, and it is essential to deal with this if it emerges, as it may well do, during the first year of work. It is not only the question of whether someone because of their sexual proclivities or their short temper might endanger children; there are some people who find that they do not like working with young people in the close surroundings of a residential unit, and this must be dealt with before it affects the atmosphere and working practices in the unit.

The probationary period must be used as Warner intended, with assessment and appraisal, and assistance to the probationer through training and personal development if there are areas on which he or she is apparently not meeting the needs of the employing authority and the children. The views of young people about the probationer should be sought and used as part of the supervision and appraisal process.

6.1.11 Locum Bureau or Bank

Children have in the past been put at risk because of the use of temporary staff who were not properly interviewed and vetted and who acted as a weak link. Where arrangements were not in place to ensure that there were suitable arrangements for cover at times of holidays and sickness, people might be drafted in to work in residential establishments on the basis that they were related to an existing member of staff, or were living as a near neighbour to the unit. Quite apart from the fact that a properly competent person should cover a vacant care post, it is risky to introduce any adult who has not been thoroughly vetted into a child care establishment where they will have unsupervised access to the children. Different solutions to the problem of finding temporary replacement staff are used by different employers. One school close to a large city is able to make use of former members of staff who still live in the vicinity. One Local Authority drafts in management or field services staff. In both cases they can be certain that the people concerned have been properly chosen and vetted.

The best solution to this problem is the bank of staff, such as there are for nurses, properly selected, vetted and inducted, who can be used wherever emergency cover is needed. In saying "properly selected, vetted and inducted", I would expect that they would be appointed in just the same way as staff are appointed to permanent posts, with the same application forms, arrangements for references, interviewing system and selection exercises, the same record checks. Induction training should take place as for permanent staff, with the added complication that they are not attached to any particular unit.

This is, however, a solution which is easier for larger Authorities to employ, and which has tended to be problematical for smaller ones with fewer units. Now, with the reorganisation of local government, there are more smaller Authorities. Perhaps consideration should be given to organisations forming themselves into consortia for the purpose of bringing together, and having access to, a bank of vetted temporary staff.

Staffing agencies should only be used if they are entirely conversant with the needs of the employing body, if all of their staff involved in recruitment of child care staff have been rigorously vetted, and if they use the appropriate selection and vetting procedures as stringently as the Local Authority must do.

6.1.12 Press cutting service

The Scottish Scouts Association, an organisation which does not currently have access to SCRO checks, subscribes to a press cuttings bureau, which gives them information about any adult who has been tried for offences against children and whose case has at some time been reported in a local or national newspaper. Their managers have found this a most valuable tool in the vetting of people who apply to be scout leaders.

6.2 Training

The Skinner Report, which says much about the importance of a skilled workforce, recommended targets for residential child care staff training levels:

> *"Local Authorities and independent organisations should aim to achieve a position in which 30% of all residential child care staff, and 90% of all senior residential child care staff hold a Diploma in Social Work or equivalent.*
>
> *Local Authorities and independent organisations should aim to achieve a position, in which 60% of residential child care staff are assessed as competent at HNC/SVQ level 3."* (Recommendations 47 & 48)[34]

There has been unfortunately less progress towards these targets than might be wished. I find it necessary to emphasise through this Review the complexity of the task that faces staff; if they are to do more than simply provide a roof over the heads of children, they must be properly equipped for it. Training is an essential part of that equipment.

6.2.1 Induction Training

> *"All residential child care staff should have 2 weeks induction training. This should be the training target given first priority."* (Skinner, Recommendation 50)

Skinner suggested that induction training should be standardised for each agency, and that new entrants should be put on a set of steps that can lead to formal training. It would appear from my contact with residential child care staff that, although agencies tend now to have systems of induction training, these are not always being used in individual establishments. It makes no sense that staff should start work in residential child care units with less induction training than they might receive if they were to start work in one of our major clothing stores. The Support Force offers a useful model package for induction training.[35]

Where staff are re-deployed into residential child care posts they must always receive induction training, and in addition an agreed training plan and its timing should form part of the re-deployment contract.

Induction training should include the safety of the children being looked after, and strategies to try to ensure it. It should also start the carers thinking about themselves; self awareness is an important part of social work training because it encourages workers to be clear about boundaries.

There is a particular problem with temporary staff; on the one hand they are "only" temporary, on the other they may have a succession of temporary jobs - some "temps" stay 3 years. If temporary staff can be squeezed out of the system by such measures as the locum bureau the problem will not arise.

6.2.2 In-Service Training

During their time working in residential child care, staff need training to meet their individual personal development goals, as shown through performance appraisal.

There will be a regular need for staff to have "short bursts" of training on particular topics, sometimes individually, sometimes as a staff group, in addition to those mentioned in the Skinner Report. Examples of these would be restraint, sex and sexuality, safe caring and recording.

Child protection will need to be covered in some detail during in-service training. It must be made entirely clear to staff at all levels in residential child care that child protection is as important in residential units as in ordinary houses, and that activity that is unacceptable in families is just as unacceptable in group homes. Staff need to learn what must be done if children are being harmed, and the procedures that must be followed.

34 Skinner, (1992) op cit

35 Support Force, op cit (1995)

6.2.3 Scottish Vocational Qualifications

SVQ3 or its equivalents are seen as essential training for basic grade care staff. There are, however, mixed feelings about the SVQ. Some employers are comfortable with it, while others find the system confusing and doubt its value in raising standards. Some care staff say they prefer it to the professional qualification in social work, because they want to stay in residential child care. Some are finding that the SVQ3 makes very heavy demands on their free time, and they are having to call a halt part way through the training until they can find more space for it. Some good caring staff are finding the emphasis on writing in the qualification makes difficulties for them, and I sympathise, but while it is demanded that basic grade staff should act as key workers for the young people, it is important that their writing skills should allow them to record clearly and well. 7% of assistant officers in charge now have SVQ3 or its equivalent, and 5% of basic grade workers have it.

However SVQs are not training at all. They are a system for assessing competence; there is no requirement at present to train those who are not yet competent so the system concentrates on those who are competent at the expense of those who are not. There is an SVQ (HNC) which means you have been assessed as competent as well as having some teaching and learning. CCETSW, quite properly, distinguish between the two.

Some employers require a minimum of HNC/SVQ3 to be treated as of Qualified Residential Care Officer status. After completion of the HNC they start the SVQ units. This can take 4 years which means that there can be staff from 3 different intakes undergoing assessment at the same time. This in turn can mean there is less opportunity for other staff to be spared for basic training courses. All the assessment activity creates the illusion of a lot of training going on when, in reality, nothing may be happening at all. There are many pressures on staffing levels with cost being an obvious one. There is a conflict between having enough staff to release people for training and not bewildering the children by having too many different adults surrounding them. We need trained staff and have to be prepared to pay the price.

According to CCETSW, the picture may not be as bad as the figures suggest. Some employers are concentrating on staff achieving a certain number of units towards SVQ, rather than the full qualification. Such staff will not show up in the statistics, but there are many more who have achieved a number of units than have received the full award. The HNC in Social Care (incorporating SVQ at Level 3) is referred to explicitly in the Skinner Report. Some employers have invested heavily in the HNC while others have concentrated on the SVQ alone. There is some ambiguity whether achieving SVQ3 without doing the HNC should count towards the targets.

There is a place for a separate training in residential child care, which could equip people to work wherever there are children living away from home. This could accord some status to a very essential profession. When the old forms of training were overtaken it was held that a separate qualification was divisive. It is, if anything, even more divisive to have SVQs for residential staff but not for field staff. There should also be an opportunity for foster carers to take an SVQ.

SVQ training should explicitly address issues related to the safeguarding of children and young people; these should be included within its Units of Competence.

6.2.4 Diploma in Social Work

The Skinner Report sees the Diploma in Social Work, which is viewed by many as primarily a qualification for field social work, as the most appropriate one for most officers in charge in residential child care. A qualification at this level confers status on residential care. Yet although it offers many appropriate skills, there are gaps in this training. It is a general course in social work. There is no requirement on anybody taking it to do a placement in a residential unit; there is little work done on the course on child development; there is even less within the course on communicating with or listening to children. As with the SVQ3, there is a need for the Diploma to address explicitly issues about safeguarding children and young people.

Currently one big difficulty about training staff to Diploma level is that at some stage many of them decide that they might have an easier life in field social work, with more status, and they leave the residential service. There is no doubt that employers have used the Diploma in Social Work mainly as a qualification for Field Workers. This tells us more about the priorities of employers and the status of residential care staff than it does about the purpose and design of the Diploma in Social Work.

The linkage between HNC/SVQ and the Diploma in Social Work is inadequate. Part of the problem must be the difficulty in making the leap from the focus on the practical and concrete in the former to the need for conceptual ability in the latter.

Some people interviewed for the Review thought that the "particular pathway" model of training is a good model for residential child care and should be developed in Scotland. The current requirements allow such pathways to be developed in child care or, indeed, residential care. This would be a desirable development.

It is presently possible to complete a Diploma in Social Work without coming into contact with children. Routeing people through a Child Care Pathway will overcome this. In 1990, 41% of officers in charge had a CQSW or equivalent, as did 30% of assistant officers in charge, and 6% of basic grade care staff. The Diploma was introduced after this time. In 1995, 65% of officers in charge, 26% of assistants and 6% of basic care grade staff had a Diploma, CQSW or equivalent.

The Diploma would also be a more effective qualification for Field Social Workers working with looked after children if the matters mentioned in the first paragraph were included on courses. It would be much better if the Diploma course was taken over 3 years. The only doubt in my mind is whether that money would be better spent elsewhere on the specific training of residential staff. But it is likely that all Scottish courses will soon be of 3 years duration. A general reduction in budgets puts the Safeguard of training at risk.

6.2.5 Management Training

Managers need knowledge and experience of the type of service they are managing, but they also need particular additional skills. When somebody is promoted to be an officer in charge, it is not enough to believe that they can simply carry forward those things they have learnt up until then; there needs to be increased input.

> *"the management tasks in the home are to translate plans and objectives into regular functioning of the home, to ensure staff are effectively deployed, briefed and trained and that the home is responsive to the individual need of each young person or child".* (Skinner 5.19)

The Skinner Report goes on to say that the management training of officers in charge is of critical importance and that they may find themselves holding a large budget with minimum training and no administrative support. It was suggested that the Scottish Office should finance and commission management training for officers in charge as a priority in 1992/93. Specific grant money was offered for this, but it would appear that in only one of the former Regions have a significant number of officers in charge and their assistants obtained management qualifications in this way.

6.3 Other Staffing Issues

6.3.1 Staffing Levels

Staffing levels should allow the unit to meet its stated objectives in work with the residents; they have an influence on the quality of care that is provided, and on the safety of the children and young people cared for. There is no recognised national standard, but some Local Authorities and other providers of residential care work to the recommendations of the Wagner Development Group, as published by the National Institute for Social Work[36].

This offers useful formulae for working out the number of staff needed to cover the unit during the waking day and at night, given the number of residents and the type of activities and tasks which must be carried out. The Development Group refers back to the Castle Priory Report[37] which identified factors to be taken into account when working out the total number of staff needed. It is clear that there must be some slack in the system to allow for emergencies, or for special occasions. There must also be plenty of time on a normal day-to-day basis for staff to talk and interact with the residents, as a group but also on a one-to-one basis.

While there will be occasions when good sense dictates that attention to an emergency means leaving one member of staff alone in a unit, rosters should not be arranged, nor plans made, to provide one member of staff on duty in the unit.

The aim should be that for a mixed residents' group the staff on duty should have both male and female members.

6.3.2 Staff pay and conditions

> *"... current salaries and conditions of service are generally insufficient to attract and retain staff able to undertake the complex tasks often involved in residential child care, and with the qualifications and training that should be brought to bear."* (Skinner, 4.3)

Staff pay and conditions can have a vital impact on the morale of the staff, and thus on the morale of the children and young people in the unit. While some types of residential child care unit (such as secure units) have favourable pay and conditions for staff, many children's homes are restricted by their pay levels as to the type of qualified staff they use. People with teaching or nursing qualifications can bring an extra quality to the work of a unit, and they should enter the service as basic grade staff, but they cannot be paid as qualified Social Workers.

6.3.3 Staff supervision

All who spoke about staff supervision in giving evidence agreed that it was important to consider it as part of staff rights. They recognised that staff should be closely supervised and that attention should be paid to their needs for support and development as an important safeguard. There was concern that supervision tends to be neglected when the agency is under stress, and that some external managers, who may not come from a child care background, were less likely to share the professional knowledge necessary to counsel staff in supervision or recognise signs of trouble; they might themselves be under pressure to think about budgets rather than people.

Most agencies record supervision sessions, and regard the recording as the property of the agency. It is not generally thought that the recording would deter members of staff from raising sensitive matters of concern in supervision, although among people who gave oral evidence there was a separation of views at this point: some thought that managers should be ready to stop recording in order to encourage a person to speak out, where others thought that a complete record might be necessary later.

I believe that it is essential that the supervisor be prepared to stop recording if it is felt to be inhibiting. If it is decided that some formal action should be taken, he or she can agree with the supervisee as to what should be recorded.

A good working relationship between supervisor and supervisee is a crucial safeguard. Where a level of trust is established, sensitive information can be shared.

36 Wagner Development Group (1990):"Staffing In Residential Care Homes" (London, NISW)
37 Castle Priory Conference Report (1969) The Residential Task in Child Care (London, The Residential Child Care Association)

6.3.4 Staff Assessment and appraisal

"Proper performance appraisal is essential to ensure that each member of staff is contributing appropriately to the achieving of a home's objectives." (Warner, 6.31)

Any child care team, and each individual member of it, however skilled, is capable of improvement. This should form the basis of performance appraisal. Staff development is a positive issue, which can lead to greater job satisfaction for staff as well as improving the home for its residents. Appraisal should be carried out on a formal basis each year, but there should be no surprises in it for staff who are properly supervised during the course of the year. It should indicate where there are training or personal development needs, and these should be met as far as possible before the next year's appraisal session. It should never be linked to performance-related pay.

6.3.5 Living In

Residential care has changed greatly from the time when there were living in house parents who would be supported by other staff. It is now far more likely that all staff will live out in their own individual accommodation. There is a fair amount of singleton sleeping in by staff and this almost always seems to involve women staff, although more it would appear by accident than design. Cover for sleeping in arrangements varies but is seen as important by all who talked about it. In many ways I regret that living in has become a thing of the past because I would prefer adults to share the home with the children. It would seem quite impracticable today and in any event I am aware that many of the offences presently coming to light involved living in staff. Staff who were living in used their rooms as a place to which they could invite children on their own. This made for a situation where abusers could more easily operate. Now, where a few living in arrangements do still exist, it is generally agreed that they should not continue for very long. Most independent boarding school houses do have living in staff.

6.4 Inspection

Inspection is important firstly because of its commitment to quality of care. It demands that all concerned should be committed to improving the service. To have inspections of almost all residential child care units is a relatively new safeguard. There are a number of expectations we could have of inspection as a safeguard

- They allow the quality of the care provided in the Unit to be checked against certain standards
- They allow the ethos of the Unit to be reported upon
- They can look at staffing levels and staff training, and how staff are handling issues such as safe caring
- Inspectors are another group of people to whom children might just be prepared to talk; they are available in the Unit, obviously investigating the Unit and asking questions about the care provided
- They may give parents a chance to complain, or to talk about something that is bothering them
- Unit staff may have a chance to talk to somebody outside normal line management
- Inspectors can look at and draw conclusions from the complaints and other logs
- They can also look at and draw conclusions from logs of violent incidents, or other important records
- They should be able to offer a clear eye going in, that can prepare an honest and direct report and make recommendations that will be acted upon.

We would expect this kind of service for all residential units for children living away from their own homes.

6.4.1 Inspection Systems

The systems in place for the inspection of children's services are complicated, and there is both overlap and omission in how they operate in practice. Some services are subject to several types of inspection. The type of inspection used depends upon the type of organisation being inspected, rather the nature of the young people using the service.

These different types of inspection are shown in relation to different types of organisation and frequency in Chart 1. Difficulties are likely where organisations are inspected by more than one body, but there are recent examples of good collaboration between inspectors.

Certain organisations are not subject to any regular inspections, for example, services run by Housing Associations or Health Trusts. Others are very infrequently inspected, for example, certain residential schools operated by Local Authority Education Authorities, which are not required to register under the Children (Scotland) Act 1995, and as such are only inspected by HMI. Some services appear to be over-inspected, for example, independent residential schools, which can receive Local Authority, HMI and the new WRP inspections.

An additional inspection can be made at any time if there is concern about a facility.

6.4.2 Inspecting Bodies

Local Authority

The Local Authority Social Work inspection units had their responsibilities extended to cover children's services in 1991. The Children (Scotland) Act 1995 will make greater demands of them. With the changes since local government re-organisation, smaller inspection units mean that the opportunity to develop specialisms such as child care within inspection teams is reduced.

Frequency of inspections: at least twice a year, one announced and one unannounced.

Social Work Services Inspectorate

SWSI carry out 5 types of inspection, but only their inspections of secure units form part of this study. A recent Scottish Office report has reviewed secure accommodation in Scotland[38]. These inspections are found to be very thorough and they deal with safeguarding issues. Standards are drawn from a range of sources, rather than one specific document, and the Inspectorate do take account of these.

Frequency of inspections: every 3 years.

HMI Reports on Schools

HM Inspectors of Schools have a responsibility to provide an independent evaluation of the education system. Until now their role has been primarily educational but under Section 35 of the Children Act 1995 they have a responsibility to inspect schools in terms of the welfare of residential pupils. They now speak of "WRP" Inspections. Where schools are also registered with Social Work Departments, Local Authority Inspectorates will inspect as well. They do not use standards documents, but have a tight methodology for the inspections that they carry out. This is based on the 8 principles of the Skinner Report, and was drawn up in close consultation with SWSI, whose inspectors are involved in several WRP inspections each year. The principles, which were drawn from the experience and expectations of children in care, now form the basis of inspecting homes and schools throughout Scotland from Glasgow to Gordonstoun. Under the Children (Scotland) Act 1995, WRP inspections cover hostels attached to mainstream secondary schools, previously uninspected.

Frequency of inspections: WRP inspections on a cycle of approximately five years, or as required; other inspections on a cycle of approximately 12 years for secondary schools, 15 years for primary schools, or as required.

38 Skinner, Angus (1996) A Secure Remedy: A Review Of The Role, Availability And Quality Of Secure Accommodation For Children In Scotland (Edinburgh, the Social Work Services Inspectorate For Scotland)

The Scottish Hospital Advisory Service
The Scottish Hospital Advisory Service can inspect health service establishments and those which are paid for by health service finance. Currently they do not inspect children's or adolescents' services unless these are linked to adult services.

The Mental Welfare Commission for Scotland
The Mental Welfare Commission has a role in the protection of children, particularly those with learning difficulties. They should receive reports of Incidents or Accidents concerning children who have a mental illness or a learning difficulty. The Mental Welfare Commission's remit requires them to make enquiries but there is less clarity about the need to alert them. It would appear that hospitals are more familiar with the task of the MWC than Local Authorities or Voluntary Organisations. The Commission is actively encouraging the reporting of incidents and accidents, which will include harm in all its senses, and it would be helpful if the Social Work Services Inspectorate did the same.

The MWC will not inspect units but they will visit individual young people aged 16 to 18 who are on Guardianship or detained under the Mental Health Act if they want a Review. Their role is much more with individuals than with groups but they will visit establishments annually and invite individuals to meet them. They would certainly feel free to comment on standards, training or external support for instance.

There has been recent recognition of a need to rationalise the service for adolescents who come within the purview of the Mental Health Act with no children on adult wards. Thankfully there are not enough mentally ill children to merit an adolescent unit in every town in Scotland, and if there was then it might get filled to justify it which would mean labelling and starting a career as a mental illness patient at a young age. The Mental Health Act has no minimum age.

Mental Health Act Guardianship is different to guardianship and can be a protective measure for 16 - 18 year olds.

CHART 1 - INSPECTION BODIES

	LA Inspection Unit	HMI	HMI Welfare of Residential Pupils Inspection	SWSI	Scottish Hospital Advisory Service	Mental Welfare Trust
Children's Homes	✓	✓ (if education is supplied on the premises)		Have the right to inspect		On the basis of individual's need/wish
Residential School (Independent) with LA SWD children	✓ if registered (with SWD voluntarily or as a result of Children (Scotland) Act 1995)	✓	✓	Have the right to inspect		On the basis of individual's need/wish
Residential School (Independent) without LA SWD children		✓	✓			
Residential School (Local Education Dept.)		✓	✓	Have the right to inspect		On the basis of individual's need/wish
Secure Unit	✓ some	✓	✓	✓		On the basis of individual's need/wish
Health Facilities		✓ (if education is supplied on the premises)			position unclear	On the basis of individual's need/wish
Hostels attached to schools			✓			On the basis of individual's need/wish
Housing Association Facilities	✓ If registered with SWD as providing residential care					

6.4.3 Comment

Inspectors are normally very good at identifying the ethos of the establishment, as well as commenting on the smaller details.

All types of inspectors like to involve at least some of the children in their inspection, by sitting down with them as a group or as individuals, and checking how they feel about the care they are getting. Many of the young people in care interviewed felt that all the residents in an establishment should meet with the inspectors. Some social work inspectors use staff from Who Cares? as lay inspectors, and they sometimes involve the young people themselves in establishments other than their own.

In residential units, there can be problems in overcoming young people's reluctance to talk, particularly if there is obvious resistance from a unit's staff group to the inspections and the inspectors are not well known, but these are being lessened as trust starts to develop. Parents' views are harder to obtain, and inspectors are trying various methods.

By looking at an establishment's records of, for example, complaints or restraint and other violent incidents, the inspectors may be able to pick up a pattern which indicates that some kind of remedial action needs to be taken. They should be checking to see what written policy the unit has on restraint or how to handle violence.

It is helpful that Local Authority inspection teams make not only one expected visit every year, but also one unexpected one. Most of the unannounced visits are pre-planned by the inspection unit, but there are circumstances which would cause them to make an additional visit. If Inspectors picked up on the grapevine that something was going wrong in the children's home; if there was a formal complaint to the inspection team about the home; if they were notified of significant changes in senior personnel, particularly the officer in charge; if there were a sudden high turnover of staff, or a lot of temporary staff had to be used. It is not always a matter of concern which makes them visit: sometimes they will drop in because they are in the area.

Inspectors need to be prepared to visit during unsociable hours, such as last thing at night, and very early in the morning. Some stay overnight.

There is clearly a need for more frequent inspections for certain types of establishments, and for the school hostels to be brought within the Local Authority inspection network. It has now been shown that it is quite possible to inspect foster care, if resources were available.

For whichever type of agency an inspector works, they need to have a knowledge of residential child care, and of the safeguards which protect children within it. As Burgner says "*Inspection units need to be staffed and resourced so that they can call on a range of professional skills - in nursing, pharmacy, nutrition and alcohol and drug misuse, in mental disability, physical and sexual abuse etc. - whenever they are needed*".[39] I noted with regret that recent changes in the Scottish Office have meant that it is no longer possible for SWS Inspectors to take colleagues from the Health Department with them on inspections; their advice had been valuable.

There is a need for national standards against which inspections can be made because standards are a method of providing a benchmark. There is a strong case for national guidance in the form and content of Social Work Inspection Reports, where there is no consistency at present.

6.4.4 Registration

Units for children and young people run by voluntary and independent organisations must be registered, and registration depends on them meeting the appropriate standards. Initial registration depends on this, and a failure to provide an appropriate standard of care at any future time can lead to registration being cancelled. Inspections are most valuable where Social Work Inspectors have the power to insist on changes for the good of residents. They have this in relation to independent care providers, because they could cancel their registration, but they do

39 Burgner, Tom (1996) Moving Forward: Review of the Regulation and Inspection of Social Services (London, HMSO)

not in relation to Local Authorities whose units are not registrable. Given the financial pressures on Local Authorities, this is a problem, which Burgner recognises by saying *"it is claimed by some that sub-standard services exist to a greater extent in the public sector and that, where they do, the timescales for remedial action to bring facilities up to standard are larger and less strictly enforced."* A Scottish Office consultation document has now gone out, suggesting that registration should be extended to establishments run by Local Authorities.

For much of the information in this section, I am indebted to The Centre for Residential Child Care, which undertook a major piece of work of behalf of the Review, a study of issues of safeguarding in the inspection process. The Centre will shortly be publishing a full report on this research.

6.5 Management Arrangements

6.5.1 Complaints Procedures

Complaints procedures are now available for use by children in care, as they are for other social work clients[40]. The use that is made of them varies greatly, but they offer real potential for young people to raise matters that are of concern to them. Complaining is quite a sophisticated activity, and many children simply want to have something sorted out as quickly and as simply as possible. They do not usually want to rock the boat and upset the staff. One Local Authority, which showed itself open to children's comments, found that 312 contacts from children with issues of concern led to only 10 formal complaints.

Despite some staff worries, there seems to be little evidence of children using complaints procedures either lightly or maliciously. It is important that children should be taken seriously when they complain, because they may test the system on small issues, holding back more serious ones until they see what reaction they have. Where organisations have developed special child-friendly complaints procedures, these are particularly successful.

Many matters which concern children can be dealt with quickly and informally, without a need to invoke complaints procedures. There are circumstances in which the formal procedures should always be used:

- any time the child or young person wishes to make a formal complaint

- if something has been raised informally, but not resolved to the child or young person's satisfaction

- if there is a suggestion by the child or young person of abuse by an adult connected with the unit of the agency or department.

The outcome of a complaint must always be properly explained to the complainant.

Some secure units and residential schools have children from a number of Local Authorities placed with them. Most Local Authorities require to be told when one of their children complains. If thirteen children from thirteen Local Authorities made a complaint about the same thing, who would see any pattern in their concern? Providers of services must report all complaints to the registering Authority, so that Inspectors and Managers can consider any patterns behind them.

The complaints log must always be kept centrally - at headquarters, by the external line manager, or with the registration and inspection team - as well as in the unit. Full information about complaints and their outcomes must be available to the Inspectors at each visit. *"Where complaints are in areas of special expertise,"* says Burgner, *" such as physical or sexual abuse, inspection units may need special training or reinforcement by outside expertise"* [41].

40 Scottish Office Circular No. SWSG5/1996 Local Authority Complaints Procedures

41 Burgner, T (1996) op cit

Parents should be informed when their children complain if that is what the children want. Parents are also able to invoke complaints procedures on behalf of children who are being looked after.

6.5.2 Child Protection Guidelines

There may be a feeling in some quarters that "looked after" children who are abused need not be brought within the Child Protection Procedures because they are already in care. This is faulty. Child protection guidelines should be followed in exactly the same way for children in residential or foster care as for children living at home with their own parents. Much has been learnt by organisations about working together for the good of children since these were first instituted 20 year ago. It is helpful that now all types of residential schools have appointed Child Protection Officers.

Those who gave evidence saw child protection work as much more complicated in residential settings than in families. There was the possibility of collusion, overt or unconscious, between social work colleagues, and it was thought that investigations needed to look at management systems as well as other issues. There was some feeling that procedures could be heavy handed, and lead to children suffering more harm than from the original incident. Some people felt that the child protection procedures had become staff protection exercises, with the real needs of the children being lost.

There are fears in some quarters that supporting children during child protection procedures may have the effect of corrupting evidence, but counselling at an early stage is very important for children's potential recovery. There is a need for supporters for both children and staff while procedures are being followed.

In some areas, where an adult is accused of child related offences, the Reporter is automatically informed by the police. The Reporters' Association feels that this is a safeguard which should be extended to the whole of Scotland, and I would endorse this.

6.5.3 Children's Panel System

We have become so used to our Children's Panel system that we tend to forget what a valuable safeguard it is. The child-centred nature of the system has always been immensely important, and continues to be so. Panel members welcome the new provision in the Children Act which will allow them to see the child alone, without parents or carers present. But they are, however, concerned about the change recently enforced by the Scottish Office following serious criticism from the European Court of Justice: parents must normally be sent all papers which come to the Panel. There is a fear that this may inhibit some report writers, and they are particularly concerned about those times when a child might want to write their own report for the Panel, but fear their parents seeing it.

In some parts of Scotland, Reporters have done a great deal of work on child-friendly communication, and on better ways of obtaining the child's point of view. However, neither the Panel members nor the Reporters whom I consulted seemed to feel that they would be likely to be used by a child who wished to disclose information about the people caring for him or her, because they are both too closely associated in children's minds with authority.

In relation to perpetrators, the Reporters are often dealing with facts about abuse, in the form either of material that has gone to the Sheriff for proof, or where abuse has been admitted to. This material might well be used by a register. There is a need for a National Child Protection Register to use this information, and any additional information from the child protection management information system.

6.5.4 Procedures and Professionalism

Procedures and protocols are valuable, and I recommend different procedures at various times throughout this Review. However, procedures are only part of the answer. Procedures, however good in themselves, can never ensure that someone is available at key moments who is sufficiently close to the child, engaged with the child's reality, to make things happen for the child, deal with problems in the long and short term, be there for the children. Agencies should commit themselves to safeguarding children through a personalised as well as a procedural approach.

Over recent years social work has become defensive, and procedurally driven. There is a danger in following procedures blindly without being sensitive to the needs of this child in this setting. It is professional judgement that makes the procedures work, and the quality of the assessment and the decision-making at each point is critical. This is part of the Social Work task, the professional task for which Social Workers are trained. It is the Social Worker's professionalism that allows him or her to make the purposeful visit to the looked after child, which helps them to keep the balance between the response in the public domain and in the private. Professionalism will help a Social Worker keep the balance between their loyalty to the task and their loyalty to their colleagues, to exercise judgement rather than to follow the rule book.

It often seems that what you do after the detection of abuse is clearer than what you do to prevent it. Increasingly, people are finding it relevant to ask whether child protection has taken over from child care. There is now a need to reduce the emphasis on procedures, and to increase the emphasis on the personal development of Social Workers, on evaluation and on training in good practice. There is a need for managers not to be too divorced from practice to understand the need to apply professionalism to the use of procedures. It is essential to have statutory regulations, but how they are applied is most important.

The professionalism of child care work needs to be strengthened.

6.5.5 Child Care Reviews

Child care reviews must be held within 72 hours after a child is received into care, within 6 weeks after and then every 6 months. The purpose of a review is to discuss the child's progress and to plan for his or her future, to make sure that the child is getting the care that is needed, and to work out how the child might be able to go home.

Either the child or the Social Worker can ask for an earlier review if they desire one. Reviews will usually involve the child, the parents, the Field Social Worker, the senior Social Worker, a senior manager who chairs the meeting, the child's carer or key worker, and the residential unit's manager if applicable. Other interested parties such as the guidance teacher might be asked to attend.

The child's safety should always be considered in reviews. Reviews are of great importance to children, and if they are cancelled suddenly the child receives the wrong message about his or her own unimportance.

6.5.6 Panel Reviews

If the Children's Panel has placed a Supervision Requirement on a child, they must review it within a year, but they can review it earlier than this. A Field Social Worker can ask for a panel review at any time. The child or his or her parents can ask for a review earlier; this can be 3 months after the panel if they were put on supervision for the first time, or if the Supervision Requirement was continued or changed in any way. A child or young person can take anyone they choose with them to the panel as their representative. Those who will attend will be the Reporter, 3 panel members, the Social Worker, the child's parents, a carer or key worker, a safeguarder if one is appointed, and any other person who is important to the child at that time.

This should be a time when the panel can review the circumstances of the child's care, and ensure that he or she is being kept safe.

6.5.7 Good Management of Foster Care

There is much that managers of residential care could learn about the recruitment and vetting of staff from colleagues who recruit and vet foster carers. They use application forms which are specific to foster care, and carefully check the information supplied on them. They make sure that applicants learn as much as possible about the task before either side is committed. They run group exercises, looking at dynamics within the groups. They tease out attitudes and value bases. They discuss the reasons why people have applied, and other more painful topics, such as abuse. They look closely at the functioning of the immediate family. They interview referees face-to-face. They run SCRO checks on adults who will be in the family home and could have unsupervised access to a foster child.

Foster carers see their training as a safeguard. They are now exposed to very thorough training as an induction to the service, and offered further training during their time with the Local Authority. If they choose to become members of the National Foster Care Association (NFCA), they will be offered training through that body also. Carers who joined the service some years ago may not be as thoroughly trained, but many of them try to make time for training when it is offered. Increasingly, training deals with the issues of safe caring.

Training is found by foster carers to help reduce stress, because they are more likely to know what to do in difficult situations. They are also helped by good social work support, on a regular basis as well as on demand, particularly from those fieldwork staff who respect their expertise and the value of the work they do. Many of them find that they are given excellent help and advice by fellow foster carers, or that they can sometimes carry on because others tell them they have been in a similar situation with a child and lived to tell the tale. If the child has had a previous placement with foster carers, they find they learn much that is helpful if they are able to contact those carers by telephone. Those who are members of the NFCA find it valuable.

When Local Authorities stick to agreements with foster carers about the ages and numbers of children they will take, and for how long, they are less likely to suffer from the burnout that leads to them giving up.

6.5.8 Allegations Procedures and Conducting Inquiries

Allegations against them are realistically feared by both foster carers and residential care staff, yet it is important that both children and other adults can make allegations and know that they will be well handled. It is critical that allegations procedures are thorough, effective and even handed, such that people can have confidence that if allegations are justified they will be proven and action taken and if the allegation is unjustified it will be shown to be false and the member of staff's position can be restored. When such confidence in the procedure has been developed we shall start to reduce the fear that staff understandably feel of having an allegation brought against them.

When child abuse by a member of staff in a Local Authority unit or by a foster carer is alleged or suspected, the Local Authority has the responsibility for both the abused child and the abusing adult. This necessitates an independent element in the investigation.

The rights of staff and foster carers must be recognised, and these include the right for support when allegations are made against them. This can be problematical, given all the different pressures that there will be on managers once an allegation is made. It can be very difficult for managers to know how best to proceed.

Some but not all organisations know what they will do if there are serious allegations against foster carers or members of staff. They have allegations procedures which are planned in advance, and which can be instituted in case of need. A good example of such procedures is contained in the guidelines on child protection prepared for the independent schools in Scotland by Professor Kathleen Marshall[42]. The Support Force also provides a guide to "Investigations and Inquiries" within its Code of Practice[43]. There are many conflicts after an allegation has

42 Marshall, Kathleen (1997) Guidelines on Child Protection Prepared for the Independent Schools in Scotland (Edinburgh, SCIS)

43 Support Force, 1995, op.cit.

been made. Children need to be protected from any (further) abuse; a residential unit needs to continue to run; if the allegation turns out to be false, there is still a strong risk of losing valued foster carers or residential care staff; if the allegation is true but not proved, the child may feel betrayed and unprotected; an innocent person's job - even their reputation - may be at risk; there is an inevitable effect on colleagues, friends, family and other children; the child who may have been harmed needs counselling and support - but not at the risk of contaminating the evidence; the person against whom the allegation is made needs support; the reputation of the Department or agency may seem to be at risk; insurance companies may want to ensure that nothing is done that will lead to compensation claims later.

There is never a good time for dealing with something like this. Allegations can be extremely threatening for all involved, and to have allegations procedures available reduces anxiety. Fewer mistakes are likely to be made, and children are likely to be better protected, where staff have guidance as to what they should be doing. Roles need to be clarified: it must be clear at the very least who is to support the child, who is to support the suspected staff member, and who is to investigate and report.

6.5.9 Vacancies

If the correct placement is to be made for a child with a foster carer, in a residential unit, a school or a secure unit, there must be choice and this depends on there being vacancies available. A really suitable placement is not only one which makes the child happier, it is one which gives the child a chance to recover from some of the more appalling things that may have happened to him or her.

It is usually safer for the child to be closer to their own home, and it certainly makes it more likely that they will be visited on a regular basis by the Field Social Worker and by parents and other family members. There are risks which come from putting the wrong children together and it is an important safeguard to be able to avoid doing this; abused children should not be placed alongside children who have abused others unless staff have been assisted to acquire the skills necessary to work with them. There are real difficulties which come when children of very different ages are expected to share the same accommodation.

Sound financial management over the last few years has meant that the number of vacancies in residential units have been much reduced, but at a personal cost to children in reduced choice. Occupancy rates averaged under 80% during the 1980s, and between 1991 and 1994 were hovering between 84% and 87%. In 1995, however, they went up to 94%.

Many Local Authorities also report a loss of choice in foster care placements, and foster carers report that they are being used for different types of caring from those in which they specialise.

This makes it less likely that they will be happy with the placement, and may increase the risk of it breaking down, or of the carer becoming disillusioned with fostering. Given that the average time for fostering before people drop out is only 7½ years, additional pressures should be avoided.[44]

6.5.10 Sex and Sexuality: Good Practice

Good practice in relation to sex and sexuality means that abuse is less likely, puts the welfare of the child to the forefront, develops the self awareness and skill of staff and is supported by an organisational policy that is carefully implemented. Openness about sexuality means that all those involved, staff and clients, are able to raise anxieties and issues before problems become dangerous and abusive.

Establishments that care for young people are increasingly learning the benefits of being able to talk about sex, sexuality and its boundaries. They are learning that training in sexual abuse alone leaves negative feelings; that staff need to move from this reaction to ways of working that are positive, using a good working language about sex and sexuality. If they do not have a language for discussing sex and sexuality, then all kinds of behaviour can be condoned for very

44 Verbal evidence from Professor John Triseliotis

fuzzy reasons, because they are never discussed openly. If training is only offered in sexual abuse, it is hard to understand "normal" sexuality; sexual expression starts to have a threatening aspect, and human contact can be seen as dangerous.

Establishments need clear policies for managing sexual behaviour, with guidelines implemented in such a way that the whole establishment understands their purpose. Clear discussion about what practices are, or are not, appropriate protects both client and worker. A lack of openness creates a climate of secrecy, which is particularly dangerous for a group of young people who may have abused or have been abused in secret. Young people in care are often confused and sad, wanting sexual relationships because they give physical comfort and a sense of belonging to another person in their own right, however fleeting, difficult or abusive the relationship.

The average parent often finds it very difficult to talk to sons and daughters about sex and sexuality. This is another area where residential child care staff are expected to be better than the average parent; many of them are already doing so.

Organisations need policies which recognise that group living creates particular difficulties when young people become sexually active; one young person's behaviour will influence the behaviour and feelings of others. However, establishments that care for young people need to accept developing sexual activity, and that teenagers in care need the sort of contraceptive care that is available to young people living at home. Ideally, information and advice are made available long before they are actually needed, and free, confidential access to the doctor of their choice should mean that young people can access help.

There is a place for the provision of written information, and for formal discussion. It must always be remembered, however, that some of the most helpful discussion takes place over the washing up, or during some other purposeful activity. It has been found that young people who have received and understood real sex education are better able to make choices for themselves, including the decision not to have sex. They may need to be helped to gain the confidence to say "No".

Training, support and policies can only reduce the likelihood of abuse, they can not eliminate it. However, we must be aware that sexual safety provides physical and emotional safety also. Because young people in care are often confused and sad, and wanting comfort from some source, this makes them more vulnerable. If we can help them to learn the facts about the better, loving kind of sex, we may make it easier for them to reject the worst.

6.5.11 Management Information

It is easier to safeguard children when we know properly what is happening to them. Part of the new openness and awareness is that we are now looking at the incidence of abuse of children living away from home, and in particular at the incidence of sexual abuse. Some Local Authorities have a much clearer idea than they did of what is happening in children's units and foster homes. Although it may be painful, this is an issue which all Authorities should be facing.

Since April 1992, Local Authorities have been progressively introducing the agreed Child Protection Management Information System. The system contains details of a child's referral and subsequent steps through the child protection procedures. However, we are not yet able to glean absolutely accurate national information from these figures, for various reasons. Local Authorities may use different definitions as to what constitutes "referral" in terms of child protection procedures. A small handful of Local Authorities have been clinging to their own statistical information systems, and have not been feeding the necessary information through to the national system. We do need reliable Scottish standard figures. We know that for the whole of Scotland for 1994 - 1995, there were 7,732 referrals to the Social Work Department for child protection. Of these 3,133 went to case conference, as a result of which the names of 1,694 children were placed on the Child Protection Register.

If all Local Authorities used the system in the way that has been agreed, we would also know how many children had to be referred because of abuse by care staff in a children's residential establishment, or by foster carers. It would be important in addition to be able to know if the child was a peer abuser living in the same residential establishment.

6.6 Speaking Out

6.6.1 Listening to Children

Many children within the care system are not used to being listened to and being taken seriously. This, connected with the problems that arise from a low self image, can make it very hard for them to talk about the things that concern them most; they may well have a feeling that it does not really matter to anyone just what happens to them. Many abused children may not know that what has happened to them is wrong, and may not understand that it is in any way out of the ordinary. It is only when they are in a context where abuse is openly discussed, that they come to see what has happened to them as abuse.

Bullies and abusers are very clever at putting young people in a position where they feel unable to tell. In encouraging children to speak up, it may be necessary to help them to understand the difference between good secrets and bad secrets and to help them to overcome the kind of guilt and shame which makes them feel that what has happened to them has been their own fault or that they have in some way asked for it. We must always remember that it is possible to love somebody who is abusing you, and not to want to lose them: this does not mean that they are not harming you, but it does complicate your position.

Children may be more likely to talk about their most intimate concerns during shared activities with adults, and it is important that staff and foster carers have enough time to allow conversations to run on. Some adults are not good at listening to children, and there is a need for Field Social Workers, residential care staff and foster carers to be trained to listen to children, to help them to talk and to give them good and positive feedback. The adults must not show that they are shocked, they should always be open to the possibility that the children they care for have been abused, and must be able to think the unthinkable. It is important that they take the children seriously and believe them. A child may choose to confide in an adult without professional status, such as the unit's cleaner; when that happens, the adult should be supported as the child's confidant so that he or she can continue to be of use to the child. Part of the training for these members of staff too must be how to deal appropriately with disclosures.

It has been found in the past, that children with a history of being abused are less likely to be believed when they talk about abuse than other children in the care system. Children in care may be considered to be manipulative, or even liars. This must not be allowed to happen. If children are to be protected, they must be taken seriously when they talk.

A significant number of people said in evidence to this Review that there is a need for children and young people to have access to external confidential counselling.

6.6.2 Awareness as part of the Culture

Fifteen or more years ago, abuse by foster carers or in residential establishments was a taboo subject, surrounded by secrecy. Adults who were in care at that time are only now finding it possible to talk about the abuse they suffered. For many, the secrecy around the topic of abuse reinforced in residential or foster care what they had learnt at home. Perpetrators use secrets as a way of ensuring the silence of the child being abused. It is for this reason very important that there should be an atmosphere of openness, not secrecy, about child abuse.

Over recent years, there has been a greater discussion of the possibility of abuse of children living away from home, and of sexual abuse in particular. Professionals are increasingly aware of the signs of abuse. In many residential units staff discuss these matters, and there are discussions between staff and the young people. Abuse forms part of the training for foster carers, and they also are encouraged to talk with young people about safe caring issues. Many staff teams are able to have clear discussions about what practices they consider to be appropriate or inappropriate in their establishments. Where staff have enough mutual trust to be able to challenge one another in small ways, and to accept such challenges in their turn, the children will be safer. When these things are clear and open, it is much easier to see when someone is acting inappropriately, much easier to spot the potential abuser. *"Discuss in your team what sorts of behaviour you will outline as acceptable and not acceptable .... Be clear and specific, and write down what you have decided"* ....

Some of those who gave evidence believed that if a young person is an abuser, this information should be made available to others living within the unit. This conflicted with the strong view that it was important to keep such things confidential to the child and the staff.

The debate is about the difference between secrecy and confidentiality. Those who argue that if you would talk openly about one boy's joy-riding you should be able to talk about another's abusing, do so on the basis that there is no reason to be more secretive about the one thing than the other. Secrecy, they say, just feeds into the atmosphere of " This is our little secret" that is used by perpetrators, and other residents will be safer if they know whom they have to guard themselves against. They would say that other things should be kept confidential, but for the good of all this should not be kept a secret. The issue is not an easy one, and deserves more thought.

What is clear is that all concerned believed that foster carers and residential care staff should always be told if a young person is an abuser. The same is true of information about a child having been abused.

6.6.3 Assertiveness Training

Children being looked after by the Local Authority often lack assertiveness, usually because the circumstances of their lives have given them a very low self-image. This is one strong reason why they are more at risk than other children who are living away from home, such as those who are attending private boarding schools, although any child who is away from home may feel less confident about asserting themselves and may particularly be vulnerable to pressure from their peer group. Assertiveness training can help to redress this.

It is a proper part of safe caring to teach children to speak up for what they will or will not accept happening to them. Children need to be told where the boundaries are, when adults and other children are behaving inappropriately, and when and how to say "No". There is material being used in schools which helps all children in a particular age group to become more assertive. I commend particularly the programme which started in Lothian Region and is now being spread to other parts of Scotland.

It is not simply in relation to abuse that children need to learn to speak up, they need to be given the confidence to take increasing control of their own lives.

It is important that assertiveness training for children and young people is accompanied by a willingness on the part of adults to listen to them; otherwise the value of the training is negated.

6.6.4 Whistle-blowing

There is now a greater atmosphere of openness about the possibility of children being abused when in residential or foster care. Because of this staff are now more likely to blow the whistle on colleagues' behaviour which seems to them to be risky.

Some Local Authorities now have simple whistle-blowing procedures in place, and actively encourage staff to speak out. The British Association of Social Workers has prepared a detailed code, which many of the people who spoke to the Review commended. Organisations responsible for the care of children should have a procedure for whistle-blowing in place well before it is needed. Where staff concerns are heard and acted upon within the organisation, there is no need for them to take the radical step of going to talk to their MP or the press.

Sometimes it will be extremely clear to a member of staff that the activities of a colleague are dubious, and should be reported immediately. Activities which are not so clearly wrong, but which raise a prickle of concern, are more difficult for the staff to handle. Where a staff team is well developed, and there is strong loyalty between its members, there may be very real conflict for staff. It has been noted by several of those who gave evidence that it is often easier for new staff members to speak out against something which worries them. People may be deterred from whistle-blowing because of the fear of losing their job, or of losing the support of the group if nobody else is prepared to stick their neck out. The procedures should recognise this, and should ensure that staff have protection while investigations are being carried on. Tom Burgner suggested that residents and staff need some "outside and impartial body" to whom they can turn for support if they need to complain or to blow the whistle.[45]

The Centre for Residential Child Care[46] says that each residential care team should *"develop a system for reporting any suspicion which will ensure that if there is a pattern it will become apparent, but if fears are groundless, they are seen to be such, without those who brought them forward being humiliated"*. Whistle-blowing is an issue which should be covered in training. After most incidents come to light staff will say they always thought there was something odd or strange about the perpetrator. In piecing together concerns in a subsequent review, it is often found there were several moments when individual staff were troubled but did not speak out. Somehow we have to get away from being wise after the event and create a climate that alerts people earlier. We need to help people to trust their intuition.

In those countries where whistle-blowing has been made mandatory, the protection of children has greatly increased. In Israel, for example, when it became an offence not to report what you know a huge increase in referrals resulted, of which only 7% were found to be groundless.

6.6.5 Protection from Defamation

Among the fears which deter people from reporting abuse, is the fear of being sued for defamation of character if the allegation is later shown to be unfounded. There is, however, legal protection under Scots Law if staff report something they have observed to an appropriate person in good faith.

> *"To be defamatory a statement must first of all be untrue. Even if subsequently shown to be untrue, the statement will be protected by "qualified privilege" if it is made to the appropriate authority "in response to a duty, whether legal, moral or social or in the protection of an interest". Unjustified repetition of the allegations to other persons will not be protected by privilege.*
>
> *The qualification on privilege refers to statements motivated by malice. If a statement, even to the appropriate authority, can be shown to be not only untrue, but motivated by malice, then an action of defamation could be successful."*[47]

6.6.6 Indicators of Abuse

It is part of the increasing awareness of abuse in our culture, that we are now able to use lists of signs to look for each of the five recognised types of abuse. With sexual abuse, the signs are often more subtle, less easily recognised than the signs of, for example, physical abuse and therefore the list of indicators for this is much longer.

In some parts of Scotland teachers are increasingly being made aware of the indicators, and they should always be part of the training for residential care staff and foster carers.

6.6.7 The Characteristics of Paedophiles

Among people giving evidence, there was some disagreement as to whether it was possible to have a checklist of things to look out for as identifiers of paedophiles. There are checklists in existence which would probably allow every adult in Scotland to be seen as a potential paedophile

45 Burgner, T (1996) op cit

46 Lindsay, Meg (1995) op. cit.

47 Marshall, Kathleen (1997) op. cit.

and which for this reason cannot be recommended. However there were some features which interviewees felt were common to many paedophiles. These are listed below, not to offer a profile but to indicate what should be included in training:

- ingratiating themselves with management - as they do with the children
- willingness to take any child, no matter how difficult, and to take children at very short notice
- interest in photographs and videos of children
- targeting situations where children are vulnerable: children's homes, single parent families, foster care, residential care, adoption and supported accommodation
- willingness to wait and prepare children, often over years, for engaging in sexual activities
- willingness to 'buy' the attention and affection of young people, by engaging their attention, by taking them home, by purchasing clothes and equipment they would not otherwise get - the 'pseudo-uncle'
- over-involvement with one particular child
- unwillingness to take responsibility for their behaviour with children, believing that it is up to children to put up the blocks
- joining in more of children's activities than you would expect
- a history in their own childhood of sexual abuse (in some cases) or physical or emotional abuse (in almost all cases)
- unwillingness to participate in conferences, training, meetings etc.
- the 'gift of the gab' and an ability to lie and conceal their background
- the ability to generate trust
- a preference for children of a particular age-range.

6.6.8 Recording

The proper and efficient use of recording is not interesting for members of staff, but it can be a very real safeguard for children. There need to be clear records about individual children, about the running of establishments, and also clear personnel records. Within units, there are certain matters which deserve to be recorded separately, such as complaints, and violent incidents including restraint by staff or violence against staff. Sexual harassment or bullying by young people would also be included in this type of record.

There are two sides to records: there is recording itself, and the scrutinising of those records in order to draw lessons from them. When they are being used properly, they can indicate dangers, and where action needs to be taken for the safety of children and young people.

6.6.9 Telephones

Since the Skinner Report recommended that children and young people in care should be able to make telephone calls in private, there has been a great expansion in the use of cordless telephones. Although there are circumstances in which the conversation can be picked up on nearby radios, these increase the possibility of children having real privacy for their telephone calls. With a telephone, they can contact Who Cares?, ChildLine, or relations or friends, to discuss issues that are of concern to them. However, care staff in some units remain suspicious about the children's need to telephone, and they place restrictions on the use of telephones, or may even try to check after the call just who the child was telephoning. Children speak of leaving scrambled numbers on telephones, so that staff cannot discover the last number dialled. The lack of privacy for telephone calls is a real source of grievance for some children in care, and rightly so.

Residential care staff have concerns about telephone costs, and agreements must be reached about these as they are in "normal" family living. Call barring systems can be used to ensure that children are unable to make calls to sex chatlines, or international calls, from the lines they use. More seriously, staff are concerned about calls from people who want to exploit the children and young people in some way, particularly drug pushers, pimps and abusers. Where they suspect this is happening, they must deal with it as they would deal with unsuitable contacts outwith the unit, in order to protect the child. However, the possibility of exploitation should not be used as an excuse to deny residents proper use of the telephone.

6.6.10 Personal and Social Development in the School Curriculum

One development for children of all ages may provide a particular benefit for looked after children. The Personal and Social Development component of the new School Curriculum is being developed in Edinburgh to allow work to be done with children on personal safety. Among other action which started in the former Lothian Education Department, a programme "Feeling Yes, Feeling No" has been brought in to help children in Primary 6 to stand up for themselves and deal with potential abusers. There are three basic concepts that the children need to learn: to say "No", to get help, to tell an adult.

The programme has already been shown to have protected a number of children from serious risk. It has now been expanded to some independent schools and to some other parts of Scotland.

Where this type of work is being done in the schools, it should be reinforced by foster carers and in children's units in the same terms as are being used in the schools. There is a need for staff to learn about the programme, and for foster carers to support it as natural parents would.

It has been shown that where teachers are trained to use the programme, and in an increased understanding of abuse, there has been an increase in referral rates of children who have been abused.

6.7 Routes of Support 1 - Adult Defenders In the System

In most families, parents are active to protect their children from harm. If children are not living with their families, others may have to take on that responsibility, to a greater or lesser extent depending on how closely the parents are still involved. Children and young people in residential care have many adults round them who can be alert for their safety, and to whom they could go if they feel unsafe for any reason. It is not possible to plan in advance just whom they may trust in a particular situation, nor indeed whether they will decide that they can trust anyone. They need to know that adults are available, so that they can choose. Children in foster care have fewer such contacts, but still have people available to them.

Certain adults are of particular value in safeguarding children who are looked after by the Local Authority. However, roles must be clearly delineated, or things go wrong, and it must be clear who is responsible for which task.

6.7.1 Manager and Other Staff: Good Practice

Within the residential unit, the main responsibility for the children's safety rests with the manager and his or her staff. It is for this reason that the calibre of staff appointed is so important. It is clear that there are at any one time units which work well for their residents, and those which are less successful. Residential child care has been referred to as the system where "the least trained and the least supervised look after the most vulnerable", as a place to store the child because nothing better can currently be found - yet it could be the intensive care unit of child care.

> *"If ever there was a labour intensive industry it must be residential child care. Staff are the really important ingredient in the care package offered to children and families; much depends on their personal and professional skills and knowledge, and the confidence which comes from them. Buildings can be improved, bedrooms can be made more attractive, but staff make or break the system. Staff are the key resource, but currently are trained too seldom and too little, insufficiently supported and sometimes appointed too casually."*[48]

The quality of the manager can set the ethos of the establishment; a person with the right experience and the right training can do much, but above all it is the quality of the person that matters.

We are always more likely to see reports of poor practice than of best practice, and indeed some real leaps forward in quality of care have come about because of inquiries into mistakes, disasters or damaging styles of care. We need to become better at recognition of good practice, at safeguarding it, praising it and learning from it.

The staff need to be able to work together as a team, with loyalty to one another, but above all loyalty to the task, knowing that the children and young people must always come first. They need to like young people, and positively to want to be working with them. Their concern for them should show in their interest and involvement, in the time spent with them which should be, in the jargon, quality time. They should be able to listen well, and not be easily embarrassed, although they should not feel they had to compromise their own beliefs for the sake of superficial popularity. They should be able to be strong and firm when necessary, but they should not be aggressive, and they should remain calm in challenging situations. There should be continuity of care for the residents, but staff members should not be burned out, and should have energy and enthusiasm to share. Residents should feel they can count on their underlying emotional support, even when they do not have approval for their actions. Finding these paragons, recruiting them and retaining them is hard; if you succeed, managing them should largely be a question of supporting them.

The first step to ensuring quality residential care is the establishment of agency policy, and aims and objectives for each residential unit. Staff should be able to feel proud of their unit, and of the work that they do. If you look at a home where the practice is bad, it is impossible to see any particular activity because the whole thing is a mess. When there is good practice in the home, any improper activity will stand out more clearly.

Safety is increasingly an issue for staff. The manager and other staff in the unit are likely to be very aware of the issues of abuse and harm. Training courses, and a greater general awareness of children in care as children at risk mean that they are alert for the safety of the young people. Much also depends on the staff knowing the children well, so that they know the ways in which they may be at risk either from others or to others, and know the things which are likely to upset them or cause them to lose their self-control.

Young people with a staff group they like and trust, where they themselves feel liked and respected, are more likely to be able to go to a key worker or another care worker if they feel at risk. Staff who really do put the needs of the young people first will also see more clearly what they must do to protect them. It will not necessarily be the key worker, nor a much respected line manager, to whom children will tell what is worrying them. It could be the laundry worker, or the gardener in a boarding school, or the cleaner in a Children's Home.

48 Skinner, Angus (1993) op. cit.

6.7.2 External Line Manager

Residential units benefit from having a line manager who knows the staff and the residents well, and is liked and trusted by them. On a day-to-day basis, line managers provide on-going support to the officer in charge, and can provide advice from a different standpoint because they are based outside the establishment. If there is a time when either a member of staff or a child needs to take a concern or a complaint outside the unit, a line manager whom they feel they know, but who is seen to have a degree of professional detachment, may be an obvious person to use. A successful external management system has good links between headquarters and individual units.

The duty of care weighs heavily on those who run children's homes, and the most stressful times tend to be from mid-evening to breakfast time and at weekends. External support from the line manager is often only available from 9a.m. to 5p.m. during the working week, not when it is most needed. Managers need to find a solution to this problem.

Organisations such as small residential schools which do not have external line managers need to find some substitute. They may find it helpful to use a consultant, or to have an independent visitor coming in on a regular basis, with the right to speak out about anything of concern.

6.7.3 Senior Managers

Senior managers need to believe in the value of residential care, and of the work of their own units. If they do believe that there is value and point to the work, they will be keen to ensure that standards are high, that young people get the best possible chance in life, and that staff are supported.

There are many different management styles, but they need to be open, honest and receptive throughout the organisation. If a senior manager is known to take a personal interest in children's units, and in the residents, they may be trusted with young people's concerns. A Director who regularly visits units and makes it clear that his or her office door really is open, may well be taken up on this at some time.

Given how important it is that staff and residents should feel pride in the unit, the interest of senior management will reinforce a feeling of value.

6.7.4 The Field Social Worker

The Field Social Worker can be one of the most important figures in the life of a child in care. As the person who is most closely involved in helping children sort out their lives, they should be the main safeguard for the child. They visit on a regular basis, they know all the background, they can see the child within and outwith the unit or the foster home. Their role is important, probably even more so with foster children than those in residential care. Their professional training has prepared them to form therapeutic relationships, and they should be able to be trusted.

Among those who gave oral evidence there seemed to be two camps on the question of whether children would tell their Social Worker if they were being abused. By and large those who thought they would do so came from the higher échelons of social work management, or from an academic background. Children, and those who care directly for them, seemed to take a less sanguine view of their relationship with Social Workers; many children see the Social Worker as the person who has taken them away from their family, and who now and again takes them out for a hamburger.

Children usually receive more than the required 3-monthly visits, but these should be used by the Social Worker to some purpose. They need to feel that the Social Worker cares about them, and that it does matter how they are getting on day by day. They must spend sufficient time together at each visit, and the quality of the interaction matters greatly. The Social Worker should be able to engage the child, to communicate with him or her, remembering the importance of listening. Social Workers may need to be trained to be pro-active: you may get answers if you ask the right questions. The child should be able to know that the Social Worker will act as their advocate. Reviews should take place as planned; if they are deferred because of pressure of other work, the child receives the message that he or she does not matter. There must be enough money in the budget to ensure that every child living away from home has a Social Worker allocated to them in a reasonable timescale and to allow children placed at some distance from the home area to be visited regularly. Recent financial stringency has led to risky situations where children either do not have a Social Worker of their own or are not visited as they should be.

The Field Social Worker is only a safeguard if he or she is sure of seeing the child alone, without residential care staff or foster carers being present.

6.7.5 Foster Child Social Worker/ Foster Carer Social Worker

If a child is in a foster placement, both the child and the foster carers need social work support, but often for different reasons. The one Social Worker should not be called upon to attempt both functions.

Foster carers need their own link Social Worker, who specialises in support for carers and can understand the problems they face and work on solutions with them. They need this however experienced they are; there is some evidence that too much is demanded of experienced carers, who may let their standards slip if they are not supported. The National Foster Care Association told me that there are more allegations involving longer serving foster parents than those who have fostered for shorter periods. There are various reasons given for this. They include that the more experienced carers are given more difficult young people to care for; that they are more likely to have sibling groups, with rivalries and sometimes a desire to hurt the carers because of jealousy; burn-out; and that they are visited less often by either their link workers or the children's Social Worker.

Groups of carers say that they find it helpful to contact a link Social Worker who is part of a team doing similar work; if their own worker is not available, they will be able to consult someone who has relevant practice.

6.7.6 General practitioner

> *"Young people should have the right to consult a general practitioner without going through staff or explaining the reasons for the consultation. In addition it is important that young people should, wherever possible, have some choice as to the doctor undertaking examinations."* (Skinner, 3.5.6)

The GP is someone outside the residential unit or foster home who may be consulted by the young person about intimate health matters. At a private consultation, the young person may share concerns about something that is happening to them. Symptoms of abuse may be noticed first by a doctor, who may then have to act to protect the child. If a unit uses a particular medical practice, staff should be prepared to spend time helping the GP understand the position of children looked after away from home, and the responsibility for their protection which rests on all who care for them.

Young people should be helped to find a medical adviser with whom they feel comfortable, and it may be important, for example, for a girl who has been abused by male relatives to have a woman doctor. In any case, young people should feel able to insist on seeing a doctor of their own sex if they prefer. Foster carers and staff must not feel they have to mediate between the doctor and the patient. They must not attempt to discourage the young person from 'bothering' the doctor. A general practitioner is the only person who has the right - or the knowledge - to say to a patient that they are making a fuss about nothing.

6.7.7 Nurse

Some people find nurses more approachable than doctors, and children who are seeing a nurse for any reason should be allowed privacy with them. In one Local Authority, a Community Psychiatric Nurse is to be made available to a group of residential units to assist with psychiatric problems like depression either in direct work with the young people or by offering advice and support to staff.

6.7.8 Children's Rights Officers

Some Local Authorities in Scotland employ Children's Rights Officers. They act as an advocate for looked after children, but often because of pressure of work have to concentrate on children living in residential units, rather than children with foster carers; some are making heroic efforts to contact all children living in foster families. They are able to take up children's complaints and concerns. Often they find that complaints can be sorted out quite informally, and in a way that makes the children feel satisfied by ensuring that matters do change. If a complaint must be taken forward formally, they are able to support the child or young person when there is a need to do so. Other staff often start out feeling defensive about Children's Rights Officers, but come to see the value of them, particularly because of the difference they can make to the atmosphere in an establishment when something is sorted out. Children tend to be positive about Children's Rights Officers, seeing them very much as a person on "their" side.

Their work usually allows them to visit residential units on a regular basis, and to get to know the children living in them before the need to pick up any problems arises. They are currently located in Local Authorities and there are arguments both for and against this. On the one hand they may not be sufficiently independent, but on the other they are able to build up the trust of the other staff and to keep in touch with developments in the service.

They are a useful safeguard, and this service should expand to cover Scotland. Given that there are currently discussions as to whether they would be better placed within or outwith the Local Authorities, it is clear that they should always retain close links with the professional network of staff in the Local Authorities with which they have most contact.

6.8 Routes of Support 2 - Others

Children need to be helped to know the routes of support that are open to them, including the Scottish Child Law Centre, Who Cares?, ChildLine and Children's Rights Officers. They need to have this information available in written form, but also to be told about it on various occasions by the Field Social Worker, foster carer or residential care worker, or others.

At one time I would have argued that the Field Social Worker should be the main route of support. I wonder now whether we need other routes partly because the Field Social Worker is too involved in bureaucracy. A child should have access to a truly independent scrutineer and advocate.

6.8.1 Scottish Child Law Centre

The Scottish Child Law Centre in Glasgow deals with the interpretation of the law in relation to children. Among their services is a telephone help line which can provide support for children living away from home and their parents. They say that most of the calls they receive from children are about some form of abusive behaviour, with the children wanting someone to talk to and for the behaviour to stop; they are often concerned about restrictions on their liberty, and about what power residential care staff have. Calls are unlikely to report serious physical or sexual abuse.

6.8.2 Who Cares?

The Skinner Report supported the development of Who Cares? in Scotland recommending that all children in care should have access to it. Recently a lottery grant has made it possible for them to expand their service further. While one or two places did not make use of their services, or had found them ineffective, the great majority of Local Authorities found them very useful and perceived the groups they ran as an effective and important safeguard. They at first found it easier to contact mainly children living in residential establishments, but are now making a very real effort to make contact with children living with foster carers.

They run some activities informally for sheer enjoyment, and these are an obvious attraction for children and young people. They hold serious discussions of issues of mutual interest for children living away from home. There is an annual conference. In some areas they meet with particular groups of children, such as girls, or young people living in secure care.

Who Cares? helps young people and children to gain self respect, and with it the confidence to raise issues for themselves. The organisation will raise issues of concern relating to particular homes or particular children. Where bathroom door locks are broken, or windows will not open and might constitute a fire risk, they will take these issues up with the relevant Local Authority. Children find they can use Who Cares? for individual and personal concerns, including abuse. Children perceive them as a useful source of information on their rights and as an advocate for themselves. Some Local Authorities appear to regard Who Cares? as a substitute for a Children's Rights Officer, and this is not advisable because Who Cares? would see its task as very different from that of the CRO. Much of the task of Who Cares? lies in dealing with groups of children expressing a corporate view, where the CRO is in a good position to take up issues on behalf of an individual child.

Who Cares? are increasingly being used by inspection teams as a source of young people who can comment on what they see in residential units, other than their own. This Review, when wishing to speak to children in care, found Who Cares? a natural way of making contact with them.

6.8.3 ChildLine

ChildLine, a voluntary organisation, provides a free telephone line "to listen to, comfort and protect children in trouble or danger". All calls are confidential. ChildLine is so well used by children and young people that the lines always seem to be engaged, and some young people give up before they are able to get through. There is, however, a dedicated line for children in care which is more likely to have lines available. Scotland has its own service.

Children and young people appreciate ChildLine, because they perceive it as being under their control. They can talk for as long as they wish on the telephone, and can cut out of the conversation at any time they choose. For this reason, children may find it possible to discuss with the voice on the telephone matters which are too painful for them to discuss with anyone else. Children may use ChildLine as a way of testing out adult reaction to something they wish to tell, and it may be a prelude to them talking to an adult whom they know. Children who disclose abuse to the confidential telephone line in the first instance, may then be able to get direct help for themselves among the people they know better. In some circumstances, ChildLine staff who are aware that something serious has been told to them, will make every effort to try to persuade the child to take action, or to help them to find somebody who can take action on their behalf.

6.8.4 Parents and Other Relatives

One reason why I am less concerned for children who attend fee-paying boarding schools than for other children living away from home is that most of the former have good links with strong, caring parents who are respected by those who run the schools. Children looked after by the Local Authority are often in a very different position. Some of them have been badly let down by their families, and will find it hard to share concerns with them. This is not, however, true of all looked after children. Some will quickly go to parents and other relatives if there is something going wrong, and will confide in them; the parent or relative will then attempt to take some action on behalf of the child. They may lack negotiating skills or feel they lack rights which boarding school parents would take for granted.

It is important for Field Social Workers and other child care staff to help the children and the parents to keep their relationships alive, even if the children have to live away from home. Privacy for meetings and for telephone calls is extremely important. Although most foster carers, Social Workers and residential care staff can quote examples of times where jealousy has led parents to make malicious allegations, it is important that professionally caring adults listen seriously to the parents of looked after children, because they can be a real safeguard.

6.8.5 School Staff

Children spend a high proportion of their working day in school. Even though some children hate and are resentful of school, it is important for many reasons that it is not made too easy for them to avoid going to it. For some the school is a place where they can form trusting relationships with adults, with whom they may be able to share sensitive information. Children of primary school age often have a close relationship with the class teacher, with whom they spend most of their day. In secondary schools guidance teachers, who have a particular responsibility for the welfare of children, may be the ones who will be trusted. Some schools employ school counsellors. Smaller schools, particularly those for children with special needs, may find that the head teacher is the person to whom children will go with something of importance.

Increasingly, education authorities are realising that they have a role in relation to protecting children from abuse. It is important that staff in schools are more aware of abuse, and of its indicators, and that they understand what to do if children start talking to them about it. Because of their training, teachers have an understanding of child development, and have learnt how to listen to and talk to children.

6.8.6 Safeguarders

A safeguarder is part of the Children's Hearing system, and until recently was appointed to prepare a report about a child's circumstances at any stage, including review, when there were difficulties and conflicts in the case. After April 1st 1997, with the Children (Scotland) Act it is no longer necessary for there to be difficulties and conflicts before they are involved. Safeguarders tend to have a background as Children's Panel members, Social Workers or lawyers.

In preparing a report to the Children's Hearing or the Sheriff Court, they have time to give to the child's case, are able to see anyone they wish and to ferret out new information. They usually find that families are open to them and trust them. As independent people with no loyalties to any organisation, they can use the courage of their convictions and go so far as to say that a placement is not right for a child. They are not afraid of causing trouble on behalf of a child. These factors make them a valuable protection for children.

Safeguarders are concerned that, at a time when their workload is about to increase, their infrastructure needs to be improved. They would see the Safeguarders Association as a way of doing this. There should perhaps also be a national body responsible for recruiting, appointing and paying safeguarders.

6.8.7 Independent Visitors

Some residential schools and other units have appointed a person, who is independent of the staffing or management, to visit the young people and take an interest in them on a regular basis. They may go in once a week to share a meal, then stay around to chat afterwards. The residents have their telephone number, on the basis that they should call if they are bothered about anything, and that the independent visitor will do their best to sort it out. Visitors are prepared to confront the staff on behalf of the children if necessary. They can raise issues which strike them as a person going fresh in to the establishment, seeing with a clear eye.

6.8.8 Friends

It often comes as a surprise to adults that children will choose first of all to confide in friends of their own age. If we stopped and thought for a moment, we would realise that this is natural, and it is what adults themselves do. Children in care can be very supportive of one another, although what happens after a friend has been told a confidence may depend on the awareness that the friend has. If they are living in a unit which has an open policy on the discussion of bullying and abuse, the friend may know well how to help the confiding child to take the matter further. Children who are being looked after also have friends outside the care system, who may understand less well what to do, but will none the less provide support and try to find a solution to the problem. Even if the problem that is shared is not a serious one, the support of a friend increases self-confidence, and the child will find in future that they can handle other issues more easily.

6.8.9 The Community

It is helpful for looked after children to be involved in normal, every-day community activities such as Cubs, Guides, a football team or a youth club. Apart from the increase in self-confidence and the fun involved, this increases the range of people available for the children to tell if anything was bothering them. The increased awareness in the community about abuse and related issues means that adults unconnected with the care system may be happy to take up cudgels on behalf of a young person they have come to know through community activities.

6.9 Other Issues

6.9.1 Code of Practice for Outdoor Pursuits

Appalling incidents where children have died on canoeing holidays, or walking in the Scottish hills, have led the Scottish Sports Council and sports' governing bodies to produce codes of practice to ensure that exciting outdoor pursuits are carried on in the safest way possible. Although there is often an element of danger which many value, those who follow the codes can ensure that young people avoid physical injury in most circumstances. Adults responsible for taking young people away from home, or for holidays away from residential units, are now likely to have been properly trained, and to follow the codes carefully.

Sports' governing bodies are becoming more concerned about adults sexually abusing young people with whom they have contact, and they have developed codes to cover this too. This is a good example of the wider community acting responsibly for the good of children.

6.9.2 Working with Adult Offenders

Sexual abuse is a type of addiction. Abusers tend to surround their activities with a great deal of fantasy, and the more success they have, the more deeply ingrained the behaviour becomes. They tend not to see themselves as responsible for what happens, but put the responsibility on to the child. Nobody is yet clear as to how effective or how lasting treatment can be, particularly while many abusers appear not to want to rid themselves of their addiction.

Some of the most successful treatment is outside prison, in the Tay Project, the first community based team working with sexual offenders. Before a sex offender is accepted on to the project, he or she has to acknowledge their own criminal behaviour. The team will continue to confront them with this. Their aim is to help people to learn to control their own behaviour, and to take responsibility for their actions. It is intensely demanding, complex work, but does appear to offer an effective way forward.

6.9.3 Working with Young Abusers

It is fortunately more possible to have success working with young abusers than with older ones. This has been shown by the handful of projects working in Britain with them. One example of these is the Halt project in Glasgow, which was established by Strathclyde Region. It takes social work referrals, and works with children between the ages of 5 and 18. The Halt project staff believe that young people may abuse in order to get power and control, and that they can learn to change their behaviour.

They will work directly with a particular child, but they also involve the staff in a residential unit or residential school and help them to work with the young person. They aim to help the young person to recognise danger points in themselves, and in the things around them. Part of this may include acknowledging what the "unsafe" areas are in a particular residential establishment, the areas where they can most easily abuse another child, or the "unsafe" times in a day. This information, which is useful to the young person in helping them to stop themselves abusing, is also useful to the staff who wish to safeguard other children. By working with young abusers, it is possible to protect other children living in the same establishment, it is possible to help the young abusers by protecting them from giving in to the desire to abuse and, by helping them to recover from their abusive behaviour, to protect young people who may come into contact with them in the future.

In Dundee, Barnardo's run the Bridge Project, which undertakes a somewhat similar task, with smaller numbers of children and without such a wide age range. There is a need for projects to help children in other parts of Scotland.

The draft Scottish Office paper on Child Protection - Guidance for Social Work Staff in Protecting Children, which has been circulated for consultation, has a chapter on young people who abuse others in residential units.

6.9.4 Buildings

Residential units which are well maintained give a message to children about their value to the people who run the buildings; they give a sense of pride, and of self worth. Poorly maintained buildings on the other hand send out a clear negative message, and this was mentioned by all the children interviewed, who were particularly concerned about failures to maintain windows, heating systems and locks on bathroom and toilet doors. They were also concerned that locks on windows might constitute a fire hazard.

The use of buildings should be carefully planned, with the staff being aware of which are safe areas for the children, and which are less safe. Smaller units are generally perceived by residents as safer, and there is agreement that the larger the establishment, the more likely it is that both sexual and physical abuse, including bullying, will happen. More than one person interviewed for the review felt that the size of the old approved schools, combined with their closed systems, had made them more vulnerable to abusers and that these dangers are now largely a thing of the past.

6.9.5 Anti-bullying Codes

Recently, there has been an increased awareness of bullying in schools, in residential units and even in adult workplaces. Bullying is no longer a taboo subject and now codes have been developed which allow it to be dealt with in an efficient manner. Those who were interviewed for the Review thought that a professional and open attitude was the best safeguard against bullying, which was agreed to be endemic in residential care. Even children who had never witnessed restraint or any form of abuse in care had experienced bullying and had participated in it. Children, in particular, felt that a regime where certain styles of communication including jokes and innuendo were allowed to go unchallenged, were not conducive to preventing bullying and violence.

Sexual harassment of girls is a form of bullying. It is seen in jokes and innuendoes, crude language, "raids" on their bathrooms and pulling off their clothes. Girls say they suffer it most when they are in a minority in an establishment.

Research has shown that when an institution creates an atmosphere in which young people feel valued and safe, there is less likelihood of violence and bullying; where unhelpful stereotypes exist and where children are bored, violence and intimidation may regularly occur.

The first thing to do is to acknowledge bullying where it exists. Work needs to be done with the bullies, showing them that what they are doing is not acceptable behaviour, and that it will not be tolerated. Reasons must be given to them as to why this is the case, because it is not always clear to bullies just what pain and distress they are causing. Work must also be done with the children who are being bullied, giving them support and encouraging them always to tell. Work needs to be done with all the children in a residential unit, or school, helping them to protect one another from bullies. Staff must learn how to be vigilant.

The Head of one fee-paying boarding school told me that he has asked his staff to remove the word "bullying" from their vocabulary, because it is more effective to talk about the different strands of bullying such as intimidation or verbal aggression or even thumping.

The Head of a special school for boys finds that some of the pupils want to emerge as top dog, and to assert themselves by extorting money or prevailing upon others to hand over their clothes. He sees them responding to the damage done to them in the past by taking things out on others. In his establishment bullying is brought out into the open, but it is the adults who have the responsibility for making the situation safe because he believes it is bad for boys to impose sanctions on other boys. Part of being an open establishment would include telling the police of serious assault. He believes that leadership should be channelled into the sports field.

There is evidence that foster carers take problems such as bullying seriously, and there are few complaints of bullying in foster care.

6.9.6 Education

When you meet an adult who as a child was in the care of the Local Authority for years, but is now successful, very often that success is due to them having had a really good education. The Skinner Report rightly emphasised the importance of ensuring that looked after children do obtain a good education. A child who is helped to get the most out of school is not only having his or her future safeguarded, they are being protected in other ways as well.

The structured day of the school ensures that the child is occupied, and that the time is used well and not for any kind of anti-social pursuits. Children who attend the same school as they did when they lived at home, feel a much better sense of continuity with their life before. Schools are a source of support from friends and caring adults, a source of protection because people you know and trust may see when something is wrong with you, it is a source of self-esteem, and it is a place where, along with your peers, you may learn self-assertiveness.

Some children talk bitterly about the way in which teachers treat them once they know they are in care. It is important that teachers understand what being "looked after" means to the children in that position, but that they should not have any preconceived ideas about all of them being the same, or having the same needs. It is as unhelpful to be too kind as it is to stigmatise all children in care as potential trouble makers. A clever school will enable children with all kinds of different abilities to have a feeling of success; if you are not absolutely sure that your home life is successful, it is very important to have some source of success in life.

I am therefore concerned that the staff who care for children in residential units should, just as much as foster carers, put efforts into ensuring that children obtain the best education they can. They need to be involved, just as a good parent would be, in ensuring that children attend school, that they do their homework at the proper time and take it to school in the morning, that their books are kept safe, that they go to school with the necessary equipment, that there are immediate contacts with the school if anything should go wrong. If there is any risk that the child will be excluded, the care staff should be in the school immediately making every effort to ensure that this does not occur. They should attend parents' evenings, and be ready to support the children whenever they have any part to play in school entertainments, or sporting activities. Care staff whose own experience of school is not happy often find this very difficult to handle, but it is essential that they learn to do it for the good of the children.

In the long run it will make their life easier. A child who is busy during the day will be ready to sleep at night, and will be making fewer demands of the staff. A child who attends school will not need to be cared for during the day, and will not need to be protected from themselves and from boredom. Bullying is more likely to happen when children have not enough to do, and feel at a loose end. If most of a child's life is well structured, then the time that they have free will be more precious to them, and will generally be better spent. It will be more difficult for them to get involved in activities which will harm them.

A Report on Safeguarding in Other Countries is given in Appendix D

CHAPTER 7

1997: A Watershed

7.1 The Convergence of Different Activities & The Impact of the Children (Scotland) Act

7.1.1 Recent Activity

The completion of this report is timed to follow the full implementation of the Children Scotland Act 1995. Since I was commissioned to undertake this task many things have happened. The full impact of the horrors of the Dunblane tragedy have been felt. The scale of abuse in North Wales, Cheshire and Merseyside has become apparent. Here in Scotland 5 people have been charged with offences against children in residential care in Edinburgh. Specific television programmes are being made on the general position and the particular position in Scotland, concerning the abuse of children entrusted to the care of someone other than their own family. The public have never been more aware that some vulnerable children may have their vulnerability compounded when away from home. The public will expect things to be tightened up; the children deserve them to be tightened. It may be a moment when the boundaries of Equal Opportunities or Civil Rights for adults can recede a little in favour of the rights of children.

Meantime a great deal is actually happening and underway since my work began and several things have come to fruition at about the same time.

The Government have published a report from Tom Burgner on the inspection and regulation of residential care including Children's Homes called for by the Secretary of State for Health in England and Wales[49]. The Minister of State in the Scottish Office said that it would be considered here so changes in the arrangements for inspection can be expected. Inspection is a major new safeguard and I have proposals to make.

The National Commission of Inquiry into the Prevention of Child Abuse established by the NSPCC, on which there was Scottish representation, have reported and their findings give cause for concern[50]. Noting the lack of clarity about abuse and harm in official statistics, they say:

> *"What estimates suggest, however, is that at least one in ten children are, at some point in their childhood, judged to be at risk of significant harm and likely to be suffering from physical, emotional, sexual or other forms of abuse or neglect. The true position is likely to be far worse than this. Furthermore, the evidence the Commission has received from victims of abuse makes it clear that abuse is seldom one-dimensional in the way official statistics suggest. Physical or sexual abuse is nearly always accompanied by emotional suffering that may be even harder to bear and last even longer".*

They point out that *"most abuse is committed by people children have most reason to trust"* - family and friends or people entrusted with their care. They believe that nearly all forms of abuse can be prevented, *"provided the will to do so is there".*

They want a Commission for Children in each of the countries that make up the UK, and for Ministers to have enhanced responsibility for children's interests. They call for more public education and awareness. They look for closer co-operation on child abuse and neglect.

49 Burgner, T (1996) op. cit.
50 Williams of Mostyn (1996) op cit

The former Government was considering a general Social Work Council but clearly was fairly lukewarm about the idea. The issue of raising standards through creating a greater sense of pride and professionalism, and the advantage to children of someone being struck off a register rather than going through an employment disciplinary route, are discussed in this report. If the employer cannot keep the wrong people out of child care then perhaps self-regulation will.

The English and Welsh Department of Health is reviewing the Consultancy Index Service and, unless it is overtaken by other events, it is likely that steps will be taken to improve the service. We have no similar service and this report has comments to make on the lack of such an index and makes some suggestions.

On The Record In Scotland was a consultative document that invited views on Government proposals to change the arrangements for access to criminal records. It drew a strongly favourable response and will lead to change which will not run contrary to anything in this report.

There is a new Police Act 1997 which contains proposals to reveal more conviction data to more people and to improve the amount of information employers in the child care and education field can receive from the police. I make recommendations that go rather further but find the presence of the new Police Act welcome. As the result of a very recent court case involving a man who did have a conviction for sexually abusing a boy, but was still allowed to be a foster carer by English and Welsh Local Authorities, the Health Minister announced plans to ensure that nobody with a past conviction for abusing children should be permitted to foster or adopt a child. Whilst I would not previously have believed that it would ever be permissable I leave this matter to the good judgement of the Scottish Office, who are reviewing the matter.

A White Paper put forward for discussion suggested radical changes in English and Welsh Social Services Departments. It did not include any major proposals in relation to the management of services for children.

A consultation exercise is underway in Scotland on the subject of the registration of Residential Establishments for Adults and Children and the promotion of national guidelines and standards.

The creation of a Paedophile Register, and the legal requirement for people convicted of the abuse of children not to seek work with them, will not of itself keep all undesirable people out of the residential situation. It will contribute to the climate being created where watchful vigilance by all will contribute to the total care of children not at home. The Chief Social Work Inspector is reviewing the arrangements for the supervision, accommodation and treatment of sex offenders in the community. However none of the major scandals in Children's Homes and boarding schools have involved individuals already convicted.

Lastly, and most importantly, there is the report by Lord Cullen into the Dunblane massacre and the Government action taken upon its receipt. A very wide range of people are being consulted on proposals for a national system of accreditation and of vetting information about adults working with children and young people. It goes to a constituency far greater than the one this report is concerned with, including clubs and groups in recreation, education, or development. Whatever flows from this review must dovetail with the outcome of Lord Cullen's report.

7.1.2 The Children (Scotland) Act 1995

The new Children Act has met with widespread approval. It was the subject of a lot of consultation which was carried out methodically and with a wide range of people. It is an important move towards the greater protection of children. A few of its provisions came into force on 1st November 1995, with the private law provisions following exactly a year later, and the rest of the Act on 1st April 1997. At that time three volumes of Regulations and Guidance under the title **Scotland's Children** were published[51]. This is the first time that Regulations and Guidance have been produced in this form for child care in Scotland, and it is intended that they should be more accessible to practitioners, and also to people closely involved in the care of

51 Social Work Services Group (1997), Scotland's Children: The Children (Scotland) Act 1995 Regulations and Guidance (Edinburgh, the Scottish Office)

children, such as parents. The price of the three volumes has been kept deliberately low, to allow as wide a circulation as possible.

It is important to acknowledge that the origins of the Children (Scotland) Act 1995 stem from a wide range of issues relating to children and families which began with the Review of Child Care Law in 1988 and was followed by two major inquiries in 1991 and 1992. The first, Lord Clyde's Report into the removal of children from Orkney, and the second, Sheriff Kearney's Inquiry into Child Care Policies in Fife. Two other reports in 1992 were also influential, the Review of Residential Child Care and the Scottish Law Commission's Report on Family Law. The White Paper, Scotland's Children: Proposals for Child Care Policy and Law 1993 notes the importance given to children's expressed needs and concerns. We must remember that throughout the long gestation period of the Act the questions now raised very specifically in this Review were not central to the concerns expressed in all of these. They were about protecting the child in his or her own home from physical and sexual abuse and increasing the general duties of the Local Authority to promote and safeguard children and young people in care. As a consequence it is inevitable that the Act, and the subsequent legislation and Guidance, does not address some of the central concerns of this Review in a more co-ordinated and comprehensive manner. Put another way, if the focus of my work had been one of the central concerns at the time the legislation was being drafted then it might have been written differently.

Before looking in detail at these central issues, I wanted to put the legislation and Guidance into context. At best they can only provide a framework from within which high quality care practice must be developed and sustained. It is widely acknowledged in the evidence given to me that the quality of current practice is uneven, whatever the limitations of the Social Work (Scotland) Act 1968 may be considered to be in relation to safeguarding children living away from home. It is important, therefore, that the new legislative demands and any subsequent amendments that may flow from this Review are carefully and consistently taken into account at a practice level to ensure that children and young people are more effectively safeguarded in the future.

It would be naive to assume that such changes in practice would not have associated costs. This point was consistently made by all of the key agencies responsible for providing child care services and is noted elsewhere in this report. It is not surprising that given the years of under-funding of, for example, residential care and the way in which it has been regarded as a placement of last resort for a long time that it may sometimes be seen to fail to safeguard children.

Residential care offers an interesting example of one of the attitudinal changes in the new Act, which has an intrinsically more positive stance on looking after children away from home than the Social Work (Scotland) Act 1968. Services were provided under Section 12 of the latter in order to prevent children being received into care. On this basis, each reception into care might be seen as a failure, with foster care being marginally better than residential care. However, services "to safeguard and promote the welfare of children" under Section 22 of the 1995 Act include fostering and residential care; it is now viewed as a positive alternative. Under the 1968 Act, residential care was the alternative to "home supervision" which included any child placed in any kind of family home, including foster care. This distinction between foster care and residential care for children living away from home is removed in the new Act.

Another attitudinal change is around the new emphasis on the importance of family links. The partnership with parents is expressed in the Guidance in Sections such as Volume 1, Chapter 1, paragraphs 22-30, but it is echoed throughout the Volumes. Not only must Social Workers share information with parents and take their views, like the child's, into account, they must "plan with the family", and the plan should form the basis of an agreement which is confirmed in writing. The plan is to be regularly reviewed "with the child and family". This expresses new attitudes to parents which will be more enabling for them, give them a greater feeling of power and reduce levels of frustration.

I split the impact of the new child care legislation into two parts. Firstly, the powers and duties set out in the Act and secondly the specific changes in the Regulations and Guidance in relation to safeguarding children living away from home.

The Act is founded on principles derived from the UN Convention on the Rights of the Child and obligations under the European Convention of Human Rights. Those explicitly relevant to this discussion are that:

- each child has a right to be treated as an individual
- each child has the right to protection from all forms of abuse, neglect or exploitation
- each child has the right to express his or her views freely and those views should be given due weight.

The Act itself places a duty on the Local Authority, Section 17(1), to safeguard and promote the child's welfare *"which shall, in the exercise of their duty to him be their paramount concern"*. Similar responsibilities are placed upon foster carers in Section 5(1). This responsibility under Section 17 includes providing *"advice and assistance with a view to preparing the child for when he or she is no longer looked after by a Local Authority"*. It continues for longer than it did under the Social Work (Scotland) Act, for now under Section 25(3) the Local Authority *"may provide accommodation for any person within their area who is at least eighteen years of age but not yet twenty-one if they consider that to do so would safeguard or promote his or her welfare"*. Under Section 29(1) a duty is placed on them, *"unless they are satisfied that his welfare does not require it"*, to provide advice, guidance and assistance to anyone under the age of 19 who was looked after by them at the time of school leaving age or after. They are now permitted to provide the same to young people under the age of 21. This will be particularly helpful to young people who do not have the support of their parents.

Throughout the Act and the Guidance there is an emphasis on the rights of the child to have his or her views heard. In a number of sections in the Act there are references to the requirement on all public Authorities and on parents to ascertain and have regard to the views of the child: Sections 6, 16, 17(4) and 25(5). The Guidance is also forceful about this, as may be seen particularly in Volume 1, in Chapter 1 paragraphs 22 - 27, in Chapter 6 paragraphs 23 - 31, and in the short Chapter 9 on complaints. This reinforces the idea that the child's views must be central, and reflects an attitudinal and policy shift. The legislation establishes the principle of the child's right to be heard and that in itself is an important source of protection for children being looked after by the Local Authority.

Sections 34 and 35 represent amendments to Section 61 of the Social Work (Scotland) Act 1968, which deals with the registration and inspection of residential establishments, other than those controlled and managed by the Local Authorities, which provide personal care or support to children. These changes to the primary legislation also make such establishments subject to the same residential child care Regulations as establishments controlled and managed by the Local Authorities thus significantly increasing the safeguards.

The role of the safeguarder is clarified and strengthened under Section 41. Whereas it had been necessary for there to be a conflict of interests before a safeguarder was appointed, the Sheriff or the children's hearing must now consider whether the child's interest makes it necessary to appoint a safeguarder and if so, must appoint one. The reasons for the decision must be stated.

The primary legislation offers a framework within which specific Regulations and Guidance can be developed towards safeguarding children from abuse.

Volume 2 of the Regulations and Guidance, Children Looked After by Local Authorities, consolidates and clarifies existing provisions in Regulations and Guidance and offers new specific secondary legislation and Guidance. The "Looked After" Regulations lift out from the old Fostering and Residential Care Regulations all matters to do with the direct care of the child and they enhance requirements to record plans, review plans and seek the child's views.

In Chapter 1, paragraphs 76 - 79 are concerned with the arrangements for monitoring placements and make the point that the frequency of visits to carers *"should be determined by the circumstances of the individual case ..... The Social Worker should ascertain the child's feelings and wishes and make a record of each visit. The record should indicate whether the child was seen and, if not, why not, and if the child was seen alone"*. Paragraph 76 is quite clear that the child and the carer should regularly be seen alone as well as together. Paragraph 77 notes that unannounced visits to foster parents may be considered necessary if there are concerns. The importance of making some visits when all the family members are present is also raised. Paragraph 78 gives some emphasis to the Social Worker developing a relationship of trust with the child. By implication this requires the Social Worker to visit the child on a consistent and frequent basis. Where there is more than one Social Worker involved with a case, that is to say perhaps the child's worker and the family's worker, *"both workers should be clear as to the division of roles and responsibilities"*. Whilst this observation may be regarded as self evident it is critical to the proper handling of the case. It avoids the likelihood of either believing the other has responsibility for a particular concern when this is not the case.

Regulation 10 of the Fostering of Children Regulations now requires carers to be subject to review at least once a year. It is recommended in the Guidance Chapter 3 paragraph 51 that such reviews should be carried out by the senior person who has responsibility for the fostering service - this is not the liaison worker. *"Consultation with the Social Workers of all children placed during the previous year will be necessary to establish how the current and any previous placements made during the year have worked out and to discover the views of children and their parents"*. It would seem important to ensure that this responsibility is clearly noted in Review Guidelines rather than a job description, and in practice it will need to be carried out thoroughly.

In Chapter 3, paragraphs 67 - 70 offer guidance on investigating allegations about foster carers stressing that the procedures *"must first and foremost protect the child's welfare"*. There is also recognition that such investigations are often inconclusive and therefore it becomes a question of risk assessment and taking account of a number of factors, i.e. the previous fostering history of the carers, their strengths and weaknesses and any particular stresses within the placement. Implicit in making such judgements is the need to consider the quality of the original assessment, subsequent reviews and the level of contact the Social Workers have had with the child and carers. The Guidance pinpoints these issues very well.

Regulation 14 of the Fostering Regulations and paragraphs 97 - 100 of Chapter 3 of the Guidance deal with immediate placements with friends or relatives who have not been approved as foster carers, and offers very specific Guidance on the issues to be addressed. Whilst by definition such placements are time limited, unless approved further by a Fostering Panel or Children's Hearing, nonetheless the point is made that visits by the Social Worker *"should be determined according to the needs of the particular child concerned"*.

Paragraph 109 identifies that in Scotland *"There is no provision for a Local Authority to arrange for a placement to be made by a private or "independent" fostering agency"*. Section 16(1) of the Fostering Regulations does however give the Local Authority the power to use a voluntary organisation to approve, review or terminate approval of carers. Section 93(1) of the Act is given as the key legislative reference in the Guidance, which is a technical clause offering an interpretation of the terms used in the Act. It defines a voluntary agency as a *"body ... whose activities are not carried on for profit"*. Responsibility and practice for deciding whether an agency is a profit or a non profit-making body rests with the Local Authority. Whilst as yet there have been no examples of private fostering agencies operating in Scotland, this provision will deter such a potential development. Unless an agency can demonstrate that they meet the definition of a voluntary agency then they cannot be considered as acting on behalf of the Local Authority. Regulation

16(4) requires the Local Authority to review the agreement with the voluntary agency at least every 12 months and the Local Authority could withdraw.

Whilst the Regulations do not prohibit foster carers from being approved by more than one Local Authority, the Guidance at Chapter 3 paragraph 114, makes the point that: *"In considering these matters it will be good practice for the Local Authority to liaise closely with any other Authority currently approving that person .... Following approval, the Local Authority should as far as possible agree procedures for consulting and notifying each other on proposed placements, the carrying out of reviews and for any important events which occur within placements"*.

The question is, should such "consulting and notifying" have been more firmly underpinned by Regulations, perhaps by making it a legal requirement? Certainly some of the written submissions I have received suggested such action.

Chapter 4 deals with residential care and confirms and refines within the Guidance the recommendations set out in the Review of Residential Care1[52]. The Annex to this Chapter includes an extended range of issues to be addressed in preparing this Statement of Functions and Objectives; they include:

- *"identifying appropriate relationships between children and staff*
- *protecting children,* and
- *dealing with complaints from children and their parents"*.

Regulation 8 of the Residential and Other Establishments Regulations (Scotland) now requires managers of residential establishments to have *"in place appropriate procedures to be followed in the vetting of staff in relation to their suitability to work in the establishment both prior to their appointment and regularly thereafter"*. This is expanded in paragraph 14 of Chapter 4 to say *"including sessional, temporary and relief staff, who have substantial access to children"*. The use of the words *"appropriate procedures"* and *"regularly thereafter"* make it clear that an SCRO check on starting work for the first time is not sufficient. The importance of staff supervision and annual documented appraisal of performance is noted in Chapter 4 paragraphs 15 and 16 together with staff training targets which were originally set out in the Review of Residential Care.

Whilst reference is made to training targets, and Regulation 6 (which is not new) deals in a general sense with the number of children who may be accommodated, which is spelt out a little more in Chapter 4 paragraph 12 of the Guidance, the question of the optimum staff to child ratio is not considered anywhere. Work was undertaken in the 1970s which emerged from a conference at Castle Priory and offered a method for calculating the numbers of staff which would be needed to work in any establishment. In today's terms, those recommendations about staffing levels should be seen as the minimum and it would be helpful to have Scottish Office endorsement of that or something fresher.

Chapter 4 paragraph 25 of the Guidance confirms that *"each establishment must have a formal complaints procedure, which ... should be easily understood and readily accessible to the children and staff"*. The importance of children having private access to a telephone and of complaints being quickly and thoroughly investigated is also noted. Consistent with these basic rights young people should have *"in normal circumstances confidential access to their General Practitioner"*. The responsibility of managers to review complaints annually, and to identify the wider implications, is also important.

The feeling of safety is one of the 8 principles identified in the Review of Residential Child Care and is given proper emphasis in paragraph 41. *"Concerns about the safety of children, for instance possible abuse, should be addressed promptly and in a way which is sensitive to the child's background and stage of development. To ensure effective arrangements each establishment should have child protection procedures agreed with the responsible agency, which are made known to children and staff"*.

52 Skinner, Angus (1993) op. cit.

The oral evidence given to me on this subject suggests that child protection work in residential settings is more complicated than in families. There is the possibility of collusion, overt or unconscious, between Social Work colleagues and investigations need to look at management systems as well as at other issues. In relation to children seeking refuge, paragraph 42 of Volume 1 Chapter 8 suggests that an independent person should be made available for the child to talk to about his or her reasons for running away. It is not difficult to think of many other circumstances in which this independent person would be of use to a child.

The whole of Chapter 8 of Volume 1 is devoted to Refuges. A young person could seek refuge from a care placement and this is another external option. The Guidance says in paragraph 43 that *"no child should have to return to a Local Authority placement in residential or foster care if he or she is afraid to return"*. If the child does not wish to return, the Guidance requires that the running away should be treated as a form of complaint unless there are compelling reasons not to do so. This is an essential safeguard for any child who has run away.

The question of care staff being properly trained in the management of challenging behaviour is noted in paragraph 49 of Chapter 4 and reference is made to the training pack "Taking Care, Taking Control" currently available from the Social Work Services Group. However a more authoritative statement from the Scottish Office is still awaited as to what physical restraints are legally permissible and in what circumstances.

There are some important new points made in relation to records and log books in paragraphs 52 and 53, in particular the need to have separate logs for different purposes, for example complaints or measures of control. All records should be cross referenced and subject to regular checks by the head of the establishment.

External management arrangements are given added prominence in the Guidance identifying in Paragraph 56 the main tasks for external managers which include:

- monitoring the experience of children
- ensuring that practice complies with legislation, Regulations and national and local Guidance
- supervising and supporting the person in charge.

The paragraph stresses the importance of the external manager visiting their residential units regularly *"to talk and listen to the children, parents and staff"*.

Chapter 5, Registration and Inspection of Certain Residential Schools, deals very specifically with child protection issues, offering Guidance in paragraphs 43 to 45 as to procedures if child abuse is suspected within the school. Paragraph 37 identifies the need for residential schools to have a complaints system and for children to have access to an advocacy service.

Volume 1 of the Regulations and Guidance Chapter 6, paragraph 73, addresses the question of safeguards for children with disabilities living away from home, noting that they *"may be particularly vulnerable and Local Authorities should have policies and measures to prevent abuse of children who are looked after in residential or foster care"*. This Chapter is of importance because it is the first time that Guidance on the legislation for children with disabilities has been brought within the Guidance on services for children. Until now, under the provisions of the Chronically Sick and Disabled Persons Act 1970 and the NHS and Community Care Act 1990, they have been included with adults. Here they are given importance, and attention is paid to their particular needs as children. Much attention is paid in the Guidance at this point to the difficulties that some children with disabilities have with communication, and to ways of overcoming these difficulties. This is a valuable safeguard for those children who would have real problems in communicating the fact that they had been abused. Particular attention is paid in paragraphs 29-31 to users' views, representations, and complaints.

Under Regulation 17 of the Arrangements to Look After Children (Scotland) Regulations 1996, children in any form of respite care for more than 24 hours are deemed to be looked after while in placement and afforded the additional protection that comes from this. If a child undergoes a series of placements during the course of a year, these can be treated as one placement for the purposes of review. There must be a medical examination before the first placement, and a plan for the child. The Guidance provides a Schedule for Reviewing Respite Care Placements in Volume 2.

Complaints have a high profile in the Guidance, and merit a whole Chapter, albeit a short one, in the first Volume. The schedule in the Residential Establishments Regulations covering matters to be included in a statement of functions and objectives spells out many safeguards, not the least of which is the handling of complaints.

It can be seen that there are a number of specific changes in primary and secondary legislation that are directly relevant to the protection of children living away from home. Much of the relevant Guidance is, however, about good practice and does not necessarily reflect changes in either the Act or the Regulations. Consequently some might consider that it carries less compulsion, but that would be to diminish the soundness and consistency of the advice and Guidance. Under Section 5(1) of the Social Work (Scotland) Act 1968, Guidance does have statutory force. To the extent to which it covers the issues raised by this Review, the Guidance offers both the Social Work manager and the practitioner a better base from which to begin to ensure that children being looked after by the Local Authority are being properly safeguarded.

The limitation of the Regulations and Guidance in the context of this discussion is that it is not comprehensive, but as already noted, given the origins of the Act, that was inevitable. The impact of the Act and the accompanying secondary legislation therefore might be described as a legislative "patchwork quilt". Such an observation is not meant to minimise the significance of the pieces that go to make up the quilt, but to simply recognise that my attention has been drawn to a number of critically important issues. These may need to be included in supplementary secondary legislation and Guidance.

There are two anomalies that are worth noting, both of which stem from comparisons with the English Children Act and their approach to setting specific practice standards. The English Regulations require under Section 22 the use of independent visitors to residential homes. Whilst it may be argued that the lack of a specific regulatory power does not stop any agency in Scotland adopting this approach, and Barnardos have done so, such a stated power would create an appropriate expectation upon Local Authorities. This raises a further question as to how best such an independent visitor might be used.

The question of inspection raises a further anomaly, in relation to the inspection standards of residential children's establishments. The position in Scotland is that the Social Work Services Inspectorate, unlike its counterpart in England, the Social Services Inspectorate, has not laid down explicit standards governing the inspection of residential child care although the Guidance provides a baseline for practice. The Social Services Inspectorate, which does lay down standards in "Inspecting for Quality: Standards for Residential Child Care Services, Department of Health 1994", focuses on the question of child protection very specifically in Sections C1, C2 and C3.

- *Children are protected from harm in the home through careful selection and vetting of all staff including volunteers and regular visitors to the Home.*

- *Children being looked after receive protection from abuse. All staff, including domestic staff and volunteers, know what action to take if they have observed or have had reported to them, possible evidence of abuse.*

- *All information of significance to the protection of children in homes is notified to the appropriate Authorities external to the Home.*

These standards are followed by criteria for "Outcomes for Children", "Home Practices" and "Management Responsibilities". It is an illustration of a comprehensive approach with detailed cross referencing to Regulations and Guidance. It must be recognised that the SSI have responsibilities to inspect Private and Voluntary Homes that SWSI do not have but, nevertheless, this offers a good basic model for the Social Work Services Inspectorate to consider adopting. There is a strong case for such a model of standards to be issued as Guidance to ensure that both Local Authority inspections, and those presently carried out by the Social Work Services Inspectorate, conform to the same criteria and such standards are consistently addressed.

The impact of the Children (Scotland) Act 1995 and the accompanying Regulations and Guidance contribute to the greater safety of children being looked after by the Local Authority. I do find it surprising that although the Act is much later than its English and Welsh counterpart, there is nothing in it equivalent to the section in Volume 4 of the English Guidance on "Child Abuse in Children's Homes". Our Guidance has either handled this issue far too delicately, or has not taken it to be of particular importance. A case can be made for there being separate supplementary Regulations and Guidance giving a sharper focus to the question of safeguards.

There is no denying that requirements under the new legislation will have significant practice, policy and resource implications for Local Authorities.

CHAPTER 8

Steps To Greater Safety

8.1 Introduction

We have to make children safer in the next millennium. There have been many reviews, working parties, study groups and inquiries, some of which are mentioned in this report. But we still have not achieved the status, support and training for staff and for foster parents that the task deserves. If you press for improvement in the future you run the risk of being seen to devalue the efforts made in the present. There are devoted adults in the world today; there are children who truly benefit from the adults providing direct care. It is a supremely difficult job calling for a climate and a level of support that do not exist but improvement is required and incremental improvement is not enough. Ten per cent better each year is not sufficient. Moving forward by small changes is not an option. There is a pressing need for radical change, whether with new money or by the redistribution of existing resources, and 1997 should see it begin, with 2000 as a target by when much of it should be achieved.

We are at a moment when several opportunities present themselves. Devolution of power to a Scottish Parliament means that Social Work policy will be enacted in Scotland. There is every reason to hope that there will be a General Social Services Council providing better regulation of people working in the Residential Child Care field. There is to be a thorough review of the Central Council for Education and Training in Social Work which can include the option of wholesale change, perhaps a Scottish CCETSW not burdened by a United Kingdom bureaucracy. The Training Specific Grant comes to an end. There is an opportunity to create a greater degree of oversight of standards, behaviour and training through a GSSC modelled on Scotland's General Teaching Council, not controlled by the professionals but by a consortium of interested parties. A small investment could bring substantial improvement to techniques of staff selection. There is the opportunity to create a National College with responsibility for seeing that Induction Courses and follow-on courses are completed by all so that no one starts work with children living away from their natural home without first being subject to some training. There is a lot of fluidity but a lot to be worked out.

The greater use of vigilant outsiders in settings that may be at risk of being too closed is a straightforward step. The system which offers support to children must be strengthened so that their views about their care can be heard. Social Work inspection has taken root and can be improved on. Greater cohesion between different inspectors from different bases is not costly.

A searching look at the organisation and remit of Child Protection Committees, and the harmonisation of Registers and reporting systems, will lead to greater information being available and objective review when abuse is suspected. When I looked at the mainstream independent boarding schools, I found many very positive changes. I believe that there remain a few areas where they can learn from publicly-funded education and child care. The Centre For Residential Child Care has already been the catalyst for improvements in services. Further investment in its work will bear fruit.

This chapter has several sections, in each of which I have recommendations to make.

8.2 The Extent of Abuse

I have tried to quantify the amount of abuse of children living away from home in Scotland but have met with only limited success. There is a dearth of hard statistics. This is something which can be tightened up without much difficulty, in the first place by ensuring that every Local Authority collects the child protection management information which the Scottish Office joint steering group agreed in March 1992 was necessary. If this information were provided in full by every Local Authority, it would be possible to see what child protection cases related to children living with foster parents or in some type of children's residential establishment, and whether the perpetrators were either foster carers or professional carers, although it might not in its present form collate information about peer abuse. The wider range of quantifying and categorising is not the business of this report but all allegations should be recorded in such a way that we should be able to monitor the number of proven cases, the number of allegations and the number of times disciplinary action is taken. What research I have been able to do leads me to believe that there is more sexual and physical abuse about than I had formerly thought, much of it by other young people, and that sadly the care and education sectors are not as safe as they should be.

In relation to sexual abuse, it is widely believed that only 5% of allegations end up in convictions. It is recognised that most offenders have assaulted many other children before they are caught and that for every known case there must be a significant number of unknown episodes. I would suppose that the same multiplier factor exists in the case of the education and care sector. However I would further suppose that the climate now is such that residential care and education are safer than they were, but there is clear evidence that this is not yet safe enough. We must be able to know how much abuse is uncovered.

The same thing can be said of physical abuse by carers. The national gathering of records should be tightened up but there are many grey areas. Children in Homes universally feel that too much use is made of restraint; neighbours complain of a lack of control. Staff are unsure of where they stand. Striking, chastising and hitting by adults in caring situations are forbidden by all employers. Wrestling to the ground is distasteful but sometimes necessary. Guidance called for in 1992 on sanctions and restraint in Scotland has not yet been forthcoming.

Abuse by peers, both physical and sexual, seems to be much more prevalent than abuse by carers. There are dilemmas about having an abused child and an abusing child in the same residential unit. Utting and Skinner both advise against, but in reality it is happening all the time. There is an issue of confidentiality: do you tell the residents of a home that a known abuser has arrived, allowing them to protect themselves, or do you accept that the abuser is another child, and allow him or her to keep the circumstances of their life a secret? It might be preferable to keep abused children in separate establishments from abusing children. However, there are insufficient resources to do this without increasing the distance at which children are placed from their homes - in itself a danger. The matter can not be ignored. One special boarding school has children who have been abused as one-third of its population and another one-third who have abused others. The Headmaster of this school is coming round to the view that it is better for all if the truth is out in the open. All the special schools and residential homes with which I have been in contact have children who have been abused in some way, normally before coming away from home, and most had a child who they know had abused others, or who was thought capable of doing so. I am aware of the counterproductive effect of generalisation or of too wide a definition and I believe the staff who met me had a balanced view. As with many of the matters with which this Report is concerned there is a need for research.

I consider bullying to be something that still happens in the residential setting, but for a number of reasons certainly no more than in the past and very probably less. To be bullied is extremely distressing and it must not be tolerated. I think that in larger establishments in the past bullying may have been used by staff as a method of control but I see no evidence of that today. Bullying is currently of great concern in the day school sector and we should not be complacent in the places where children are living away from home, but I think staff are well aware of it and that the position is manageable. Young people in Children's Homes have told me they are bullied more at day school than in the Unit. This may be because of staff ratios and smaller numbers. Continuous reminders are needed and bullying should be routinely on a staff meeting agenda, a feature in induction training and in in-house team training programmes.

I make no apologies for dwelling on the "harm" part of the Remit but I have been concerned to keep the concept within bounds and not to lose credibility. The population of young people being cared for away from home includes a mix of the most privileged and the most disadvantaged. A boy may have been sent to boarding school because his parents wished to spend a great deal on his education, or because caring adults unrelated to him believed that this was the only way to cope with the problems that he now has. Whatever the intention when it is decided that the young person should not remain in their own home for 52 weeks of the year, there may be features in life away that are themselves harmful.

Damage can be caused by the wrong sort of care. The Literature Review has highlighted the disruption to children caused by multiple placements and changes in educational provision. Skinner said very strongly in his 1992 report:

> *"The establishment of an environment in which young people feel safe and secure is the first priority. This entails the establishment of routines within the unit and definitions of acceptable behaviour which are understood by everyone - both staff and young people. Security is provided for children and young people through continuity of care and experience in an environment which is predictable and consistent. Physical and emotional security are the basis for healthy growth and development and residential care must provide this before anything else can be achieved."*[53]

There is reason for serious alarm at the information position. A joint central Government and Local Authority Working Party met in the early 1990s and prepared a system for gathering statistics about the abuse of children. The results of their work, called the Child Protection in Scotland Management Information, arranges for the collection, by child referred, of information about the placement of a child immediately prior to referral, the main category of abuse or risk, and the relation of the abuser, or source of concern, to the child. There are weaknesses in the system, such as there being no place for coding "teacher" except as "other person known to the child". Despite the weaknesses the system could be helpful - but it was not universally used even before local government reorganisation as 3 major Regions would not participate in the standard management system but used analogous systems of their own from which they furnished information in a different way. There is no point in gathering national statistics unless they are gathered in a standardised way. Local Authorities must be pressed to complete the returns to a common format. From the information available it would seem that in the year 1994/95 in half of Scotland there were 12 occasions when a foster parent or a residential child care worker was recorded as the primary suspected perpetrator of some type of abuse leading to recording on the Child Protection Register.

The Social Work Services Group Statistics Branch costs about £350,000 a year to run. It is not within my remit to go into the whole field of statistics gathering but I suspect there is information stored and never used. This particular information is vital; it is literally about saving lives. Perhaps the whole information reporting system needs review and overhaul; this small part of the whole system was reviewed 5 years ago but is not working properly. Worse, it is reported that some Local Authorities are thinking of investing less in this information. There is no need to recall the working party that established the system to go over their work again. What is required is the universal implementation of their advice.

It is impossible not to have some sympathy with Local Authorities. They feel beset and overburdened. You have the daily round of pressure; old ladies wandering, violent young men marauding, meals on wheels to provide, babies abandoned, but there are still forms to fill in. Forms are presently filled in in a manner that does not allow the best analysis and is invariably stale. This cannot be countenanced.

53 Skinner, Angus (1993) op. cit.

There is no reason why there cannot be a common format for child protection registers. It might require a one-off capital expenditure to equip Local Authorities with the same hardware and software, but it would not be very substantial. There are those who believe a National Child Protection Register would be helpful and certainly it could grow from a common system. The data provided would include the number of allegations of abuse of looked after children, the type of abuse involved, the alleged perpetrator by category (including staff, carer, volunteer or another child) and whether the allegation is proved. Despite the fact that the average retail outlet can tell each day by how much the stock of tinned food has been reduced, far more vital information in this setting is not readily available.

Consideration should be given to ways of logging initial and subsequent abuse and for the Child Protection Register to be notified of an incident of abuse of a child living away from home by adults or by peers. An Annual Report should be submitted to the Secretary of State on all activity but in particular commenting on this specific issue.

Reading the Literature Review, I am struck by the number of times that the author has to state that there is little or no British research on a particular topic. Above all, I am aware that although we have one inquiry after another, often repeating at the end many of the same recommendations, there is as yet no British research which looks at abuse in institutions as a topic in its own right. It is time to take a more pro-active stance on this in relation to the Scottish system.

We need studies of the incidence of abuse and neglect of children living away from home, in different types of settings;

- Residential care (covering different types of establishments, residential homes, residential schools etc.)
- Foster care
- Boarding Schools
- Hospitals/Psychiatric Units
- Prisons

I am particularly concerned that there is even less information about abuse in foster care than there is about abuse in residential settings. We need research into the experiences of children and young people in out-of-home care settings using their own words as far as possible. Complaints procedures need to be evaluated, as a measure established to reduce the abuse of children living away from home. The work of Children's Rights Officers and other advocates for children should be studied.

There are no studies of the aetiology of abuse which differentiate between abuse as a result of recruiting unsuitable or unstable staff, deliberate targeting by potential abusers, and pressures put on inexperienced or overworked staff. This would suggest that there should be a standardisation of reporting procedures. If abuse by residents is a greater problem than abuse by staff then why does this situation arise, and how do we deal with it? Boarding school education and long stay hospital care have not been properly studied since Dartington and the Coram Foundation did so in the 1970s. It is high time to take another look.

Recommendation 1: National Statistics must be gathered from a common format of Child Protection Registers. The recommendations of the Working Party of 1992 that reported on Child Protection in Scotland Management Information should be implemented in a standard way across Scotland.

Recommendation 2: An Annual Report must be made to the Secretary of State by the Child Protection Committee of all child protection activity that includes specific comment on children living away from home.

Recommendation 3: There should be studies of the aetiology of the abuse of children living away from home and research into abuse in foster care.

8.3 Support for Children

Much has been written about the need to listen to children and a lot has been done in legislation and Guidance to ensure that their views are heard. I was very struck by the range of people who said that children do not misuse the complaints system. One English NSPCC team offer a complaints service to an English city and have logged 150 complaints from children in care in 18 months, of which one-quarter had child protection involvement, and where they believe only 2 were mischievous. A clients' complaints officer in a Scottish city believes she has never had a vexatious complaint from a child. Many people have told me that young people do not normally complain maliciously and I subscribe to that view.

Such records as I have had access to would suggest that managers may not always put the same construction on things but, by and large, adults have got much better at believing children. I had misgivings about the introduction of formal complaints procedures, but am now glad to recognise that they have their place and are a useful weapon in the defence armoury. Whilst there is something of a backlash at present over the perceived paramountcy of children's views I do not think any ground should be conceded over complaints systems, but rather that they should be improved, made more child-friendly and extended. A lot of good work has gone on in attempting to achieve this but there is still room for improvement. The Scottish Council of Independent Schools have done a very good job indeed with child protection guidelines for fee paying Boarding Schools and should be encouraged to offer them a model complaints procedure also.

The young people I have met do not share the view that we are getting better at hearing children and dealing with their complaints. They tell me of bureaucratic drag and of not getting answers. They are not too bothered about form filling - if there is a problem they want it sorted out. Every complaint from a young person, however informally raised, however apparently trivial, must be dealt with as quickly as possible; its outcome must be discussed with the complainant. It is helpful to think in terms of a pre-complaint stage - staff, including care staff and teaching staff in independent boarding schools, should be trained in handling complaints. Policies should be more specific about how it will be decided what constitutes a serious complaint to be handled formally and other complaints to be handled informally. This begs the question of what is serious and agencies must determine this. Certainly physical and sexual abuse are serious, but questions of pocket money or whose turn it is on the snooker table may be less so. Again the issue of professionalism in judgement versus a dependency on procedures is important. The procedures are of benefit in contributing to the safety of those living away from home, but it is essential that where a child makes a serious complaint they are offered support and are informed of the outcome of their complaint by the person who investigated it. I also believe that all records of complaints, including those in Secure Units, must be provided to Inspectors for monitoring. Further, all establishments must maintain complaints logs which are reviewed by external managers. Complaints should be summarised and monitored statistically in terms of the types, source, and outcomes. Trends should be noted and investigated.

Recommendation 4: Complaints procedures should be more child and parent friendly. SCIS should launch a model complaints procedure and distribute it to all their member schools.

Recommendation 5: Staff, particularly care staff and teaching staff, should be trained in handling complaints. Where a child makes a serious complaint they must have support and be informed of the outcome of their complaint by the person who investigated it.

Recommendation 6: All establishments must maintain complaints logs which are reviewed by external managers. Complaints should be summarised and monitored statistically in terms of the types, source and outcomes. Trends should be noted and investigated. Records of complaints, including those in secure units, must be provided to Inspectors for monitoring.

There are times when a Local Authority Department, or other agency providing residential care for children, needs the help of an independent agency in investigating a serious complaint or allegation. There are not many suitable agencies for them to use in Scotland. However, there are more agencies which can provide a choice to the child of support and advocacy.

The Scottish Child Law Centre provides a free 'phone service for under 18s, and an advice line, on 4 days per week. Most of the calls they receive from young people relate to some form of abuse, albeit quite minor.

ChildLine runs a separate Scottish telephone helpline service on a budget of just under £500,000 annually, £36,000 of which comes in the form of a Scottish Office grant. They answer between 500 - 700 calls every day, but estimate that as many calls again cannot be answered, because of a lack of telephone lines. They do have a telephone number solely for children in care and it is much easier for children to get through on this line. It worries me that a service, which children show so clearly they appreciate, is short of the money to provide enough lines so that children are not left with either an engaged tone or an answer 'phone. I believe that an increased grant from the Scottish Office would encourage others to give to an expanded ChildLine service in Scotland.

Children 1st, the former RSSPCC, do post-abuse counselling, usually with adults who were abused as children but also with children. With younger ones, they often work through play. They would not, I think, see themselves acting as an advocacy service for children and they have withdrawn from an investigative role. The NSPCC in England and Wales are playing an increasingly important part in helping Local Authorities, in particular, to combat the problems of harm and abuse away from home by way of providing independent visitors, investigations or support for children's rights. It is a matter for regret that in Scotland there is no comparable body providing authoritative and well founded independent support, advice or criticism.

The support given to Who Cares? after the Skinner Report has been fruitful, and recent growth has been helped by lottery funding. Many children and young people in care value their support particularly because it comes from people who have been in care themselves. I would wish to see their grants from all sources remain about the present level, in order to allow them to consolidate the good work they do.

There are a handful of full-time Children's Rights Officers in Scotland and others who have children's rights work as part of their remit, and I have been impressed by the things they do, the way they do them and the value they bring. As the role of the Field Social Worker changes there is a feeling that they are not generally seen in the light of children's advocates as they once were. Of course there are Social Workers who are important figures in the child's life but for various reasons not all are able to be this. In addition Social Workers often have to advocate what they see as best for the child so that if children want their own views expressed at Panels or Reviews they may prefer to ask the Children's Rights Officer to do this for them. I would be apprehensive about Children's Rights Officers if they were seen to undermine the role of the Field Social Worker, but that does not seem to be the case because often their role is different. I don't like the name but no one has yet thought of anything better.

Children's Rights Officers are helpful to the looked after population and I would want them to be accessible to all children living away from home. The independent Boarding Schools would probably look askance at the prospect of someone with the right to enter and pursue something on a child's behalf. On the other hand most of them have someone outside the school whose name is promulgated as a person to go to if there is a concern. If that person were to feel that they were getting out of their depth then I would want them to have someone else - attuned to the needs of children and good at communicating with them - to turn to. The Children's Rights Officer could fill this role.

By the same token, it makes little sense to have coverage by people with a children's rights remit in a few parts of Scotland only. I would suggest that national coverage by a group of people in touch with one another would make a lot more sense, bearing in mind the high regard given to those Children's Rights Officers who do exist.

I am aware that there is now a powerful head of steam pressing for a Children's Commissioner, an Ombudsman. I do not believe that this Safeguards Review allows me to add my voice to that lobby no matter what respect I have for the individuals in it. The Child Care Law Review completed in 1990 called for a Child Welfare Commission, the Scottish Child Law Centre advocates a Commissioner for Children, Children in Scotland have a similar view. I do not believe the group I am reporting on justify such a role by themselves; however, if such a role were to be created for all children in Scotland and given power, with a range of local staff for children themselves to go to, I would support it so long as these special children looked after away from home had priority attention.

Meantime I would prefer a network of about 15 full-time Children's Advocates and Advisors, born of the Children's Rights Officer service, to be deployed throughout Scotland with appropriate clerical help. There are two views about the location of such people. If they work within the Local Authority they are brought into close touch with Social Workers, Teachers and others who grow to respect and trust them - I have found much evidence of Social Workers initiating contact with the Children's Rights Officer on behalf of a child. If they work outwith the Local Authority they have an independence visible to the child, to the parents and to others who are concerned. Being within the Local Authority entails support and management; it also means they have some power to influence planning and development. Just being a free floating independent group probably brings chaos. On balance I prefer the independence that comes from being outwith the Local Authority but would want them to be included in an existing organisation. I believe it would be possible for ChildLine to discharge this function although they would have to be very careful not to distort their existing service. They could readily provide the management for a network of Children's Advocates who would effectively be ChildLine Field Workers.

Recommendation 7: The availability of ChildLine should be increased by way of increased Scottish Office grant in the expectation that that would attract more money still. Who Cares? should be retained and the level of grant should be maintained at the present level.

Recommendation 8: The help of Children's Rights Officers should be available to all children living away from home not exclusively the looked after population alone. Central Government should consider a nation-wide network of children's advocates. Funding should be made available to provide a number of people to be spread across Scotland and supported.

It is important that steps are taken to promote the risk and danger components in the Personal And Social Development Curriculum in schools. There is some reason to suppose that personal and social education programmes are better handled in the state sector than the independent sector. Children living away from home should be exposed to this teaching along with everyone else. Because an undue proportion of young people in children's homes are not at school then their staff need to find ways to make up for this.

It is essential that senior figures pay more attention to the loss of educational opportunities experienced by many looked after children. It is a fact that far too many looked after children are not attending school and greater efforts must be made to achieve better attendance. The excluded child misses normality and may lose contact with his or her peers. Part of the problem is that the residential child care staff themselves may not have had much in the way of education and do not attach sufficient importance to it. Day school staff may tend to see exclusion of a looked after child as a less serious matter because they believe that, as the child is in care, the care staff will do what is necessary. In practice the excluded child places additional demands on the care staff. It would be helpful if there was an obligatory case conference before exclusion took place but that is not practicable because it would not apply to everyone else. Nevertheless there should be an obligatory case conference within 48 hours of a looked after child being excluded with a view to finding clear planning for alternative education or alternative activity; a representative for the excluding school or for the Education Department should be obliged to attend in order to identify a suitable alternative placement or domiciliary educational resources. It is the Education Authority that has responsibility for the education of children in care and the Social Work Authority and staff who have a responsibility to press for it. No statistics concerning the exclusion of looked after children are collected on a national basis, but it is distressing to learn from one Local Authority, that keeps its own records, that there are times when more children of school age in residential care are not at school than in school.

The provision of a refuge as permitted by the new Children (Scotland) Act may well constitute a new safeguard. It is unlikely to prove attractive at a time of financial constraint and has to be balanced against other demands particularly when there has been virtually no new development. However being in a refuge is safer than being on the streets and it might be possible to find a large establishment that could open up a satellite when required. This is discussed again later on.

Some people will see the Field Social Worker as main plank in offering support for looked after children. They are not normally relevant to children in independent boarding schools. The Children (Scotland) Act requires Social Workers to visit looked after children at intervals of not less than 3 months but does stipulate that this may need to be much more frequent. There is a great deal of Guidance at the moment and I am reluctant to advise that visiting should always be more often. We have to leave room for professional judgement. The National Foster Care Association report that their research into allegations would indicate that the longer a foster parent has offered a service the more likely it is that there will be an allegation against them. It would be unwise to reduce the need to visit the longer the child has been in the placement. Rather than recommend Guidance being offered on exactly what the Social Worker should be expected to do and achieve when visiting a looked after child I would prefer to rely on improved training. Social Workers should, of course, ask looked after children whether anyone has hurt them - some children will not tell until they are asked. There is a principle of the primacy of protecting children not only when they are in their own homes. Existing advice on the conduct of reviews insists on the child being seen alone.

Recommendation 9: Steps should be taken to promote the risk and danger components in personal and social development curriculum in schools.

Recommendation 10: More attention must be paid to the loss of educational opportunities experienced by many children in care. In particular there should be an obligatory case conference within 48 hours of a looked after child being excluded from school.

8.4 Selection, Recruitment and Staffing

There are concrete and specific things to be done with selection to improve the safety of youngsters in foster care, Boarding Schools or Homes. The first two are to build on the present criminal conviction system efficiently run by the SCRO and to devise a Consultancy Index holding information from sources other than the police.

There is potential for conflict between the needs of children living away from home and the needs of those responsible for their care. Article 19 of the United Nations Convention on the Rights of the Child ordains that:

> **"States parties shall take all appropriate legislative, administrative, social and educational measures to protect the child from all forms of physical or mental violence, injury or abuse, neglect or negligent treatment or exploitation, including sexual abuse ...."**

While Article 17 of the International Covenant on Civil and Political Rights states that:

> *"No one shall be subjected to arbitrary or unlawful interference with his privacy .... nor to unlawful attacks of his honour and reputation; everyone has the right to the protection of the law against such interference or attacks".*

We have to protect the child but protect the privacy of the adult as well. I believe we can get this balance.

In Scotland we are fortunate to have the Scottish Criminal Records Office. Police checks are made routinely and are the very minimum that society expects in the protection of our children - we must at least keep convicted people out. The problems that Scottish employers have when recruiting south of the border will be reduced in future when the Police Act provides a better system for England and Wales through their Criminal Records Agency. However, it is important to remind ourselves constantly that police checks are no substitute for good recruitment arrangements and selection policies.

The police have a crucial role and the technology available to SCRO can react very quickly. We are at a moment when improvements can be made to existing arrangements. Not enough use is made of the fact that residential child care staff are in a notifiable occupation as defined in the Police (CC) Circular 4 of 1989.

SCRO checks are made on first appointment. The new arrangements provided under the Police Act 1997 mean that there will be criminal conviction certificates, criminal records certificates and enhanced criminal records certificates. The latter are applicable in respect of those who will be regularly involved in caring for, training, supervising or being in sole charge of persons aged under 18.

SCRO will be approached for a check when an appointment is about to be offered. The check will now reveal convictions but also some other information such as cautions, factual information about known associates, decisions not to prosecute, and acquittals in some circumstances. The civil liberties line in the sand is important, but the legislation permits the sensitive use of this information. The check will be initiated by the applicant and forwarded by the prospective employer's authorised counter signatory. These checks can be made when a provisional offer of appointment is to be given or when required by a professional body. One of the present dilemmas is how to create a professional body without a profession.

Considerable responsibility falls on the prospective employer to ensure that the person they are appointing is the person he or she claims to be, and it would be advisable for this to be done thoroughly using at least two forms of identity check such as passport, driving licence or credit card as well as checking the National Insurance number and birth certificate which will be needed anyway. The police themselves believe that fingerprinting of all people working with children when their name is first put forward would overcome the risk of someone giving a false name or a false date of birth at that time, or a false occupation if arrested later. While it would appear that the public mood is ready for sweeping change this might be seen as going too far, although I for one would welcome the demonstration that we care that much for our children - and that was also the response of staff I met.

It is important to go beyond the comparatively simple business of obtaining a criminal bill of health at first appointment, and we should look to an ongoing arrangement that guarantees to reveal subsequent transgressions that may not come to the notice of the employer. It is practice in some parts of Scotland for there to be two-yearly checks on foster carers and the local police may well tip off their local Social Work Director that an employee will be appearing in court or has given them grave cause for concern. This can be improved on - in the case of teachers, arrest will lead to the General Teaching Council being notified.

The technology exists for the SCRO to know when someone who has already been checked comes to the notice of their colleagues in one of the Forces. It is quite possible to construct a list of people who work with children, who have been SCRO screened and whose identity was confirmed on appointment. SCRO could know when someone on that electronic list was charged or convicted. They could notify the employer or some "professional" body.

This would eliminate any need for an annual criminal records checks that I would otherwise feel I had to advocate. The "list" could start to be constructed from an appointed day in a rolling fashion with all new appointments, that excluded existing employees, or by a one-off start-up with back record conversion; a census when all employers report the names, dates of birth and National Insurance numbers of their staff. I favour the latter alternative. The "list" would be updated for the employees name when someone leaves and/or starts work elsewhere by way of tear-off slip and pre-paid envelope on departure or appointment - at the moment SCRO do not know who the employer has appointed, they check but get no feedback.

Where a member of staff drives a minibus it is common practice to check the driving licence on an annual basis. The same sort of thoroughness should apply to criminal convictions and, quite frankly, an employer should be told that a boarding school matron, for instance, has been found to be in the possession of drugs or has committed some other offence that reflects on her ability to care for children. They would be if she was to be newly recruited.

There will have to be one-off capital costs to enable the SCRO to uprate their existing systems. It has been accepted, or at least suggested, that in implementing the Police Act 1997, the financial arrangements will reflect the fact that existing organisations already make checks.

Lord Cullen recommends an Accrediting and Vetting Agency. In most of the boarding school and children's home field we do not need the accreditation because they are registered; foster parents are approved. It is open to some doubt whether the consultation following Lord Cullen's report will lead to a police checking system for youth leaders, or indeed for Sunday School teachers, that is as thorough as I recommend for the residential arena. If it did then residential workers can be subject to the same screening as youth leaders; if not then the standards for residential workers should not be lowered.

Recommendation 11: The SCRO should maintain a list of people who have already been vetted. This list will enable the police to inform employers, or a new register, of people employed in residential child care who have committed an offence.

Using the list of SCRO vetted people, or using the census referred to above, means we can create a new General Child Care Register funded by subscription and run by a Council with the power to strike names off, to monitor supervision and appraisal arrangements, deal with complaints and create standards of conduct and practice. A primary function would be the protection of service users. Teachers finance their register with a levy of £15, and £10 per year thereafter. The UKCC discharges a similar responsibility for trained nurses from a subscription of £1 per month. The number of people working in residential establishments, who are not teachers, is insufficient to pay for an administration with that sort of subscription and it would probably need to be about £30 per year per person together with some start-up costs from central Government. It would be healthy and underline a sense of belonging to a group that wants to self-regulate if the individual paid the fee rather than the employer. It would have to be tax deductible which would have a small cost for the Treasury.

Up until now Central Government has been lukewarm about a General Social Services Council. Recently there has been talk of a General Teaching Council in England and Wales and there are more hopeful signs about a GSSC. If this is to come about all well and good. Otherwise this group of staff and this group of children must be treated differently.

Each person on the General Residential Child Care Register would have a PIN and the new Council would be informed of offences. If a General Social Services Council grew from this proposal so be it, but otherwise let us make a start with this group to underline their importance. The Social Care Association have a Code of Conduct which should be commended to employers. The UKCC, which governs the training of nurses, creates standards and is the instrument of registration, has a similar Code of Conduct. The big distinction between nurses and teachers on the one hand and residential Social Workers on the other is that the former are registered when they are trained. We should aim for registration even though people are not yet all trained. SVQ3 could serve as a datum with a particular day specified and arrangements for people working in care settings without qualification to be provisionally registered. Child minders are registered by Local Authorities after a vetting process that is probably superior to that for residential Social Workers and inferior to that for foster parents. There are 75,000 registered teachers in Scotland and a similar number of registered nurses.

Teachers and nurses should, like Social Workers, have an SCRO check at the commencement of their training not on its completion.

Recommendation 12: A General Residential Child Care Register should be created and funded through subscription after initial start-up costs have been met if no General Social Services Council is created with residential child care staff included in the first tranche.

The lack of a register of people unsuited to care for children is obvious and must be remedied. A Consultancy Index which holds the names not simply of those convicted but also of those who have been dismissed, or who have left and would not be re-employed, must be maintained. "Dismissed" is straightforward; the person's behaviour may have been completely inappropriate although it may not have merited prosecution. Dismissal is a fact, and a fact to be recorded with the knowledge of the individual. In the event of someone leaving either "by being required to resign" or simply where there have been concerns and the agency would not re-employ, then that agency must tell the departing employee that they would not re-engage and that the name will go on to the Index. It could be the responsibility of the employer to take the action to inform the Index and inform the ex-employee. It will be the task of the Index holder to inform prospective new employers of the fact that the name is on the Index. It will be the task of the prospective employer to check against the Index before making an appointment.

No one wants duplication or too many doors to knock on. Without Lord Cullen's Report I would have advocated an Index to be maintained in the Scottish Office or by the proposed General Residential Child Care Council with an obligation placed on employers both to use the Index when recruiting and to put names on it when there is ground for so doing. Lord Cullen's advice may well lead to a much bigger Index than one needed for foster carers and for staff in Boarding Schools and Children's Homes. It may cover all Youth Clubs and Church football teams for example. If it is possible to fit the need for security of the very small group of children living away from home into a wider register, all well and good. If the level of information in a Cullen Index is less than residential care needs, then a separate register will be required.

This list or register or Index should contain the names of people who have been dismissed from care employment. It should also include people who have left and whom the employer is prepared to declare they would not employ again. Equally people who have been transferred to a desk job within the organisation to take them away from children should have their names entered on this Index. The person will have to be told that their name is being recorded in this way and there will have to be an appeal mechanism to challenge this action or to register their disagreement. It will be up to the employers to put names on the Index and up to prospective employers to interrogate the Index. This may have to be a stand-alone Index exclusively dedicated to residential child care provision, but if the outcome of the Cullen consultations are satisfactory it could be a part of that.

When a central Consultative Index is established we have to determine whether the register holder is the person who goes to the SCRO every time to check someone's record or whether it is the prospective employer. The question of where the Index is actually held will have to await the outcome of the post Cullen Consultation. The options are at the SCRO, who would have to step outside their primary role and be paid to act as an agent, a new General Residential Child Care Register or some central body such as the Scottish Office or perhaps COSLA. The more lists the more room for muddle, the more bureaucracy and the more work for the initial employer. I would favour the General Residential Child Care Register if that recommendation were to be accepted.

Recommendation 13: There should be a new Consultancy Index created for those with access to children.

Since the Warner Report and the subsequent work of the Support Force in England and Wales, recruitment practice has improved. The Support Force Code of Practice is a first class piece of work and should be commended to all employers. In England and Wales the Department of Health issued Section 7 circulars - that is to say circulars with more authority to them - about the implementation of Warner's proposals. We need similar action in Scotland. The Scottish Office should commission work to put the Support Force Code of Practice into a Scottish context - not a very big job - and then endorse it as a way for Scottish employers to act. It would be appropriate for the Centre for Residential Child Care to undertake this work in conjunction with COSLA.

Recommendation 14: The Scottish Office should require the recommendations in the Warner Report to be implemented. Special procedures should be created for all appointments to residential care and to boarding schools including teaching staff. The Scottish Office should commission work to put the Support Force Code of Practice into a Scottish context.

There is a problem in getting some employers, particularly Local Authorities, to see that the care of children is so special and so important that recruitment procedures should be different. The interviewing of at least one referee is a case in point - you would not do this for an architect or librarian but you must do it for residential child care staff, if necessary by telephone. There is no reason why there should not be a knock for knock arrangement between employers by way of commissioning a colleague in another part of the country to undertake the interview, indeed this might be more objective. Such an exchange would need a common structured interview guide. A compulsory probationary period of appointment is another. Perhaps it is acceptable to employ a new clerical officer on a permanent contract but new staff with access to children should have a period of closely supervised practice with appraisal before the employer is finally committed to them. It is argued that employment legislation permits unsatisfactory people to have their employment terminated within the first year, but decisions can drift; a probationary period forces an employer into making a decision at a particular time and to have been discussing attitudes and approach with the new member of staff as the months pass, with the opportunity to review progress and improve practice. It also creates an expectation that supervision and appraisal will be a routine part of future employment. Induction training is a firm Skinner recommendation and money has been allocated in the specific training grant which ends in 2 year's time but should continue while it is still needed. Whilst I have found there to be induction training programmes available in many places I have found less actual training. Local government reorganisation has meant some new Local Authorities have been writing new programmes rather than getting on with the old ones. Support Force offered an excellent model programme. I believe the probationary period following induction to be imperative, and that it should only be followed by ratification when SVQ Level 2 has been achieved. The Prison Service has implemented something fairly similar with some success. If we aim a little higher and reflect an expectation that everyone should be capable at least of SVQ Level 3 it will be possible to miss out Level 2 and substitute a requirement to achieve 6 out of the 12 units needed for Level 3.

Recommendation 15: There should be a compulsory probation period for all new employees with an initial 2 week induction period. The probation period should be ended, and a permanent appointment offered, only when SVQ Level 2 or above has been achieved.

I discussed in Chapter 6 my concerns that the new COSLA Code of Recruitment takes the generalist approach without particular reference to recruiting staff who work with children, and does not recognise the potential conflict between good child protection policies and equal opportunities policies. They make a suggestion about "where references are sought" that opens up the possibility that references may not be sought. "Applicants should be asked whether references can be taken up before the interview" - a reference taken up on the successful candidate only puts the referee in a difficult position when the candidate knows he or she is the only obstacle. While every effort must be made to treat candidates in the same way a reference is an important tool to have before the interview.

On the other hand I wrote in Chapter 6 about how impressed I have been with some of the material emerging from the consortium of 7 Local Authorities - one of which was Scottish - set up after Support Force reported. For a variety of reasons this work stopped before they moved on to develop it. The fruits of much activity now lie dormant and comparatively modest investment by the Government, perhaps £50,000 for each of three years, would regenerate it and help improve selection - and subsequent support - enormously. The work that stands ready for development and universal practice includes job analyses for Residential Social Workers and Officers in Charge, interview training and a structured interview guide, as well as recommendations concerning best test practice and selection techniques.

A public relations campaign, funded by central Government, underlining the importance of these roles within the community, and stressing that there is a formidable selection process might attract good calibre candidates rather than deter them.

Recommendation 16: Funding for 3 years should be offered to the Scottish Consortium developing the earlier work undertaken by 6 English Local Authorities and Tayside supported by a firm of recruitment consultants. This should ensure standards of selection are improved and that the process is seen as the start of continuing support and supervision with monitoring of the success, or weaknesses, of the selection system.

The report by Norman Warner in 1992 spelt out clearly his view of the need for supervision, appraisal and personal development plans. It would be helpful if the Social Work Services Inspectorate provided some impetus to propel this forward. Supervision as a style is widely accepted but the practice varies. From the safeguards standpoint Warner is quite specific and his Recommendation 43 says:

> *"Employers should ensure that supervision is seen as the normal means by which staff are able to raise with their line manager any concerns about the welfare or treatment of a child; but that staff have access to advice about a child outside the line management chain and are able to raise any concerns through an independent staff support service."*

Guidance from the Scottish Office is important. Work undertaken by Stirling University, following the publication of the Skinner Report, on supervision is helpful and could be developed. The Scottish Office should require appraisal systems to be introduced with a personal development plan for all staff including teachers and nurses in residential care.

Staff appraisal of residential child care staff has yet to take root throughout all agencies and I think is at present better handled by voluntary organisations than by Local Authorities. Two main reasons are offered for the resistance to it - that we do not do it for other staff and that the Unions do not like it because it may lead to performance related pay. It is my belief that neither of these concerns is valid and that the reasons are much more about a changing social service world that bewilders and causes people to react to the next new thing, missing the mundane and overdue staffing practice issues. There is every reason to take more care with child care staff; they are dealing with a most important commodity, and the more we put them through special hoops the more special they will become and feel. The view expressed to me by a UNISON official about performance appraisal was clear and concise - it should be part of everyone's job and there is no problem as long as the issue of appraisal and pay are kept separate.

Recommendation 17: By building on the work done by Stirling University the Scottish Office should offer guidance on staff supervision. Employers should insist on appraisal and a personal development plan for all staff in residential care including teachers and nurses. Performance appraisal should not be linked to pay.

It is important that staff understand their duty to report concerns about the well-being of a child and the behaviour of an adult. An understanding of this responsibility should be checked at interview. The core task in residential care is protecting and safeguarding and the duty of the post must be included in the job description. All staff should have an exit interview on leaving the service, and the safety of the children should be discussed to see if there is now a moment when they can speak even if previously they remained mute. Staff should always have access to a named person, other than their line manager, to whom they can go with suspicions or concerns. Staff will not complain if they think they will not be believed, or that someone more powerful will be listened to.

Recommendation 18: The duty to report concerns about the well-being of a child should be discussed at interview and should form part of the job description. All staff should have an exit interview on leaving the service. Staff should always have access to a named person, other than their line manager to whom they can go with suspicions or concerns.

There should be regular staff meetings, probably at the rate of one a week, at which safety should always be an agenda item minuted after discussion. Safety should be discussed at supervision sessions and minuted. The hallmark of a well run establishment is that it allows a child to be safe. It cannot be stressed too strongly that the whole culture of the agency and the unit must be open; open to be challenged, open to be discussed, open to be disciplined, open to the outside. External management and the most senior management must be part of the culture to be open.

Recommendation 19: Safety should always be a standing agenda item for staff meetings, and safety should be discussed at supervision sessions and minuted.

Banks of relief staff should be available to ensure that staffing can be maintained at a safe level. This is done in many Local Authorities at the present time but it is not yet universal. Relief staff, and volunteers, must be vetted on the same basis as permanent staff and should not be allowed to graduate from job to job without re-interview for the new role.

Recommendation 20: Relief staff and volunteers must be vetted carefully and should not be allowed to move from job to job without re-interview for the new role.

Personal Development Plans for staff are occasionally to be found and work goes on in some agencies to identify training needs. They are now an integral part of work in many other places, for example in the Scottish Office, and are a core ingredient with Investors in People. Practice in residential care is a long way short of Warner's Contract, where the development of staff is linked to that of the Home and the organisation, with a signed undertaking that staff will, for example, undertake SVQs and their employer will provide them.

I would not presume to advise on the precise detail of the compilation of staff personal files. However I would advise that they be retained for some considerable time after a member of staff has left in all cases, whether or not the person left under a cloud. The plethora of investigations that have been taking place recently about events that took place some time ago, in relation to people not previously under suspicion, leads me to suppose that all staff files must be kept, probably for 25 years, if necessary by way of micro fiche.

Recommendation 21: Staff files should be kept for a substantial period, probably not less than 25 years.

All in all there is little point in going over the Warner and Support Force ground again. Their recommendations and proposals need to be translated to Scotland and rigorously pursued by the Scottish Office, by employers, by training agencies, by Inspectors and by staff themselves.

8.5 Training

I am tempted to advocate changes so radical as to cause consternation in all quarters. The main burden of my song is that pride has gone from the job, people look for "better alternatives" to residential care, the public have no understanding of the complexity of the task, the staff are undervalued and their calibre needs improving. We may have gone so far down our current path that only a total upheaval will get the standards of care right. I am concerned that the Social Work model may not be the right one for residential care. The Diploma in Social Work at the moment provides "cradle to grave" training, while we are concerned with the under 21s. There may for residential child care staff be more affinity with youth workers, psychiatric nurses, occupational therapists and others. The Diploma in Social Work is sometimes described as the passport out of residential care - so that one can only wonder why good staff came to work directly with children if they really want to get out into a different kind of job. Career patterns, week-end working and levels of remuneration may be factors in this choice. Fundamentally we have to recruit and train people who want direct involvement with young people who are sometimes damaged, with the rewards that come from helping them overcome their difficulties and enjoying their company - without wanting to abuse them! Residential Child Care should be seen as a different kind of Social Work from Field Work, requiring its own skill and experience. Very little training explicitly addresses safeguarding children and young people. It is implicitly expressed as a value statement for the Diploma of Social Work. The generic nature of training courses mean that the specific needs of children are subsumed under options or specialisms or pathways.

So long as men were losing their lives in wars or colonising empires there were legions of worthy women to devote themselves to children who could not stay at home. Without this option, we must find a suitable alternative. There is evidence that a group of people of the right calibre does exist. Many of them are already working in residential child care.

Today's task is not mundane; it is much more than diversion or nurture. It is a sophisticated business that needs the cream in the way of staff. We have long talked of two levels of status and training; we were always striving to level up the residential worker to the field worker. Now perhaps is the time to leap frog and have greater expectations of the residential worker as the crucial figure for children living away from home in care units, and to a lesser degree in Boarding Schools.

It is important to spell out that residential child care be not accepted as a lifetime job. It is demanding and exhausting. A qualification that includes the ability to work as a Field Social Worker opens the door for people to move into and out of residential work. In some areas of child care we seek to introduce adults whose age is relevant to the child's age in reflecting the natural child rearing years. If we applied that to residential child care, where the young people are mainly 12 - 18 we would be talking of adults aged 30 - 53. This is, of course, too rigid but we do need to equip people with the training or qualification to move out and move back. This is not the same thing as the so called "passport to leave" when people who are not committed have been recruited and then trained. Those who had previously been trained teachers, nurses or occupational therapists can move in and out of their former setting.

Meantime, while there is pressure to increase the number of qualified staff in residential child care we have to note that there are now concerns raised in hospital circles that going for Graduate Nurses may be to the detriment of old fashioned hands-on care. I would be concerned at the prospect of staffing Children's Homes with qualified Social Workers who felt they should be office bound, establishing networks, doing assessments and referring people elsewhere because that is what they believe their field work colleagues do.

There is talk of an "enhanced role" for the diploma holder in a residential setting as though somehow they are too good for the ordinary task. The ordinary task, the daily task, the routine job is demanding and vital and will be done better by trained people if their training is more relevant. The Diploma course does not at present do enough to equip people to work with children. The radical change I have contemplated, and have rejected, was to separate residential care from Social Work outright and to reinvent the old Certificate in the Residential Care of Children and Young People built up to Diploma level.

In the real world we have gone down the SVQ route and although many are disappointed that more has not happened yet, the die is cast. What is needed, urgently, is for SVQs, HNCs and Social Work Diplomas to knit together and also to match up to university systems. SVQ4 is now available in Scotland although no one has yet achieved it. SVQ4 does not feature in the training targets because it had not then been devised. We can, at a stroke, level up the training target for SVQ3 to be SVQ3 or 4. There is a pressing need for equivalence. Fundamentally there are in Britain two systems of qualification for adults. Within the universities there are certificates, diplomas, degrees, honours degrees and post-graduate work. Vocational qualifications are available for a whole range of industries, including the social care industry, with 5 levels of competence, of which Level 5 would be post-professional. Although SVQ3 in social care is quite well established, there is no proposal for social care Level 5 and we have not really established social care Level 4. The Diploma in Social Work is seen as ahead of SVQ Level 4, and Level 5 is seen as not being needed because of post qualifying training. A professional qualification is a different thing to a vocational qualification: a Diploma in Social Work is not a vocational qualification, and SVQ4 is not a professional qualification.

Social Care is not alone in having difficulty in getting vocational, professional and academic awards to dovetail and also avoid duplication. At present it would seem that CCETSW understand what the connections between qualifications are but neither employers nor staff have been convinced.

CCETSW believe there is a third system of qualification for social care, and that is their continuum. This needs fresh impetus. The qualification systems need to be developed in ways which do not compete with one another, but which are interconnected. We need to create a system where SVQs and HNCs can get into that framework. We need also to provide courses that can get practitioners a CCETSW post-qualifying award and contribute to a BA degree. Post Qualifying Awards do not feature in the training targets which gives the impression they are not meant for residential staff thereby underlining their second class status.

You can convert a vocational qualification to a professional qualification by a shortened diploma course. The SVQ as a vocational qualification has only a limited amount of teaching, and indeed, can have no teaching at all. The 2 year Social Work diploma course is made up about half time in practical placements and about half time in the lecture theatre. It would appear sensible to use a conversion course: it would seem that the amount of practical experience the SVQ3 holder already has may mean they only need to do part of the diploma course in order to convert the vocational SVQ3 to a professional Diploma in Social Work. The SVQ4 holder, particularly those who had achieved SVQ3 in conjunction with HNC, must be recognised as eligible to do a shorter course leading to the Diploma. However progression step by step from one SVQ level to another is not encouraged as it is seen to be too time consuming

Above all we need to bring in new people. We have to make the job so attractive, so valued and recognised that high calibre people want to be there. When qualified Field Social Workers were in short supply an emergency course was devised. After Utting reported in England they developed a Residential Child Care Initiative to train up existing staff to the diploma level. Interestingly there is some evidence that many of these people have remained in residential child care.

I believe that there are two main ways to bring new blood in. One is to turn trained teachers, occupational therapists, or psychiatric nurses into Social Pedagogues by giving them a course that matches the existing course but recognises and builds upon their earlier training. They would be recruited at a salary level that is on the top two points of the unqualified scale with a Personal Development Contract expecting completion of supplementary training on a part time basis within two years. The other is to move towards a mature students training programme along the lines of the one just started in Kent with Department of Health funding which is to be expanded.

A Social Pedagogue would be someone who works with children and young people in a variety of settings and would not only be found in residential care and in schools but as Intermediate Treatment Workers, as Youth Workers and as Children's Advocates - essentially deployed to help the whole child develop, not simply education in a school setting. Haydn Davies Jones explains that social pedagogy:

> *"includes personality development, the acquisition of social skills and competencies, the education of feeling and the emotions, the attainment of an appropriate independence and the preparation for adult life in all its forms, social, political and cultural".*[54]

I am impressed by the work of the Caldecott College, which has grown out of the work of the Caldecott Therapeutic Community for children in England. The College offers 2 main courses. The first is a part-time one year foundation Certificate in Therapeutic Child Care. Those who undertake it include not only new and unqualified staff but also those with more experience in working in children's residential units. They have 180 students on it this year. It is not yet linked with NVQ although it might well be so at Level 3 or Level 4. It does not yet contribute to any part of the Diploma in Social Work. An interesting feature of this course is that they have taken 21 of their students on a mature student programme, and these are able to claim income support or unemployment benefit and travelling expenses while attending the course. The certificate course is accredited by a university and is worth 60 points at university level 3. Their other course is a 2 year part-time Diploma in Therapeutic Child Care which is part of the CCETSW post-qualifying framework and leads directly to the PQ award and a degree. It is the only Diploma in Therapeutic Child Care in the country. The Diploma course would be a suitable vehicle to turn teachers, occupational therapists, youth workers, registered mental nurses, health visitors and perhaps experienced SNNEBs into social pedagogues. I would wish to see their activity reflected in Scotland.

There is now an advanced certificate in residential child care at the University of Glasgow, on a part-time basis over 18 months, which again might be tailored to convert people from other professions to Social Pedagogue. I am quite sure of the wisdom in attracting people from other professions into therapeutic work with children cared for away from home. I am less sure what the children themselves would make of the term Social Pedagogue. Perhaps Social Educator, or the old Scottish Tutor, is better. CCETSW have been funding discussion and intend to develop with employers, universities and colleges a post qualifying course which could be validated at a number of academic institutions which can be accessed by staff across the country. People with a Social Work qualification, who complete such a course, would receive an academic award and credits towards a post qualifying award. Those from other walks of life, with their own professional qualification, would only get the academic award unless their own parent profession chose to give post qualifying credits. Nevertheless a teacher, nurse or youth worker with a validated certificate on top of their own qualification would contribute significantly to a boarding school or residential unit.

54 Madge, Nicola (1994) Children and Residential Care in Europe (London, National Children's Bureau)

Recommendation 22: A new Social Pedagogue role should be created by training Social Workers, Youth Workers, Teachers, Nurses, Nursery Nurses, Occupational Therapists on courses such as those provided by the Caldecott College or now available at the University of Glasgow.

In Northern Ireland they have made valiant efforts to recruit only trained staff. There are pockets in Scotland, the old Grampian and the new Dundee for example, where they have been successful. It may not be possible for us to establish a deadline by which we would only employ qualified staff, but we could establish a date after which no new recruit comes to the end of a probationary period and is offered a permanent contract without a personal development plan that establishes when training will be completed. January 1st 2000 will allow a 2 year lead-in time.

Recommendation 23: A date should be established after which no new recruit comes to the end of their probationary period, and is offered a permanent contract, without a personal development plan which establishes when training will be completed.

I do not want to rule out diploma holders from residential care; quite the reverse. I want a mix of people where those trained exclusively in social work would need to do a third year of supervised practice in child care. If we could achieve a staff group of, say, 8 where 2 have the Diploma, 2 were Social Pedagogues with another background, and 4 were home grown SVQ3 and 4 we would be getting somewhere.

I have been very struck by the number of different people who have said to me that the Diploma in Social Work does not really train people to work with children. CCETSW published clear notes for programme planners on the teaching of child care in 1991 but, anecdotally at least, there seems to be a gap between what is planned and what is learned. Unless a person's life experience has given them an understanding of children at different ages, they often find it very hard to communicate with them. They may not have an understanding of "normal" human growth and development, so it is hard for them to see when a child's behaviour expresses something other than normality. If they do not have a proper understanding of normal sex and sexuality, it may be harder for them to face the problems that arise out of sexual abuse. It is important that a Field Social Worker whose case load is primarily children should have spent some time on their course doing a placement in a residential unit.

Whether or not individual staff members in residential units are undergoing their own personal training, there is a need for in-service training for members of the staff group as a whole. Anyone working with "looked after" children will need not only training on the issues mentioned above for the Diploma in Social Work, but other matters too. They need to learn more about safe caring, and about normal sex and sexuality, so that they have a proper context in which to learn about sexual abuse, paedophile behaviour, and peer abuse. They need to learn about behaviour management, but also to be properly trained in restraint and in methods of restraint in the context of rewards and sanctions for behaviour. Training in methods of restraint should be repeated at least yearly. They need to learn about the risk and danger programmes for children which are carried out in schools, so that they can back up these programmes in the unit. They need to learn about bullying. If staff in a particular unit work on these issues together in training, they are in a better position to develop a policy for the unit in working on them in practice.

Recommendation 24: Thought must be given when planning in-service training to include matters of safety for children and young people. There should be greater emphasis in particular with safe caring, normal sex and sexuality, sexual abuse, paedophile behaviour and peer abuse. There is a need for staff to learn more about behaviour management, proper training in restraint and methods of restraint.

The University of Strathclyde have looked at ways of developing standard modules of in-service training that could help bring an academic backup to the SVQ system as well as build up a system to access degree courses. The Social Care Association, in conjunction with the Church of Scotland, are trying to establish some training and teaching to underpin SVQs. To drive this sort of proposal forward, to give residential staff a better chance to learn, to establish the opportunity for further training after SVQ3 or 4, and above all to get first induction training for everyone before they begin work, to a level that means more than it does today, we require a National College.

Ideally no one should be working in residential child care without going through a nationally recognised form of induction training provided by an approved institution. Everyone should get the same induction training and one National College should franchise others. Responsibility for standards and control should rest with one body which deals with the curriculum. All accredited training for residential child care, from induction through to management, should be the responsibility of the Scottish National College. Things have simply got to be different to the way they are; training must be linked to the system of vetting and to the register. The registration process must specify recruits have gone through the training process. Requirements for registration must be laid down, one of which would be an appropriate induction. Staff should not be allowed to work with children and young people without their names being on the register and the money needed to provide the way to meet the requirements must be made available.

There will be manpower planning problems. Staff are needed suddenly but urgent vacancies must be covered from a standing pool. Scottish Fire Brigades are able to train personnel before sending them out to fight fires and nothing less should be acceptable for the task of looking after children.

Such a National College could be based on an existing institution or be a completely fresh start. It would have to have an outreach capacity, recognise the SVQ system and avoid providing basic Diploma in Social Work courses offered in a large number of academic institutions already. Training for Inspectors is an example of the sort of more detailed work to be undertaken as well as the courses that would equip professions allied to Social Work to work in residential child care.

Recommendation 25: A National College should be developed providing induction training, learning support for SVQs, post qualifying training and 'conversion' training for SVQ holders to obtain the Diploma in Social Work, and for those who have other qualifications to obtain a Diploma in Therapeutic Child Care.

I have recently been able to see some good work being done in in-service training with primary school teachers about paedophiles and sexual abuse. I hope to see this type of work expanded throughout the country to all Local Authority day schools. Meanwhile, I believe we are missing an important opportunity if we do not use the time when teachers are being given their basic training to help them to learn about sexual abuse, paedophiles and bullying. Teachers may be an important safeguard for children, but unless they know how to react if they notice something out of the ordinary, or if a child discloses something to them, they may be harmful rather than helpful to the child. Social Work professionals would be able to advise on the content of a suitable course on these issues. It need not take long, but it would create an awareness that would be valuable not only for the teachers being trained, but also for the colleagues with whom they discuss issues in the staff room in future.

Recommendation 26: Teacher Education Institutions should ensure that all teachers are trained about sexual abuse, paedophiles and bullying in their pre-service training.

As far as vocational qualifications are concerned we are in midstream and now is not the time to change horses. SVQ3 and SVQ4 should be retained. However, much more work needs to be done dovetailing vocational qualifications to the other forms of qualifying and of training. The HNC, the Diploma in Social Work, post qualifying courses and SVQs must fit together.

Vocational, professional and academic qualifications must be harmonised.

I have referred earlier to the need for more candidates to work in residential child care. When better arrangements are in place for recruiting (Recommendation 16) and when there is nationally agreed induction training (Recommendation 25) and a register created (Recommendation 12) consideration should be given to matching funding from central Government and employers for a national recruitment campaign designed to build the status and respect the job deserves.

8.6 Inspections

In Chapter 6 I wrote of the expectations I would have of inspections as a safeguard for children. It is not the job of an Inspector to go into a unit in order to find abuse, but rather to look at the standards, the quality and type of care that are provided and whether safeguards are in place that would make abuse less likely to happen. They report back on what they find, and as long as the body which manages the homes implements the recommendations they make, they have a role in the gradual improvement in the standard of care for children.

In talking about their work, Local Authority Social Work Inspectors say that they go out of their way to discuss with children the care they are receiving in the units. They make it clear to staff that they are ready to listen to them. They are people to whom children, their parents and the caring staff might just choose to talk if they were worried about the activities of anybody around the unit.

There are too many different inspection systems, which seldom make contact with one another. There is good work being done, but it makes little sense for some inspections to be carried out by Local Authority Inspectors, and for some Inspectors to be nationally deployed, such as the HMIs who now have the responsibility for the welfare of residential pupils, or the Social Work Services Inspectors who inspect secure units. It is worrying that there are, for example, Health Service and Housing Association units which are not inspected at all.

I was impressed by many of the arguments in Tom Burgner's review of the regulation and inspection of Social Services[55]. He was writing about the situation south of the border but many of his recommendations could well be applied in Scotland. I believe that it is important that we have national benchmark standards, and that Local Authority Homes should be registrable.

Recommendation 27: Registration, and therefore the possibility of de-registration, should be required for a Local Authorities' own units.

There should also be national Guidance on the scope and format of inspection reports. There should be national practice standards for residential child care as well as standards for inspection, and they should match each other.

Tom Burgner, who believes that it is wasteful for over 100 Authorities in England and Wales each to draft their own standards, suggests that there is a need for national benchmark standards, defined by statutory regulation, to ensure adequate care. He believes there should also be national methodologies for registration and inspection, and national Guidance on the scope and format of inspection reports. At present, each Local Authority in Scotland may insist on a Home meeting their individual standards if children are to be placed there. This could lead to problems. In theory, it might be necessary for staff going to restrain a child to ask him or her first what Local Authority area they are from, and therefore what method of restraint should be used with them.

Service agreements with bodies which run homes must reflect the standards document which has been agreed by the Local Authority. If the resources which are available do not come anywhere near to matching the standards which have been agreed, that removes relevance from the standards. It would be much more sensible for benchmark standards to be set at a level below

55 Burgner, Tom (1996) op. cit.

which no resources must fall, and then for there to be general efforts to improve the standards to meet very proper aspirations. Tom Burgner suggests that higher standards might be adopted at local level, so long as the local bodies were able to justify any additional costs involved.

Recommendation 28: There should be more standardised formats for Inspection Reports that allow easier monitoring and there should be national standards for inspection together with associated Guidance for Inspectors. Training should be provided about their role.

He is also concerned about the number of different bodies which inspect. Among his suggestions for the rationalising of inspection systems is the idea that there should be joint inspection units run by the Local Authority and Health Authority together, or that there should be a new local statutory body, funded jointly by the Local Authority and the Health Authority, which would determine local care standards and have regulatory responsibilities.

I believe that this arrangement would work well for adult services, but that for children's services something rather different is needed. There are far fewer Inspectors devoted to work in children's services than there are to work in Nursing Homes and other types of care homes for adults. Some small Local Authorities have few children's services to inspect.

In Scotland there are 15 Health Boards, 8 Police Boards, 32 Local Authorities, 28 Local Authority inspection teams and the Reporter Managers are grouped in 7 areas. If we created Joint Boards for inspection purposes, democratic accountability would be retained, at least as far as social work was concerned, and so would professional control. I believe that there is something special about care for children which would make it entirely appropriate for their inspection service to be separate from that for adults; many of the Inspectors would not agree with me, but I would argue quite strongly for a specialist service.

The boundaries of Health Boards and Local Authorities in Scotland are not coterminous but recognise each other. The same thing can be said about Reporter Manager boundaries. All Local Authority inspection services could be grouped by Health Board areas which is probably right for adult services but not big enough for the smaller children's service. In this case the Local Authorities could be grouped by Reporter Manager area. Another possibility would be to match the groupings of the HMI.

Recommendation 29: There should be joint Inspection Boards for children's services with groups of Local Authorities banded together.

Responsibility for the Welfare of Residential Pupils inspections should remain with the HMI, but whatever future structure there is for Local Authority inspection services, there must be much closer linkage with HMI. One way of achieving this, and also to bring a Social Care perspective to all boarding school inspections, would be for the HMI to invite Local Government Inspectors to become involved. The present arrangements do not include a role of Associate Inspector but such a title should be considered.

There should be a National Inspection Forum with representatives from all Inspectorates on it to allow more collaborative working, the sharing of knowledge and to develop common standards and methodology.

Recommendation 30: There should be closer links between Local Authority Social Work Inspectors relating to children and HM Inspectors of Schools. Local Government Inspectors should be invited to assist when HMIs inspect boarding schools. There should also be a national standing committee on inspection with representatives from all Inspectorates relating to children on it, to allow more collaborative working and the sharing of knowledge to develop.

I have found that SWSI Inspectors are perceived to be providing the best quality of Social Work inspection in Scotland. However, they are currently inspecting a very small number of units, and on a less frequent basis than Local Authorities inspect other units for children. There is no logic in inspecting secure units less frequently than other residential child care units - rather the reverse, they should probably be inspected more frequently than anything else. There now seems to be little point in secure units being inspected on a different basis from other residential care units for looked after children, and one option might be for the responsibility for their inspection to pass to the Local Authorities. The SWSI Inspectors' skills and methodology are valuable however and it is important that these should be handed on to the Local Authorities to use, whatever decision is made about inspecting the secure units. If registration stays with central Government, and it probably should, then there would have to be related inspection. A compromise would be for the Local Authority inspectors to visit secure facilities twice a year as they would for other units and for SWSI to inspect them every five years.

All Local Government Inspection Reports should be kept centrally and monitored. It would probably be most appropriate for this function to be carried out by the Social Work Services Inspectorate who will need space to undertake this new task.

Recommendation 31: Secure Units should be visited at the same frequency as other residential child care units.

Recommendation 32: Copies of all Local Government Inspection Reports should be held centrally and be monitored and it will be appropriate for this function to be carried out by the Social Work Services Inspectorate. The registration of secure units should remain with the Secretary of State.

The national benchmark standards should include standards for "safeguarding young people from abuse": the Centre for Residential Child Care argues that just as you would have standards for fire safety, so you should have standards for children's safety. It should be possible to base an entire inspection on safeguarding standards alone.

I have no evidence that this is the case but it is possible that children in foster homes are more vulnerable than children in residential settings. There are fewer officials visiting and Children's Rights staff do not find it easy to go in. Foster caring should be brought within the inspection process. One Scottish region has done this on a pilot basis, with success. Burgner is particularly concerned about private fostering agencies, which do not currently operate in Scotland, but he does believe that any regulatory mechanism applied to private agencies should also apply to the voluntary agencies and "so far as possible" to the statutory sector. I believe that the body which inspects residential child care should also inspect foster care. Perhaps this should concentrate on the arrangements for fostering, but I would want Inspectors to at least meet a sample of carers and children.

Recommendation 33: Foster care should be brought within the inspection process.

There are a surprising number of places where children are living away from home as well as boarding schools and children's homes.

A significant number of children are in hospital or health facilities. Guidance is offered in three particular publications "At Home in Hospital - A Guide to the Care of Children and Young People" (1993), "Children 1st - A Study of Hospital Services" (1993), "Caring for Sick Children - a Study Of Hospital Services in Scotland" (1994). Certain problems are identified. There are differences in standards between wards in dedicated children's departments and adult speciality wards. Most adolescents are admitted to adult wards.

The statistics gathered by the Scottish Office Department of Health show that almost 700 children under 18 spent over 30 days in hospital acute services in 1994 of whom 600 were under

15 and for almost 500 this was a continuous stay. More than 1,000 young Scots under 18 went to a psychiatric hospital or unit in 1994 of whom 200 were between 5 and 15 with a mean stay of nearly 3 months.

The full rigours of inspection apply to some places while others, that are really little different, do not get the same external examination. There are schools run by Local Authority Education Departments which only receive inspections by Her Majesty's Inspectors of Schools. There are a few health service units that are not subject to any kind of inspection. Services for children run by Health Trusts outside hospitals should be visited by Scottish Hospital Advisory Service who should call upon Local Authority Social Work Inspectors to assist. There are children in day school hostels which have just been made subject to HMI/WRP inspections. The number of hostels has gone down, but they are still a significant feature in areas where the population is scattered. There are for example 150 children in hostels in Lerwick. Such children may well be away from home for 4 nights a week, although some stay for 7 nights a week, but they can be there for several years and really are no safer, and no less safe, than lots of other children living away from home. Hostels attached to mainstream secondary schools should be inspected by Local Authority Inspectors on the same basis as children's homes.

The new Welfare of Residential Pupils inspections for boarding schools, introduced by the Children (Scotland) Act, is to be welcomed but the frequency of visits is too low. Set against the context of day school inspection of every 12 or 15 years then a strike rate of every 5 years for welfare of residential pupils inspection sounds reasonable. But the whole ethos of the school, the whole regime, even the whole staff can change in 5 years. Why inspect Local Authority and voluntary society children's homes twice a year and a boarding school every 5 years, or 10 times less often? There is a need to rationalise the frequency of visits and to include some facilities not inspected at all. Secure units and services run for children by the health service should be visited on the same frequency as other residential child care units. It is my belief that WRP inspections should be undertaken annually but it may be more realistic to suggest at this stage they should take place every 3 years.

The Guidance should be changed so that the small group of residential special schools run by Local Authority Education Departments, which currently under Section 34 of the Children (Scotland) Act only have HMI inspections, are inspected under Section 35 by the Local Authority inspection team.

Recommendation 34: Local Authorities must be more effective at inspecting and enforcing changes to their own resources especially their own residential schools.

Recommendation 35: Boarding Schools need to have the welfare of residential pupils inspections at least every 3 years.

Recommendation 36: Schools run by Local Authority Education Departments, and hostels attached to mainstream secondary schools, should be inspected by Local Authority Inspectors as well as by HMI.

Recommendation 37: The Scottish Hospital Advisory Service should inspect residential resources for children run by Health Trusts, calling upon Local Authority Social Work Inspectors to assist.

The focus of inspections is rightly the life of the children within the residential unit. However, if that unit is run by a parent body which is itself not committed to the proper standards, and to employing staff of the right calibre not only in the unit but also at Headquarters level, there are bound to be problems within the establishment. There may be times when it will be necessary to inspect the parent body also, and to check the functioning of the Headquarters and its staff.

Recommendation 38: Consideration must be given to inspecting the parent body as well as its satellite units.

The principal link between a residential unit and the Headquarters of the organisation is the immediate external line manager. He or she is the most visible "outsider" whose role all staff and all children should understand and feel free to make use of. The external line manager should not usurp the role of unit Head but be a clear superior that both the unit staff and the Headquarters trust. He or she is someone Inspectors should make a point of meeting. This is practice in some Local Authorities already but it should be made mandatory.

Recommendation 39: The Local Authority Inspectors should always meet with the external line manager at every inspection.

Guidance for Inspectors must be improved and reflect the same sort of standards applied to under 8s. Every inspection of a child care establishment must involve as Inspector at least one person with a full knowledge and experience of residential child care issues, and work should be undertaken to train a group of young people who have previous (but not current) experience of living in residential care and boarding schools to join inspections. Training for Inspectors should include joint training for HMIs and Local Authority Inspectors in areas where there is common concern. The English OFSTED/National Children's Bureau pack would be useful for this.

More work is needed to ensure that recommendations from Local Authority Social Work Inspectors are enforced. Penalties other than closure alone should be considered. Closure is not always in the children's interests, and can in some circumstances be seen as a sledge hammer to crack a nut, and thus not used so nothing is done. Local Authorities must be more effective at inspecting and enforcing changes to their own resources especially their own residential schools. HMIs have routine follow up procedures.

8.7 Boarding Schools

When I looked at the fee paying boarding schools to which parents chose to send their children, I found that there was less evidence of abuse occurring, although there is still potential for it to happen. There have been documented cases of abuse recently, and it is something which worries children enough for them to telephone ChildLine about it. Although most children living in this type of school have the protection of regular contact with caring parents, they are still living away from home, and we must be sure that everything possible is done to safeguard them. I have been impressed by the work done by SCIS (The Scottish Council of Independent Schools), which seems to me both valuable and important. SCIS is forward-thinking, and has recently done very positive pro-active work to ensure that children in independent boarding schools are safeguarded. They are skilled at persuading school boards of the value of what they propose. It is for this reason that I believe it would be extremely helpful if they were to launch a model complaints procedure and distribute it to all their member schools. A procedure that came from SCIS might overcome the wariness that some schools feel about complaints, and pupil power.

The work that SCIS has done in producing guidelines on child protection is a model of its kind, and is apparently much appreciated by schools. It would be helpful now if SCIS would increase general understanding by writing to all Local Authority Social Work Departments to explain their involvement with their member schools, and to offer help to Departments in their dealings with them. Mutual understanding would also be much helped if all independent schools had annual meetings with the Local Authority Child Protection Teams or other representatives of the Local Authority.

Recommendation 40: Greater understanding of each other's role and needs would follow from meetings, on a routine basis, between schools and Local Authority Social Work Departments.

I am concerned that the HMI's WRP inspections are only to be on a 5-yearly basis. Immense changes are possible in a school over that time. Ideally, I would like to propose annual inspections, but must recognise that resource implications are too grave for a service which is already quite well stretched. For this reason I am proposing that the WRP inspection should take place at least every 3 years.

There are occasions on which boarding school pupils are boarded out, rather than living within the boarding houses of the school. There is little routine boarding out, but it may happen that a house unit needs to be repaired and refurbished and the pupils are placed with people chosen by the school in the local community. Occasionally a child with parents living abroad may need to be placed with somebody for part at least of the holiday period. I am used to the care taken by Social Work Departments when placing children with foster carers, and can only be concerned that few of these boarding out placements are done with the same type of thoroughness that is applied to foster care. The task of caring will, of course, usually be much easier, but the vetting of carers must be rigorous to ensure that the wrong type of adults are not taking children into their homes.

Section 35 of the Children (Scotland) Act 1995 is clear that there is a duty placed on Education Authorities and on managers to safeguard and promote the welfare of children accommodated inside or outside the school when placed for the purposes of education. During school holidays the position is different and I believe the Private Fostering Regulations - which were not swept up into the Children (Scotland) Act - apply.

I have similar concerns about the appointment of guardians. A significant number of school pupils are from overseas, and are rightly given a named guardian in this country while they are away from their parents. It is important that the guardian keeps in good contact with them and is a fit person to discharge their responsibility. Careful checks and vetting are essential. Any possibility of the school appointing people directly connected with it as guardians should be avoided. SCIS are preparing Guidelines for Guardians and should be encouraged in that task.

It is expected that all who run Residential Care Homes are vetted to ensure that they are proper fit persons to do so. The same must also be true of Governors and managers of boarding schools. They should have to give references and be vetted for convictions, just as any member of the school staff will.

Recommendation 41: Care must be taken when boarding schools place children with local families and in the appointment of Governors and Guardians.

Under Section 99 of the Education (Scotland) Act 1980 there are 4 grounds for de-registering schools. None of these refer specifically to the welfare of the child, and now that Section 35 of the Children (Scotland) Act 1995 ensures that those responsible for schools providing residential accommodation have a duty to safeguard and promote the welfare of the child or young person while accommodated in the school, there must be a power to ensure that those schools which do not do so adequately can be closed. I would therefore propose that there should be new ground for de-registration.

Recommendation 42: There should be a new ground for deregistration under Section 99 of the Education Act 1980 "failure to provide adequately for the welfare of the child".

Local Authority schools in Scotland must use teachers registered with the GTC, but other schools have the freedom to employ whomever they wish as teachers. Some schools have used this wisely, and have benefited from it. However, there is a danger in this freedom: it would be possible for a teacher struck off by the GTC to obtain work in a boarding school, without the school's managers learning that the teacher had been discharged as unsuitable to work with children. An abusing teacher who is unable to find work in the public sector could in theory easily become employed in the private. It would be wrong to go back over all the appointments made of non-GTC teachers in past years and declare that they were unsuitable. However, I am convinced that in future we should insist on GTC-registered teachers for all new appointments to ensure that the safeguard of the General Teaching Council Register is in place for all school pupils, regardless of the type of school that they attend. If schools want to recruit untrained teachers they will not be on the register, in which case they should be treated, for employment and vetting, as residential care staff.

There is another way in which children in boarding schools may be less safe than children in children's residential units. Many boarding schools tend not to see their children as at risk from improperly vetted care staff, and the education sector is hardly aware of the work that has been done for and since the Warner Report. Because recruitment and vetting procedures in children's residential care now put up better barriers against the paedophiles and abusers, those who actively seek to work in a place where they may abuse children may move to a sector where there are fewer safeguards. It is therefore important that these safeguards are used by boarding schools, just as they are in the care sector. It is time to ensure that all house staff and residential care staff in boarding schools are vetted and selected in the same way as care staff in children's homes.

Because of the better discipline in most boarding schools, they may have different ratios of staff on duty caring for children at night from those which must be used in children's homes. Whilst I have not uncovered this practice, if this was ever to mean that there is only one member of staff on sleeping-in duty at night caring for a large boarding house of pupils, then it must be discouraged. There are dangers in this practice if a child has an accident or a serious illness, or if there is a fire in the boarding house. There are other dangers if the singleton worker has abusive tendencies. It is essential that boarding schools ensure that numbers of house staff are sufficient, and that no member of staff is working alone with a large number of pupils at night.

There is considerable confusion about which schools fit into Section 34 of the new Children (Scotland) Act and which fit in to Section 35. The definitions are not very tight. To recommend all schools with any child with a disability be inspected by Local Authority Social Work Inspectors might bring too much focus on one child and might even be a bar to admission. It would be better to invite HMI to make a practice of asking Local Authority Inspectors to become involved.

8.8 External Eyes

Reports of inquiries of homes where abuse has occurred would indicate that these homes tended to operate in a closed way, with comments from people outside the system being discouraged. Most residential units for children are far more open now, and this in itself constitutes a safeguard. I believe that we should be ensuring that there are a number of people, responsible for looking after the welfare of individual children, or of the establishment as a whole, going into a Residential Child Care Unit on a regular basis. There is also a need for some additional people to go into foster homes.

We would gain by the use of Appointed Persons, as required by Regulation 22 of the Children's Homes Regulations which followed the English Children Act. This Regulation "*requires monthly visits to all Homes by those responsible, or by their representatives...... and a written report of such visits should be made to those responsible for the Homes. An important purpose of these visits is to ensure that the day to day conduct of the Home is seen by someone not involved in its operation and who can provide an independent report to the responsible Authority .... the purpose of visiting and the items to be covered ... should also include a check of the records of sanctions imposed on the children, the Home's daily log and the physical condition of the premises. But visitors must always be given an opportunity for private conversation with any child, other family member or staff member who requests it; and should always report on their observations of the children*"[56]. They could be deployed in Scotland through the Safeguarders Association, through Children 1st, or they could be a Local Authority member or appointee. They must be seen to be outwith the management line, but have the opportunity to report direct to the Board of Governors or whatever constituted body is responsible. Some independent units in Scotland, notably those run by Barnardos, are already using Appointed Persons, with success.

> ***Recommendation 43: The role of the Appointed Person to visit each establishment should be created and guidance provided.***

56 Social Services Inspectorate (1997) The Children Act 1989 Guidance and Regulations Volume 4 Residential Care (London, HMSO)

Some boarding schools already use Independent Visitors for children who can make themselves known to a group of children, and be available to them if there is anything they wish to discuss. Once an advocacy network has been set up for Scotland, the Independent Visitor would be able to call upon the services of the network on behalf of children in boarding schools.

Recommendation 44: There should be an Independent Visitor for children in boarding schools.

I would expect that most complaints from children would be dealt with as quickly as possible, as near to the source of the complaint as possible. However, there will be times when it would be important that an independent person should hear complaints from children. This could be undertaken by Children 1st, or some other local arrangement might be made. If Children's Rights Officers were to be made into a new advocacy network for the whole of Scotland, they could undertake this work, except that this would mean they would turn themselves into judge and jury when their principal task should be to support the child in making the complaint.

Recommendation 45: There should be a willingness to involve an independent person to hear complaints from children.

Children who are living away from home and who do not have immediate access to a parent lack a safeguard which others have. This is as true of looked after children as it is of children in boarding schools whose parents live on the other side of the world. There are usually arrangements to appoint guardians for school children, and I have already indicated the ways in which I would like this system to be improved. The befriender, independent person or guardian should have responsibilities in relation to one child only, would be expected to keep in regular contact and to visit not less than once per month. Such a person would be an important additional safeguard for children in foster care without immediate access to their parents, and in particular those where a Parental Responsibilities Order has been made. One from an appropriate racial background should always be appointed for a black child in residential or foster care.

Recommendation 46: Every child living away from home without immediate access to a parent should have a befriender or independent person or guardian appointed. This is particularly important for those children for whom the rights and powers of a parent have been assumed by the Local Authority.

The former Lothian Region had a Child and Family Charter. Any child who had exhausted the complaints procedure under the Charter but still felt that his or her complaint had not been satisfactorily resolved could contact the Child and Family Charter Adjudicator, who would consider what needed to be done to preserve the rights of the child. He has a right to obtain all information relevant to the pursuit of a complaint, to make visits and arrange appropriate meetings. The essence of his authority is 'persuasive'. This system could be expanded through Scotland to provide help for children who are living away from home or are aggrieved for one reason or another. Interestingly this was a recommendation in the Utting Report.

Recommendation 47: Adjudicators could be created along the lines of the Child and Family Charter of the erstwhile Lothian Region.

I would not expect all "external eyes" to be external to the Local Authority or Voluntary Body. A key figure in the protection of children should be the dedicated line manager, outside the children's unit, who specialises in child care or better still in residential child care, having had experience of work within it. They need to understand children's residential care well, so that they can see clearly what is happening within the units for which they are responsible. Small Local Authorities may not be able to provide such a dedicated member of staff, and in these circumstances it would be important that Local Authorities should be able to come together along Regional Planning Committee lines, in order to appoint a member of staff who can have this responsibility for the Homes which they each individually run.

Recommendation 48: There should always be a dedicated line manager who specialises in child care or better still in residential child care. It may be necessary for some Local Authorities to band themselves together in respect of their residential child care provision.

As I have said above I do not believe it falls within my remit to advise the creation of a Children's Ombudsman for this comparatively small number of children. However, should a Commissioner for Children or Ombudsman be created, and if that person has staff resources placed at his or her disposal, it might be unnecessary to create the advocacy network.

As with Inspectors, Directors of Social Work are not likely to catch abusers themselves but they should be open to a direct approach by children. Heads of Voluntary Agencies are much more visible in children's units than senior Council staff but that reflects the different nature of the job. Social Work Directors have a quasi-parental role as the most senior figure in the "corporate parent" and should pay more heed to this part of their job than some other aspects. This must be recognised by Councillors and other staff. The most important reason for paid Heads of Agencies, Governors and Managers visiting establishments is to demonstrate the openness of the organisation and the accessibility of everyone in it.

Recommendation 49: The need for time to be set aside by senior figures to visit establishments must be recognised by employers.

As discussed in Chapter 7, the role of Safeguarders will change under the Children (Scotland) Act, in that it will no longer be necessary for there to be difficulties and conflicts in a case before they are involved on behalf of children. It is very likely that this will result in a growing role. At present there is no formal structure for safeguarders created by Government although some money has recently been granted for training.

There may be a benefit in having them discharge some of the safeguarding and advocacy functions recommended in this report. At the moment their Association is not well resourced, and some grant aid would improve this and facilitate them taking on additional functions.

Recommendation 50: Funding for the Safeguarders Association should be increased.

A few Independent Reviewing Officers have now been introduced in Scotland. Their posts are separate from the normal line management system in a Social Work Department, and dedicated to chairing Child Protection Case Conferences as well as reviews of children in care. Because they are not in the same line management chain as the Social Worker or key worker for the child or young person, they are able to take a more "arm's length" approach to the issues faced by them. Part of their task is to raise the profile of individual children at their own reviews. They should always be asking about the safeguards and whether they are in place to protect the child. A few people conducting the large number of reviews would mean that they would become more expert. The new Children Act Guidance refers to this but financial constraints forbid deploying additional staff. The reviews are, however, being conducted by someone and it may be a question of re-arrangement rather than growth.

The Skinner Report, wishing to provide extra support for parents of looked after children, recommended that Parents' Associations should be developed to allow them some degree of mutual support. Sadly, I have found no examples of these existing in Scotland. Each Local Authority should now be taking steps to create Parents' Associations for their own looked after children. Many parents will not want to be involved, but I would expect that in the long run there would be gains not only for the children of members of Parents' Associations, but for looked after children in general.

Recommendation 51: Steps should be taken by the Scottish Office and by Local Authorities, possibly by way of Section 10 funding, to seek to create Parents Associations for looked after children.

It is hard to keep a children's home feeling like a home if too many outside people have the right to come and go and there are dangers in bringing in too many external eyes. However, these proposals would cause few additional visits each month, and if they are well handled by staff would add to the well-being of children and young people.

8.9 Investigation And Monitoring

Some Local Authorities have in the past found reasons for not reporting cases of abuse of looked after children to Child Protection Committees, in the belief that they should be able to use management arrangements to sort out any problems. The Child Protection Guidelines used in different parts of the country do not necessarily make specific reference to abuse by professional staff or substitute carers; they are unlikely to refer to peer abuse.

All instances of abuse by carers should be reported to Child Protection Committees. They should be treated as events of the utmost gravity. The Child Protection Committee should then initiate a composite review along the lines of part 8 of the English "Working Together" document, and conducted in the fashion recommended by the Bridge Child Care Consultancy service.

Following local government reorganisation, many Child Protection Committees cover a small area of responsibility. They should be grouped together in order to be able to invite a neutral and objective view to be taken by stepping outside the boundaries of one Local Authority. Reporters are deployed by Local Authority areas and their managers by Sheriffdoms. An appropriate grouping would be by Reporter Manager areas.

The Local Authority may be big enough to have an identifiably separate part of itself which can conduct the investigation into any abuse. If this is not the case, a neighbouring Local Authority may be able to do so, or if there are difficulties in arranging this, an outside, independent body should be used.

I am concerned that a child can be abused in a residential unit or foster home without anybody outside the Social Work Department hearing anything about it. The Child Protection Register must be notified every time there is an incident of abuse of a child living away from home. This would include abuse perpetrated by peers, which is sometimes not treated as seriously as it merits. Each Child Protection Committee must submit an Annual Report to the Social Work Services Group on its activity. I recommend that in future these reports should be to the Secretary of State, and that each Report should include a specific category for abuse of children living away from home.

It is present practice for the circumstances surrounding the death of a child in care to be reported to the Secretary of State. It might be appropriate to involve the Child Protection Committees in this and for them to do the report.

Recommendation 52: There should be a composite review of any instance of abuse by carers. They should be undertaken by Child Protection Committees who should be reorganised in clusters of Local Authorities to enable objective investigation by another agency if this is deemed appropriate.

I have already revealed my concern about the national gathering of statistics from Child Protection Registers, and raised the possibility of a National Register. The Child Protection Committees do not concern themselves much with individual sets of circumstances. It is worth considering a fresh look at the purpose and functions of Child Protection Committees either by a piece of research or by special SWSI inspection. The Child Protection Registers have grown away from the non accidental injury registers with the result that we have moved away from expressing concern and we need to get back to recording concern. It would be a good moment to review the role of Child Protection Committees and to establish that we are sure their remit is the right one.

Recommendation 53: The work of Child Protection Committees and the use of their Registers should be reviewed.

All establishments caring for children living away from home should have a procedure which enables staff to blow the whistle when they have any concerns about the safety of children and young people, however tenuous the basis for the concerns may be. Loyalty to the task of safeguarding children should be the key to behaviour. The organisation should make it clear that they would always prefer to be able to prove fears groundless, than to miss anything that is endangering or harming a child. A duty should be placed on staff to report any suspicions they have about children being put at harm or risk. A few Local Authorities already have guidelines written for staff to encourage them to take action. Staff must always be reassured that they will be both protected and supported if they "whistle blow" in line with the guidelines. Staff should be in no doubt that a duty is placed on them to report any suspicions they have about children being put at harm or risk.

Recommendation 54: All establishments caring for children living away from home should have a procedure which enables staff to "blow the whistle".

I am aware that unfortunately many young people do not trust the organisation which cares for them well enough to believe that if they say anything against a member of staff, they will be protected from any reprisals. In the case of peer abuse, they may fear what the abuser will do to them. For this reason, I believe that it is helpful, as an additional safeguard, to interview children and young people as they leave one type of service for another, or at the end of their time in care. Under these circumstances, young people may be able to propose improvements to the service they have just left or in a few cases they may indicate that there has been abusive behaviour which must be stopped for the good of others. It would be up to the Local Authority or Voluntary Organisation to decide whether these interviews were best carried out by the Field Social Worker, by the Children's Rights Officer, if available, or by the External Line Manager but ideally the child would choose.

Recommendation 55: All young people should be interviewed as they leave services by way of an exit interview.

In the care system it is easy to become insensitive and lose a freshness of approach. We have to be constantly on the alert to the real needs of children and how to meet them. Child protection and safe caring policies should both be regularly reviewed.

There is the issue of mandatory reporting of child abuse and neglect. Many countries now have laws which lay a duty on various professionals and others to report any abuse of children. In Scotland, until now, only the Local Authority has had a duty to report suspicions that a child is in need of care and protection: this is usually interpreted to mean Social Workers. The Children (Scotland) Act extends the mandatory duty to police constables. There is debate as to whether others such as teachers and health visitors should have a mandatory duty to report, apart from a professional responsibility, but there is real concern that this would block a child's access to confidential advice.

8.10 Children in Prison

The number of Remand Unruly Certificates for under 16 year olds was 9 in 1992, 13 in 1993, 28 in 1994 and 67 in 1995. The number of under 16s in Longriggend averages 40 per year. Once you are over 16 there is no real distinction made for those under 18 and there is a good case for creating a separate wing at Polmont Young Offenders Institution. The number of 15 and 16 year olds going directly to penal establishments, other than Longriggend or Polmont, rose from 151 to 160 to 210 in the years 1993, 1994 and 1995. 20 or 30 16 year olds go to prison every year for fine default.

There are far too many children in penal establishments either because of a misuse of remand to give them a taste of prison or because there are inadequate alternatives. I am loath to recommend an increase in the number of places in secure units but I would rather children were placed there than in the Remand Centre or Young Offenders Institutions. We need to explore the possibilities of remand fostering in order to create more space in the existing secure units and also to follow up the experience of the Close Support Units established in Lothian in the early 90s. Dundee Social Work authority are now moving in this direction using Scottish Office funding. The Scottish Office report A Secure Remedy suggests there should be Close Support Units in every Scottish city.

Recommendation 56: The number of young people in penal establishments must be reduced, and no child under 16 should be in one at all.

8.11 Help for Young Abusers

Young abusers need help from a suitable programme. The Halt Project in Glasgow and the Bridge Project in Dundee are models that need to be developed elsewhere using, in part, crime prevention funding. A key issue is the lack of psychiatric and of psychological services. We have to identify the need for psychological support and then seek to ensure it is provided through the Health Boards' purchasing strategy.

Recommendation 57: Further programmes for helping young abusers need to be initiated with Central Government funding, part of which can be crime prevention funding.

8.12 Refuges

The Skinner Report recommended that Local Authority managers and inspection units should gather information on absconding from residential homes and schools and investigate patterns, causes and solutions and a Scottish Office working party is preparing proposals for doing this. It is intended to pilot new reporting arrangements late in 1997 and introduce a new scheme that helps quantify and analyse the episodes of absconding or of children going missing in 1998.

I am saddened but not surprised that a high proportion of children and young people looked after away from home run away from their residential units, or the caring foster family. As has been seen, runaways are at great risk of harm. I am therefore glad that there is now statutory provision within the Children (Scotland) Act for a child to take refuge in a residential establishment, with a designated foster family or other approved carer, or in an establishment designed as a refuge. I am aware that there are mixed views about the value of refuges, but I believe that as long as they protect children from the dangers of living rough, or sleeping in unsuitable places, and having to fall into crime to support themselves, they are necessary. Unless they are given publicity, it is hard to imagine a child running away in distress finding his or her way to one. However, some Authorities may fear that by giving information about refuges they encourage running away.

There is a problem of where to locate a refuge. Presumably a city is the right place but resources will not stretch to 4 or 5; on the other hand what use is a refuge in Glasgow to a child in Aberdeen? Perhaps a large unit - by definition that now means a school - could have a house nearby that could be staffed up at short notice.

Recommendation 58: A pilot scheme for a refuge should be established.

8.13 The Centre for Residential Child Care

The Centre for Residential Child Care, which was a direct result of the Skinner Report, is proving to be a success. It is playing a key role in improving the quality of residential care for children and young people in Scotland. Some people would like to spread its success in terms of care of children to the residential care of adults, but I am convinced that it must retain its specialism in children, and not dilute its very real quality and its very real purpose by embracing the residential care of others. On the contrary, the time is now ripe for its role to be strengthened and augmented. I am impressed by the role that the Dementia Centre of the University of Stirling has played in raising the awareness of dementia, not only in Scotland, but even outwith the UK. We have seen the Centre for Residential Child Care beginning to have a role of this nature, and it is important that its profile is now raised.

It is time for it to have a broader-based committee chaired by an eminent and prominent public figure. Its funding, which runs out in 1999, needs to be continued after that date but it should also be increased in order to allow the Centre to expand. The University of Strathclyde should be encouraged to introduce, and base in the Centre, a Chair in residential child care studies, possibly by seeking a foundation to create this professorship. Wherever possible and appropriate, research money should be focused on the Centre; this will help it to increase its role as a centre for excellence.

We need a powerful influential body to press the case for residential child care and press the cause. A National Development Group with a remit to draw public attention to the vital nature of the task and to pursue recommendations, for example those of the Skinner Report, and to point out lapses in a forthright and open manner is required. The Scottish Office Report "A Secure Remedy" calls for a national planning group for secure units. This could be expanded to take on part of the role I am looking for, but it is likely to pursue non-residential programmes and I believe we need something that concentrates exclusively on residential programmes. There is a need for a national body whose job it is to analyse, distil and convey the lessons and the messages from the vast amount of official literature in the form of enquiry reports, committee reports and Audit Commission reports. The more bodies the more overlap and the best way forward is to augment the Centre for Residential Child Care still further through a powerful Board. Funding is presently due for review; it should be continued and increased.

Recommendation 59: The profile for the Centre for Residential Child Care should be raised, it should receive increased funding and a Chair in residential child care studies should be created.

I have been concerned that there is very little choice of placement available for children now. Occupancy levels in residential units, combined with a general shortage of foster carers, mean there is not currently any real variety of alternative resources to chose from. Yet the safety of children is enhanced if this is available. It would now seem that Field Social Workers do not expect to be able to choose the right placement for a particular child, and often go simply for the first available place, grateful to have been able to find somewhere. The Centre for Residential Child Care has a data base of resources, which they are more than happy to make available to Social Workers, and it should be much better used than it is currently.

There should always be a choice of placement. Before advocating an increase in the resources available, which may well become necessary if the numbers go up as I believe they will, action should be taken to ensure proper use is made of the data base. The ability to choose a placement, and for instance avoid putting a child into a position where there may be a concern about the impact on another child, means safer planning. Local Authorities must recognise they cannot provide all the things they need and must look to one another to ensure a range of placement opportunities.

Recommendation 60: Every step should be taken to ensure there is always a choice of placement. Greater use should be made of the Centre for Residential Child Care's data base of resources.

8.14 The Children (Scotland) Act 1995

The new Children (Scotland) Act which finally came into force on April 1st this year makes a significant improvement in the structure set up to protect children from harm. The Guidance is detailed and may be more detailed than we have seen before. There is evidence that we are not very good at following up national reports and reviewing how far we have gone in achieving the implementation of recommendations. The new Act can provide a means of sweeping up on several fronts. At some point it will be necessary to examine, in the light of experience, whether the Act, Regulations and Guidance are seen to be effective in providing adequate safeguards. The timing of this Review does not permit an examination of how the Act is working in practice. It is too early to recommend change and the Act must be given time to bed down but it is likely that separate supplementary Regulations and Guidance to the Children (Scotland) Act 1995 will be needed to give sharper focus to the question of safeguards.

Recommendation 61: Any review of the Children (Scotland) Act 1995 conducted in the future must pay heed to the impact, or lack of impact, the Act may have had on the issues raised in this report.

8.15 Conclusion

We must make 1997 a watershed when the protection of children entrusted to the care of others, be they in boarding schools, children's homes, hospital or hostels, is improved. This will come about only by recognition of the extent of the problem, by the use of the appropriate formal structures, and through continued vigilance.

We are in a period of financial restraint. Both Central Government and the Convention of Scottish Local Authorities agree that resources allocated to Local Authorities for residential child care have reduced. I must therefore be aware that recommendations which call for greatly increased expenditure are unrealistic. Nevertheless this is an important issue: we are talking about the safety of children.

We must be sure that we are spending money wisely. Lord Williams of Mostyn showed the financial costs of child abuse in his report[57] and they are high. The human costs are high too.

There are certain key planks to my thinking in terms of drawing up recommendations aimed at ensuring greater safety for children living away from home:

- **Better recruitment arrangements** mean trying to avoid recruiting the wrong people. We can never guarantee to keep out the predatory abuser or the slipshod carer but we must try, and be seen to try. The more the recruitment process emphasises the child protection aspect, the more new employees will understand that observation, awareness and concern are part of the culture. The more good staff that are recruited the greater the chance that they will help avoid the retention of bad staff.

- **The need to raise the status and professionalism of the care task** simply reflects the fact that children living away from home are often the most vulnerable. Compare the Health Service: if you are ill you get treated in one way. If you are very ill you get treated in another; you go to special facilities with skilled experts. Children in care, and children who need special boarding schools, must go to centres of excellence with exceptional staff. There is also every reason to suppose that the parents of children in fee paying boarding schools want well qualified staff caring for their children out of school hours as well as good teachers within school hours. This means training, support, appraisal, supervision, standards and the sort of regulatory body offered to Teachers and to Nurses.

- **The need for information** reflects a need for a greater understanding of what goes on: information for child and parent about the access to help, better reporting of incidents, more research, and improved statistics-gathering.

- **A culture that simply does not tolerate abusive behaviour** is required. The more open the residential setting, the safer the children. The uppermost management of the organisation, the middle manager and the unit manager are responsible for creating this culture.

It has been said that strong belts and strong braces don't make good trousers; procedures and guidelines can help but the fundamental fabric is the culture.

57 Williams of Mostyn 91996) Childhood Matters: Report of the National Commission of Inquiry into the Prevention of Child Abuse (London, the Stationery Office)

APPENDIX A

Oral Evidence

I have not named below everyone who gave oral evidence. Those unnamed include colleagues in the Social Work Services Inspectorate and Social Work Services Group.

Who Cares? were instrumental in introducing us to groups of young people. Their evidence was some of the most valuable material we were given but they remain anonymous.

Local Authority Social Work staff who gave oral evidence have included groups of residential care workers, and individual officers responsible for children's services, personnel, children's rights, complaints, registration and inspection, and fostering. A group of Headmasters in the West of Scotland met especially and were very helpful.

I am very grateful to all those who gave their time and their thought to this Review.

Association of Directors of Social Work, Children & Families Committee

Jane Aldgate, Professor of Social Work, Leicester University

Ian Baillie, Director of Social Work, Church of Scotland

Norma Baldwin, Professor of Child Care & Protection, Dundee University

Peter Bates, Director of Social Work, Dundee City Council & Colleagues

Anita Bennie, Senior Legal Officer, Scottish Child Law Centre

George Bishop, Director of Human Resources, Perth & Kinross Council & Colleagues

Betty Bridgeford, Director of Social Work, Perth & Kinross Council & Colleagues

Lorna Brownlee, Scottish Office, Education & Industry Department

Liz Burns OBE, Director, Volunteer Development Scotland

J. W. Caithness, Headmaster, Aberlour House & Colleagues

Alexander Cameron, Director of Social Work, South Lanarkshire Council & Colleagues

Children's Panel Advisory Group members

Susan Clark, Scottish Director, National Foster Care Association

Dick Clough OBE, General Secretary of Social Care Association

Dr Bronwen Cohen, Director Children in Scotland

David Colvin CBE, Assistant Director (Scotland), British Association of Social Workers

Father Tom Connelly, Roman Catholic Church in Scotland

Liz Cook, Community Nurse Education Officer, Royal College of Nursing

Representatives of the Convention of Scottish Local Authorities

Bill Deans, National Board for Nursing, Midwifery & Health Visiting

Guy Dehn, Public Concern at Work

Alan Dickson, Director, Capability Scotland & Colleagues

Norman Dunning, Director, Enable

Michele Elliot, Director, Kidscape, London

Chief Superintendent Hugh Ferry, Scottish Criminal Records Office & Colleagues

Alan Finlayson OBE, Child Law Consultant & Temporary Sheriff

Donal Giltinan, Scottish Director, British Agencies for Adoption & Fostering

Dan Gunn, Governor in Charge, Polmont Young Offenders' Institution & Colleague

Alex Hamilton, Assistant Director, Social Work Department, Aberdeen City Council

Sue Hamilton, Principal Officer Personal Safety, Edinburgh City Council

Jim Harding, Director & Chief Executive of NSPCC, London & Colleagues

Andrew Hardwick, Principal, Caldecott College & Colleagues

Liz Harrison, Director,Saville & Holdsworth Ltd.

Mary Hartnoll CBE, Director of Social Work, Glasgow City Council & Colleagues

Highland Council, Directors of Social Work, Education & Personnel

Ann Houston, Director, ChildLine Scotland

Jim Howden & Jill Lewis, Tay Project

George Irvine, Director of Social Work, North Ayrshire

Mark Irvine, Head of Local Government, UNISON

Cathy Jamieson, Principal Officer, Who Cares?

John Jillings & North Wales Enquiry Team

Adrianne Jones, Chair of Support Force for Children's Residential Care

Gerald Lee, Director, Quarrier's Homes

Meg Lindsay, Director, The Centre for Residential Child Care

Ian Macaulay, Assistant Director, Western Isles Social Work Department & Colleague

Alastair MacDonald, Governor of Longriggend Remand Centre & Colleague

Paul Machell, Chairman, Scottish Independent Special Schools Group

Jim Mackay, Assistant Chief Constable, Tayside Police

Hugh Mackintosh CBE, Divisional Director, Barnardos, Scotland

Norman Macleod, Reporters' Association

Alan MacPherson, Registrar of Independent Schools & Colleague

Ranald Mair, Headmaster, Geilsland School

Keith Makin, Director of Social Work, Dumfries & Galloway Council & Colleagues

Kathleen Marshall, Child Law Consultant

Ruairidh Martin, Principal Educational Psychologist & Colleague, Western Isles Council

Christine McCarlie, Director, Halt Project

Leslie McEwan, Director of Social Work, Edinburgh City Council & Colleagues

Chris McGregor, Social Work Commissioner, Mental Welfare Commission for Scotland

Janet McGregor, Acting Head of Personnel, NHS Scotland

Ron McKail, Headmaster, Oakbank School, Aberdeen & Colleagues

Douglas McKelvie, Social Work Education Adviser, CCETSW

John McLachlan, Divisional Education Officer, Shetland

Ivan Middleton, Consultant

Professor Alan Miller, Chair, Scottish Council for Civil Liberties

Rosemary Milne, Free-lance trainer in Child Care

National Foster Care Association members with Sandra Moody

Joe Nee, Educational Psychologist, North Lanarkshire Council

Angela O'Hagan, Development Officer, Equal Opportunities Commission, Scotland

Gerry O'Hara, Director, National Children's Home & Colleagues

Richard Parker, Personnel Department, Falkirk Council

Fiona Philipson & Jim Boyle of Bridges Project

Jan Raitt, Police Division, Scottish Office

John Rea Price OBE, Director, National Children's Bureau, & Colleagues

Rainer Reinardy, Camphill Rudolph Steiner Schools, Aberdeen & Colleagues

Chief Inspector Jim Reynolds, Paedophile Unit, Scotland Yard

John Robertson, Rector, Dollar Academy & Colleagues

John Rowell, Head of Crime Prevention Unit, Scottish Office

Mrs Fraser & Mr McCall of Scottish Safeguarders Association

Michael Sawyer, Director of Social Work, Fife Council & Colleagues

David Scott, Head Teacher, Donaldson's College for Deaf people

David Shelmerdine, Chief Executive, Scottish Council, the Scouts Association

Roger Singleton CBE, Senior Director, Barnardos, England & Colleagues

Judith Sischy, Director, Scottish Council of Independent Schools

Susan Smith, Project Development Officer, Scottish Council for Voluntary Organisations

Dr Elisabeth Sowler & Dr Patrick Brooks, Department of Health, Scottish Office

William Spencer, Chief Constable, Tayside

Harvey Stalker, HM Chief Inspector of Schools, Scottish Office

Daphne Statham CBE, Director, National Institute for Social Work

Ivor Sutherland, Registrar, General Teaching Council for Scotland

John Triseliotis, Professor, University of Edinburgh

Sir William Utting, Social Services Inspectorate & Colleagues

Dr Eileen Vizard, Consultant Psychiatrist

Joe Wake, Secretary, Scotland Central Bureau for Educational Visits and Exchanges

Clive Walsh, Director, BASW, England & Colleagues

Norman Warner, Managing Director, Warner Consultancy & Training Services

Lorraine Waterhouse, Professor of Social Work, Edinburgh University

Patrick Webb, Principal, Harmeny School & Colleagues

West of Scotland Headmasters' Support Group

Mr D Whitehead, Deputy Director, Cheshire County Council Social Services Department

Carole Wilkinson, Director of Social Work, Falkirk Council & Colleagues

Arthur Wood OBE, Chief Executive of Children 1st & Colleagues

Ray Wyre, Principal Adviser, Faithfull Foundation

APPENDIX B

Written evidence

Written evidence takes 2 forms: material specifically written for the Review, and other material sent to me because it would be useful for the Review. Included in the latter are:

- social work committee reports
- internal documents such as standards documents or procedures
- child protection guidelines
- public information
- unpublished papers
- the evidence sent to Lord Cullen on the topic of the vetting of adults who have access to children

This material was enormously useful but is not listed below.
The following also provided written evidence to the Review:

Association Of Chief Police Officers In Scotland
Association Of Directors Of Social Work
Association Of Heads Of Special Schools
Professor Norma Baldwin, University Of Dundee
Barnardo's
British Agencies For Adoption And Fostering
British Association Of Social Workers
Caring For Children
Central Council For Education And Training In Social Work
Childline Scotland
Church Of Scotland Board Of Social Responsibility
College Of Paediatrics And Child Health
The Commission For Racial Equality
Convention Of Scottish Local Authorities
Ruth Emond, University Of Stirling
John Jillings and the North Wales Inquiry Team
National Foster Care Association
National Institute For Social Work
National Society For The Prevention Of Cruelty To Children
Public Concern At Work
Royal College Of Nursing
The Royal National Institute For Deaf People
Scottish Independent Special Schools Group
Sense Scotland
The Social Care Association
Who Cares? Scotland
Cathie Wright & Associates

APPENDIX C

Bibliography

Asquith, Stewart, Ed. (1993) **Protecting Children: Cleveland to Orkney: More Lessons to Learn?** (Children in Scotland, HMSO)

Association Of Reporters To Children's Panels (1992) **Submission To The Orkney Inquiry**

Baker, Heidi & Caraher, Martin (1995) **Do It Yourself: The Process Of Developing A Drugs Information Resource For Children** (London, Home Office)

Baldwin, Norma (1991) **The Power To Care In Children' s Homes** (Aldershot, Avebury)

Batty, Daphne & Cullen, Deborah, Eds.(1996) **Child Protection: The Therapeutic Option** (London, British Agencies for Adoption & Fostering)

Borland, Moira (1996) **Review Of Statements Of Functions And Objectives In Residential Child Care** (Edinburgh, Social Work Services Inspectorate for Scotland)

British Association of Social Workers (1995) **'Whistleblowers': Guidance For Social Services On Free Expression Of Staff Concerns** (Birmingham, BASW)

Buist, Maureen & Fuller, Roger (1997) **A Chance to Change: An Intervention With Young People Who Have Sexually Abused Others** (Edinburgh, Scottish Office Home Department Central Research Unit)

Bullock, R., Little, M., Milham, S. & Mount, K. , Eds (1995) **Child Protection: Messages From Research** (London, HMSO)

Burgner, Tom (1996): **The Regulation and Inspection of Social Services** (London, Department of Health & the Welsh Office)

Caldwell, Beth & Rejino, Erlinda (1993) **Ensuring That All Children And Adolescents In Residential Treatment Live In A Protected, Safe Environment** (Residential Treatment for Children & Youth, Vol. 11, no. 1)

Castle Priory Conference Report (1969) **The Residential Task in Child Care** (RCA)

Centre for Residential Child Care (1996) **Approaching Adulthood: Quality Standards & Guidelines In Planning Services For Young People Who Are Leaving Care** (Glasgow, The Centre for Residential Child Care)

Children's Rights Development Unit (1994) **Scottish Agenda For Children** (Glasgow, Children's Rights Development Unit)

Children (Scotland) Act 1995 (London, HMSO)

Children Act 1989 (London, HMSO)

Cleland, Alison (1995) **Guide to the Children (Scotland) Act 1995** (Glasgow, Scottish Child Law Centre)

Clyde, James J. (1992) **The Report Of The Inquiry Into The Removal Of Children From Orkney In February 1991** (Edinburgh, HMSO)

Convention Of Scottish Local Authorities (1996) **A Code On Recruitment And Selection** (Edinburgh, CoSLA)

Cullen, The Hon. Lord (1996) **The Public Inquiry Into The Shootings At Dunblane Primary School On 13 March 1996** (London, The Stationery Office)

Curtis, Myra (1946) **Report of the Care of Children Committee** (London, HMSO)

Department of Health & Social Services (1996) **Making The Right Choice: A Guide To Using The Pre-Employment Consultancy Service** (Belfast, Department of Health & Social Services)

Department of Health & Social Services (1996) **Our Duty to Care: Principles of Good Practice for the Protection of Children and Young People** (Belfast, Department of Health & Social Services)

Draper, Alan G. (1996) **Child Sexual Abuse: Report commissioned by the Bishops' Conference of Scotland**

Elliott, M., Browne, K., & Kilcoyne, J. (1992) **Child Sexual Abuse Prevention: What Offenders Tell Us** (Child Abuse & Neglect, Vol 19, No. 5)

Elliott, Michele (1992) **Protecting Children: Training Pack for Front-Line Carers** (London, HMSO)

Finlayson, Alan F. & Newman, Alison J (1993) **Complaints From Young People In Care: A review of present and planned arrangements with recommendations for future action** (Edinburgh, Lothian Regional Council)

Finlayson, Alan F. & Newman, Alison J. (1993) **Listen - Take Seriously What They Say** (Edinburgh, Lothian Regional Council)

Fitzgerald, John (1993) **The Management Of Case Reviews: A Guide And Model Process For Area Child Protection Committees** (London, the Bridge Child Care Consultancy Service)

Francis, J., Thomson, G.O.B., & Mills, S. (1996) **The Quality of the Educational Experience of Children in Care** (Edinburgh, The University of Edinburgh)

Fraser, Carole et al. (1993) **Corporate Parents: Inspection of Residential Child Care Services in 11 Local Authorities** (London, Social Services Inspectorate, Department of Health)

Gough, D.A., Boddy, F.A., Dunning, N. & Stone, F.H.: Abridged version edited by Laybourn, A., & Harvey, J. **The Management Of Child Abuse: A Longitudinal Study Of Child Abuse In Glasgow** (Edinburgh, Scottish Office Central Research Unit, 1993)

Gulbenkian Foundation (1993) **One Scandal Too Many... The Case For Comprehensive Protection For Children In All Settings Report of a Working Group** (London, Calouste Gulbenkian Foundation, 1993)

Harper, Nigel (1996) **Children Still In Need: Refocusing Child Protection In The Context Of Children In Need** (London, Association of Directors of Social Services & NCH Action for Children)

HM Inspectors of Schools (1995) **The Welfare Of Residential Pupils: WRP Inspections: Guidelines**

Home Office (1996) **On The Record: The Government's Proposals for Access to Criminal Records for Employment and Related Purposes in England and Wales** (London, HMSO)

Home Office Department of Health , Department of Education & Science & the Welsh Office (1991) **Working Together Under the Children Act 1989: A Guide To Arrangements For Inter-Agency Co-Operation For The Protection Of Children From Abuse** (London, HMSO)

Home Office in conjunction with the Department of Health (1992) **Memorandum Of Good Practice On Video Recorded Interview With Child Witnessses For Criminal Proceedings** (London, HMSO)

Howe, E (1992) **The Quality of Care: Report of the Residential Staff Inquiry** (London, Local Government Management Board)

Hunter, Mic (1990) **Abused Boys: The Neglected Victims Of Sexual Abuse** (Fawcett Columbine, New York)

Jones, Adrianne (1996) **Report Of The Examination Team On Child Care Procedures And Practice In North Wales** (London, HMSO)

Kearney, Brian & Mapstone, Elisabeth (1992) **The Report Of The Inquiry Into Child Care Policies In Fife** (Edinburgh, HMSO)

Kendrick, A., Fraser, S., Borland, M. & Harvey, J (1992) **The Review of Residential Child Care in Scotland: The Three Supporting Research Studies** (Edinburgh, the Scottish Office Central Research Unit)

Kendrick, Andrew & Macquarrie, Alan, Eds. (1996) **A Better Kind Of Home?: Proceedings Of The First Annual Conference of the Centre for Residential Child Care** (Glasgow, The Centre for Residential Child Care)

Kendrick, Andrew (1995) **Residential Care In The Integration Of Child Care Services** (Edinburgh, Scottish Office Central Research Unit)

Kendrick, Andrew (1995) **The Integration Of Child Care Services in Scotland** (Children & Youth Services Review, Vol 17, Nos. 5/6)

Kilgallon, William (1995) **Report Of The Independent Review Into Allegations Of Abuse At Meadowvale Children's Home And Related Matters** (Northumberland County Council)

Kirkwood, Andrew (1993) **The Leicestershire Inquiry 1992** (Leicester, Leicestershire County Council)

Laming, Herbert (1996) **Progress Through Change: The Fifth Annual Report of the Chief Inspector, Social Services Inspectorate 1995/96** (London, HMSO)

Levy, Allan & Kahan, Barbara (1991) **The Pindown Experience And The Protection Of Children: The Report of the Staffordshire Child Care Inquiry 1990** (Stafford, Staffordshire County Council)

Lindsay, Meg (1995) **Discovering The Person Behind The Disability** (Glasgow, The Centre for Residential Child Care)

Lindsay, Meg (1995) **Guidance For Residential Workers Caring For Young People Who Have Been Sexually Abused And Those Who Abuse Others** (Glasgow, The Centre for Residential Child Care)

Lindsay, Meg et al. (1995) **Physical Restraint - Practice, Legal, Medical & Technical Considerations** (Glasgow, The Centre for Residential Child Care)

Lowe, Kevin & Flynn, Ronny (1994) **Choosing To Foster: The Challenge To Care: Leader's Guide** (London, National Foster Care Association)

Macaskill, Catherine (1991) **Adopting or Fostering a Sexually Abused Child** (London, Batsford)

Madge, Nicola (1994) **Children And Residential Care In Europe** (London, National Children's Bureau)

Marshall, Kathleen (1995) **Guidelines On Child Protection prepared for the Independent Schools in Scotland** (Edinburgh, SCIS)

Mellor, Andrew (1993) **Bullying And How To Fight It: A guide for families** (Edinburgh, The Scottish Council for Research in Education)

Miller, Sheriff Colin Brown **Ayrshire: Report**

Morgan, Roger (1993) **School Life: Pupils' Views On Boarding** (London, HMSO)

Morris, Sally & Wheatley, Helen (1994) **Time To Listen: The Experiences Of Young People In Foster And Residential Care** (London, Childline)

National Foster Care Association (1994) **Safe Caring** (London, National Foster Care Association)

National Youth Work Agencies (1996) **Vetting And Supervision Of Adults Working With Children: a Submission to Lord Cullen**

Nixon, Stephen & Verity, Pat (1996) **Allegations Against Foster Families** (Foster Care, January 1996)

Nolan, The Rt. Hon. Lord (1995) **Standards In Public Life: First Report Of The Committee On Standards In Public Life** (London, HMSO)

Norrie, Kenneth McK. (1995) Children (Scotland) **Act 1995 - Green's Annotated Acts** (Edinburgh, W. Green/ Sweet & Maxwell)

Parry-Jones, William Ll. & Maguire, Roseann (1996) **Mental Health Services For Children And Young People In Scotland: A National Review** (Glasgow, University of Glasgow Department of Child And Adolescent Psychiatry)

Peggie, R.G.E. (1993) **Setting Up A Complaints System: Good Practice Note** (Edinburgh, Commissioner for Local Administration in Scotland)

Price Waterhouse & National Institute for Social Work (1996) **Reports Of Two Feasibility Studies** (Loondon, Department of Health)

Rose, Nick & Dehn, Guy (1997) **Abuse in Care: A Necessary Reform** (London, Public Concern at Work)

Roskill, C., Richards, D., Davies, M., & Gildersleeve, G. (1991) **Working With Child Sexual Abuse: Guidelines For Trainers And Managers in Social Services Departments** (London, Department of Health)

Savage Young & Associates (1993) **Report On Recruitment And Selection Of Staff In Children's Residential Care** (Edinburgh, Savage Young & Associates)

Scottish Office (1992) **Effective Intervention Child Abuse (Mark 2): Guidance On Co-Operation In Scotland** (Edinburgh, HMSO)

Scottish Office (1996) **On The Record In Scotland: Proposals for Improved Access to Criminal Records** (Edinburgh, The Scottish Office)

Scottish Office Education Department (1993) **Curriculum and Assessment in Scotland: National Guidelines: Environmental Studies 5 - 14** (Edinburgh, The Scottish Office)

Scottish Office Education Department (1993) **Curriculum and Assessment in Scotland: National Guidelines: Personal and Social Development 5 - 14** (Edinburgh, The Scottish Office)

Shiner, Michael & Newburn, Tim (1996) **Young People, Drugs And Peer Education: An Evaluation Of The Youth Awareness Programme (YAP)** (London, Home Office)

Skinner, Angus (1996) **A Secure Remedy: A Review Of The Role, Availability And Quality Of Secure Accommodation For Children In Scotland** (Edinburgh, The Social Work Services Inspectorate for Scotland)

Skinner, Angus for The Social Work Services Inspectorate for Scotland (1993) **Another Kind Of Home: Agenda for Children and Young People** (Edinburgh, HMSO)

Social Services Inspectorate (1991) **The Children Act 1989 Guidance And Regulations: Volume 3 Family Placements** (London, HMSO)

Social Services Inspectorate (1991) **The Children Act 1989 Guidance And Regulations: Volume 4 Residential Care** (London, HMSO)

Social Services Inspectorate (1991) **The Children Act 1989: The Welfare of children in Boarding Schools: Practice Guide** (London, HMSO)

Social Services Inspectorate (1992) **Independent Schools With Boarding -An Induction Framework For Social Services Inspectors, Trainers And Managers** (London, HMSO)

Social Services Inspectorate (1993) **A Place Apart: An Investigation into the Handling and Outcomes of Serious Injuries to Children and other matters at Aycliffe Centre for Children, County Durham** (London, HMSO)

Social Services Inspectorate (1993) **Evaluating Performance In Child Protection: a framework for the inspection of Local Authority social services practice and systems** (London, HMSO)

Social Services Inspectorate (1993) **The Inspection Of The Complaints Procedures In Local Authority Social Services Departments** (London, HMSO)

Social Services Inspectorate (1993) **An Abuse Of Trust: The Report Of The Social Services Inspectorate Investigation Into The Case of Martin Huston** (Belfast, Department of Health & Social Services)

Social Services Inspectorate (1995) **Caring For Children: A Study Of Residential Care In Northern Ireland** (Belfast, Department of Health & Social Services)

Social Services Inspectorate (1994) **Standards For Residential Child Care Services: A Handbook For Social Services Managers And Inspectors, Users Of The Services And Their Families** (London, HMSO)

Social Services Inspectorate (1994) **Second Overview Report Of The Complaints Procedures In Local Authority Social Services Departments** (London, Department of Health)

Social Services Inspectorate - Wales & Social Information Systems Ltd. (1991) **Accommodating Children: A Review Of Children's Homes In Wales Vol.1** (London, HMSO)

Social Work Services Group (1996) **Report Of The Working Group On Residential Care Home Registration Procedures** (Edinburgh, Scottish Office Home Department)

Social Work Services Inspectorate for Scotland (1993) **Local Authority Complaints Procedures 18 Months On** (Edinburgh, The Scottish Office Home & Health Department)

Support Force for Children's Residential Care chaired by Adrianne Jones (1995) **Code Of Practice For The Employment Of Residential Child Care Workers** (London, Department of Health)

TACADE (1990) **Skills For The Primary School Child: Promoting the Protection of Children** (Salford, TACADE)

Thain, Michael (1996) **Homelessness and the Children (Scotland) Act 1995** (Edinburgh, Shelter Scotland)

Thomas, Jerry **A Framework For The Prevention Of Sexual Abuse In Institutional Settings**

Triseliotis, John & Marsh, Peter (1996) **Readiness To Practise: The Training Of Social Workers In Scotland And Their First Year In Work** (Edinburgh, The Scottish Office Central Research Unit)

United Nations (1992) **Convention On The Rights Of The Child** (London, HMSO)

Utting, Sir William (1991) **Children In The Public Care: A Review Of Residential Care** (London, HMSO)

Van Riesen, Wendy (date unknown) **Feeling Yes, Feeling No: A Sexual Assault Prevention Program For Young Children: A User's Guide** (Vancouver, National Film Board of Canada)

Vizard, E., Monck, E., & Misch, P. (1995) **Child And Adolescent Sex Abuse Perpetrators: A Review Of The Research Literature** (Journal Of Child Psychology & Psychiatry, 36, 731-756)

Vizard, E., Wynick, S., Hawkes, C., Woods, J., & Jenkins, J. (1996) **Juvenile Sexual Offenders: Assessment Issues** (British Journal of Psychiatry, 168, 259-262)

Volunteer Development Scotland (1995) **Protecting Children: A Code of Good Practice for Voluntary Organisations in Scotland working with children and young people** (Stirling, Volunteer Development Scotland)

Wagner Development Group (1990) **Staffing in Residential Care Homes: A Handbook Of Guidance On The Calculation Of Staffing Establishments And The Deployment Of Staff** (London, NISW)

Warner, Norman (1996) **Creating A Home From Home: A Guide to Standards** (London, The Residential Forum)

Warner, Norman (1992) **Choosing With Care: The Report of the Committee of Inquiry into the Selection, Development And Management Of Staff In Children's Homes** (London, HMSO)

Waterhouse, L. & Carnie, J. (1990) **Child Sexual Abuse: The Professional Challenge to Social Work and Police** (Edinburgh, Scottish Office Central Research Unit Papers)

Waterhouse, L., Dobash, R. & Carnie, J. (1994) **Child Sexual Abusers** (Edinburgh, Scottish Office Central Research Unit)

Westcott, Helen & Cross, Merry (1996) **This Far And No Further: Towards ending the abuse of disabled children** (Venture Press for British Association of Social Workers, 1995)

Westcott, Helen L. (1991) **Institutional Abuse of Children - from Research to Policy: A Review** (London, National Society for the Prevention of Cruelty to Children)

White, Tom (1992) **Report Of The Committee Of Enquiry Into Children And Young People Who Sexually Abuse Other Children** (London, NCH)

Williams of Mostyn (1996) **Childhood Matters: Report of the National Commission of Inquiry into the Prevention of Child Abuse** (London, the Stationery Office)

Wyre, Ray **Conference Handouts** (Wakefield Police)

APPENDIX D

Work Undertaken by the National Institute for Social Work: Safeguarding in Other Countries

D1 The National Institute for Social Work were invited by the English and Welsh Children's Safeguards Review Team to look at safeguards operating in other countries for children living away from home. Although the remit came from the Department of Health, it was agreed that the work should be done on behalf of the Scottish Children's Safeguards Review Team also. The NISW produced a paper "Safeguarding Children Living Away from Home in Other Countries: Western Europe and the USA". This is a summary of that paper.

D2 Methodology

Questionnaires were sent to 50 known contacts involved in the field of child welfare throughout Western Europe and the United States of America and for comparison purposes to Israel and Canada also. 14 completed questionnaires were returned. It is believed that the small numbers completed were due to the short timescale involved and to language barriers. For those countries where no returns were made, information was obtained from available literature.

D3 Points of Interest Arising from the Research

D3.1 Staffing

The reports on the different countries do not all give a name for members of staff working with children in residential units. However, Belgium, Finland and Germany all employ "educators". Denmark uses "pedagogues" and the Netherlands and Sweden use "social pedagogues". Other staff working in residential units in Sweden are psychologists and family therapists and the Netherlands state that an increasing number of psychiatrists and psychologists are working in residential child care.

D3.2 Training

Other countries demand quite a high level of training. In Denmark, the Union of Pedagogues campaigned for and obtained the right to a 3½ year long training. In Sweden, social pedagogues do a 3½ year university training and Social Workers a 4 year training. The USA says that a Degree is needed in most residential child care agencies. Under the social work programme in Norway, it takes 3 years to work for a Certificate or Diploma and increasingly, people are doing a fourth year post graduate year in administration or child care. Staff in Finland tend to come from educational backgrounds. Luxemburg has mandatory training in residential child care. In Germany there is a stated percentage of staff which should be qualified (but the figures were not given to NISW) and in-service training is a requirement.

D3.3 Registers

Germany has state licensing for educators and Social Workers, and in Ireland there is a campaign for a state register of child care workers. In Denmark, personal files are checked when someone applies for a job in child care; these contain information about any crime or offence affecting work with children: serious offences such as child abuse will stay on file for life and lesser criminal offences will stay on file for 5 years. In France, checks are made with the President of the General Council or the Prefect of the Department on the "moral qualities of the candidate".

In the USA, criminal checks include the child abuse register, which includes people who may not have been prosecuted but who "have been found to abuse/neglect children".

D3.4 External Eyes

In Israel, each Home has external staff such as educational supervisors and psychological counsellors who keep in close contact with the children. Austria uses visiting specialists such as psychologists.

D3.5 Standards

British Columbia in Canada says they are developing standards of care. In the Netherlands, there are guaranteed standards for residential child care facilities. Israel says that their standards cover such things as the numbers of children in the group, child:staff ratios, nutritional standards, health care and staff training. In Denmark, standards include child:staff ratios. Germany has Regulations as to how to carry out inspections of residential child care and what should be considered. In France, Inspectors have the authority to close down Homes.

D3.6 Foster Carers

Foster carers in Portugal get support from inter-disciplinary teams of Social Workers, teachers and psychologists. In the USA, private agencies check weekly on children in foster care. In Denmark, foster carers are allowed a maximum of 4 children and foster care is inspected through supervisory visits from Social Workers and pedagogues. Israel has "periodic evaluations" of foster carers.

D3.7 Complaints

Both the USA and Finland expect children to take any complaints they may have to their Social Workers. Many Homes in Finland often have a time set aside where children can approach the Director of the Home with any grievances. Israel says the children can go to various staff with complaints and they name among these Social Workers, psychologists, teachers, the Head of Home or the Ombudsman. There is an additional safeguard in Israel because the placement agency is separate from the care agency, and any child can approach staff from the placement agency with complaints. In the Netherlands, one of the tasks of the Youth And Welfare Services Inspectorate is to take complaints from children, parents and guardians.

D3.8 Ombudsmen

A number of countries now have some form of Ombudsman. Israel, Norway and Sweden all use the title of Ombudsman for the person fulfilling this role, and the Ombudsman in Sweden acts not only as the spokesperson for children but also gives information to parents and professional staff who are working with children. In Belgium, the youth judge acts as a children's Ombudsman and in France the Juge Des Enfants acts as an Ombudsman. In Germany an Ombudsman service is provided by the Landesjugendamt. Finland and Luxemburg are both discussing the possibilities of appointing Ombudsmen. Belgium and the Netherlands both use the "Confidential Doctors Centre" system and say that anyone can take complaints there.

D3.9 Telephone Service

Finland, France, Italy and Sweden all provide a special telephone service for children.

D3.10 Privacy

Sweden makes it mandatory that when a case is reviewed, the child and the Social Worker must have the chance to be alone together.

Safeguarding Children Living Away from Home from Abuse: A Literature Review

by Andrew Kendrick

Department of Social Work

University of Dundee - 1997

Acknowledgements

I would like to thank Nichola White, research assistant to the literature review, for her hard work in tracking down material. Roger Kent and Mary Thomas of the Children's Safeguards Review Team have provided constant support, advice and encouragement throughout the process of writing this review. My thanks to all those people who have guided me in the direction of relevant research and literature, sent me copies of papers and reports, and confirmed those areas where material does not exist. Finally, my gratitude to Norma Baldwin for her comments on drafts of the review.

Andrew Kendrick

Contents

Introduction

Article 19

1. States Parties shall take all appropriate legislative, administrative, social and educational measures to protect the child from all forms of physical or mental violence, injury or abuse, neglect or negligent treatment, maltreatment or exploitation, including sexual abuse, while in the care of parent(s), legal guardian(s) *or any other person who has the care of the child...*

Article 20

1. A child temporarily or permanently deprived of his or her family environment, or in whose best interests cannot be allowed to remain in that environment, shall be entitled to *special protection* and assistance provided by the State...

(The UN Convention on the Rights of the Child, emphasis added)

In 1992, the Report of the Committee of Inquiry into the Selection, Development and Management of Staff in Children's Homes expressed concern that "there have been so many Inquiries whose findings seem to have gone largely unheeded by the service as a whole" (Warner, 1992, p. 6). Five years later, cases of widespread abuse in children's homes in different parts of the country continue to hit the headlines and Doran and Brannan write:

> The lack of research and the piecemeal implementation of recommendations following a number of inquiries leaves one feeling that professionals have not addressed their 'responsibility' for the abuse and protection of children. We all have an active part to play and should not displace the problem solely onto the abuser - we have a collective responsibility for every child in our care and under our protection (Doran and Brannan, 1996, p 155)

The abuse of children and young people living away from home is a matter of serious concern around the world. Increasingly, professionals and the public in different countries are waking up to the fact that child protection is not just an issue about children in their own homes and the literature on the abuse of children living away from home reflects this: in Ireland (Gilligan, 1996) in Australia (Single, 1989; West, 1996); in Canada (Overton, 1993); in Germany (Conen, 1995); in Greece (Agathanos, 1983). The harrowing pictures of the conditions in which children lived, and the abuse they were subjected to, in the institutions and orphanages of the countries of Eastern Europe and of China shocked the West. Tolfree draws parallels between the past experience of institutional care in the West and the current experience in the developing world where "many institutions are large, overcrowded, poorly resourced, understaffed, neglectful and, in some cases, overtly abusive" (Tolfree, 1995, p. 60).

In the USA, efforts to address the identification and prevention of abuse of children in out-of-home care have been taking place for over twenty years. The Child Abuse Prevention and Treatment Act (P.L. 93-247) which was enacted in 1974 established the National Center on Child Abuse and Neglect (NCCAN) (Howerton, 1987)[1]. States must meet certain criteria laid down in the Act, including the requirement for independent investigations of reports of suspected child abuse in out-of-home care and the extension of the definition of "persons responsible for the

1 The Child Abuse Prevention and Treatment Act was amended in 1978, extended in 1981 and amended and extended in 1984 (Howerton, 1987)

welfare of a child" to include those persons providing out-of-home care (Howerton, 1987; Nunno and Motz, 1988; Nunno, and Rindfleisch, 1991; Rindfleisch and Nunno, 1992).

In the spring of 1977 a major conference on institutional abuse of children was held at Cornell University (Garrett, 1979; DHHS, 1980; Rindfleisch and Nunno, 1992). In the same year in San Francisco, a preventive demonstration project was funded to: increase public awareness of the problem of child abuse and neglect in out-of-home care; increase reporting of suspected incidents of abuse; prevent incidents of abuse and neglect through training; and provide remedial action in facilities where abuse occurred (Gil and Baxter, 1979). Between 1979 and 1984, NCCAN sponsored 15 research, training and demonstration projects on abuse and neglect in residential institutions (Rindfleisch, 1988a).

Even in the USA, however, Nunno and Motz comment that the issue of abuse in out-of-home care is not a primary focus, and most states are making slow progress of developing adequate laws, procedures and programs to address the problem.

> The tendency of the child welfare system to minimise or deny the problem of maltreatment of children in residential care continues. Children in care settings rarely have an effective public voice or effective legal advocacy; therefore the system is slow to respond (Nunno and Motz, 1988, p. 522)

Despite the continuing concerns expressed in the US literature, the issue of abuse and neglect in out-of-home care has been identified at both state and national level for some twenty years. In the UK, by contrast, the abuse of children living away from home has only been addressed much more recently. There has been little in the way of systematic research and responses to the problem have frequently been in reaction to inquiries into high profile cases of abuse and neglect. In 1991, government guidance for England and Wales on inter-agency co-operation for the protection of children from abuse - *Working Together* - explicitly addressed the protection of children living away from home.

> Children in accommodation provided for them as a service are entitled to the same level and standard of protection from harm as is provided for children in their own homes. ACPC [Area Child Protection Committee] procedures should include a clear policy statement that their agreed local arrangements for the handling of child abuse cases apply in every situation where an allegation of abuse is received in respect of such a child. (Home Office, 1991, p. 33)

The guidance discusses children in both foster care (section 5.19) and residential settings (section 5.20) and addresses abuse by other children, by visitors and by staff (Home Office, 1991, pp. 33-36).

This review is intended to draw together knowledge on abuse and other harm experienced by children and young people living away from home. It aims to inform all those working with children and young people so that we can better promote the well-being of children and young people in care settings; ensure that they are safeguarded from abuse and other harm; and provide the *special protection* to which they are entitled.

The review highlights the points of weakness and vulnerability in care settings which have allowed children and young people to be abused and neglected but also emphasises the safeguards and controls which are necessary to protect their interests.

The review starts by considering the definition of abuse in out-of-home care and identifying the way in which it differs from abuse in the family. It will look at the different forms of abuse and other harm which affect children who are cared for away from home: the physical, sexual and emotional abuse of children, but also 'programme abuse' and 'system abuse'. Drawing on evidence from research and inquiries into specific cases of abuse, the extent of abuse by staff in residential establishments (including boarding schools, hospitals and penal institutions) and by foster carers will be identified and the factors linked to abuse in out-of-home care settings will be discussed. We will next look at issues concerning the response to abuse in out-of-home care: the denial of abuse and the barriers to reporting abuse; the investigation of abuse in residential and foster care; and the crucial aspect of supporting the child or young person who has been abused.

Much of the research in the United States is based on the mandatory reporting of abuse in out-of-home care and the review will discuss mandatory reporting legislation as well as sex offender registers and community notification laws which are established in other countries.

Black children and children from minority ethnic groups are disproportionately represented in the care population and issues of racism and abuse will be discussed. Children with disabilities are particularly vulnerable to abuse and the specific issues relating to the abuse of this group of children will be reviewed. A high proportion of children in residential care run away or go missing and the factors involved in running away will be addressed, as will the linked issue of child prostitution.

Children and young people are not only abused by staff or carers, they suffer abuse at the hands of other young people. Bullying is an often hidden torment to children and young people living in residential establishments and the sexual abuse of children by other young people is also a serious concern. The review will address the scale of the problem and ways of preventing bullying and sexual abuse. Young people also frequently harm themselves while in care and the review will look at the issue of suicide and self-harm, as well as abuse of alcohol and drugs.

Finally, the review will look at creating a safe and secure environment. This will focus on the importance of listening to children and the ways in which this can be achieved, such as complaints procedures, children's rights officers and advocates, and telephone help-lines. It will also focus on staffing issues such as the recruitment, assessment and selection of carers and staff, and the need to support staff through supervision and training.

One of the issues in doing this review has been highlighted by Mercer (1982):

> A discussion of the prevention of institutional abuse has led us and will always lead us to a whole complex of issues touching on virtually every aspect of residential programming. This complex of issues might be boiled down to a basic question - what constitutes good, or at least acceptable, residential child care? (Mercer, 1982, p. 129)

There are then, no hard and fast boundaries in terms of the literature and research which could be included in the review. Some of the decisions on what has been covered have had to be determined to a degree by feasibility given the wide-ranging scope of the review and the limited time-scale for carrying it out. My own background is in social work and child care research and from this starting point, I have reviewed the literature relating to hospitals, boarding schools and prisons. Inevitably, some sections of the review will be more developed than others.

The literature review was carried out between September 1996 and February 1997. Keyword searches were undertaken on five literature databases: BIDS (Bath Information and Data Services); ASSIA (Applied Social Science Index and Abstracts); CAREDATA; MEDLINE, and ENB Health Care Database. A limited keyword search of the Internet was carried out. A request for material was posted on the Cornell University Child Maltreatment list-server and requests for reference material were made to the Centre for Residential Child Care, the Scottish Council for Research in Education (SCRE), Action for Sick Children, the National Foster Care Association Scotland; the Howard League for Penal Reform; and Penal Lexicon. A bibliography produced by the National Children's Bureau was also used. In addition, requests for material were made to a number of individuals who have carried out work in this field.

The remit of this literature review has meant that it has focused on the most negative aspects of the care of children and young people living away from home. Children suffer a range of harm in out-of-home care; from the worst excesses of systematic physical and sexual abuse to abuse of their rights to privacy, dignity and respect. The most conscientious carers acknowledge that at times they have overstepped the line into abusive behaviour.

> I have been guilty of punishing children (and adults), depriving them of their rights, taking away their liberty in some temporary fashion, or even (and, thank God only very occasionally) of hitting them or hurting them. And I admit to the same treatment of my own children in my own home. I believe nearly every care worker (and parent) with substantial experience has punished the people she or he works with - mentally, emotionally or physically - and, much more frequently, has in some way wished to punish without doing so (Burton, 1993, pp. 64-65; see also Baldwin, 1990; Berry, 1975)

In focusing on the negative aspects of abuse and harm, the good and excellent practice in providing children and young people a positive experience that goes on in residential establishments and foster care up and down the country must not be forgotten. The aim, however, must be to ensure that all children and young people receive that positive experience.

Definitions of Abuse in Out-of-Home Care

A crucial problem concerns the point at which acts of commission or omission are defined as abusive. This is not just an issue about abuse in out-of-home care but relates to broader debates in child protection. The recent overview of research in child protection highlighted that there is no absolute definition of abuse

> There are many definitions of abuse in the legal and scientific literature. Most describe abusive *incidents*, especially beating, sexual interference and neglect of children. But policy makers, researchers and practitioners are likely to consider the *context* in which such incidents occur before they will define them as abusive (HMSO, 1995, p. 11)

This issue of the threshold of abuse has been identified as creating major problems in the identification of, and response to, abuse in out-of-home care (Nunno and Motz, 1988; Rindfleisch and Rabb, 1984b; Rabb and Rindfleisch, 1985; Thomas, 1995).

An early and useful definition of abuse in out-of-home care was provided by Gil (1982):

> "... any system, program policy, procedure, or individual interaction with a child in placement that abuses, neglects, or is detrimental to the child's health, safety, or emotional and physical well-being or in any way exploits or violates the child's basic rights. This abuse of children in out-of-home care is of three types: physical and sexual abuse; program abuse, and system abuse" (Gil, 1982, p. 9).

Physical and sexual abuse is like abuse which occurs in family situations but is perpetrated by the professional carer or foster care (Gil, 1982; see also Harrell and Orem, 1980).

Programme abuse occurs when "programs within a facility are below normally accepted standards; have extreme or unfair policies; or rely on harsh, inhumane, or unusual techniques to teach or guide children" (Gil, 1982, p. 10; see also Powers et al, 1990). Gil includes in this: over-medication, inappropriate isolation, mechanical restraint, and disciplinary techniques. Shaughnessy (1984) gives an example of one facility where aggressive boys were overfed "until they were too obese to cause any behavioral difficulties" (Shaughnessy, 1984, p. 314). Robin (1982) discusses the situation of 'status offenders'[2] in psychiatric hospitals, many of whom have been abused in their family. He argues that it "is in the normal course of treatment that many children are abused" (Robin, 1982, p. 82) through the use of locked doors, depersonalised rules and regulations, seclusion and isolation, and the use of drugs for the management of disruptive behaviour. Two cases of programme abuse in the UK have been the purported 'behaviour modification' of the 'pindown' regime in Staffordshire residential establishments (Levy and Kahan, 1991) and the 'regression therapy' perpetrated by Frank Beck in Leicestershire (Kirkwood, 1993)[3].

Gil suggests that the third type of abuse, system abuse, is the most difficult to define, acknowledge or correct and gives examples of the damaging effect of 'foster care drift' and multiple placements to highlight the abuse "by the immense and complicated child care system, stretched beyond its limits and incapable of guaranteeing safety to all children in care" (Gil, 1982, p. 11). Kahan states that:

2 "... status offenses are those noncriminal behaviors such as incorrigibility, running away, and truancy that are considered illegal because of a child's age." (Robin, 1982, p. 79)

3 See below, page 159.

> ... stability and continuity are not only essential for good care but they are the necessary conditions for a child to grow up well (Kahan, 1994, p. 104)

However, over a number of years, research in the UK has highlighted the disruption and harm caused to children and young people by multiple care placements and changes in educational provision (Audit Commission, 1994; Berridge, 1985; Berridge and Cleaver; 1987; Cliffe with Berridge, 1991; Department of Health, 1991; Kendrick, 1995; Social Services Inspectorate, undated a; Triseliotis et al 1995). Shaughnessy (1984) also describes "misplacement and misdiagnosis" as a kind of institutional abuse and "maintaining the child or client in an inappropriate environment may be a further form of abuse when other, more appropriate facilities are available" (Shaughnessy, 1984, p. 313). Thomas discusses the wider political and economic context of child welfare services and argues that the adoption of systematic methods of service delivery can lead to the failure of welfare rather than to its success (Thomas, 1982).

Garbarino suggests that, in addition to general definitions of abuse:

> ... we define the broader domain of maltreatment in out-of-home care as acts of omission, commission or permission (acts perpetrated or promoted by the child welfare system, child care policies, a child care organisation, a specific program or a specific procedure) that violate the goals of out-of-home care, thereby harming the child.
>
> A situation would be considered harmful if it -
> (1) endangers the protection, security, and/or safety of the child;
> (2) prevents the child from obtaining basic care and satisfying basic physical and emotional needs;
> (3) places obstacles in the way of the child's development or severely restricts the developmental opportunities available to the child;
> (4) prevents the child from participating in the special care and treatment that he or she needs for adequate developmental progress
>
> (Garbarino, 1986, cited in Cavanagh, 1992, p. 20)

A number of authors have proposed categorisations of abuse in out-of-home care which, while similar in some respects, also have important differences. Garrett (1979) proposes four categories of institutional abuse:

Physical Abuse and Neglect: includes physical mistreatment, lack of care that results in illness or other physical difficulty, and medical or chemical abuse.

Sexual Abuse: when the institution and/or its staff permit or participate in involuntary sexual activity with or among residents, or any sexual activity by individuals unable through age or capacity to make a reasonable choice.

Emotional and Intellectual Damage: failure to provide an opportunity for each child to achieve his/her potential for emotional and intellectual growth constitutes a pervasive form of abuse, difficult to define but possible to identify and observe.

Social Damage and Labelling: social damage from labelling can ensue from the fact of institutionalisation itself, limiting the child's potential for fulfilment (Garrett. 1979, pp. 62-63)

Groze (1990) also presents four categories of abuse which were used in a state reporting process of institutional abuse. These were:

Abuse; the intentional or non-accidental use or threat of physical force by a person responsible for a child's health or welfare, aimed at hurting or injuring the child or knowingly causing or permitting any person to intentionally injure a child.

Sexual abuse; any sexual activity prohibited by state law, including sexual exploitation or procuring or knowingly causing or permitting any person to injure or sexually abuse or exploit a child.

Neglect: a wilful act of omission which directly results in a child suffering or being exposed to risk of suffering physical injury or emotional injury and includes the failure to furnish food, clothing, shelter, or withholding medical attention from the child.

Inappropriate treatment; means harm or threatened harm to a child's health or welfare which is caused by any violation of statutes, regulations, written rules, procedures, directives, or accepted professional standards and practices which is not otherwise classified as abuse but which results in, or creates the risk of injury to the child. (Groze, 1990, pp. 230-231)

Rabb and Rindfleisch (1985) categorised eight types of institutional abuse and neglect. As well as *physical maltreatment, sexual maltreatment, failure to provide,* and *emotional maltreatment* which are similar to previously mentioned categories, they include:

> *Failure to supervise.* An adult caregiver's failure to provide monitoring, guidance, structure, restraint or discipline necessary to protect a child from harm....
>
> *Questionable moral behavior.* A caregiver's engaging in behaviors in a child's presence which are illegal, immoral, or inappropriate for a child to observe, and which are likely to encourage a child to violate legal, moral or community standards...
>
> *Harmful restraint/control.* Methods of limiting behavior which harm or endanger a child, including isolation and medication
>
> *Setting up.* Caregiver deception, gross inconsistency or unrealistic expectations which result in substantial provocation or predictable failure of a child
>
> (Rabb and Rindfleisch, 1985, p. 287)

Bibby (1996) comes at the definition of institutional abuse from a different direction. He is concerned with the wider issue of organised abuse and considers that institutional abuse is a sub-set of organised abuse.

> Institutional and ritual abuse are but specialised forms of organised abuse
>
> *Organised abuse* is the systematic abuse of children, normally by more than one person
>
> It is characterised by the degree of planning in the purposeful, secret targeting, seduction, hooking and silencing of the subjects
>
> (Bibby, 1996, pp 5-6; see also, Gough, 1996; Kelly and Scott, 1993)

He suggests that while previous definitions have attempted to define organised abuse in terms of numbers, and relationships between perpetrators and victims, this definition "directs our thoughts towards the *systems* used by perpetrators" (Bibby, 1996, p. 6).

Most recently, in the UK, the National Commission of Inquiry into the Prevention of Child Abuse recommended the following definition of system abuse.

> System abuse may be said to occur whenever the operation of legislation, officially sanctioned procedures or operational practices within systems or institutions is avoidably damaging to children and their families (Williams of Mostyn, 1996, p. 5).

System abuse is considered to occur when: children's needs are not recognised or understood so they are not considered separately from those of adults; services are unavailable because they do not exist, are inadequate or inaccessible; services are so poorly organised, managed, monitored or resourced that they permit unskilled and unsafe environments; services for children with emotional and behavioural disorders are so poorly defined and co-ordinated that organisations can avoid or shift responsibilities; there are unnecessarily intrusive procedures or practices which undermine children or their families (Williams of Mostyn, 1996, p. 5).

Abuse in Residential Care

Introduction

> Young people and children should feel safe and secure in any residential home or school (Skinner, 1992, p. 21)

In 1979, Garrett wrote of the USA that accurate data on abuse of children in residential institutions was almost non-existent (Garrett, 1979, p. 60). As we shall see, this is the current situation for the United Kingdom and much of the systematic information on abuse in residential care comes from the United States. A major barrier, however, to detecting and measuring the extent of the problem concerns the general lack of clarity about what constitutes institutional abuse (Rindfleisch and Rabb, 1984a; 1984b; Powers et al, 1990)[4]. There are major barriers to the reporting of abuse and it must be accepted that the figures presented from studies based on reported abuse will therefore tend to be underestimates of the actual incidence of abuse.

In the United Kingdom there is a lack of systematic information on the extent of abuse and neglect of children and young people in residential establishments (Westcott, 1991a; Westcott and Clement, 1992) and since "there is no central mechanism in this country for reporting or recording investigations and findings regarding institutional abuse, we remain ignorant of its true scope" (Doran and Brannan, 1996, p. 157). Several major inquiries, however, have highlighted the fact that the problem is more widespread than had previously been recognised: Kincora boys' hostel in Belfast (Hughes, 1986); 'pindown' in Staffordshire (Levy and Kahan, 1991); Ty Mawr in Wales (Williams and McCreadie, 1992); Castle Hill School in Shropshire (Brannan et al, 1993a, 1993b) ; the Beck case in Leicestershire (Kirkwood, 1993). More recently, the extensive abuse which took place in residential establishments in Cheshire and the North-west of England was highlighted by the conviction of Keith Laverack for the sexual abuse of children over a period of twenty years (Ward, 1997; Connett and Calvert, 1997). In Wales, a tribunal is under way to investigate allegations of widespread abuse in children's homes and 175 people who have made allegations of abuse will give evidence (Brindle, 1997).

Research Evidence from the USA

Rindfleisch and Rabb (1984a) conducted a nation-wide survey of 1,700 residential establishments in the USA and obtained information about the establishments, the residents and staff, and specifically, the number of complaints of abuse and neglect in the establishment. 1,100 establishments returned questionnaires and based on the returns, an estimated 2,692 complaints were made in the 1,700 residential establishments; 617 of these were confirmed. However, site visits to 12 residential establishments in four states to validate these figures suggest that "the number of complainable situations may be substantially larger than the number reported in our survey data" (Rindfleisch and Rabb, 1984a, 39).

> Despite the lack of consciously developed case finding systems to protect children in residential facilities, it is our impression that the rates of occurrence of complainable situations in residential facilities may be twice as large as rates of occurrence in families (Rindfleisch and Rabb, 1984a, p. 39)

4 For some residential care is inherently abusive and according to this view all residential institutions should be closed as quickly as possible (Savells, 1983; see also Garrett, 1979; Rindfleisch and Rabb, 1984b; Turnbull, 1995).

Blatt and Brown (1986) present information on 232 reports of alleged child abuse and neglect incidents made between October 1980 and September 1983 in New York State Office of Mental Health (OMH) operated psychiatric facilities. These were incidents of physical, sexual or emotional abuse and institutional abuse as defined by Gil (1982) as programme or system abuse were not studied. The 232 allegations were broken down into: excessive corporal punishment (47.4%); lacerations, bruises, welts, fractures, burns (24.6%); lack of supervision/inadequate guardianship (13.8%); sexual abuse (13.8%); child's drug or alcohol use (3.0%); and inappropriate restraint (0.4%) (Blatt and Brown, 1986, p. 175). The 232 allegations involved 174 different children with an average age of 14.6 years (OMH population average age was 14.3 years). 68% were males and 32% were females exactly the same as the OMH population. 40% were white; 36% were black and 13% were Hispanic, with a larger proportion of the children being black than in the OMH population (29%) (Blatt and Brown, 1986, p. 176).

Groze (1990) collected information from the files of a large southwestern state agency which investigates allegations of mistreatment of children in the custody of the state residing in state-operated and private mental heath, child welfare and juvenile correctional institutions. 609 allegations were made in the two years, 1985/86-1986/87: abuse (22.1%); neglect (15.8%); sexual abuse (6.6%) and inappropriate treatment (55.4%). 490 of the allegations were 'ruled out' and 110 were confirmed[5]. The rate of confirmation of the different types of abuse varied markedly: 3.1% of allegations involving neglect were confirmed; 9.7% of abuse allegations; 22.5% of sexual abuse allegations; and 25.3% of inappropriate treatment allegations. Thus three-quarters of the confirmed reports were for inappropriate treatment; 11.8% for abuse; 8.2% for sexual abuse; and 2.7% for neglect (Groze, 1990, p. 234). In confirmed cases, the average age of the victim was older for sexual abuse (16) and younger for neglect (11.7). Most of the victims were male although over half the victims in cases of sexual abuse were female. Most of the victims were white and the proportion of non-white victims ranged between 22.2% (sex abuse) and 38.5% (abuse) in the different categories of abuse (Groze, 1990, pp. 235-236).

> The finding that *inappropriate treatment* is the most common mistreatment alleged and confirmed suggests that the majority of staff who mistreat youths in institutions do so by violating statutes, regulation, written rules, procedures, directives, or accepted professional standards and practices. These behaviors are most effectively addressed by appropriate supervision, consultation, and training (Groze, 1990, p. 239)

Further work was carried out in New York State by Blatt (1992), who analysed a random sample of 510 reports of alleged child abuse and neglect made to the New York State Child Abuse and Maltreatment Register between 1986 and 1988. The allegations were distributed: fractures (0.9%); internal injuries (0.2%); lacerations (34.8%); burns (0.7%); excessive corporal punishment (10.3%); drug use (3.6%); lack of medical care (2.7%); sexual abuse (17.2%); educational neglect (0.4%); emotional neglect (0.7%); lack of food, shelter, clothing (1.3%); lack of supervision (5.1%); inappropriate restraint (22.1%) (Blatt, 1992 p. 500). The average age of children reported as abused neglected was just under 14 years and the age distribution was very similar to that of all children receiving residential services (Blatt, 1992, p. 499).

Rosenthal et al (1991) describe 290 reported incidents of abuse and neglect in family foster homes, group homes, residential treatment centres and institutions in Colorado. 38% of complaints (102 of 272; 18 cases missing) were of incidents in residential treatment centres; 14% (38) in group homes; and 11% (30) in institutional settings. In each setting physical abuse referrals were most common (53 - 64%); sexual abuse referrals were second in frequency (20 - 27%); and neglect referrals were least common (16 - 20%). Confirmation of referrals varied according to setting. 39% of institutional referrals (11 of 28) as compared to only 18% (7 of 38) of group home referrals and 19% (19 of 100) of residential treatment centre referrals. Group home and institutional victims of alleged abuse were 13.8 years old on average and residential treatment centre victims were 14.0 years old (Rosenthal et al, 1991, pp. 252-253).

5 Figures in Table 1 (Groze, 1990, p. 234) do not add up to 609.

Finally, in relation to the US research, Spencer and Knudsen provide data for the state of Indiana between 1984 and 1990 regarding total complaints and 'substantiated/indicated' reports of physical and sexual abuse and neglect in foster homes, schools, day-care homes and centres, residential homes, state institutions, hospitals and other facilities (Spencer and Knudsen, 1992). This data was combined to provide weighted averages of the number of substantiated/indicated cases per year for physical and sexual abuse and a rate of maltreatment was calculated. Over the period, the rate of maltreatment in residential homes was 120.35 per 1,000 children, at least seven times the rate in any other type of out-of-home care. The child maltreatment rate in other forms of care was: foster homes 16.93 per 1,000; state institutions 8.88; hospitals/other facilities 15.66. Sexual abuse was the most frequent form of abuse in residential homes with a rate of 70.20 per 1,000 children, compared to 33.43 per 1,000 for physical abuse and 16.72 per 1,000 for neglect. In state institutions the rates were: sexual abuse - 6.14 per 1,000; physical abuse - 1.70; and neglect - 11.04, and in hospitals and other facilities: sexual abuse - 8.54 per 1,000; physical abuse - 5.70; and neglect - 1.42. These figures compare to a maltreatment rate in the child's family home of 11.59 per thousand: sexual abuse - 2.42 per 1,000; physical abuse - 2.97; and neglect 6.20 (Spencer and Knudsen, 1992, pp. 488 - 489).

Evidence from the Inquiries

In December 1981, three residential staff of the Kincora Boys' hostel were convicted and jailed for a series of offences including buggery, gross indecency and indecent assault spanning the 1960s and 1970s. The Royal Ulster Constabulary investigation of Kincora uncovered allegations of sexual abuse in other residential establishments which led to the conviction of four others (Hughes, 1986, p. 2). The Kincora scandal was entangled with allegations that there had been an official "cover-up by Unionist politicians and paramilitaries and by police and British military intelligence" (Kelly and Pinkerton, 1996, p. 46). The Hughes Inquiry concluded that there had not been a 'cover-up' (Hughes, 1986, pp. 190-191) but Kelly and Pinkerton suggest that, in emphasising administrative systems and methods of staff selection, "both the political dimensions of the case and what it had to say about power relations between young people and adults within residential care were neatly side-stepped" (Kelly and Pinkerton, 1996, p. 46)[6].

In Staffordshire, at least 132 children were subjected to 'pindown' between November 1983 and October 1989 (Levy and Kahan, 1991). The Inquiry concluded that the children subjected to the "narrow, punitive and harshly restrictive experience" of 'pindown' suffered to varying degrees "the despair and the potentially damaging effects of isolation, the humiliation of having to wear night clothes, knock on the door to 'impart information'" and of having "all their personal possessions removed; and the intense frustration and boredom from the lack of communication, companionship with others and recreation" (Levy and Kahan, 1991, p. 167). 'Pindown' was described as "intrinsically unethical, unprofessional and unacceptable (Levy and Kahan, 1991, p. 167).

The Inquiry into Ty Mawr Community Home concluded that there "was an over masculine culture at Ty Mawr"[7] and that there "was a degree of low level physical violence (slapping, cuffing, knuckling, that is striking on the head with the knuckles) by certain members of staff." (Williams and McCreadie, 1992, p. 33). The Inquiry carried out a review of suicides, attempted suicides or threats to self-harm and concluded:

> **In many ways,... Ty Mawr unfortunately became the whipping boy in respect of incidents, many of which could not be sensibly connected to Ty Mawr and certain of which Ty Mawr was not to blame for.** There were undoubted deficiencies at Ty Mawr, of structure, planning and resources. The institution and the staff were being asked to deal with young boys in circumstances which were impossible (Williams and McCreadie, 1992, p. 51)

In 1991, Ralph Morris, the Principal and joint owner of Castle Hill Independent Special School was sentenced to twelve years imprisonment having been charged with sixteen specimen counts

6 Christopherson (1989) discusses examples of institutional abuse in the context of sex rings where the syndicated ring "is a well structured organisation geared to recruiting children to provide pornography or other sexual services on a commercial basis" (Christopherson, 1989, p. 35). He cites Kincora as an example of a syndicated ring, although the Inquiry concluded that the abuse was not linked to child prostitution (Hughes, 1986, pp. 199-201)

7 See also Kirkwood (1992) and Jones (1994) for discussion of the sexist and racist culture in the Leicestershire children's homes and at Castle Hill School.

of offences ranging from physical assault to indecent assault and buggery (Brannan et al, 1993a, p. 2). Brannan et al comment that "the control and seduction of a great number of young boys proved to be an underlying motivation for the conception and growth of Castle Hill School" (Brannan et al, 1993a, p. 6).

> Within the school a regime developed over a period that was utterly restrictive, where fear was used to exercise control. Ralph Morris' management style was totalitarian with ultimate control being vested in him. There was a subculture within the school involving himself and the boys. He operated a hierarchical system whereby some older and more senior boys were afforded special privileges... These favoured pupils presented as a fearful and vindictive corps and were used to control those who dared to go beyond the clearly defined limits. There were many examples of boys being assaulted by members of this elite task force at Ralph Morris' instigation (Brannan et al, 1993a, pp. 7-8)

Also in 1991, Frank Beck, an officer-in-charge of children's homes in Leicestershire, was found guilty on 17 counts involving sexual and physical assault including four offences of buggery and one of rape. Two other children's home staff were convicted of charges of indecent or common assault (Kirkwood, 1993, pp. 1-2)[8]. The Leicestershire Inquiry also identified other cases of sexual abuse in children's homes and while it concluded that the evidence did not tend to support that a paedophile ring was operating, "during the period 1973 to 1986 there was an alarmingly high number of child sexual abusers at work in Leicestershire Children's Homes" (Kirkwood, 1993, pp. 295-296). In the children's homes run by Beck, there was "a regime of physical, sexual and emotional abuse" (Kirkwood, 1993, p. 309) and many children found "his treatment approach which became known as 'regression therapy'... threatening, violent and humiliating" (Kirkwood, 1993, p. 56).

Research Evidence from the UK

The National Association of Young People in Care (NAYPIC) made an early attempt to highlight abuse in the care system in the UK. They studied the cases of fifty young people who had complained to them in a three month period (Moss et al, 1990). NAYPIC found that "65% of the young people... were sexually abused whilst in care" and "85% of female young people said they had suffered sexual assault" (Moss et al, 1990, pp. 4-5). Over three-quarters of the young people reported that they had been physically abused in care and the "complaints varied from being hit whilst arguing with staff, up to and including systematic, severe physical abuse" (Moss et al, 1990. p. 5).

A further attempt to provide more detailed information on institutional abuse was carried out by the NSPCC. A survey of NSPCC teams and projects in March 1992 identified 84 cases of alleged abuse in residential or educational settings over the previous year (Westcott and Clement, 1992). The authors acknowledge that the sample is unrepresentative as it is likely that these are particularly severe cases. Two-thirds of the children involved (63%) were male and one-third were female; 12% of the children were under 10 years; 43% were between 10 and 14 years old; and 45% were between 15 and 17 years of age (Westcott and Clement, 1992, p. 7). A large number of children (42%) had been placed in the residential establishment because of previous abuse. The majority of children (69) suffered sexual abuse; 16 suffered physical abuse; 4 suffered emotional abuse; 6 suffered from inappropriate restraint and 9 suffered other forms of abuse (Westcott and Clement, 1992, p. 11). In half the cases, the perpetrator was a peer, in 43% of cases it was a staff member, and in the other cases it was a sibling. The majority of abusers were male (81%). For the 25 staff perpetrators where their age was known, the majority (19) were aged 40 and above (Westcott and Clement, 1992, p.11).

A more recent account of abuse in residential establishments has been provided by ChildLine (Morris and Wheatley, 1995). They provide an analysis of calls made by 539 children in England and Wales and 137 children in Scotland in 1992/93 over the first six month of the lines' operation.

8 A fourth member of staff who was arrested died before he could be brought to trial (Kirkwood, 1992, p.1)

Over a quarter of the boys (18) and 11% of the girls (24) from England and Wales and eight callers from Scotland reported bullying and violence from other residents as their main problem. Allegations of current sexual abuse were made by 25 children in England and Wales. In 9 cases, male residents were the perpetrators, in eight cases it was male residential staff and in most of the remainder, the abuse had occurred on home visits (Morris and Wheatley, 1995, p. 54).

The most comprehensive survey of institutional sexual abuse in England and Wales was carried out by Gallagher, Hughes and Parker (1996) in the context of a national survey of organised sexual abuse. Questionnaires were sent to every police force (N=43), Social Services Department (N=116) and NSPCC team (N=66) in 1992 requesting information on each case of organised, ritual or institutional abuse between January 1988 and December 1991 (Gallagher, Hughes and Parker, 1996, p. 216). Institutional abuse was defined as, "a case in which an adult has used the institutional framework of an organisation for children to recruit children for sexual abuse" (Gallagher, Hughes and Parker, 1996, p. 217). The authors had doubts about the reliability of the findings in that they believed that agencies had reported only a small proportion of high profile cases, "such as those involving allegations of ritual abuse or large numbers of perpetrators and children" (Gallagher, Hughes and Parker, 1996, p. 218).

Of the 211 cases reported to the national survey, there were 45 cases of institutional abuse and 16 (8%) were in residential institutions (Gallagher, Hughes and Parker, 1996, p. 218).

Information on the abuse of children and young people is also available from research looking more generally at residential care. In their study of special residential schools, Grimshaw and Berridge detail the extent of abuse of 67 children who had had been resident in the schools for at least a year, although data was not collected from staff about where the abuse had occurred or the perpetrator of the abuse. Four per cent had definitely suffered physical abuse and 6% sexual abuse. One fifth (21%) were reported to have "experienced some form of suspected or confirmed abuse; 13% had experienced suspected or confirmed physical abuse and 13% similarly sexual abuse..." (Grimshaw and Berridge, 1994, pp. 103-104). They concluded:

> For a proportion of children, admission to a residential school did not mean that they were fully protected from abusive experiences. Clearly the system of management and inspection of such schools needs to reflect this unfortunate reality (Grimshaw and Berridge, 1994, pp. 103-104).

Triseliotis et al (1995) studied social work services to a sample of 116 teenagers over a 12 month period. Fifty-five young people experienced 78 residential care placements and, in interviews, "two young people spoke of incidents when they had been assaulted by staff and both had formally complained about it" (Triseliotis et al, 1995, p. 181).

Research on perpetrators of child sexual abuse has also indicated to some degree the extent of abuse in care settings. A study of social work, criminal justice and health service case files for a sample of 501 child sexual abusers found that "6% of the sample were known to the victim in their capacity as foster or adoptive parent, male residential care-giver or a male who was in care with the victim" (Waterhouse et al, 1994, p.16).

Programme Abuse

The research discussed here has, for the most part, focused on physical abuse, sexual abuse and neglect. Two cases of programme abuse in the UK have been the subject of major inquiries: the pindown regime in Staffordshire residential establishments and the 'regression therapy' or 'regressive therapy' perpetrated by Frank Beck in Leicestershire (Levy and Kahan, 1991; Kirkwood, 1993). We saw above that in the 1980s, large numbers of children were subjected to the pindown regime.

The practice of 'pindown' varied considerably but the Inquiry identified the following common features:

> ... firstly, isolation for part of the time in a part of a children's home cordoned off as a 'special' or Pindown unit; secondly, removal of ordinary clothing for part of the time and the enforced wearing of shorts or night clothes; thirdly, being told of having to earn 'privileges', and fourthly being allowed to attend school or a 'school room' in the unit, and changing back into shorts or night clothes after returning from school. (Levy and Kahan, 1991, pp. 119 - 120)

The Inquiry went on to detail the features of 'full pindown' or 'total pindown':

> ... firstly, persistent isolation in a part of a children's home cordoned off as a special or Pindown unit; secondly removal of ordinary clothing for lengthy periods and the enforced wearing of shorts or night clothes; thirdly, persistent loss of all 'privileges'; fourthly, having to knock on the door to 'impart information', for example, a wish to visit the bathroom; and fifthly, non-attendance at school, no writing or reading materials, no television, radio, cigarettes or visits (Levy and Kahan, 1991, p. 120)

While acknowledging that the 'pindown' regime had a purported 'philosophy' to give children intense individual attention, the Inquiry considered that this was "never to any significant extent put into practice; and was in any event a pipe dream due to lack of sufficient staff and lack of qualified and experienced people" (Levy and Kahan, 1991, p. 167).

In Leicestershire, Frank Beck developed a purported treatment approach known as 'regression therapy' or 'regressive therapy'.

> Quite apart from a volume of allegations made since 1989 by former residents in Children's Homes of sexual and physical assaults upon them by Mr Beck and other care staff over the years, there have been significant complaints about the treatment methods that were used. They are significant because young people found the treatment to which they were subjected in the name of therapy to be abusive in itself (Kirkwood, 1993, p. 62)

'Regression therapy' involved dealing with young people as with a child under five: for example, dressing the child; spoon-feeding or using baby bottles; using dummies[9]; "the apparently bizarre use of the paraphernalia of babyhood in the treatment of adolescent boys and girls" (Kirkwood, 1993, p. 57). The rules also allowed for the provocation of children but this frequently led to the persistent verbal and physical abuse of children and young people and there was "a wealth of evidence of the violence of confrontation, provocation and often unwarranted physical restraint from witnesses who had been broken down to make them amenable to regression treatment" (Kirkwood, 1993, p. 67).

Recently, the National Commission of Inquiry into the Prevention of Child Abuse wrote:

> The catalogue of abuse in residential institutions is appalling. It includes physical assault and sexual abuse; emotional abuse; unacceptable deprivation of rights and privileges; inhumane treatment; poor health care and education. This is especially disturbing because many of the children in residential institutions have already been deeply harmed... (Williams of Mostyn, 1996, p. 19)

Boarding Schools

Little research on abuse has been carried out in boarding schools or independent schools. In relation to bullying, Walford states that the "competitive situation in which schools find themselves means that writers from within the schools are likely to play down any problems, and

9 This is taken from "Ratcliffe Road Adolescent Unit - Rules Governing the Treatment of Children and the Conduct of Staff" (reproduced in Kirkwood, 1992, pp. 82-83)

it is rare for outside researchers to be given the chance to find out" (Walford, 1989, p. 84; see also Geddes, 1994). In the 1960s, Lambert and Millham (1968) conducted research in "66 boarding schools for ordinary children in England and Wales recognised by the Department of Education and Science" and includes "26 public schools…; 18 other independent schools…; 7 others are called progressive schools…; 15 others are directly maintained by LEAs…" (Lambert and Millham, 1968, p. 3). Their book *The Hothouse Society* is based solely on the writings of some 12,000 children in boarding schools. Evidence of sexual abuse of boys by staff[10] was identified in four of the 66 schools and in these four schools "it was mentioned by over three quarters of the boys in all age groups, often many times over even when it had no relevance to the questions asked" (Lambert and Millham, 1968, p. 272).

More recently, abuse in boarding schools was researched in relation to the operation of the ChildLine Boarding School Line. This was set up following a case of serious sexual abuse by staff in a private boarding school; Crookham Court (La Fontaine and Morris, 1991). Over 130,000 children are estimated to attend boarding schools, two-thirds of whom are boys and most are 13 years and older. The Boarding School Line received 10,315 calls between January and July 1991; 1,012 of these resulted in some form of counselling with the production of a case note/log (La Fontaine and Morris, 1991, p. 10). While the line had calls from children in all types of schools: special schools; independent and maintained schools; single-sex and mixed schools; and were from weekly and termly boarders, in the vast majority of cases schools were not identified, even by type. Half of the calls were made from telephones in schools and over a quarter from a public telephone box. Most of the callers were aged between 12 and 15 years and girls called more often than boys, although more boys attend boarding schools than girls. The main problem of each caller was identified from the case-note, although callers may have had several concerns. Over a third of the calls related to two main problems: bullying (19.8%)[11] and sexual abuse (15.3%).

34 cases (3.5%) were classified as sexual harassment (sexual remarks and sexual behaviour that did not involve touching the child): most were reported by girls and in 21 cases male teachers were the perpetrators of the harassment (La Fontaine and Morris, 1991, p. 18). Sexual abuse "involving physical contact and ranging from touching and kissing to intercourse" was reported in 155 calls with just over half the calls coming from boys. In 110 of these cases, the alleged perpetrators were staff of the boarding schools: in five cases, the allegation was made against the Headmaster; in seven cases, a Housemaster; in 97 cases, a teacher; and in one case, the Matron (La Fontaine and Morris, 1991, p. 28)[12]. In a quarter of the cases, the callers indicated that other children were being abused by the same person.

5.5 percent of the calls involved physical abuse and this was the third largest problem for boys. In seven of the cases "it appeared that the problem was corporal punishment which was regularly used by the member of staff concerned" (La Fontaine and Morris, 1991, p. 26).

> However, this category of complaints largely referred to the actions of staff, the majority of them men. The calls were about teachers, four Headmasters among them, who either lost their tempers or regularly showed their displeasure in physical assaults (La Fontaine and Morris, 1991, p. 26).

Morgan, in his report on the views of boarding school pupils, found that "a small minority of staff were described by pupils as using idiosyncratic punishments" and that while some of these were harmless, they also included "slapping, pulling, and other forms of striking pupils, and use of inappropriate physical restraint" (Morgan, 1993, p. 70). Some pupils had tried to raise concerns about the risks of abuse by staff with other staff members but without success (Morgan, 1993, p. 45).

Hospitals

There is very little research and literature on child abuse which takes place in hospitals.[13] We saw above that Spencer and Knudsen included hospitals[14] in their study of the rates of abuse in different out-of-home care settings. The maltreatment rate in hospitals/other facilities of 15.66

10 Referred to as "sexual deviation on the part of staff" (Lambert and Millham, 1968, p. 272)

11 This will be dealt with in more detail in the section on `Bullying'

12 The figures presented in Table 4 on page 28 are slightly different to those presented in the text on page 22.

13 The abuse of children with disabilities in hospitals and psychiatric settings is dealt with in the section `The Abuse of Children with Disabilities',

14 This research included `hospitals and other facilities'

per 1,000 children was the second lowest rate. Sexual abuse was the most frequent type of maltreatment in hospitals and other facilities: 8.54 per 1,000; followed by physical abuse - 5.70; and neglect - 1.42 (Spencer and Knudsen, 1992, pp. 488 - 489).

In the UK the literature is very limited and in an overview of the changes in the care of children in hospital and the areas of concern which still remain, there is no mention of the abuse of children or child protection in hospitals (Belson, 1993). The Royal College of Nursing, however, has recently prepared guidance "to raise awareness among nurses and their managers of the complex issues which need to be addressed in the light of recent cases where children have been harmed by nurses and other health care staff caring for them" (Royal College of Nursing, 1996).

Much of the literature which is available concerns the case of Beverley Allitt. Between February and April, 1991, three children died suddenly on Ward Four of Grantham and Kesteven General Hospital and a baby died shortly after discharge from the ward. Nine other babies and children collapsed unexpectedly, some of them more than once. Beverley Allitt was found guilty of four murders, three attempted murders and six instances of grievous bodily harm (Clothier, 1994, pp. 5-6). The Clothier Report identified a number of issues relating to absences through sickness while undergoing qualifying training and recruitment and found that "virtually none of the procedures in the hospital's recruitment policy was followed when Allitt was appointed" (Clothier, 1994, p. 22). Clothier states that:

> In fact, Occupational Health did not find any reason to reject her on health grounds and, since she had no criminal convictions, it is likely that she would have been appointed whether or not these checks were carried out promptly. Nevertheless, this series of failures to follow normal procedures is extremely worrying. Procedures to prevent unsuitable people from being employed on a children's ward should be rigorously applied. (Clothier, 1994, p. 22)

Clothier also criticised nurse staffing levels on the ward as inadequate in terms of both numbers and experience; consultant staffing was inadequate; management of the ward did not provide leadership and was criticized for "dilatory and ineffective action when apprised of suspicions of foul play". Senior management was criticized for "a general laxity of operational procedures within its responsibility and for indecisiveness in the later stages of the crisis" (Clothier, 1994, p. 125).

The Clothier Report identified only two previously reported cases of nurses attacking child patients. These appeared in the *New England Journal of Medicine* in 1985. In 1980/81, there was a dramatic increase in the mortality rate in the cardiology ward of a Toronto children's hospital. Investigation found that deaths were linked with digoxin poisoning. Although one nurse was arrested and accused of administering these overdoses, she was later released when it was found that a child had been poisoned when she was not on duty. Suspicion fell on a second nurse but she was never arrested. In the second case in Texas, USA, an unusual increase in the number of deaths and arrests in the paediatric intensive care unit of a large medical centre was found to be linked to the presence of one nurse. Clothier states that although she was never charged in respect of these incidents, "she was charged and convicted in 1984 on one count of attempted murder" (Clothier, 1994, p. 78)[15].

The Allitt case was linked to the form of child abuse which has become known as Munchausen Syndrome by Proxy.

> This term, first introduced by Professor Roy Meadow in 1977, is applied to a situation in which factitious injury or manifestation of illness is inflicted on others. The victims, usually children, suffer in a way that is comparable to the self-inflicted suffering of those with Munchausen syndrome (Clothier, 1994, p. 77)[16]

15 Repper gives details of this case and states that the nurse "was convicted of the murder of six babies at the private clinic" (Repper, 1995, p. 303)

16 For a recent review of Munchausen Syndrome by Proxy, see Donald and Jureidini (1996). This article argues that there needs to be explicit acknowledgement that Munchausen Syndrome by Proxy is child abuse; that there needs to be a narrower and much more rigorous definition of Munchausen Syndrom by Proxy; and that it needs to be managed in terms of child protection procedures and practice.

The Clothier Report states that in nearly all cases of Munchausen Syndrome by Proxy, "the abuse has been perpetrated by mothers on their own children, although there have been cases involving father, grandparents and other relatives or carers, but not nurses in a hospital setting" (Clothier, 1994, p. 77) . Clothier goes on to say that because of confusion surrounding its meaning, they did not "find the term Munchausen Syndrome by Proxy helpful in the context of our Inquiry" (Clothier, 1994, p. 79).

Following on from the Allitt case, Repper (1995) reviewed the literature on Munchausen Syndrome by Proxy to assess the incidence of this syndrome among health care workers. Repper found that "at least 14 criminal trials have occurred between 1975 and 1993 in which health care providers were associated with epidemics of adverse patient outcome" (Repper, 1995, p. 302). However, only four of these led to convictions. Repper argues that while the consideration of the similarities between Munchausen Syndrome by Proxy in parents and in health care workers is complicated by the more complex system of relationships, "there are potentially similar characteristics and dynamics in terms of the motivators and rewards for the behaviour demonstrated: the need to belong, the need for attention, recognition, revenge, success, power, control" (Repper, 1995, p. 302). She details five cases of children harmed by their carers (a baby-sitter, a foster mother, and three nurses) which share features of Munchausen Syndrome by Proxy.

> The evidence of a previous history of self-harm or suspicious behaviour in several of the cases cited suggests that careful attention to the backgrounds of nurses at the point of selection and employment is essential. It also confirms the importance of ongoing supervision and appraisal of health care workers (Repper, 1995, p. 303).

A number of articles have discussed the implications of the Allitt case for the protection of children in hospitals and tend to focus on issues relating to the recommendations of the Allitt Inquiry: the sickness record and mental health of those seeking entry into the nursing profession and the involvement of occupational health services: the practice of coroners and the involvement of paediatric pathology services; monitoring equipment; reporting of serious untoward incidents; and the staffing levels on children's wards (Allen, 1993; Friend, 1993; Glasper and Whiting, 1993; Leenders, 1995; Lunn, 1994; MacDonald, 1995, 1996; Rogers, 1993; Royal College of Nursing, 1994).

Long (1992) discusses the case of a registered nurse convicted of four counts of indecent assault on two 13-year old boys and sentenced to two years in prison. The offences took place while Philip Donnelly was director of nursing services at Booth Hall Children's Hospital in Manchester and occurred both in his office and outwith the hospital. The article focuses on the fact that the United Kingdom Central Council for Nursing, Midwifery and Health Visiting (UKCC) Professional Conduct Committee, although finding him guilty of professional misconduct, allowed him to remain on the register and continue in practice. Long concludes that the case shows "to the profession that gross acts of indecency and misconduct will be tolerated among its members" and that a "message has been sent to the British public that the governing statutory body of nursing cannot be trusted to act responsibly to prioritize public safety before the career interests of an individual practitioner" (Long, 1992, p. 9).

> … the Council has failed to protect the public. Moreover, since it represents the profession, and there is no mechanism for the members of the profession to challenge its decision, then the Council has also failed the profession (Long, 1992, p. 9)

The Royal College of Nursing guidance focuses on issues relating to protection of children from sexual abuse of children (Royal College of Nursing, 1996). The guidance highlights that respect for privacy and dignity is a right for all children. Principles for good practice where work requires care of an intimate or personal nature include: negotiation with and explanation to the child and the child's main carer; presence of a parent or other carer if care of an intimate nature is to be given in a community setting; awareness of accepted cultural and social norms of the society the child comes from; promotion of self-care where possible involving the child's main carer;

responsiveness to the child's reactions; the child's personal preferences should be documented in the care plan to ensure consistency of approach; the results of actions should be documented and concerns reported; and all nurses should have a supervisor working closely with them (Royal College of Nursing, 1996).

Penal Institutions

Of all the settings covered in this review, abuse of young people by staff in penal institutions appears to be the least well documented in research and other literature. The Howard League for Penal Reform Commission of Inquiry into Violence in Penal Institutions for Teenagers under 18 looked at three types of prison: young offender institutions (YOI) holding teenagers serving sentences; remand centres (usually attached to a YOI) and local adult prisons holding teenagers on remand (Howard League, 1995a). The remit of the Commission was to investigate the extent and causes of violence and included "all forms of bullying, fighting, intimidation and abuse carried out by young people or staff... also... self-harm and suicide which are often directly linked to physical or verbal intimidation" (Howard League, 1995a, p. 5). The concerns of the Commission in relation to abuse of young people by staff focused on the use of physical control and restraint.

> Commissioners found no evidence of prison officers routinely "cuffing" prisoners (although a couple of officers said they had physically threatened bullies). Some governors emphasised their intention to prevent such behaviour, including the Governor of Feltham who has recently dismissed two members of staff following allegations of assault. However, a number of prisoners complained of excessive force being used during restraint (Howard League, 1995a, pp. 43-44)

The report of the Commission dealt in depth, however, with the issues of bullying and violent assault by young people, and self-harm and suicide. The Commission's findings, along with other literature on these issues, is dealt with in detail below.

Factors in Abuse in Residential Settings

The Isolation of Residential Care

> Institutions function as a closed system with their own established policies and procedures for operating and for defining their contacts with the outside world (Nunno and Motz, 1988, p. 523; see also Harrell and Orem, 1980)

Berridge and Brodie, in discussing the Leicestershire and Ty Mawr cases, identify the social isolation of the units and "problems may thus have been more likely to have remained undetected" (1996). While Berridge and Brodie suggest that this isolation had not occurred in the 'pindown' case in Staffordshire, Wardhaugh and Wilding argue, that "in common with many other institutions where corruption of care has taken place, there was a marked sense of isolation and conservatism, both within the institutions themselves and within the county's child care services as a whole" (Wardhaugh and Wilding, 1993, p. 22). The physical and geographical isolation of residential establishments also reduces visits by professionals and families. There is thus more potential for the denial of abuse than in the wider community.

> Local authority, educational and childcare establishments which are situated long distances from the placing authorities or the children's families and are not networked into the larger organisation feature in a significant number of investigations (Doran and Brannan, 1996, p. 159; see also Spencer and Knudsen, 1992; Sullivan et al, 1987).

Many staff working in residential facilities believe that the incidence of harmful acts and omissions is exaggerated (Gil and Baxter, 1979; Rindfleisch and Rabb, 1984a). Reports of maltreatment tend to originate from outside institutions and:

> Children isolated in institutions are much less subject to external scrutiny, have fewer outside contacts and are therefore less likely to be reported (Powers, Mooney and Nunno, 1990, p. 86)

Children in residential establishments are themselves "particularly isolated, both socially and geographically..., again mirroring the kind of isolation experienced by abusive families" (Westcott, 1991, p. 12).

The power imbalance between adults and children is exacerbated by the residential environment:

> Weakness and vulnerability are characteristics of long-stay patients in mental handicap hospitals or geriatric hospitals, or of children in care. They have little power or influence, little knowledge of how the organisation works, little awareness of how to assert their rights or how to call to account those on whom they often depend for the basic elements of living (Wardhaugh and Wilding, 1993, pp. 11-12; see also Crossmaker. 1991; Westcott, 1991a)[17]

This is a crucial factor in inhibiting children from reporting abuse and has been highlighted in Inquiry reports (Hughes, 1986; Levy and Kahan, 1991, Kirkwood, 1993).

> Children in institutions are frequently described as a 'voiceless' population, having no control over decisions affecting their current and future placements, and no influence over the quality of care they receive (Westcott, 1991a, pp. 12-13; see also Brannan et al, 1993a, 1993b; Gil and Baxter, 1979; Nunno and Motz, 1988)

Siskind also stresses that children in institutions are often particularly vulnerable to sexual abuse "because of their developmental lags and insecurities and their increased reliance on adults" (Siskind, 1986, p. 15).

Management and Organisation

Berridge and Brodie, in their comparison of the Staffordshire, Ty Mawr and Leicestershire Inquiry reports, identify three common features of management.

> In all three instances line management of facilities and heads of homes tended to be ineffective or non-existent. Line managers also had minimal, if any, direct contact with units and so were in no position to observe malpractice, assuming of course that they would have recognised it. Adequate complaints systems were not in place (Berridge and Brodie, 1996, p. 184)

Wardhaugh and Wilding stress the "absence of clear lines and mechanisms of accountability" as a factor in institutional abuse where:

> management... often neglects its responsibility to know what goes on, to set appropriate standards and to insist on staff accountability. Front-line staff are frequently simply left to get on with things (Wardhaugh and Wilding, 1993, p. 24)

Siskind discusses a number of 'administrative styles' which have been identified with patterns of institutional sexual abuse: an autocratic director, protected by strong political and administrative networks, discourages participation by staff and residents in shared decision-making; emphasis is placed on the difficulty of handling residents and on control; reliance is placed on theoretical or ideological models which tend to distance and dehumanize relationships with residents; and an oppressor mentality promotes hostility toward females, children or minorities (Siskind, 1986, p. 20; see also Crossmaker, 1991; Wardaugh and Wilding, 1993, Westcott, 1991a).

17 Elliott et al, from interviews with 91 child sex abusers, report that "... nearly half (49%) of the offenders reported they were attracted to children who seemed to lack confidence or had low self esteem. As one man commented, "you can spot the child who is unsure of himself and target him with compliments and positive attention" (Elliot et al, 1995, p. 584)

Pay and Conditions of Residential Staff

Durkin (1982a) stresses the fact that institutional work brings out the worst in child care workers. Baldwin cites research which showed how the attitudes of child care workers on the causes and handling of delinquency changed from being 'quite enlightened and permissive' when they started working in residential care to being "much less permissive", and showing "punitive, unenlightened views, shared with other personnel" (Baldwin, 1990, p. 150) when they had done the job for some time[18]. Residential workers are often overworked and underpaid and they have little say in decision-making (Agathanos, 1983, Baldwin, 1990; Gil and Baxter, 1979; Nunno and Rindfleisch, 1991; Powers, Mooney and Nunno, 1990; Siskind, 1986; Spencer and Knudsen, 1992; Wardhaugh and Wilding, 1993; Westcott, 1991a).

> Abuse seems to occur when adults are unable to cope with the stress under which they live and take out their frustrations on troublesome, vulnerable children (Durkin, 1982a, p. 17; see also Harrell and Orem, 1980; Powers, Mooney and Nunno, 1990; Sundram, 1986; Westcott, 1991a)

> *"It's just a nine-to-five job. All they are bothered about is the pay cheque at the end of the week. They don't give a toss about young people's views or privacy. If they have a bad day at home or something, then they take it out on the people who are around them - the kids"* (Safe & Sound, 1995, p. 7)

Nunno and Rindfleisch also point out that child care staff have conflicting demands placed on them with little support (Nunno and Rindfleisch, 1991, p. 296). Generally, they are poorly trained and inadequately screened (Gil and Baxter, 1979; Powers, Mooney and Nunno, 1990; West, 1995; Westcott, 1991a).

> Like abusive parents, child care workers are left overstressed, isolated and without a sufficient support system (Nunno and Rindfleisch, 1991, p. 296).

Tired caregivers suffering from burnout may abuse children (Maslach, 1983, in Dowd and Daly, 1992) and a number of authors have identified the way in which burnout is characterised by increasing negative attitudes towards clients or children including depersonalisation and dehumanisation (Edwards and Miltenberger, 1991; Maslach and Jackson, 1981; Mattingly, 1981; Swanson, 1987)[19] . Harrell and Orem suggest that "institutional maltreatment often results from the gradual development by a staff member of a *pattern* of reacting impulsively and impatiently to residents and of resorting more and more frequently to physical solutions to the problems of confrontation and challenged authority (Harrell and Orem, 1980, p. 16; see also Wardhaugh and Wilding, 1993).

> "Burn-out" can also contribute to an institutional climate in which there is greater potential for sexual abuse (Siskind, 1986, p. 19)

McGrath (1986) highlights the potential for the alienated, burnt-out child care worker to influence practice in a unit or team:

> This domineering, influential team member, skilled at introducing elements into team practice and team climate which are disconcerting or downright distasteful, often bullies other team members into collusion, into accepting and even executing utterly unpalatable practice (McGrath, 1986, p. 60)

Harrell and Orem (1980) have suggested that high child to adult ratios may contribute to incidents of maltreatment and Blatt and Brown (1986) found that staff to child ratio was one of the factors related to abuse incidents. Stressors such as staff lay-offs and the movement of groups of children to new living areas were also related to abuse incidents (Blatt and Brown, 1986, p. 178). Blatt (1992) found that episodes of suspected abuse and neglect were more likely to occur between 5.00 p.m. and 8.00 a.m. and that early morning (7.00 a.m.) and early evening (7.00 p.m. to 9.00 p.m.) had particularly high incident rates.

18 See also the discussion below, page 221.

19 For a review of the literature on stress and burnout in relation to residential child care, see Kendrick and Fraser, 1992.

> These times coincide with the times that youngsters are getting up and dressed in the morning, and finishing dinner and getting ready to go to bed in the evening - times that are typically some of the most chaotic parts of the day. They are also times when less programming is available and professional staff are typically not working (Blatt, 1992, p. 514)

Haddock and McQueen (1983) developed a battery of screening tests to identify an employee's potential for child abuse: "Milner's Child Abuse Potential Inventory[20], the Minnesota Satisfaction Questionnaire, and a General Information Form..." (Haddock and McQueen, 1983, p. 1022). This battery of tests was administered to a sample of "21 identified abusive employees and 21 non-abusive employees employed or previously employed by out-of-home care institutions in Southern California" (Haddock and McQueen, 1983, p. 1022).

Haddock and McQueen (1983) found that 17 subscales of the Minnesota Satisfaction Questionnaire were significantly related to abusive behaviour in child care employees (Haddock and McQueen, 1983, p. 1023) and three were identified by multiple regression analysis as among "the "best" 8 items, which accounted for 73% of the variance" between the two groups (Haddock and McQueen, 1983, p. 1024). MSQ-10 Independence measures an employee's satisfaction on the chance to work alone on the job and "it appears that the abusive employee is dissatisfied in the chance to isolate himself and to work independently of others" (Haddock and McQueen, 1983, p. 1024). MSQ-4 Advancement measures an employee's satisfaction in the hope of advancement or promotion and MSQ-2 measures an employee's satisfaction in the feeling of accomplishment he receives from the job.

> One of the major eliciting behaviors identified by child-care staff in this study's pilot interview was not seeing progress in the child. When minimal progress with the child is experienced, the job becomes more frustrating and less rewarding. Pines (1977) study on employee "burn-out" reported that staff members who were experiencing a sense of success had a much more positive view of themselves and their clients... Abusive employees apparently do not experience this feeling of success (Haddock and McQueen, 1983, p. 1027; see also Poteat et al, 1989; Atten and Milner, 1987)

Haddock and McQueen (1983) found that the abusers in their study had more children and that "abusive caretakers were 1.5 times more likely to be married even though they were statistically matched with a similar non-abusive employee" (Haddock and McQueen, 1983, p. 1027). The abusers also tended to consume more alcohol. Blatt (1992) found that the average age of workers accused of abusing or neglecting children was 31.9 years and younger workers (<35 years) were over-represented as alleged perpetrators compared to the staff work-force (Blatt, 1992, p. 504). Over three-quarters of the alleged abusers were male in marked contrast to the proportion of males in the work-force where over two-thirds of the groups of workers largely responsible for the direct care of children are female.

Durkin suggests that there are two ways to address the issue of stress: to change the way adults cope with the stress or to relieve the strains placed on them and that the latter may be more fruitful than the former.

> To achieve this, we must address the strains that are placed on child care workers: conflicting demands, too much work, too few rewards (Durkin, 1982a, p. 18)

Durkin presents the model of the *educateur* as a way of reducing the stress of the child care role. The *educateur* is a trained generalist; "an overseer of the group life, who organizes daily routine" and has the responsibility and commensurate training and authority to organise children's lives and to use other professionals on a consultative basis (Durkin, 1982a, pp. 18-19)[21].

> This would provide the potential for workers to develop a serious career in child care and for attracting appropriately trained and motivated individuals... The professional child care specialist or *educateur* model would also lessen the powerlessness and isolation that have proven so detrimental to institutional abuse of children. (Durkin, 1982a, pp. 19)

20 The Child Abuse Potential Inventory and other assessment instruments for physical child abuse are reviewed in Milner (1991); see also Milner et al, 1984; Milner and Robertson, 1985; Robertson and Milner, 1985; Robitaille et al, 1985; Monroe and Schellenbach, 1988. However, as discussed in the section on Recruitment and Selection, extreme caution must be used with such predictive tools. Milner (1991) stresses that multiple measures should be used and tests should be used alongside interviews and observation (Milner, 1991, pp. 58-59)

21 In the context of `pindown' in Staffordshire, Crimmens discusses the higher levels of professionalisation of residential care staff in European countries such as Belgium and Holland, and the role of the "social pedagogue" in residential care (Crimmens, 1994)

Targeting of Residential Care by Paedophiles

> Tony never sexually abused any of the boys while they lived in the three homes where he worked. Instead he groomed them, very slowly, very patiently to acquire their trust. When they left care, Tony kept in touch. Soon they were visiting his home on a regular basis. Then the buggery would begin (Downey, 1992, p. 12)

Tony abused 50 boys over a 30 year period from the age of 25. He met them at youth clubs, sailing and canoeing and he did courses in outward bound activities. He worked in three residential establishments before he was convicted of two charges of buggery and eight of gross indecency.

> **Tony**
> *All my life I groomed and conned parents and boys. All the way through my job I conned the senior people above me and I have bluffed my way through that. It makes me feel like shit to know there are thousands of people out there doing it still.*
> (Downey, 1992, p. 13)

The literature stresses that paedophiles target work settings and activities which will give them access to children whom they can abuse: schools (Sullivan et al, 1987, p. 256); hospitals (Royal College of Nursing, 1996); youth work (Cullen, 1996); coaching of sporting activities (Dispatches, 1996).

> As with any area of work in which adults have close and continuous interaction with children and young people, residential child care settings - in which there will be many children who are particularly vulnerable because abuse will have already become an integral part of their personal history - are likely to attract those individuals who might seek to take advantage of the position of responsibility and authority in which they are placed (NCH, 1992, p. 16; see also Brookhouser et al, 1986; Marchant and Page, 1992)

Research of child sexual abusers has also identified the ways in which they target their victims. In interviews with 91 child sex abusers, Elliott et al found that:

> The offenders used more than one type of strategy to approach the children or their families. Most often they offered to play games with the children, or teach them a sport, or how to play a musical instrument (53%). Many also gave bribes, took them for an outing, or gave them a lift home (46%)... It is highly significant that 48% of the offenders isolated their victims through babysitting. (Elliott et al, 1995, p. 585).

Colton and Vanstone give a detailed account from in-depth interviews with seven men who worked with children and who sexually abused them.

> The amount of convergence between career and abuse motivation varies from the explicit, to the implicit, to an apparent absence of any. It is clearest in the case of Harry, who saw in voluntary work the opportunity to form relationships with children... Kim closely links the invitation to engage in voluntary work - again with no checks - and his awareness of the potential in the situation to abuse. Similarly, although he makes no connection himself, James very quickly offered to undertake other staff members' sleep-ins when he first took up employment in a children's home. The fact that he later reveals this tactic as part of his broader strategy to manipulate the system so that he could abuse the boys in his care strongly suggests a pre-determination to use his employment for that purpose (Colton and Vanstone, 1996, p. 180)

Doran and Brannan (1996) state that there are two principal archetypes of institutional abusers. They are not explicit about whether they are talking primarily about child sexual abusers but their discussion of "the 'grooming' stage" would suggest this. The first is "the charismatic, articulate, well-networked 'caring professional' who is usually part of the leadership of the institution" while the second is "not well integrated into the social network of the institution and could be characterised as just an isolated, but dutiful, staff member who is perhaps over-helpful to colleagues and children, and frequently does things outside normal duties" (Doran and Brannan, 1996, p. 158; see also Downey, 1992).

Jones (1994) uses Weber's concepts of 'traditional' and 'charismatic' domination to analyse the authority structure in Castle Hill School and the sexual and physical abuse perpetrated by Ralph Morris.

> ... the appeal of the charismatic leader, particularly one who has risen through the ranks of institutions himself, coupled with the opportunity to become his disciple, may offer such vulnerable children the sense of self-esteem and power that has been so lacking in their own lives (Jones, 1994, p. 72)

Jones further argues that the combination of charismatic and traditional authority may be "particularly attractive to the agents of rational-legal authority in the placement of children labelled as "maladjusted." (Jones, 1994, p. 74). He suggests that current mechanisms of "rational-legal regulation from the outside looking in" cannot succeed and there needs to be a greater understanding of the way in which charismatic and traditional authority structures operate in institutions.

> The institutional abuser ranges from the disturbed person who lacks impulse control to the worker who feels excessive fondness for children and whose sexual involvement with them is both a disturbed expression of affection and as symptom failure in more acceptable sexual relationships. Most frequently, institutional sex abuse is an impulsive and isolated act committed by a worker with no history of abuse but with clearly unresolved sexual conflicts and significant emotional immaturity (Siskind, 1986, p. 18)

However, this focus on the abuser must not detract from the broader organisational, social and political issues which are crucial in understanding abuse in residential care (Baldwin, 1990, Westcott, 1991a). Pringle discusses the broader issues of abuse by men and he argues that "if the male potential for abuse is so organically linked to both masculinity and entrenched patriarchal structures as suggested in this paper" (Pringle, 1993, p. 16), then the role of men in care services must be questioned.

Abuse in Foster Care

Introduction

The literature on the abuse and neglect of children in foster care placements is scarce, particularly in the UK (Kendrick, 1994; Thomas, 1995). We have seen that there is a developing literature about abuse in residential settings but relatively little has appeared on the incidence of abuse by foster carers. In 1986, however, Roberts, discussing the issue of fostering children who had been sexually abused, commented that, given the rate of child sexual abuse in the general population, "it must be happening in some foster homes at the moment" (Roberts, 1986, p. 10). Pringle goes further and argues that "such evidence as does exist points in one direction: fostering seems as unsafe as residential alternatives" (Pringle, 1993, p. 5). In the USA, Rindfleisch and Rabb also write that there "is widespread concern among public child protection agencies, both at state and local levels, that the occurrence of abuse and neglect in foster family care is a matter of greater urgency than is abuse and neglect in child welfare institutions" (Rindfleisch and Rabb, 1984b, p. 206; see also Gustavsson and Segal, 1994, pp. 95-97).

Research Evidence from the USA

Material from the United States on child abuse and neglect in substitute family care tends to be more systematic than that available in this country. Cavara and Ogren (1983) describe the development of a protocol for the investigation of institutional abuse and neglect of children in Hennepin County Community Services Department in 1980 and their paper focuses on abuse which occurred in family foster homes. They comment first on the large number of investigations which were carried out. Hennepin County has approximately 570 foster homes and in the 18 months studied, there were 125 investigations. Investigation findings have to be categorised as either:

> *Substantiated*: An admission of the fact of abuse or neglect or a confirmation deemed valid (i.e. bruises)
>
> *Not Substantiated:* The complaint, although it may have been made in good faith, is found to have no substance
>
> *Unable to Substantiate:* Insufficient evidence for a substantiated report is present, but there remains reason to suspect abuse or neglect
>
> (Cavara and Ogren, 1983, p. 288)

The paper gives details of 81 "substantiated" and "unable to substantiate" incidents. These were of three types of abuse: sexual abuse, neglect and physical abuse. There were 5 incidents of substantiated sexual abuse and 6 that were unable to be substantiated; 8 substantiated incidents of neglect and 20 unable to be substantiated; and 16 cases of substantiated physical abuse and 26 unable to be substantiated (Cavara and Ogren, 1983, pp. 290-291). Thus almost one quarter (23%) of reported incidents were substantiated and two-fifths (42%) were unable to be substantiated[22]. Since social workers were initially reluctant to make a finding of substantiated abuse without irrefutable evidence, Cavara and Ogren do not distinguish "substantiated" and "unable to substantiate" incidents in most of their analysis; "in the belief that they are more

22 Figures were not given for the breakdown of "not substantiated" incidents, so it is not possible to calculate comparative substantiation rates.

representative of institutional abuse" (Cavara and Ogren, 1983, p. 291). In the 11 sexual abuse cases, 9 of the victims were male and 9 were female. One child was under 3 years of age, seven were between 4 and 12 and 10 were 13 or older. In the 28 neglect cases, seven of the 50 victims were aged 0-3, 27 were 4-12, and 16 were 13 or older. There were 60 victims in the physical abuse cases; 35 male and 25 female. Four were aged 0-3, 35 were 4-12, and 18 were 13 and older[23] (Cavara and Ogren, 1983, pp. 290-91).

All the perpetrators in the 11 sexual abuse cases were male. In the 28 neglect cases, the foster mother was considered to be the perpetrator in 19, the foster father in 2 and both in 7 cases. No figures are given for the perpetrators of physical abuse. The authors found three factors which distinguished the study families from the general foster family population: there was a higher proportion of single mothers (46% compared to 30%); they tended to have been licensed for a greater length of time (64% were licensed over 4 years compared to 47%); and a higher proportion were childless (34% compared to 17%) (Cavara and Ogren, 1983, p. 292).

Rosenthal et al (1991) describe 290 reported incidents of abuse and neglect in family foster homes, group homes, residential treatment centres and institutions in Colorado. 38% (102 of 272; 18 missing cases) of the reported incidents took place in foster homes (50 incidents of physical abuse, 22 of neglect, and 30 of sexual abuse). Overall, 29% of the cases were confirmed (56% of sexual abuse cases, 18% of physical abuse cases, and 28% of neglect cases). 38% of the reported incidents in foster homes were confirmed. Males were the predominant victims of both physical abuse and neglect while females were the predominant sexual abuse victims.

325 perpetrators were identified from 261 reported incidents (29 cases missing). Foster carers were identified in 45 cases of physical abuse, 34 of neglect and 20 of sexual abuse. Foster siblings were identified in 7 cases of physical abuse, 9 of neglect and 15 of sexual abuse. A point with important policy implications to be taken from this study is the number of foster siblings perpetrating sexual abuse. This can be linked to the findings that sexual abuse by non-parental adolescent care-givers is more common than that by older non-parental care-givers (Margolin and Craft, 1990; Margolin, 1991).

In discussion, Rosenthal et al suggest that multiple factors lead to abuse. There are shortages of foster homes because of low remuneration. This creates pressure to license as many homes as possible. Further, the emphasis on placing children in the least restrictive setting leads to difficult, behaviourally disturbed children being fostered. There is also a lack of adequate support for foster carers because of large caseloads.

> These events combine with stress in the family home - perhaps the husband is laid off at work - to create a tension-filled setting. A foster child reacts to this tension with provoking behavior and is abused. The children are removed, placed in another home, and a similar cycle repeats. The county investigation assigns blame to the foster family, (Rosenthal et al, 1991, pp. 257 - 258)

However, Molin, although not discussing abuse explicitly, also makes the important point that because of the chronic shortage of foster care, there are pressures on the agency to see placement problems as stemming from a bad match or frankly attributed to the child; "there is a cost to categorizing a setting as unable to care for any child rather than simply unsuitable for a particular child" (Molin, 1988, p. 244).

We saw above that Spencer and Knudsen (1992) compared the rate of maltreatment in various out-of-home care settings. Foster homes had a maltreatment rate of 16.93 per 1,000: sexual abuse - 5.23 per 1,000; physical abuse - 9.31; and neglect - 2.38. Spencer and Knudsen give a limited amount of information about the perpetrators of the abuse and "custodians were involved in sexual abuse in foster homes in 78 percent (60/77) cases... child perpetrators were involved in 6% of the foster home cases" (Spencer and Knudsen, 1992, p. 488).[24]

23 The ages of 3 children were unknown.

24 Figures on perpetrators of abuse were for the years 1987-1990. Equivalent figures for physical abuse were not presented.

Zuravin et al (1992) present information about foster home characteristics associated with confirmed maltreatment of a foster child and compares this to a random sample of foster homes where foster children had not been reported for maltreatment. The sample consisted of 62 foster homes with at least one confirmed maltreatment report and 234 foster homes where there had not been a report (Zuravin et al, 1992, p. 560). Sexual abuse was the most prevalent type of abuse, occurring in 48% of the maltreating homes, followed by physical abuse (39%) and neglect (29%)[25]. The perpetrator was a foster parent in almost two thirds of the sexual abuse cases and almost all of the physical abuse and neglect cases. The authors found few correlates between maltreatment and foster home characteristics.

> Eight variables… were associated with maltreatment. At application, maltreating homes were more likely than were comparisons to include younger mothers…, mothers with health problems, and fathers with less than high school education…..; to be restricted regarding placement of certain types of children; and to be regular foster homes. At relicensing, maltreating families were more likely than were comparisons to have foster children who shared bedrooms with each other or with foster parents, to have younger foster mothers, and to have had one or more negative conditions (i.e. foster parent health problem, income, age etc.) (Zuravin et al 1992, p. 262)

However, attempts by the authors to develop predictive models from characteristics at licensing and relicensing were unsuccessful (Zuravin et al 1992, p. 262).

In a study of the Casey Family Program, Fanshel et al report that 15% of a sample of former foster children revealed that someone in their foster home had tried to 'take advantage of them sexually' (Fanshel et al, 1990, cited in Pringle, 1993). However, these figures have been criticised on methodological grounds (Pecora, 1991, cited in Pringle, 1993).

In her study of rape and sexual abuse, Russell (1984) interviewed 930 adult women residents of San Francisco. Sixteen percent (152) of this sample had at least one experience of incestuous abuse before they were eighteen. 74 of the 186 cases of incestuous child abuse occurred within the nuclear family.

> Forty-two women reported an incestuous relationship with their fathers before the age of 18 (including 27 biological fathers, 15 step, 1 foster, and 1 adoptive father). (Russell, 1984, p. 186)

Evidence from the UK

In the UK, as Pringle (1993) points out, evidence tends to be more anecdotal (see also Sone, 1992). However, some studies do have information relating to abuse in foster and adoptive families. In research which focused on the issues of caring for sexually abused children in foster placements, Macaskill (1991) gives details of the abuse. She studied 66 foster families although she acknowledges that these families do not constitute a representative sample since they were nominated by the 11 social services departments and 8 voluntary agencies who agreed to take part in the research. The placements of 80 children were studied in depth and the research found 8 cases of abuse in previous foster or adoptive placements. The foster or adoptive father was the abuser in 5 cases and the foster mother's boyfriend in another case. In one case the abuse was perpetrated by the foster mother and in one case by a foster brother (Macaskill, 1991).

In the Triseliotis et al study of social work services to teenagers, 27 young people experienced a total of 37 foster care placements during the study year (Triseliotis et al, 1995, p. 99). Two girls were sexually abused in foster care, one by the male foster carer, and one by "a family friend who had taken her in on a private fostering basis" (Triseliotis et al, 1995, p. 190).

La Fontaine studied 204 cases referred to the child sexual abuse unit of a London hospital between 1981 and 1984 (La Fontaine, 1990). Details are given of 259 perpetrators in these cases (220 perpetrators where the victim was a girl and 39 perpetrators where the victim was a boy).

25 Percentages add to more than 100% because homes involving more than one type of abuse were included in the count for each

Four per cent of the perpetrators abusing girls and three per cent of those abusing boys were classified as a foster father or foster brother. In addition to this, three adoptive fathers perpetrated the sexual abuse. This compares to only one case where the perpetrator was a worker in a children's home (La Fontaine, 1990, p. 121).

The ChildLine analysis of calls made by 539 children in England and Wales and 137 children in Scotland also gives details of abuse in foster care (Morris and Wheatley, 1995). In the English study, 24 of the children known to be in foster care reported being sexually abused.

> Foster brothers were the most common perpetrators of sexual abuse reported on the line, accounting for 11 of the 24 cases in foster care... A significant factor seemed to be the age difference between the predominantly male abusers and the foster child; the abusers were commonly two or three years older. There were also children who were being abused by a foster father figure, either a live-in partner or a boyfriend regularly visiting the house (Morris and Wheatley, 1995, pp. 38-39)

Twenty of the children reported being physically abused and information from the ChildLine study "indicated that physical abuse from carers was more of a problem for children in foster than residential care" (Morris and Wheatley, 1995, pp. 39). In most cases (13) the abuser was the foster father, in 5 cases both foster parents were abusers, and in the other two cases it was a parent or the abuser was unknown.

> Children commonly described the physical abuse taking place when their foster mother was out, at work in the evening or socialising. Another group described foster fathers who drank regularly and were more likely to hit them when drunk. Some girls said the abuse started when they became involved in relationships with boys. Others described foster parents who used physical abuse as a form of discipline (Morris and Wheatley, 1995, p. 40)

The most recent study of abuse in foster care was carried out by NFCA and the University of Birmingham as part of an international study of allegations of abuse (Verity and Nixon, 1995; Nixon and Verity, 1996). A survey of social services and social work departments was conducted in 1995 seeking information on: the type of procedures used in investigating allegations of abuse; the nature of support of and communication with foster carers; the removal and return of foster children; and whether foster carers continued to foster during and after investigations (Nixon and Verity, 1996, p. 11). 59 departments returned questionnaires and these departments had accommodated 13,333 children in 7,719 foster homes during 1994. 305 reports of abuse were investigated during the year under study, representing 4% of foster homes. Just over one-fifth of the cases (67) were substantiated and in a further fifth of cases investigating staff were not able to determine whether or not abuse had occurred (Nixon and Verity, 1996, p. 11). In 44 cases the foster carers' own child was the alleged perpetrator: 12 cases were substantiated; in 12 cases there was no determination of whether abuse had occurred or not (Nixon and Verity, 1996, p. 12).

Comparison of Abuse in Foster Care, Residential Care and the Family Home

Reflecting possibly the high profile nature of some of the scandals of abuse in residential care, there has been an assumption that abuse of children in care tends to take place in residential homes. Waller and Lindsay, for example, state that opportunities for abuse are greatest in residential care (Waller and Lindsay, 1990). La Fontaine's figures and the evidence from ChildLine suggest that this might not be the case. Pringle (1993), while acknowledging that more research is required before an absolute judgement can be made, argues that foster care seems just as unsafe as residential care. He cites his experience in working in an independent agency which specialised in family placement of teenagers who were 'difficult to place' and/or who had been sexually abused. He states that "it was common to take referral of adolescents who had been abused in local authority foster placements" (Pringle, 1993, p. 6). Spencer and Knudsen's study, however, shows rates of abuse in foster homes which were much lower than those in residential homes.

There is also evidence that abuse is more prevalent in foster care than the general population. A Canadian study of the abuse of children in foster care estimates that proportionately children in care are more susceptible to being abused (Dawson, 1989, cited in Waller and Lindsay, 1990). In New York a report from the central registry suggests that fatalities in foster care due to abuse and neglect, although small in absolute numbers, may appear at two to three times the frequency of the general population (New York State Department of Social Services, 1980, cited in Nunno and Motz, 1988). The rates of physical and sexual abuse in foster homes in Spencer and Knudsen's study were also higher than the rates in the family home (Spencer and Knudsen, 1992, p. 489).

> In foster homes, physical abuse is the most likely form of maltreatment... sexual abuse is over twice as likely to be reported in foster homes and over thirty times as often in residential homes, as in the child's own home (Spencer and Knudsen, 1992, p. 488).

Bolton et al (1981) and Benedict et al (1994) specifically compared the rate of child maltreatment reports in foster placements with that of the general population. Bolton et al analysed a 50% sample of child maltreatment reports referred for investigation to the Maricopa County unit of the Arizona Department of Economic Security's Child Protective Services from the beginning of 1976 to the end of 1978. This yielded a sample of 5,098 cases and 114 of the 11,653 children involved were foster children. Comparing these figures to the total number of children in foster care during the study period, Bolton et al estimate that approximately 7% of foster children were at risk of living in families reported for suspected child maltreatment. This compared to 2% for children in the general population (Bolton et al, 1983, pp. 41-42). Although a slightly higher percentage of reports were substantiated in non-foster homes than in foster homes (35.4% compared to 29.8%), this was not statistically significant and the authors conclude:

> Given the level of scrutiny faced by the foster family - subjected to frequent observations by a trained social worker - it is not surprising that there is a regular occurrence of being reported for suspected maltreatment. Some question as to the social worker's ability to increase the capacity of that family to deal with the needs of the foster child does arise when faced with the information that, within this specialized home, the rate of substantiated maltreatment is equal to that in homes in the general maltreating population (Bolton et al, 1983, p.51)

An analysis of basic demographic variables found that the foster parent group reported for maltreatment tended to be older, to have a higher income and to have higher rates of marriage than the general population. The authors acknowledge that this is as would be expected. However, they also note that the foster parent group reported for maltreatment also tended to be older than foster parents in the community, raising questions about the role of foster parents' age in the conduct and success of placements (Bolton et al, 1983, pp. 49-50).

Benedict et al (1994) describe the prevalence, types, and severity of maltreatment reports in family foster homes in Maryland, Baltimore and compare these to non-foster families in the community. Information on reports of maltreatment in Baltimore city foster homes was obtained from Child Protective Services records for the years 1984-1988 and statistics on reports of maltreatment in non-foster families was provided by the Department of Social Services for some of the years of the study period. 443 reports were received on 285 foster families over the five years. Physical abuse alone was alleged in over 60% of reports, neglect in 17.4% and sexual abuse in 10.7%. 10.5% of reports involved more than one maltreatment type. Over 55% of sexual abuse cases were substantiated compared to less than 9% of physical abuse cases. Substantiation of neglect allegations varied between 20% and 40% of the cases over the time period (Benedict et al, 1994, p. 580). In substantiated cases, the most frequent physical abuse injuries were cuts or bruises with 7.2% of children having more serious fractures or burns[26]. Intercourse or attempted intercourse was involved in almost two-thirds of the substantiated sexual abuse cases, the remainder involving fondling, harassment, or exposure by the perpetrator. Inadequate supervision by the caretaker occurred in just over one-third of the substantiated neglect cases, neglect of the

26 Severity or type of injury was not known in a quarter of the cases.

child's physical health care in just under one-third, and neglect of hygiene, nutrition and household sanitation were involved in 20% of cases (Benedict et al, 1994, p. 580).

Foster carers were the designated perpetrators in over 80% of the physical abuse and neglect allegations, but were designated in only 40% of the sexual abuse allegations; foster siblings and others were more frequently designated as perpetrators (Benedict et al, 1994, p. 580).

While reports involving foster families accounted for only 1.1% of all reports over the five years, when compared to non-foster families they were significantly more likely to be reported for all types of maltreatment. They were seven times more likely to be reported for physical abuse, four times as likely to be reported for sexual abuse and twice as likely to reported for neglect. There were significant differences in distribution of the different types of maltreatment in the two groups, with a smaller proportion of physical abuse reports in non-foster families (35.9%) and a larger proportion of neglect cases. This may be accounted for by the different criteria for report in the two populations since no corporal punishment is allowed in foster care. Sexual abuse was involved in similar proportions of reports in both groups. While we have seen that foster families were seven times more likely to be reported for physical abuse, there was a much lower substantiation rate (8.9% compared to 36.6%). The substantiation of sexual abuse was similar in the two populations.[27] The authors suggest that while the "high reporting may reflect the agency's policies related to corporal punishment,... the low substantiation may reflect more closely community norms of discipline or other issues related to foster care, such as the shortage of homes and the agency's reluctance to close a home perceived as good in the past (Benedict et al, 1994, p. 283). Although the substantiation rate for physical abuse was much lower for foster families, foster homes still had almost double the risk (Ratio 1.77) for a substantiated report than non-foster families (Benedict et al, 1994, p. 282).

While it is difficult to ascertain the exact scale of abuse in foster care, it cannot be disputed that it occurs, and with a frequency which makes surprising the lack of detailed study.

27 Comparison of substantiation rates was not possible for neglect cases.

Responding to the Abuse of Children Living Away from Home

Introduction

Rindfleisch N. and Rabb J. (1984a), in visits to 12 residential establishments in four states, carried out to validate results of a national survey, found that, in general, the monitoring and investigative elements of the child protection system in each agency and each state had an ad hoc quality (Rindfleisch and Rabb, 1984a).

> There seemed to be little consistency even within residential institutions in the way abuse and neglect were identified and investigated (Rindfleisch and Rabb, 1984b, p. 212)

Rabb and Rindfleisch used vignettes developed from actual cases to study assessment of harm to the child, and assessment of whether it was abuse or neglect by six groups of people involved in institutional care: residential managers; direct caregivers; public child welfare workers; residential board members; foster parents; and children in care. They found that respondents "appeared to be more cautious in judging abuse/neglect than in assessing the situation as harmful" (Rabb and Rindfleisch, 1985, p. 293). They suggest that this is because a judgement of abuse/neglect requires action to be taken and "indicates that it is easier to agree that harm has been done than it is to agree that something ought to be done" (Rabb and Rindfleisch, 1985, p. 293).

Denial of Abuse

Institutions may be reluctant to report incidents of abuse because they fear damaging their reputation, and the possible loss of their credibility, referrals and licence (Durkin, 1982a; 1982b; Gil and Baxter, 1979; Harrell and Orem, 1980; Powers, Mooney and Nunno, 1990; Sullivan et al, 1987).

> In the authors' work with educational programs for deaf children in which sex abuse occurred, they have seen staff and students threatened and coerced into not talking to investigators, records destroyed, and children who sought therapy intimidated and ostracized... the reaction was denial, lying, "stonewalling", and a "gestapo-like" martial law environment as the crisis peaked (Sullivan et al, 1987, p. 258)

Placing agencies may also be reluctant to disturb the situation in relation to the most difficult young people who are placed in last resort placements (Rindfleisch and Rabb, 1984b, p. 213).

Bloom (1992) suggests that the single greatest impediment to adequately protecting residential clients from sexual abuse is the attitude that "it can't happen here." (Bloom, 1992, p. 133). Brannan et al (1993a; 1993b) highlight that a significant feature in the investigation of abuse at Castle Hill School was the "disbelief of other professionals and parents and their initial inability to accept and comprehend the sheer volume and extent of the abuse" (Brannan et al 1993b, p. 273). There was similar disbelief on the part of police officers in Leicestershire which led to complaints against Frank Beck not being investigated (Police Complaints Authority, 1993).

Single (1989) also addresses issues for the child sexual assault victim and the child care worker when the alleged offender is a fellow professional. She points out that the "difficulties of disclosure may be particularly increased in cases in which the alleged offender is a professional person, especially one involved with child protection or child care" (Single, 1989, p. 21). Single suggests that some workers "may, at least initially, lose their 'professional' stance and may react to the allegations in ways similar to members of incestuous families, that is, by denial" (Single, 1989, p. 22) and this may impede or delay the investigation of the child's allegation.

> *"Morris had [total] hold over our lives at the school, at home, the lot. He had us right where he wanted us, under his thumb. He was a very convincing man."* (Young person from Castle Hill School, cited in Doran and Brannan, 1996, p. 165)

Barriers to Reporting Abuse

> In many cases there is a failure on the part of would be reporters to recognize incidents or circumstances as abusive or as an environment injurious to the health and welfare of the child in residential care (Nunno and Motz, 1988, p. 523)

Nunno and Motz suggest that since most reporting systems are geared to familial abuse reports, they do not address the anxiety or the fear of the institutional maltreatment reporter, the nature of institutions to protect themselves, or the information and support needs of the investigator to initiate an effective response (Nunno and Motz, 1988, p. 524).

> Individuals who suspect (or know) that institutional child abuse is occurring may have valid concerns about reporting incidents, which explains their frequent reticence. Such concerns may be personal in nature, such as the fear of losing their jobs or the desire to avoid becoming involved in what is usually a messy business at best, or may reflect attitudes regarding the system, be it the county Children's Protective Service agency or the institution, which may be ineffective or bureaucratic (Durkin, 1982b, p. 110; see also Sullivan et al, 1987)

Rindfleisch (1988b) argues that there are three types of barriers to reporting maltreatment in residential settings. The first arises from the conflict between "the assertion by professionals that only they can regulate themselves and the increasing recognition of children's rights" (Rindfleisch, 1988b, p. 55). Most occupations argue that only a group of peers has a right to say when a mistake has occurred and this "attitude may be extended to complete silence concerning mistakes of a member of the colleague group, because the very discussion before a larger audience may imply the right of the layperson to make a judgment; and it is the right to make the judgment that is most jealously guarded" (Rindfleisch, 1988b, p. 55). The professional community justifies this by claims about: the doctrine of "in loco parentis" where the facility has the rights of parents to judge whether it is culpable of abuse or neglect; the concept of "in the child's best interest" where what has been done is for the child's own good; "best professional judgment" which is based on the presumed expert and specialised knowledge of staff; and the "argument of limited resources" which is invoked to reduce the degree of administrative culpability (Rindfleisch, 1988b, p. 56).

The second type of barrier comes from the general absence of consensus about what constitutes abuse and neglect (Rindfleisch, 1988b, p. 57).

The third type of barrier to reporting is organisational in nature.

> For while there is widespread agreement among administrators of children's residential facilities that program monitoring, professional rapport with the residents, and an "open door" policy are sufficient to assure the safety and security of residents, reporting of maltreatment has been negligible (Rindfleisch, 1988b, pp. 54-55)

In a study of the factors that influenced the willingness to report, Rindfleisch and Bean (1988) presented 598 respondents with 1 of 8 events depicting adverse acts or omissions of residential facility staff and were asked what action they would be likely to take. Of the different types of abuse depicted, sexual and physical abuse and failure to supervise led to increased willingness to report as did higher levels of assessed severity of maltreatment. The position of staff involved also affected willingness to report maltreatment in that there was more willingness to report abuse "when a social worker was depicted in an event, in contrast to a supervisor or child care worker" (Rindfleisch and Bean, 1988, p. 518). However,

> ... the effects of these factors were modest when they are compared with the effects of the four items which tapped the respondents' commitment to report adverse events even if reporting threatened the agency's funding, resulted in anger from one's peers, or the loss of one's job... commitment to residents' welfare was strongly and positively related to that willingness (Rindfleisch and Bean, 1988, p. 518)

In the US, the failure to report out-of-home maltreatment has resulted in both criminal prosecutions and a number of civil actions seeking money damages from workers, their supervisors and their agencies (Besharov, 1987, pp. 401 - 402; see also Harrell and Orem, 1980). While employees of agencies may be justifiably discharged or suffer other employment actions for failure to report suspected maltreatment, Besharov highlights the concern about adverse employment action because an employee did make a report. He gives examples of workers being demoted or fired because they had reported maltreatment of children by their own agencies and while it is difficult to know how often this occurs, "enough cases have become known so that four states... have now passed specific legislation to protect employees who report in good faith" (Besharov, 1987, p, 405; see also McHale, 1992; Vinten, 1994). Besharov calls for all states to enact such anti-retaliation legislation and Harrell and Orem consider that "there is a priority need for legislation to protect "whistle blowers" in institutions" (Harrell and Orem, 1980, p. 21). Durkin writes:

> Those who report will find the first experience of bringing charges of child abuse to be the hardest. They need active supporters or, at least, confidants. The experience is difficult and lonely, particularly when it threatens job security and future employment (Durkin, 1989b, p. 113)

Skinner (1992) makes the recommendation that:

> Persons receiving allegation, or suspicious themselves, about possible abuse of young people or children in residential care should inform the police without hesitation (Skinner, 1992, p. 62)

Investigation of abuse

Specialised investigative procedures for institutional abuse are rare and "... child protective services are entering an environment within which they possess no immediate credibility, no claims to expertise, no reputation or track record to fall back on" (Thomas, 1985, cited in Nunno and Motz, 1988, p. 525). Because of lack of knowledge in this area, child protective workers often fail to recognise incidents involving overuse of, improper or inappropriate restraints or medication as abusive. Nunno and Motz also suggest that in the USA, the child protective system all too often gives allegations of abuse and neglect lower priority than the situation merits, leading to delays in investigation, and Gil stresses the fact that there can frequently be a conflict of interest when licensing workers investigate those facilities they have licensed (Gil, 1982, p. 8).

> It seems clear that the federal requirement of independent investigation of out-of-home maltreatment report has had to cover a diversity of administrative conditions and situations at the state level. It is cause for concern, however, that despite this language in the federal rules, a wide rage of standards for defining independent investigations is reflected in reported state practices (Rindfleisch and Nunno, 1992, p. 707).

Reducing the potential for conflict of interest in decision making should be a major concern to the administration of the institution, child protection services, and any licensing or regulatory body. They stress the need for the development of clear written formal agreements worked out by licensing and child protective services administration based on specific legal and regulatory authority to enforce or monitor the corrective actions mandated by the results of the investigation (Nunno and Motz, 1988, pp. 525-526).

In the UK, there is also a lack of formalised, written procedures and policies for dealing with abuse allegations (Westcott, 1991a) although *'Working Together'* states that for children in residential settings, "there must be clear written procedures on how suspected abuse is dealt with, for children and staff to consult and available for external scrutiny" (Home Office, 1991, p. 34). 'Working Together' stresses that where there are investigations of allegations or suspicions of abuse perpetrated by a member of a social services department's own staff, they:

> ...should, as far as possible, include an independent element. This could, for example, be a representative from another SSD or the local NSPCC (Home Office, 1991, p. 35)

In relation to the abuse of young people at Castle Hill School, Brannan et al comment that the:

> "... sad reality is that the eventual success of the inquiry came about following the failure of the pre-existing machinery to effectively investigate and co-ordinate previous concerns. This is not meant to be a criticism of agencies or the individuals involved, rather an indication of the need for a corporate, co-ordinated approach. (Brannan et al, 1991, p. 9)

Nunno and Rindfleisch highlight the low reported substantiation rates of allegations of abuse in out-of-home care and argue that using "familial investigating procedures ignores the basic differences between familial and state care of children and may contribute to the phenomenon of low substantiation rate," making a compelling case for specialised intervention units (Nunno and Rindfleisch, 1991, p. 302). Motz and Nunno (1988) advocate a state-level regulatory team which, as well as having an investigative function, could make policy, assist in defining institutional abuse, drawing up identification and reporting procedures; and monitor and review cases after the investigation is complete. One advantage of such a team is that the overview they gain from reviewing cases provides information to assist budget and legislative initiatives, and the development of training. The team should be interdisciplinary and should have representation from the medical, legal, educational, social work, and law and enforcement professionals. They suggest that the institutional abuse review team would need to look at whether existing responses to familial abuse address issues relating to abuse in out-of-home care. The review team should consider whether: the state's definition of child maltreatment is sufficient; current reporting and investigation procedures allow immediate and safe access to the child; investigation procedures allow for ensuring the immediate safety of the child, removing the child, transferring or suspending the alleged perpetrator, closing the facility, and contacting law enforcement officials; assessment procedures are appropriate; corrective action recommendations address the incident and any systematic or administrative problems contributing to the incident.

The team should consider the following issues in a review:

1. Interagency co-ordination and co-operation in the investigative process;
2. Appropriateness of placement;
3. Licensing violations;
4. Previous incidents involving the facility and the child;
5. Staffing patterns within the facility or investigation unit;
6. Legal issues, such as current state labor law, civil service statute, employment agreements, and placement agreements;
7. Law enforcement issues, including the due process rights of the staff and care facility;
8. Medical and psychological issues;
9. Child care agency hiring, orientation, training plans, and procedures.

(Motz and Nunno, 1988, p, 450)

Rindfleisch and Rabb (1984a) found that incidents which were reportable were handled informally or if reported, were dealt with as failures in performance of the worker rather than as an infringement of the child's rights The issue is defined as a staff problem not as a problem of mistreatment (Rindfleisch and Rabb, 1984a, p. 37). Baldwin (1990) makes a similar point in her research with residential workers in one local authority in England where she found that "a tendency to look at shortcomings of individual staff members when things go wrong still seems very common" (Baldwin, 1990, p. 149).

> ... in spite of an expressed commitment to the development of a clear analysis of how services could be improved, there were many occasions during the project when senior staff in the department would discuss particular situations where problems had occurred, as though faults could be explained simply as a result of personal inadequacies of staff. Examples where the inability of staff to keep control of difficult young people, where excessive force had been used to restrain someone, or the failure to provide a constructive plan for a young person 'acting out'. (Baldwin, 1990, p. 149)

Doran and Brannan (1996) also suggest that:

> In an effort to minimise and deal with this guilt, Morris and Beck were elevated to the status of being cunning deviants, which had enabled them to operate despite the good offices of all the agencies involved. The reality is that in both cases (and many others) basic but thorough checks and monitoring systems would have either prevented the regimes developing at all or, at worst, stopped them at a far earlier stage (Doran and Brannan, 1996, p. 161)

Bloom stresses that the first duty of the agency is to protect the child and:

> Removing the potential source of harm - suspending the alleged abuser - clearly demonstrates the agency's commitment to protecting the child. For other types of abuse the author recommends a case-by-case determination of the appropriateness of suspension (Bloom, 1992, p. 134)

White also raises the question of whether suspension of staff is always the best approach, and while "welfare of children must be a foremost concern,... employers have to take a decision about the purpose and benefits of suspension rather than it being automatically imposed" (White, 1993, pp. 135-136; see also Warner, 1992). He suggests that there is a role for the Area Child Protection Committee in this, bringing together the range of expertise in this forum for the benefit of young people in residential care (White, 1993, p. 136).

The family should be informed of the allegations and what is being done about them, how the child is being protected and helped to work through this crisis. A multi-service plan is necessary to support the child since a child alleging sexual abuse by a staff member is frequently scapegoated by peers and staff members; staff may try to dissuade the child from holding to the allegation; and they may distance themselves emotionally from the child, blaming the child for seducing the staff member (Bloom, 1992 p. 135; see also Durkin, 1982b).

While clearly affirming its primary duty to the children, the agency must safeguard the rights and dignity of the alleged abuser. For other staff it is essential to communicate clearly and unambiguously what has been done and what will be done in response to the abuse allegations. While staff must be kept fully informed as events happen, it is important that the focus is kept on the normal operation of the regular program (Bloom, 1992; Durkin, 1982b).

> Forthright, unambiguous management of the abuse-related circumstances, paired with clear and direct communication of the agency's response to the situation, will help to counteract the natural tendencies to be secretive and defensive (Bloom, 1992, p. 140).

Bloom suggests that all "shareholders": board of directors; major referral sources, clients, staff members and the community at large are entitled to candid and unambiguous communication about the incident. One senior administrator should be designated as the person in charge and all information and communication should be channelled through this one person. An abusive situation should serve as a signal to initiate a risk management analysis of the agency which should review hiring practice, orientation, training, supervision and articulated philosophy. The communication network should also be reviewed to ensure that it is an open system in which information flows freely (Bloom, 1992).

Kelleher (1987) highlights the fact that when abuse occurs within an institutional setting, the response models are far more limited than in cases of abuse within the family.

> When abuse is substantiated, the guilty staff member is often fired and possibly prosecuted, and the child victim is sometimes relocated to another setting. End of intervention (Kelleher, 1987, p. 344)

Kelleher describes a systematic program review which was undertaken by the state child protection agency following a case of sexual abuse in a cottage-based group care facility for children. Separate from the abuse investigation, this evaluation identified nine key areas for special attention: treatment; child profile; staff issues; training; physical plant issues; education; medical; abuse-related issues; and the role of the state's child protection agency (Kelleher, 1987, p 348).

> By separating investigation and substantiation strategies from post-evaluation strategies, state agents can base after-the-incident intervention on an ecological model..., thus making an investment in the long-term welfare of a program by providing recommendations for program changes. (Kelleher, 1987, p 350).

Response to Allegations of Abuse in Foster Care

Interestingly, in the UK, there appears to be as much literature on the problem of foster carers dealing with allegations of abuse than on the incidence of abuse by foster carers. In a UK survey, 519 foster carers returned questionnaires of whom 177 had experienced an allegation. Foster carers were frequently poorly informed about the investigation and investigations were often protracted. Foster carers considered that there was a need for better support during investigations; more information; improved legal assistance; better policy and procedures; and better preparation of carers on safe caring and discipline (Nixon and Verity, 1996; see also Hicks and Nixon, 1991; Seymour, 1990; Sone; 1992). NFCA has stressed the importance of a code of practice where foster families have been accused of abuse and they should have: the right to be told of the substance of the allegation; to be heard by people not directly involved in the complaint; to place on record their perception of events; to a second medical opinion where physical abuse is alleged and medical evidence is being presented; to proper investigation by competent, experienced and independent people; to support both during the investigation and after it has made its findings; to receive decisions in writing; and the right to appeal (Lowe and Verity, 1989).

In the United States, Carbino (1991, 1992) has also stressed the importance of policy and sets out the characteristics of a constructive policy. Staff members and foster carers should be prepared and trained for the reality of allegations. Information needs to be provided about the fact that allegations occur; that the agency will investigate all reports; about the process of the investigation and the decision-making process; what rights foster carers have and do not have; and what resources are available for the support of the foster carers. Throughout the investigation of allegations of abuse, foster carers need to be reminded of resources for information on exactly what the involved agencies are likely to do and what the likely time frame is. Constructive policy should avoid unnecessary or unplanned removals of children. Input of the foster family to a fair and thorough investigation should be guaranteed and support for the family should be provided for interviews and hearings. Timely information on the progress of the investigation and a written notice of the final disposition of the investigation and what it means should be provided (Carbino, 1992, pp. 502 - 504). Following disposition of the report, the foster family should be reminded of agency procedures for this phase, what is likely to take place, and what the avenues for review and appeal of decisions are (Carbino, 1992, p. 506).

Carbino makes little mention of the fact that abuse does take place in foster care. Macaskill devotes a chapter in her book to the trauma of allegations but does place this in the context of sexual abuse taking place in foster care. The lack of preparedness was a common feature. The research indicated that the idea of being accused of sexual malpractice had not occurred to over one-third of the foster families.

> An absence of basic information resulted in some families engaging in a reckless type of parenting which failed to take cognisance of the child's sexual history (Macaskill, 1991, p. 104).

When an allegation of abuse did take place, the lack of information continued and foster carers were often unaware of what was taking place. Given the emphasis on the importance of professionals listening to the child and believing the child's story, Macaskill writes that it is "grossly unfair to expect substitute families to take on a sexually abused child without explaining to them how crucial the abused child's words will be if any allegation does occur" (Macaskill, 1991, p. 109).

Macaskill sets out a list of recommendations based on the experiences of foster families:

a) Every local authority and voluntary agency needs to devise clear guidelines for handling allegations.

b) The importance of alerting every foster and adoptive family to the potential risk of allegations of sexual abuse being made against them.

c) Familiarize every substitute family with the opportunity to consider changes which may be essential in their lifestyle to protect all family members against allegations. Repeat this exercise in a specific way whenever a new placement occurs, taking into consideration the unique factors in each child's history.

e) Ensure that the following issues are clarified at the outset of the placement:

- Who will offer support should an allegation occur?
- What type of support will be available (including support for other children in the family)?
- For what length of time will support be available?

(Macaskill, 1991, p. 109; see also Kendrick, 1994)

Placement Endings following Abuse

Rosenthal et al (1991) give details of the response to allegations of abuse for 116 referrals of abuse in out-of-home care in Colorado (these were a sub-set of 290 referrals). Victims were removed from the placement in 44 per cent of all incidents (49 of 111; 5 cases missing) and in 78 per cent of confirmed incidents (31 of 40; 1 case missing). Sexual abuse referrals were most likely to result in removal; 92 per cent (23 of 25) compared to 54 per cent of neglect referrals (12 of 22) and 29 per cent of physical abuse referrals (14 of 64). The figures for confirmed reports were 94 per cent (17 of 18); 70 per cent (7 of 10) and 58 per cent (7 of 12) respectively. Children were removed more frequently from smaller settings; foster placements and group homes than from larger establishments (Rosenthal et al, 1991, p. 254).

One third of the placement settings closed following confirmed cases of abuse and "as size of setting increased from foster home to group home to residential treatment center to institution, the probability of closing decreased." Sexual abuse referrals were most likely to result in the closure of the care setting while physical abuse referrals were least likely to do so (Rosenthal et al, 1991, p. 254).

In Cavara and Ogren's study of abuse in foster care in Hennepin County, some details are given of the actions taken following the incidents of physical and sexual abuse. In the eleven substantiated and 'unable to be substantiated' sexual abuse cases, licenses were revoked for seven families, two families withdrew from fostering, and no action was taken in relation to two families (Cavara and Ogren, 1983, p. 290). In relation to physical abuse licensing actions are only given in relation to the 20 abusing or neglecting foster fathers: "in these instances, the following licensing actions were taken: revocation, 2; withdrawal, 6; probation, 1; contracting, 2; no action, 9" (Cavara and Ogren, 1983, p. 292).

Professionals' Reactions to Abuse

Single describes the complex and strong reactions of fellow workers involving feelings of anger and rage, distress and depression, despair and guilt at "having 'missed' subtle cues in the child which may have alerted them to the situation" (Single, 1989, p. 22, see also Marchant and Page, 1992, p. 35). Single also points out that there is a high acquittal rate when compared to other child sexual offenders and "the devastating effects of acquittals in child sexual assault cases, which may intensify the distress and damage to the child" (Single, 1989, p. 26). Acquittals also have serious implications for the agency and:

> Perhaps the most difficult situation which workers in this area face is that in which the workers believe the child's allegations, but the alleged offender is acquitted and returns to work in the child protection agency. This produces major stress in such agencies, with a general feeling that the child protection service is, in a sense, a 'sham' (Single, 1989, p. 23).

Supporting the Child or Young Person

> **Andy**
>
> *I got no support during the investigation - nor did my family. You shouldn't have to ask for that kind of support - it should be available straight away. The police treated me pretty well but the interviews were pressurised and I felt I was being hassled for more and more information. They told me that they believed me - and I think they meant it. But I was given no information or advice about who to speak to. My family were the only ones who gave me any support, and they were under a lot of pressure and needed help themselves.*
> (Safe & Sound, 1995, p. 4).

Clayden (1992) discusses the importance of offering support for victims of institutional abuse and describes the free confidential helpline operated by Leicester NSPCC, providing telephone and face-to-face counselling and advice for adult survivors of abuse in care, their relatives, and former members of staff.

> The children and young people had their sense of trust shattered. We had to offer a service in which they could feel confident. Many feel massively betrayed: they were removed from their families to a place that was supposed to care and nurture them. They express anger with their abusers and the system. They have found it very difficult to trust the NSPCC (Clayden, 1992, p. 21)

In the Castle Hill case, the investigative team "set up a helpline and gave a commitment to always being available in addition to making arrangements for support systems in their own areas" (Brannan et al, 1993, p. 273). Single (1989) also stresses the importance of supporting the victim of sexual abuse by a professional worker through the Court process. She suggests that it is important that high quality legal representation be made available to the child and that a high quality assessment of the child by a professional worker skilled in this area be carried out in order to "give an expert opinion of the child's cognitive functioning and mental state, the child's personality, the effects of the abuse and the validity of the child's allegations" (Single, 1989, p. 27). Post-court support is also crucial and Brannan et al state that the "team should facilitate counselling therapy and compensation claims on behalf of the victims" (Brannan et al, 1993, p. 274).

Mandatory Reporting, Sex Offender Registers and Community Notification

Mandatory Reporting of Child Abuse

In the 1940s and 1950s a number of medical studies in the US identified the possibility of physical abuse of children and in 1962, Kempe et al published the influential '*Battered-Child Syndrome*'. The following year the US Department of Health, Education and Welfare Children's Bureau published a proposed, model statute for mandatory reporting (Sussman, 1975, p.247). By 1966 all states except one (which later did so) had enacted mandatory reporting legislation (Kalichman, 1993, p.11). Originally, mandatory reporting laws focused on the duties of physicians to report physical injuries (Sussman, 1975; Hutchison, 1993; Lindsey, 1994; Giovannoni, 1995) and "was designed to overcome doctor's unfamiliarity with the syndrome, their unconscious barriers against the conception of parental abuse, and their unwillingness to get involved in social and legal proceedings" (Sussman, 1975, p. 270).

> Most commentators appear to agree that the law should be focused on custody and protection of the child before all else and not upon punitive action against the perpetrator (Sussman, 1975, p. 249)

Giovannoni stresses that mandatory reporting laws do not in themselves establish the basis for state intrusion into situations of child maltreatment nor mechanisms for intervention, "these laws merely established a new gateway for entry into the system" (Giovannoni, 1995, p. 489).

While all states require physicians to report cases of suspected child abuse, either explicitly or by inclusion in "any" person, there has been a legislative trend to widen the range of mandated reporters to include other medical professionals, teachers[28] and social workers and an increasing number of states require reporting by "any person" (Hutchison, 1993). All states require mental health professionals (psychologists, social workers, psychiatrists and counsellors) to report suspected abuse. Some states have also mandated specific professionals to report suspected abuse; such as pharmacists, religious healers and commercial film developers[29] (Kalichman, 1993, p. 24). There has also been a widening of the types of abuse included in the legislation.

A number of issues have been identified in relation to mandated reporting and child protection. There has been a huge increase in the number of child abuse and neglect reports. Lindsey (1994) presents figures which detail the rise from 6,000 reports in 1963 to just under three million in 1992. This increase has led to "the most fundamental change in child welfare during the 1980s" (Lindsey, 1994, p. 44).

> Child Protective Services (CPS) (covering physical abuse, sexual abuse, and neglect reports, investigations, assessments, and resultant actions) have emerged as the dominant public child and family service, in effect "driving" the public agency and often taking over child welfare entirely (Kamerman and Kahn, 1990, p. 7, cited in Lindsey, 1994)

However, this increase was not accompanied by a comparable increase in resources "because laws were expected to improve services without additional costs" (Lindsey, 1994, p. 44; see also Hutchison, 1993; Giovannoni, 1995). Giovannoni argues that it is this that has created discontent with mandatory reporting laws since:

28 For a discussion of school personnel and mandatory reporting, see Mahoney (1995)

29 Usually specifying suspected sexual abuse or exploitation indicated by sexually explicit photographs of children.

> Within CPS systems, various "screening" practices and "risk assessment" techniques have been developed. These involve the establishment of criteria for not responding to reports, not investigating them, or, if investigated, constricting the criteria used for processing cases further into the system...(Giovannoni, 1995, p. 488; see also Zellman and Antler, 1990)[30]

This is linked to issues both around the over-reporting of suspected abuse and the under-reporting of suspected abuse. There is a high rate of unsubstantiated reports; Deisz et al (1996) cite figures of 54% of all reports being either unfounded or unsubstantiated with wide variations in substantiation rates in different states and jurisdictions; "in New York State, recent statistics indicated that 66.4% of the reports from social services sources and 71.4% of the reports initiated by mental health sources were unfounded" (Deisz et al, 1996, p. 276).

> When a professional requires only a minimal level of suspicion to report, usually resulting from subtle signs of abuse, he or she has exercised a lenient criterion, or low reporting threshold. Children with unexplained changes in behavior or who appear emotionally distressed..., or who present with unexplained anxiety and somatic disturbances..., provide examples of such cases... The mandatory reporting system, by design, accepts a high rate of false identifications in order to maximize rates of accurate detection of child abuse. The objective of the reporting system is to cast a wide net to capture as many actual cases of abuse as possible (Kalichman, 1993, pp. 70-71)

Hutchison argues that while the failure to substantiate reports is not clear evidence that inappropriate cases are reported since it may reflect inadequate technology, in that professionals do not know how to adequately assess the risk faced by children, or inadequate allocation of resources, "it calls into question the assumption that reporting laws allow for accurate identification" (Hutchison, 1993, p. 58).

Deisz et al found that a gap seems to exist between therapists as mandated reporters and child protection workers and that:

> ... the therapists in this study typically had a more expansive or broadened concept of what was reportable whereas CPS workers tended to have a limited definition that was somewhat instrumental in focus. (Deisz et al, 1996, p. 284)

Hutchison calls for the revision of mandatory reporting laws:

> Efforts should intensify to simplify and specify definitions to eliminate as much of the vagueness as possible. More specifically, definitions should be narrowed to include only manifest *serious* harm to child, parental behavior that threatens imminent *serious* harm to child, or acts of sexual exploitation (Hutchison, 1993, p. 62)

Finkelhor (1990), however, argues that the substantiation rate of suspected child abuse reports is similar to the conviction rate for violent crimes.

> Finkelhor explains in detail the social tolerance for high rates of arrests to ensure public safety and that this same logic provides the rationale for lenient child abuse reporting criteria prescribed by law (Kalichman, 1993, p. 72)

Giovannoni stresses that concentration on the issue of over-reporting draws attention away from the issue of under-resourcing of child protective services:

> Efforts at reducing demand by manipulating reporting laws or reporters' behavior, or the establishment of screening and risk assessment devices, may, in time, solve the problem of overreporting. Such devices may make system statistics look better and the systems may even run more smoothly as a result of their use. Unfortunately for children, the wrong problem may have been solved (Giovannoni, 1995, p. 500)

30 Besharov (1984) discusses lawsuits against child welfare agencies for failing to accept reports for investigation, failing to investigate adequately or failing to place a child in protective custody. This article also discusses liability for the abuse or neglect of children in foster care.

The other issue concerning mandatory reporting, however, relates to under-reporting by mandated reporters. Kalichman reviews the research on underreporting:

> Surveys have repeatedly shown that approximately one third of professionals have had contact with at least one case of suspected abuse in their professional work that they have declined to report... Similarly, the 1986 Study of Nation Incidence and Prevalence of Child Abuse and Neglect found that only one third of the 1,273,200 cases of abuse suspected by professionals were reported... (Kalichman, 1993, p. 3)

Zellman and Antler (1990) found that the potential reporter's attitude toward the effectiveness of the local Child Protective Services was an important predictor of failure to report (see also Crenshaw et al, 1994).

> Recent data in California suggest that approximately 9 per cent of children who are reported for child abuse and neglect receive any services other than investigation and assessment. Thus, more than 90 percent of children receive no services (Lindsey, 1994, p. 51)

Issues of protecting confidentiality in the treatment situation and the perception that reporting might worsen the child's situation have been linked to under-reporting (Kalichman, 1993; Zellman and Antler, 1990) although this is "despite evidence that reporting can have minimal adverse effects on treatment and can even be positively integrated into professional relationships" (Kalichman, 1993, p. 78). Mandated reporters also have concerns about negative personal consequences such as lost time or income or the risk of a lawsuit (Zellman and Antler, 1990, p 32; see also Kalichman, 1993).

Kalichman sets out three arguments for future directions for legislation and policy in mandatory reporting of child abuse. The first rejects the idea of statutory reform but attention should be given to other elements of the child protective system. Reineger et al (1995), in a study of a state-mandated training programme on child abuse and reporting requirements, stress the importance of education and training in relation to mandatory reporting.

> We must teach procedures. Even when they recognize abuse, professionals don't know what to do with the information. We must educate them. (Reineger et al, 1995, p. 68)

They conclude that unless "professionals who come in contact with children know how to identify and report child maltreatment, the statutes are meaningless" (Reineger et al, 1995, p. 68). We have also seen that child protective services have severe resource problems and "social commitment to child protective service reform would, therefore, build a stronger foundation for reporting" (Kalichman, 1993, p. 188).

The second argument suggests that there should be reform of the mandatory reporting laws themselves although "there is little consensus on the degree to which specific components of the law are to be revised and how such changes will most benefit child protection" (Kalichman, 1993, p. 188). Those advocating reform have focused on the need to change: definitions of child abuse which provide clear and objective parameters for reporting[31]; standards for required reporting which explicitly define both *knowledge* and *reasonable suspicion*; immunity for reporters to include a second type of immunity for professionals who do not report in good faith; and, in specific circumstances, guaranteeing therapist-client confidentiality, for example in treatment work with offenders (Kalichman, 1993, pp. 188-196).

Finally, suggestions for "systemic reform" have included "proposed flexible reporting options for mandated reporters with specialized training in child abuse" (Kalichman, 1993, p. 197).

Walters (1995) discusses Canadian mandatory reporting legislation from the point of view of the psychology profession. Since 1980, in Canada:

31 For a study of the effects of differently worded statutes on reporting of suspected child abuse, see Kalichman and Brosig, 1992.

> Provincial and territorial governments have responded to the need to identify children in need of protection through legislation mandating individuals to report instances of child maltreatment to authorities delegated with the responsibility of coordinating protective services (Walters, 1995, pp. 164-165)

Since each province and territory has its own legislation, there is variation in definitions of abuse, in the time frames associated with the duty to report, and in the processes once a child has been identified as being in need of protection (Walters, 1995, p. 165).

> ... *all persons* who believe on reasonable grounds that a child is (may, or has been, depending on the particular jurisdiction) in need of protection are duty bound to report their suspicions to an agency designated by the region's Minister in charge of protective services protection (Walters, 1995, p. 166)

In addition, some provinces and territories, place an explicit duty on professionals who learn of child abuse in the course of their professional duties. Different jurisdictions require different degrees of certainty on the part of reporters; some require "reasonable grounds to believe" that a child is in need of protective services; some "emphasize suspicion as adequate grounds to report" (Walters, 1995, p. 167). Few of the jurisdictions outline precise penalties for failure to report; in some jurisdictions it is only an offence for a professional to fail to report; and in others the legislation does not explicitly make non-reporting an offence.

> ... all duty to report statutes intentionally waive the ethical and legal requirement of professional confidentiality in the specific case of reporting children in need of protection (Walters, 1995, p. 166)

In Australia, all States and Territories except two, have legislation requiring the compulsory reporting of at least some types of child maltreatment (Tomison, 1996). In Queensland, mandatory reporting is limited to medical practitioners while in the Northern Territory it includes "any person not being a member of the police force". In other States and Territories different ranges of professionals are included: medical practitioners, dentists, school teachers and principals, child welfare and child care workers, social workers, psychologists, pharmacists, dentists, police officers (Tomison, 1996, p. 8). In Victoria, a phased implementation of mandatory reporting was halted after the first phase which mandated police, doctors, nurses and teachers to report child maltreatment, because of the significant increase in reports and the resultant demands on services (Tomison, 1996, p. 7). States and Territories also differ in the types of maltreatment to be reported, in some it is limited to physical or sexual abuse while in others all forms of abuse have to be reported.

In Ireland, there has been wide ranging support for the introduction of mandatory reporting (Gilligan, 1996). Recently, Barnardos, the Dublin Rape Crisis Centre and the Irish Society for the Prevention of Cruelty to Children have again urged for provisions which would legally oblige all those with responsibility for the care of children to report suspected or actual abuse or neglect of children to the health board and/or the Garda. The measure would also give those who report in good faith legal indemnity and would clarify the structures for reporting abuse (O'Connor, 1996).

The UK does not have mandatory reporting laws and "only local authority social workers, health and social service board social workers (in Northern Ireland) and police have a *duty* to report suspicions that a child is in need of care and protection" (Williams of Mostyn, 1996, p. 45). In the early 1980s, mandatory reporting was considered by the *Review of Child Care Law* working party but the idea was rejected (Bell and Tooman, 1994; Lyon, 1996). In Scotland, the extension of the mandatory duty to report was considered during the parliamentary process of the Children (Scotland) Act 1995, but it was felt that more needed to be known about the experience of other countries (Marshall, 1996). Considering that professionals may feel mandatory reporting could adversely affect victims' confidence in them, or discourage the disclosure of abuse because of fear of the consequences, the National Commission of Inquiry into the Prevention of Child Abuse suggests that there should be "encouragement to disclose information and suspicion of abuse, combined with greater flexibility of action and the exercise of professional judgement within the formal systems" (Williams of Mostyn, 1996, p. 45). There should also be public education of the fact that child protection procedures are not necessarily invoked immediately and that there are intermediate stages (Williams of Mostyn, 1996, p. 45).

Bell and Tooman argue that since mandatory reporting was rejected in the *Review of Child Care Law*, there have been significant changes in the provision of welfare services, particularly the purchaser/provider split, and that these are impacting on child protection. They conclude that:

> ... reporting laws in the United States combined with training programmes for all mandated reporters have increased the number of reports of suspected child abuse and have emphasized and legitimated the role and responsibility of *all* professionals in the protection of children. Such laws are therefore worthy of consideration in other jurisdictions, particularly in the UK (Bell and Tooman, 1994, p. 354)

Marshall also calls for an investigation into "the outcomes for children in countries with wider mandatory reporting duties" (Marshall, 1996, p. 254).

Sex Offender Register and Community Notification

In the United States, the 'Jacob Wetterling Act'[32] encourages states "to adopt laws requiring released sex offenders to register with law enforcement agencies in their communities and allowing law enforcement to disseminate information about sex offenders including their names, addresses, and photographs" (Lewis, 1996, p. 90). The Act requires states to enact a registration system for child sex offenders by 1997 or lose 10% of the state's share of federal grants for local and state crime-fighting programmes (Earl-Hubbard, 1996, p. 796). As of January 1996, forty-six states had enacted child sex offender registration laws (Earl-Hubbard, 1996). Most of the state registration laws set out the offences that require registration.

> For the most part the statutes focus on sexual assaults, including forcible rape and sodomy, and sexual abuse of children, including incest. Several statutes also target promoters of child pornography and child prostitution. Lesser crimes such as indecent exposure or public indecency are enumerated in some of the states. A few states require registration for relatively benign offenses: adultery in Arizona, bigamy in Louisiana, and voyeurism in Ohio (Bedarf, 1995, p. 888)

Some states focus their registration laws exclusively on child sex offenders and some focus on habitual sex offenders (Bedarf, 1995, p. 888).

All of the states require the offender to give his name, address, and conviction data when registering. Some states also require: a work address and phone number; social security number; vehicle identification or driver's licence number; blood type. Most states require fingerprints and photograph on registering and a small number of states require a blood sample, saliva sample or hair sample (Earl-Hubbard, 1996, pp. 802-803).

Bedarf argues that although registration laws are intended to address the high recidivism rates of sex offenders, research shows "that recidivism for sex offenses is relatively low" (Bedarf, 1995, p. 893).

> ... if actual recidivism rates motivated registrations laws, drug dealers and burglars should be the prime targets of registration laws, rather than sex offenders (Bedarf, 1995, p. 898)

32 The Jacob Wetterling Crimes Against Children and Sexually Violent Offender Registration Act is part of the 1994 Violent Crime Control and Law Enforcement Act (Lewis, 1996, p. 89).

Bedarf also argues that registration laws have not fulfilled the goal to improve law enforcement by providing the police with information to use in subsequent investigations of sex offenses (Bedarf, 1995, p. 899). Resource issues have meant that registration laws have not worked effectively. In California, it is suggested that up to 90% of registration information is inaccurate since although initial compliance may be high, offenders frequently do not notify of a change of address. Earl-Hubbard comments that the penalties for failure to register tend to be minor (Earl-Hubbard, 1996, p. 812).

> Police generally rely on offenders' voluntary compliance with the change-of-address notification requirement, or on tips from concerned citizens. Police do not follow up on sex offender registrants because they lack the time, personnel, and money to pursue violators of the Act (Bedarf, 1995, p. 902)

In 1996, 17 states complied with the federal guidelines in regard to community notification laws (Earl-Hubbard, 1996). The debate about community notification laws centres around the tension between the wish to protect society - especially children - from recidivist sex offenders and the protection of the rights and liberties of individuals.

> Understandably, communities and lawmakers want both to prevent sex crimes and crimes against children and apprehend the perpetrators of these abhorrent offenses. On the other hand , sex offender laws substantially infringe the rights and liberties of individuals who, although found guilty of a sex crime or crime against a child in the past, have served their time in prison and been released (Lewis, 1996, pp. 90-91).

Bedarf notes four basic models of community notification: mandatory self-identification; discretionary police identification; public access to police book; and public access by telephone.

The self-identification model requires the offender to identify himself in the community. In Louisiana, child molesters, upon grant of parole, must notify neighbours and the superintendent of the school district in which he resides, of his name, address, and conviction. The parole board may also order the sex offender to make known his status by such means as signs, bumper stickers or labelled clothing. As these are requirements of parole, the duty to comply with them expires with the term of parole (Bedarf, 1995, p. 904; Jerusalem, 1995, p. 241).

In the second model, the police have discretion about the release of information about convicted sex offenders to the community. In Washington state, the "statute gives police wide discretion in deciding whether to release information, what kind of information to release, and how to disseminate the information" (Bedarf, 1995, pp. 904-905). Community notification generally consists of "door-to-door flier distribution and posting signs with the offender's photograph, address, and explicit details of his offense history" (Earl-Hubbard, 1996, p. 810).

The third model allows individuals to view information about sex offenders. In California, individuals can go to their local sheriff's office and see registration data and photographs of child sex offenders. "The information consists of a photograph and physical description of the offender, his name, age, zip code, and a list of his registrable sex offenses" (Bedarf, 1995, p. 905).

Finally, Californian legislation also allows people to check whether an individual is a registered child sex offender by telephone. "Callers must provide very specific information, such as the exact street address, birth date, or detailed physical description of the person in question, in order to verify registration status (Bedarf, 1995, p. 905).

Bedarf outlines the benefits of community notification laws.

> Community surveillance of sex offenders augments police surveillance. Under hundreds of watchful eyes, it is more difficult for a sex offender to escape into anonymity (Bedarf, 1995, p. 906)

This may have a deterrent effect if registered sex offenders believe the chance of detection is more likely in the future. Community knowledge of sex offenders may also prevent sex offenses in that individuals "can tailor their behavior to reduce the risk of vicimization by identified sex offenders" (Bedarf, 1995, p. 906; see also Jerusalem, 1995, Freeman-Longo, 1996; Earl-Hubbard, 1996).

However, a number of arguments have been made against community notification laws. Freeman-Longo (1996) writes:

> Many of the more recent legislative actions appear to be the result of emotional public responses to violent crime rather than based upon fact and research that these laws will make a difference in the frequency of a particular crime. Public notification of sex offender release is one example of what may be feel good legislation that in the long run may result in consequences we will live to regret (Freeman-Longo, 1996, p. 96)

There have been numerous instances of vigilantism and attacks on registered offenders since the community notification laws have come into effect (Freeman-Longo, 1996, p. 96; Earl-Hubbard, 1996, pp. 824-825) and "evidence from Washington state shows that 26% of sex offenders identified under the community notification law have been subjected to some form of harassment" (Bedarf, 1995, pp 908-909).

Jerusalem maintains that public knowledge through community notification laws cannot protect society from repeat offences. Registration affects only a small proportion of sex offenders; those convicted. Secondly, "there is concern that public notification may provide people with a false sense of security" (Jerusalem, 1995, p. 247). Thirdly, the stigmatising effect of community notification on sex offenders may make them more likely to re-offend.

Bedarf also argues that:

> By informing the public of a sex offender's presence, community notification laws jeopardize an offender's chances of reintegrating into society and leading a productive life. Community notification laws destroy the anonymity that is crucial to reintegration. (Bedarf, 1995, p. 910; see also Earl-Hubbard, 1996, pp. 854-856)

The U.S. literature also questions the constitutionality of registration laws, particularly community notification laws. Earl-Hubbard concludes:

> ... the laws have overstepped the bounds of punishment acceptable under the Eighth Amendment. By their vagueness, dissimilarity, and lack of notice to those who enter a state's borders, the laws also deny offenders the notice necessary for procedural due process guaranteed by the Fifth and Fourteenth Amendments. Furthermore, by their unquestioned and unchallenged procedure for determining when to notify a community, the laws deprive offenders of a liberty interest without the opportunity to be heard (Earl-Hubbard, 1996, p. 861)

Bedarf states that legislatures "should resist the temptation to jump on the community notification bandwagon, and courts should seriously consider invalidating community notification laws as cruel and unusual punishment" (Bedarf, 1995, p 939; see also Lewis, 1996, pp. 116-117).

In Australia, the Crime Prevention Committee of the Parliament of Victoria has recommended that the Victoria Police establish and maintain a sex offender register. This would involve the lifelong registration of all adult offenders and requirements for adolescent sex offenders register for a period of five years (summary offences) or until they are 21 years of age (indictable offences). Registration should include sex offenders released from custody and those serving their sentence in the community and sex offenders must register within 10 days of being released or commencing their community based sentence. Failure to register or provide false information would be an indictable offence. The Committee suggests that the register should include: name, date of birth; address of residence; source of employment; physical description; set of fingerprints; DNA sample and photograph (Parliament of Victoria Crime Prevention Committee, 1995; Tomison, 1995).

In June 1996, the Home Office published a consultation paper on proposals for:

> strengthening the arrangements for supervising convicted sex offenders following their release from custody...;
>
> extending the power in the Criminal Justice and Public Order Act 1994 so as to enable samples to be taken for the purposes of DNA testing from convicted sex offenders who are serving a prison sentence which was imposed before that power came into force...;
>
> requiring sex offenders to notify the police of their address and any subsequent changes to it, so as to provide the police with a register of the current whereabouts of convicted sex offenders;
>
> introducing provisions to prohibit sex offenders from seeking employment involving access to children; and
>
> providing supervised access by defendants to victim statements and photographs in sexual offence cases...
>
> (Home Office, 1996, p. 1)

The proposal to introduce provisions to prohibit sex offenders from seeking employment involving access to children has been taken forward in a further consultation paper which sets out the proposed offence for anyone convicted of a qualifying offence to:

> (1) seek work or training involving unsupervised contact with children;
> (2) accept an offer of work or training involving unsupervised contact with children;
> (3) offer services or agree to provide services involving unsupervised contact with children;
> (4) enrol on a training course which will involve having unsupervised contact with children.
>
> (Home Office/Scottish Office, 1997, p.3)

In regard to the register of sex offenders, the consultation document states that the purpose of requiring sex offenders to notify police of a change of address would be "to ensure that the information on convicted sex offenders contained within the police national computer was full and up to date" (Home Office, 1996, p. 8). This would help the police in identifying suspects when a crime has been committed, could possibly help them to prevent such crimes, and might act as a deterrent. In proposing who should be required to register, the consultation document states that:

> a balance must be struck between the need to protect the public and the justice of placing a burden (and potential stigma) of registration upon individuals who may have paid their debt to society and might not reoffend (Home Office, 1996, p. 8)

Therefore the requirement would best be targeted on offenders who have committed offences sufficiently serious to attract the possibility of custody. The consultation document asks whether the requirement to register should be automatic on conviction; at the discretion of the court; or should be automatic only for more serious offences (Home Office, 1996, p. 9). The consultation document acknowledges some of the issues identified above surrounding open access to registers:

> Unrestricted availability of criminal records information could have a number of undesirable outcomes: the register could be used by those who wished unlawfully to harass those on it; it could be used to locate victims...; and it could be used by sex offenders as a means of networking (Home Office, 1996, p. 12)

The register would be accessed therefore, only by the police and bodies with whom access arrangements have been made.

Ivory (1996) sets out the civil liberties implications of the proposals and states that while many would regard the proposals for electronic tagging, registration and the creation of an offence of seeking work with children "as striking a fair balance between the civil liberties of serious sex offenders after their release and the right of the public to be protected from further offences" (Ivory, 1996, p. 21), the potential impact on far less serious offenders has alarmed some observers.

> Gay groups have been particularly angered by the extensive list of offences covered by the Home Secretary's consultation paper... Among the 32 separate offences listed in Annex A are 'indecency between men', 'solicitation by a man', and, most bizarre of all, 'homosexual acts on merchant ships' (Ivory, 1996, p. 21)

There is concern that "the proposals may be a Trojan horse whose occupants could run riot through the whole criminal justice system. Might it be sex offenders today, other classes of offender tomorrow?" (Ivory, 1996, p. 21; see also Freeman-Longo, 1996). However, the proposals set out in the consultation document have been supported by the National Commission of Inquiry into the Prevention of Child Abuse (Williams of Mostyn, 1996, p. 43).

Racism and Abuse

Darren
I hate being in care because I am always picked on because of the colour of my skin. But whenever I complain to the staff, they just ignore me. Therefore, I often get into fights and I'm the one they label as the troublemaker
(Marrett, 1991, p. viii)

There has been a recognition that services provided for black children and their families often do not address their specific needs, along with institutional and individual racism (Ahmad, 1990; Ahmed et al, 1986; Barn, 1993; Black and In Care, 1992; Caesar et al, 1994; Cliffe with Berridge, 1991; Moss et al, 1990; Thanki, 1994). In a study of care placements in one inner-city local authority, Barn considered that there were encouraging moves in terms of the placement of black children in racially and culturally appropriate foster care and towards anti-racist working in residential care (Barn, 1993). However:

> It is troubling to note that black children are severely disproportionately represented in care, enter care twice as quickly as white children... There was less preventive work done with black families. While greater efforts were made not to admit white children into care, the same was not true for black children... (Barn, 1993, p. 120; see also Ahmad, 1990; Cheetham, 1986; Moss et al, 1990; Utting, 1992)

Barn highlights the fact that there is little information on the experience of black children in care. At the first national conference of black children in care, held in 1984, overt racism was highlighted.

> Racist remarks from staff and other white children were not uncommon. It was also stressed that staff in these residential homes had little or no knowledge of the experiences of black people in this society or of black cultures, and therefore racial conflicts between children could not be amicably resolved. (Barn, 1993, p. 9; see also Marrett, 1991)

Moss et al, in their study of the cases of 50 young people (60% of whom were black or from a minority ethnic group) who had complained to NAYPIC, found that racial abuse and racism was a common complaint.

> In the secure unit for girls we looked at, staff used sexist, racist and verbal abuse as a means of control and to humiliate and degrade the young people (Moss et al, 1990, p.9)

Barn's study does not look at children's experiences in placements in depth, but does give one example of a young girl being physically abused in a foster placement (Barn, 1993, p. 79).

The *Who Cares?* Trust and the National Consumer Council carried out a questionnaire survey of young people in care through the magazine Who Cares? Sixty-eight of the 626 young people who responded were black or from a minority ethnic group and there were three complaints of racial abuse (Fletcher, 1993, p. 64). The Social Services Inspectorate found that in some homes there were examples of racist comments and jibes which went unchecked by staff (Social Services Inspectorate, undated b, p. 40) and the Howard League Commission also identified a number of complaints about racist abuse by both staff and young people; with evidence of right-wing National Front influence in some prisons (Howard League, 1995a, p. 39 - 40).

Caesar et al studied the work of the Barnardo's Adolescent Placement Service (APS) which provided specialist family placements for adolescents, many of whom were African-Caribbean.

> The nature of the project meant that all of the young people placed in it had experienced trauma and/or abuse - be it emotional, physical, psychological, sexual or racial - when previously in the care of their natural family, adoptive family, foster carers, children's home, secure unit or any combination thereof (Caesar et al, 1994, p. 39)

Interviews with ten young people gave insight into previous placement experiences. One member of a sibling group contrasted their current placement with black foster carers with a previous long-term placement with white foster carers.

> 'You've got freedom and you don't have too much "slavery". You can go out when you want with your friends and it's ok. You're not bullied about or hit or anything. They (community parents) are always caring and they don't just spoil one person. I couldn't say we're not spoilt, because we are all spoilt! What we are talking about is that they've not just spoilt their own kids and left us three out'. (Caesar et al, 1994, p. 41)

Caesar et al concluded that placements with black families provided by APS had "also helped provide the young people with an important understanding of, and confidence in themselves as Black young people. Previous placements, often in White families, had been unable to provide this" (Caesar et al, 1994, p. 94; see also Small, 1986). Buchanan et al (1993) found that "many residential and foster carers living in predominately white areas did not have the necessary awareness to meet black children's needs and yet were sometimes placed in a situation of having to do so" (Buchanan et al, 1993, p. 5; see also Cliffe with Berridge, 1991). Maximé (1986) highlights the emotional harm caused by racist practice which denies black children and young people a positive sense of their racial identity (see also Marrett, 1991).

Simms (1995) emphasises the fact that the Children Act 1989, in making it a duty to consider the racial origin, ethnicity and linguistic background of the child, "takes into account, for the first time, the multi-ethnic and multi-cultural nature of our society" (Simms, 1995, pp. 53-54). Simms provides principles of good practice and examples of how improved standards might be implemented and measured to promote equality in residential settings. These cover: food/diet; clothing; cosmetics; social development and positive identity; language; accommodation; education; religion; and health (Simms, 1995, pp. 55-57).

> Working towards equality is about making a shift within our thinking which can be reflected within our practice. However, the most valuable resource for social work change in achieving equality is "good practice". Good practice is dependent on each professional's commitment and ability to fully seek and utilise all the necessary components of antiracist and anti-oppressive practice principles (Simms, 1995, p. 58)

Abuse of Children with Disabilities

Introduction

> *"I was put in straightjacket. I just cracked up in the sideroom. Trying to get ways to tell people what was happening. Punishment was to scrub floors with scrubbing brush. They kept hitting me across the face, with towels, stripped me of my clothes - had to wear pyjamas"*
> (Man with learning difficulties abused as young person and adult by hospital staff)
> (Westcott, 1993, p. 16)

> It is... society's response to disability that may lead to increased abuse and vulnerability of disabled people, more than the disability or any other attribute of the abuse victim (Westcott, 1991b, pp. 253-254; see also Authier, 1987; Brookhouser et al, 1986; Kennedy and Kelly, 1992)

While the particular vulnerability of children and young people with disabilities has been highlighted over recent years, "... there has been little systematic investigation of the factors relating to the maltreatment of handicapped children" (Ammerman et al, 1989, p. 335).

> This is particularly surprising given that (1) disabled and impaired children are often overrepresented in abused and neglected samples, and (2) many handicapped children and their families have characteristics that in nondisabled populations are considered to be high risk factors for maltreatment (Ammerman et al, 1989, p. 335; see also, Walmsley, 1989).

The abuse of children with disabilities is made more complex because:

> ... there are two separate linkages:
> 1. ... abuse may be implicated in the creation of disability
> 2. ... children with disability may be differentially targeted for abuse
>
> The possibility that abuse might compound a pre-existing disability must also be borne in mind.
> (Kelly, 1992a, p. 159; see also Galbally, 1993)

Garbarino discusses three major forms of harm as a result of child abuse: *medical problems* such as nutritional deficiencies, hearing loss or brain damage; *developmental problems* such as "mental retardation", language deficiencies or impaired motor skills; and *psychological problems* such as "extremes on most dimensions of personality... as well as general unhappiness, poor attachment, and inadequate peer relations" (Garbarino, 1987, p. 8; see also Sinason, 1989; Vizard, 1989; Westcott, 1991b).

> ... handicapping conditions may well be the *result* of maltreatment early in life and then become the *cause* of maltreatment in later interactions with parents, peers, teachers, and other caregivers. (Garbarino, 1987, pp. 8-9).

The use of residential and specialist facilities by children with disabilities has also been identified by many authors as increasing the likelihood of abuse.

> Handicapped children, including deaf youngsters, are disproportionately likely to be institutionalized at some point in their lives. When they are institutionalized, they are at even greater risk for maltreatment, because of their difficulties in communicating, as well as their (and their family's) inordinate dependence upon the institution for special services (e.g. the residential school attended by the child may be the only resource available in the state). (Brookhouser et al, 1986, p. 153; see also Galbally, 1993; Kelly, 1992a; Sullivan et al, 1991; Utting, 1991; Westcott, 1993)

In the UK, research by Westcott (1993) identifies children with disabilities as additionally vulnerable to abuse precisely because of the settings in which they are placed. Nine adults with learning disabilities and eight adults with physical disabilities were interviewed about their experiences of abuse both as children and as adults. Many of them had spent long periods in hospitals, psychiatric institutions or special schools and "for this group many of the abusive incidents to be reported occurred in these hospitals and institutions" (Westcott, 1993, p. 14). The interviewees identified the settings they were put into and their experiences in those settings as a factor in their abuse (Westcott, 1993, p. 17).

> Disabled interviewees themselves pinpointed the following contributory factors: physical and social isolation; lack of choice; lack of physical and psychological resources to defend oneself; physical immobility; and the ability to 'switch off' one's body at will. This latter factor arises from the frequent intrusive behaviour displayed by able bodied professionals and other adults (Westcott, 1993, p. 33).

The institutional context of abuse is also identified as exerting additional pressures against telling about the abuse (Westcott, 1993).

Degener also raises the issue of the experience of children with disabilities of intrusive medical examinations and treatment and its implications.

> They might have to undergo repeated therapy and surgery, all of which are likely to produce in the child negative feelings towards his or her own body. If a child has never been allowed to say 'no' to being touched by doctors, nurses or even parents, how can we expect the child, or later the woman, to resist a sexual attack (Degener, 1992, p. 154; see also Galbally. 1993)

Cross (1992) identifies some of the abusive aspects of medical intervention itself where "children have been denied adequate pain control" and some "children with physical impairments, because of the nature and relative frequency of surgery, have suffered greatly from preventable pain. (Cross, 1992, p. 194).

Incidence of Abuse of Children with Disabilities

Much of the information on the relative incidence of institutional abuse of children with disabilities comes from the work of the Center for Abused Handicapped Children at the Boys Town National Institute for Communication Disorders in Children. Sullivan et al (1987) studied 100 deaf children who received evaluation and/or treatment services at the Center. "Sixty-four per cent of the deaf youth attended residential schools. Of these, 40 were abused in the school, 10 in the home and 15 at both the school and home" (Sullivan et al, 1987, p. 29; see also Brookhouser, 1987b).

Sullivan et al (1991) studied "482... consecutively referred children and adolescents with identifiable handicapping conditions and documented maltreatment who were evaluated at the Center... over a 4-year period" (Sullivan et al, 1991, p. 189). House-parents in residential schools or other institutions were responsible for 24.2% of sexual abuse perpetrated by females and 7.2% of physical abuse perpetrated by females, while house-parents were responsible for 15.3% of sexual abuse perpetrated by males and 13.8% of physical abuse perpetrated by males (Sullivan et al, 1991, p. 191).

> Children who attended residential schools were significantly more likely to be victims of sexual abuse than children who attended school in mainstreamed settings (Sullivan et al, 1991, p. 192)

Knutson and Sullivan (1993) present information on a group of 351 children referred to the Center... who presented with specific communication difficulties (associated with a hearing impairment, a speech and language impairment, or a cleft palate). It was found that while neglect and most emotional abuse took place in the child's home, over 60% of the sexual abuse and approximately 40% of the physical abuse took place in residential schooling (Knutson and Sullivan, 1993, p. 9).

Identification of Abuse

Identifying abuse, particularly sexual abuse, is a complex and difficult task with able-bodied children, and is much more difficult where the child has a physical or learning disability (Westcott, 1991b).

> Problem behaviour is too often accepted as normal for people with mental handicaps, so that symptoms which may signal alarm in a child or young person without handicaps are perceived as the inevitable consequence of the handicap (Walmsley, 1989, p.7)

Elvik et al also discuss problems related to the medical examination of "developmentally disabled" children and adults in a residential setting (Elvik et al, 1990).

Another major issue in identification may be a child's difficulty with communication. The attempt to communicate about an abusive experience "may be misunderstood, disregarded, or discredited because of the handicapping condition" (Authier, 1987, p. 237; see also Brookhouser, 1987a).

Kennedy (1992) discusses the issues for child protection work in the use of different communication methods for children with disabilities, for example: British Sign Language for deaf children; deaf blind manual alphabet for deaf blind children; Makaton signs and symbols for children with learning disabilities; Paget Gorman signed speech (PGSS) for children with language disorders; communication boards for children with cerebral palsy or multiple disabilities (Kennedy, 1992, pp. 170-175; see also, Marchant and Page, 1992; Sullivan and Scanlon, 1990). Kennedy concludes that such communication systems "can enable good work (albeit rather more basic and simplistic) with abused children with disabilities and communication differences" (Kennedy, 1992, p. 176). However, the difficulties are "compounded by our limiting of the vocabulary disabled children use in order to deny their sexuality" (Kennedy, 1992, p. 176; see also Authier, 1987). Limitations of vocabulary may also impact on identification of other forms of abuse. Marchant and Page give an example where "the child did not have the words 'shut' 'smack' or 'hit' on her word board" (Marchant and Page, 1992, p. 7). Some children have such impaired communication/ language capacity that they cannot use such systems; others do not have access to skilled teaching in the systems; and there is also a lack of persons skilled in using the systems (Kennedy, 1992).

Knutson and Sullivan stress the role of specialist staff in identifying the abuse of children with disabilities.

> The high rate of out-of-home maltreatment in the communicatively impaired sample and the high rate of residential placements in the sexually abused groups strongly suggest that aural rehabilitation specialists and speech-language pathologists should be sensitive to abuse in residentially placed populations (Knutson and Sullivan, 1993, p. 9).

Brookhouser et al similarly highlight the role of the otolaryngologist.

As a primary physician for most deaf children, the otolaryngologist must be able to recognize signs and symptoms of sexual abuse, as well as to initiate appropriate referrals both to insure the safety of the child and to comply with state reporting requirements (Brookhouser et al, 1986, p. 157).

Responding to Abuse

Marchant and Page highlight the gross inadequacies of services to provide therapeutic work for children with disabilities who have been abused.

> ... we had major difficulties in accessing any kind of help for these children, and the feeling was not only of falling between stools, but of amazement at the number of different stools available to fall between (Marchant and Page, 1992, p. 31)

Sullivan and Scanlan (1990) discuss the effectiveness of psychotherapeutic intervention techniques for children with disabilities who have been sexually abused. 72 young people who attended a residential school for the deaf had been "sexually victimized more than once by dormitory staff, family members, and/or older students" (Sullivan and Scanlan, 1990, p. 32; see also Sullivan, 1993).

> Preliminary data on handicapped victims of sexual abuse suggest that the children are emotionally traumatized and require therapeutic intervention (Sullivan and Scanlon, 1990, p. 135)

Half the young people underwent psychotherapy[33]. One year after the start of therapy, the treatment group had significantly lower scores on the Child Behaviour Checklist which was used to record behavioural problems and competencies.

> Therapy with the girls was found to be particularly effective in alleviating symptoms of depression, aggression, and cruelty. For boys, the treatment groups had significantly lower scores on the aggression, hyperactivity, delinquency, immaturity, hostile withdrawal, and uncommunicative scales (Sullivan and Scanlon, 1990, pp. 32-33)

Kelly (1992b) raises another issue which needs to be addressed in responding to the abuse of children with disabilities and this concerns the failure of the criminal justice system to take account of the needs of these children. In particular, Kelly expresses concern about the delays in cases coming to court; the lack of concern to create supportive conditions for the children such as the provision of screens; and "abusive defence tactics" (Kelly, 1992b, p. 189, see also Westcott, 1993).

Prevention through Education

Craft and Hitching (1989) describe the adaptation of Kidscape material for use with older children with special educational needs. They consider that sex education programmes have a vital part to play in the protection of children with disabilities because they: give a context for teaching about the cultural and legal parameters of sexual expression; can be the setting for work on self image and self assertiveness; can give students not only the confidence to talk about situations which make them feel uneasy but also the vocabulary with which to accurately describe events and behaviour; and sex education programmes help students identify adults in whom they can confide.

> ...planned and purposeful teaching, supported by staff and managers who are aware of, and sensitive to, the issues involved is a contribution to safety which we must not neglect (Craft and Hitching, 1989, p.36; see also Sullivan and Scanlon, 1990)

33 The nontreatment control group was possible because parents of half the young people refused the offer of free psychotherapy services for their child (Sullivan and Scanlan, 1990, p. 32).

Runaways and Child Prostitution

Running Away

Estimates suggest that children and young people go missing approximately 100,000 times in the UK every year (Abrahams and Mungall, 1992; Payne, 1995) and:

> ...there is evidence that a substantial proportion of those young people run away from residential care homes, so they are directly the responsibility of the social services; they are likely already to have experienced serious difficulties in their lives; and running away is likely to increase their vulnerability to problems still further (Payne, 1995, p. 334)

Abrahams and Mungall, in a study of running away in four sample police force areas, found that 4,166 young people were reported runaways from home, 1,826 from residential care, and 76 from foster care. However, young people in residential care were more likely to run away repeatedly, so that almost three-fifths of the 102,000 estimated runaway incidents were young people in residential care (Abrahams and Mungall, 1992, p. 9)[34].

> The 40 establishments which recorded the highest numbers of runaway incidents accounted for 58% of all recorded runaway incidents from residential care, and 34% of all reported runaway incidents overall, a very high proportion (Abrahams and Mungall, 1992, p. 17).

The 'top 40' residential establishments with high runaway numbers varied widely in size and type which "implies that aspects of the regimes in operation, or of the group dynamics in residential resources may influence running away behaviour" (Abrahams and Mungall, 1992, p. 17).

Rees, in a study of running away amongst young people under 16 in Leeds, found that one in seven of all young people run away and stay away for at least one night before the age of 16 and "for many young people, even if they come to no physical harm, running away is a lonely and frightening experience" (Rees, 1995, p. 66). Running away was a much more common experience for young people in residential care and 80% of the young people surveyed in children's homes had run away compared with 14% of those surveyed in schools (Rees, 1995, p. 66). Almost half the young people in residential care interviewed by Triseliotis et al "said that they had left the placement at least once without permission" (Triseliotis et al, 1995, p. 181). While half of these were 'occasional' absconders who were only away for a few hours or at most a day, the 'habitual absconders' "had run away more than four times and for some there had been periods when it was a daily occurrence. Absences were also longer, sometimes exceeding a week or more" (Triseliotis et al, 1995, pp. 181-182).

Stein et al (1994) carried out research with young people in contact with four Children's Society street-work projects. 102 young people completed questionnaires and 36 were interviewed. Seventy percent of the young people had lived in substitute care and 84% of these had lived in a children's home; 57% had experienced foster care; and 17% had been placed in secure care (Stein et al, 1994, p. 21). Most of the young people from residential care had started running away before they went into care which "means that we can't simply view young people who run away from care as "absconders". Instead we need to view their running away within the context of their lives" (Rees, 1995, p. 66).

34 Abrahams and Mungall do make the point that while some parents may be reluctant to report their runaway children missing, in contrast, residential care staff may be less reluctant and are likely to report a missing child in accordance with agency policy (Abraham and Mungall, 1992, p. 7) and "most runaway incidents from care included in the study consisted of a young person simply absenting her or himself from where they were otherwise supposed to be, not of a dramatic row followed by the young person storming out" (Abrahams and Mungall, 1992, p. 24)

> As a result of running away, attention is often drawn to the family situation and this can lead to the young person being removed from the family and placed in substitute care. Once in care, many young people continue to run (Stein et al, 1994, p. 44)

Kufeldt and Nimmo (1987) studied runaway and homeless youth in Calgary. Over a one year period 489 young people were interviewed and two distinct groups were identified: "runners" who tend to leave their homes with the intention of not returning and thus their runs are extended; and "in-and-outers" who run away as a temporary coping mechanism. Fifty-three percent of the "runners" were from child welfare facilities (Kufeldt and Nimmo, 1987, p. 540).

Payne suggests that there are five categories of 'missing person': *Runaways* (missing people) tends to be applied to young people who go missing and implies an element of 'spur-of-the-moment' decision-making in response to some fairly immediate social pressure in their immediate surroundings; *Throwaways* (rejected missing people) refers to people (particularly children) who are thrown out of their home; *Pushaways* (people forced to go missing) refers to the situation where the members of the person's social network forces them to leave, for example in situations of physical or sexual abuse or domestic violence; *Fallaways* (people who have lost contact) where relationships which were once important fall away until all contact is lost. *Takeaways* (people forced out of contact) includes kidnappings for criminal intent such as sexual or physical violence and also parental abductions (Payne, 1995, p. 337).

The main reasons for running away include problems at home or in care, including verbal, physical and sexual abuse; rejection; school problems; general unhappiness (Abrahams and Mungall, 1992; Payne, 1995, p. 341; Rees, 1995, p. 68; Stein et al, 1994, p 39). The main factors identified by young people as contributing to their running away from substitute care included: being taken into care feeling outside the control of the young person; negative experiences of the care system; not wanting to be in care; poor relationships with staff (young people feeling ignored or not listened to); peer pressure; bullying; running away for excitement (Rees, 1995, pp. 68-69; Stein et al, 1994, pp. 35-40). Running away was "often a response in situations were the teenagers felt powerless or hopeless in relation to an immediate crisis or longer-term prospects" (Triseliotis et al, 1995, p. 182).

In the US,

> Research has demonstrated an alarming incidence of abuse and neglect among today's runaway and homeless youth population... Several studies have shown that a much higher rate of childhood sexual abuse has been found among runaways than among the general population... Farber and his colleagues (1984) found that 75% of the 199 runaways in their sample had been subjected to severe maltreatment in the year prior to running away (Powers et al, 1990, p. 88; see also Janus et al, 1995).

There are considerable risks associated with young people going missing.

> Even if a 'missing persons incident' is of short duration, young people may still be placed at risk of abuse or exploitation in order to obtain care or somewhere to live; they may become the victims of crime; or they may take to unconventional lifestyles, including crime, drug and alcohol abuse, and prostitution, in order to survive (Payne, 1995, p. 343).

Stein et al (1994) found that over half the young people (56%) had stolen or shoplifted while they were away, and at least one in seven (15%) had provided sex for money (Stein et al, 1994, p. 44).

Janus et al (1995) investigated runaways' experiences of physical abuse and in addition to the abuse they experienced prior to running away, a large proportion had experienced physical abuse on the street: over half had been punched; two fifths kicked; one quarter had been assaulted with a weapon or had their head banged on wall or floor or been thrown around a room (Janus et.al, 1995, p. 440).

> What is clear from these data is that middle- and late-aged adolescents are not able to protect themselves from physical risk. Neither gender nor increased age prevent them from experiencing a broad array of criminal assault (Janus et al, 1995, p. 443).

Perhaps the most concerning finding of this study was that "over half the youth who identified assailants reported them as employed in or involved with institutions dedicated to their care" (Janus et al, 1995, p. 443).

> The implications are sobering. Not only are these youths physically assaulted at home, not only are they subject to assault from intimate partners and friends as well as casual acquaintances and predators alike when they reach the street, but once they have left home, they are subject to assault in those institutions to which they turn for assistance (Janus et al, 1995, p. 443).

Kufeldt and Nimmo (1987) found that almost three-quarters of the "runners" and over a half of the "in-and-outers" had been approached to take part in illegal activities:

> For the in-and-outers, [the street] is perhaps a cry for help or a respite. For the runners it may begin as a respite but becomes an escape. The sad reality, and the motivation for our research, is that it is no true escape. The continuation of the spiral is the abuse, neglect, and exploitation that exists on the street. The culmination may be maturation into the exploiters of the next generation of runaways or the lost and lonely derelicts and bag people. The sad and final outcome for some may be death (Kufeldt and Nimmo, 1987, p. 540)

Abrahams and Mungall (1992) argue that there needs to be a co-ordinated approach between police and social work to young people who run away. Since a significant proportion of runaway incidents originate from a relatively small number of residential care homes, there needs to be an active response to evidence of a pattern of going missing which should involve reporting within the agency, investigation of reasons and preventive action within the home.

> In particular there needs to be awareness that frequent running away by several young people from a single home may indicate abuse or other failings in the management or practice in the home (Payne, 1995, p. 346).

The Inquiry into the police investigation of complaints of child abuse in Leicestershire children's homes between 1973 and 1986 found that "in almost every case the contact between the Police and abused child came about as a result of the child being missing from a Children's Home" (Police Complaints Authority, 1993, p. 168) but complaints of abuse were not believed and the children were returned to the children's homes where they had been abused.

There is also a need to provide support to a young person in re-integrating on their return and in resolving the difficulties which led to the runaway incident in the first place.

> Both help with reunions and investigation of local patterns of help require much more effective co-operation between local agencies likely to be involved, especially the police and social services departments, together with other agencies which offer residential care for young people (Payne, 1995, p. 346).

Stein et al stress that:

> Just as attempts to improve the quality of life in families could contribute to the prevention of running away, so improving the quality of life in substitute care may prevent young people running again and for longer. Strategies to improve resourcing, service delivery and staff training would have a general impact; more targeted programmes addressing the reintegration of runaways into substitute care settings could have a similarly beneficial effect (Stein et al, 1994, p. 119).

> Angela: Care needs changing a lot - a lot - they need to be more careful on who they are employing - and people in homes have been abused that much they just turn to work - out on the street - when I first started working I said, "oh well, I might just as well go out and get paid for working rather than getting abused by someone" - that's when I first started working (O'Neill, Goode and Hopkins, 1995, p. 14).

While there is very little literature and research on child prostitution in the UK (Jesson, 1993; Barrett, 1995), a clear link is made between residential care and prostitution; with a significant number of children and young people involved in prostitution who are, or have been, in the care of local authorities (O'Neill, Goode and Hopkins, 1995; Lee and O'Brien, 1995; Childright, 1995).

Jesson (1993) describes three perspectives on prostitution: the traditional structuralist perspective in which the emphasis is on "male biological appetite" and there is "social containment of female sexuality within marriage for one man (monogamy), which simultaneously allows male sexuality to be satisfied by prostitution" (Jesson, 1993, p. 520); 'the prostitutes' perspective which emphasises "a discourse of legally recognized work, choice and civil rights"; and the feminist perspective which sees prostitution as "an institution which reflects the oppression of women in society, or the sexual exploitation of women by men" and is thus "felt to be an undesirable occupation, which adds to women's exploitation" (Jesson, 1993, p. 521). However, Jesson suggests that these three perspectives shed little light on the question of young women in care who become involved in prostitution and argues that it is important to distinguish between the behaviour of adult women and that of adolescent women. Drawing on the work of Weisberg (1985), Jesson lists a number of background characteristics which she states, "tend to have a chronological, sequential order".

- the home environment is unstable (not an original biological family)
- the children tend to come from broken homes where they have often experienced physical and emotional abuse
- the children have experience of early sexual activity, often sexual abuse within the family experience
- the children have a history of poor school attendance
- the children run away from home, and from *care institutions*

(Jesson, 1993, p. 524, emphasis in original)

In their research with young people in care and who have left care, O'Neill, Goode and Hopkins identified a number of experiences of the care system expressed by the young people. These included: the fear and loneliness of moving into care; problems around fitting in and 'going along' with the group even if it means prostitution; lots of moves between homes or from foster care to residential care; lack of privacy; daily harassment, abuse and incivilities; and the problems of leaving care - not being adequately prepared, living in temporary accommodation, unemployment, difficulties in entering or maintaining college courses (O'Neill, Goode and Hopkins, 1995, p. 16).

Lee and O'Brien state that the evidence "clearly points to a prevalence of disruption and discord in the early lives of young people involved in prostitution. It shows sexual abuse, neglect, school problems, unemployment and running away are particularly associated with prostitution" (Lee and O'Brien, 1995, p. 12). Prostitution is then a survival strategy for life on the streets and "many of these girls and young women enter prostitution with all the associated risks, in order to <u>survive</u> as they are denied an adequate income by any other means" (O'Neill, Green and Mulroy, forthcoming).

> The issue of young people providing sex for money as a means of survival came across powerfully in the information we gathered from young people and professionals. This is an issue of particular concern, as many young people would have experienced the abuse of power within their birth families and were then exposed to the abuse of adult male power on the streets in order to survive (Stein et al, 1994).

So, as Jesson emphasises, the link between early sexual abuse and prostitution may not be a direct one, but rather that sexual abuse leads to running away (Jesson, 1993, p. 526; Finkelhor et al, 1986; Ennew, 1986; see also Joseph, 1995).

Lee and O'Brien (1995) consider that the Children Act in England provides the framework for responding to children and young people involved in prostitution.

> The Children Act provides for the development of services for children and young people in need and many young people involved in prostitution will have a series of needs that are not being met. The Act also provides for interagency work on child protection and emergency intervention when the welfare of a child is at risk (Lee and O'Brien, 1995, p. 21).

However, they stress that the law "whilst recognising the need to protect young people from sexual abuse and exploitation, also allows for children as young as ten to be prosecuted for offences relating to that abuse" (Lee and O'Brien, 1995, p. 31) and "the police are increasingly using the criminal justice system to respond to younger women on the street and involved in prostitution" (Lee and O'Brien, 1995, p. 47). They conclude that:

> If more consideration is to be given to the welfare of young people and less use made of the criminal justice system for dealing with young people involved in prostitution, it is essential that the police service places more emphasis on its obligations and powers under the Children Act and less on its ability to caution and arrest young people (Lee and O'Brien, 1995, p. 35).

The National Commission of Inquiry into the Prevention of Child Abuse also stressed that the emphasis of criminal proceedings should be placed "on the identification and prosecution of clients and pimps who exploit children through prostitution" (Williams of Mostyn, 1996, p. 47).

Jesson found that social work responses also tended to be punitive "in the sense of controlling the young woman's social freedom and residential movements, between children's homes and often into secure accommodation" (Jesson, 1993, p. 528). O'Neill, Goode and Hopkins (1995) stress that the system of residential care needs to be adequately funded, staffed and resourced to meet the needs of children and young people in care and that any interventionary strategy should start with the need to train residential care staff (O'Neill, Goode and Hopkins, 1995, p. 16).

> The local authority survey findings suggest that very few child care workers have experience of developing an understanding of the behaviour of adolescent prostitutes or of developing appropriate long-term interventions (Jesson, 1993, p. 529).

Lee and O'Brien also argue that there needs to be "an increased recognition of children and young people's rights to be consulted and the full introduction of children's care plans are likely to reduce young people's estrangement from their families and their negative experiences of residential care" (Lee and O'Brien, 1995, pp. 53-54). They stress the importance of interdepartmental communication and planning of services at both national and local level. O'Neill, Green and Mulroy (forthcoming) pick up on this theme from a youth work perspective and stress that "a multi-agency response to young people's needs must mobilise to change the current socio-legal situation so that protection, harm minimisation and the welfare of the children and young people is absolutely paramount" (O'Neill, Green and Mulroy, forthcoming; see also Williams of Mostyn, 1996, p. 47))

Bullying, Peer Abuse and Self-Harm

Jas
"... I was physically abused by two other young people because I didn't fit their particular set of 'rules'."
(Safe & Sound, 1995, p. 3)

Rob
"... I was assaulted by male and female staff and I was also bullied by other young people all the time. Staff encouraged this sort of bullying by other residents as a way of controlling you"
(Safe & Sound, 1995, p. 6)

Gwynn et al (1988) emphasise that the group living experience has a profound impact on the socialisation and rehabilitation of emotionally disturbed young people and that while the peer group can make a contribution to positive social development, "the interpersonal problems of emotionally disturbed children may make group living a barrier to treatment... the peer culture influence in residential centers is generally negative, one in which antisocial values are reinforced while prosocial values are undermined, negatively reinforced, or punished" (Gwynn et al, 1988, p. 104).

> There is a growing awareness that bullying does not just affect the lives of children in schools but extends to many other organisations in which numbers of people have to live and work in close proximity. There is an increased concern about bullying in the work place, armed forces, hospitals, residential institutions such as children's homes, and homes for the aged - and, most certainly in prisons (Tattum, 1995, p.18).

Bullying can be defined as "the behaviour of one person or group which causes distress to another person or group as a result of physical threat, assault, verbal abuse or threats" (Support Force for Residential Child Care, 1996, p. 63). Connell and Farrington (1996) identify three key elements:

> First, there is physical, verbal or psychological attack, threat or intimidation that is intended to cause fear, harm or distress to the victim. Second, there is an imbalance of physical or psychological power, with a more powerful person, oppressing a less powerful one, or with several people ganging up on a victim. Third, there is a continuous series of incidents between the same people over a prolonged time period (Connell and Farrington, 1996, p. 75).

Despite the extensive literature on bullying in schools, there is a very limited amount of research that has been carried out on bullying in institutions and there is little basic data about its prevalence, frequency, or nature (Connell and Farrington, 1996, p. 78).

Extent of Bullying and Victimisation

Connell and Farrington carried out two pilot studies in the summer of 1992 and summer of 1993 at an open-custody facility for young offenders in Ontario, Canada. There were 10 residents at each point of study and all were white, male young offenders aged between 16 - 18. 70% of residents were involved in bullying, just under half as bullies and a quarter as victims. There was no overlap between bullies and victims. While the majority of current bullies (6 out of 9) had also been bullies in previous custodial facilities and all had previously been in custody, "the five victims were the only subjects who were serving their first custodial sentences" suggesting that "their lack of experience in custody might well have been a contributory factor to their victimization" (Connell and Farrington, 1996, p. 86).

> Bullies were given high status, often by both staff and residents, and it was the common opinion that being a bully gave you "jail respect". The majority of residents felt that bullying was just a normal part of life in custody and helped to establish and maintain the "hierarchy" (Connell and Farrington, 1996, p. 85).

Browne and Falshaw (1996) describe factors related to bullying at the Glenmore Youth Treatment Centre which offers specialised secure care facilities for severely disturbed and anti-social young people aged between 13 and 18 years. Of 44 young people involved with the Youth Treatment Service over a 6 month period, almost half (47%) regularly bullied their peers and over half (56%) were frequent victims of bullying. Three-fifths (58%) of the incidents involved violent assault. One-quarter (27%) of the young people were neither bullies nor victims, but just under one-third (30%) were both bullies and victims (Browne and Falshaw, 1996, p.124). There was a significant relationship between bullying behaviour and sexual harassment toward others on the units. Bullies were significantly more likely to have come from broken homes and to have committed violent crimes. All had a history of aggression, fighting and bullying in previous schools. Bullying at school was significantly associated with a high number of care placements, a higher number of special schools, under-achievement, educational special needs, vandalism and criminal property damage, car crime, thieving and violent crime. The victims who never bullied had a history of being bullied at previous schools and a history of alcohol abuse(Browne and Falshaw, 1996, p. 125).

The Howard League Commission of Inquiry into Violence in Penal Institutions for Teenagers under 18 also found staff condoning bullying, particularly with young people serving sentences:

> While prison staff appear far more comfortable working with sentenced prisoners, better relationships often go hand in hand with unwritten rules, and the use of bullying and the prisoners' own pecking orders as mechanisms of control... *I don't exactly know what makes a good nick... It's generally a question of knowing when to turn a blind eye... Good "barons" can be helpful if they don't get into too much and stick to stuff that's safe like cannabis...* (Howard League, 1995a, p. 27).

All the prisons visited by the Commission saw reducing bullying as a major priority, reflecting the extent of official concern but "even in the "better" institutions it is clear that a culture of verbal threats, "taxing" and competing regional loyalties is deeply entrenched" (Howard League, 1995a, p. 34). Bullying was seen as part of the "natural order" of prison life by many of the young people:

> *... everyone does it. If I don't someone else will. You've got to learn to stand up for yourself... I'm doing them a favour really. I don't hurt anyone... I usually only have to look at them.* (Howard League, 1995a, p. 38).

Little (1990), in his study of young offenders in a remand centre and a youth custody centre, found that "actual violence between prisoners is rare" (Little, 1990, p. 124). Fights were planned but involved little physical violence; "Pugilists, adversaries in combat, have a respect for each other when the episode is complete" (Little, 1990, p. 136). However, a recent survey carried out between April 1994 and December 1995 in two adult male prisons and two Young Offender Institutions, found high levels of victimisation (Edgar and O'Donnell, 1997). The authors argue that because of the subjective nature and 'looseness' of the concept of bullying, "it is easier to think of preventive strategies for well-defined behaviours" (Edgar and O'Donnell, 1997, p. 15). Victimisation is defined in terms of "six discrete behaviours: assault, threats of violence, verbal abuse, cell theft, robbery, and social exclusion" (Edgar and O'Donnell, 1997, p. 16). The survey found that, in the previous one month period, one in three young offenders had been assaulted; half had been threatened with violence; over half had received hurtful insults; a quarter had suffered cell theft; and, one in ten were the victims of robbery (Edgar and O'Donnell, 1997, p. 16). A quarter of young offenders were both victims and victimisers in the previous month.

> Assault, verbal abuse, and threats of violence were largely mutual. The behaviour tended to be reciprocated, and the roles of victim and victimiser were fluid. These types of victimisation were *egalitarian*. Robbery, exclusion and cell theft were quite different. There was little overlap. Those who were excluded or robbed were not likely to have excluded or robbed others. These types of victimisation tended to be *hierarchical* (Edgar and O'Donnell, 1997, p. 16).

Skett et al (1996) provide further evidence of the levels of violence. In one young offender establishment, adjudications records for 1994 were examined to identify reports relating to "rule 47 para 1 (Commits any assault), para 4 (Fights any person), para 17 (Uses threatening abusive insulting words or behaviour), para 21 (In any way offends against good order and discipline) and para 22 (Attempts, incites, assists any of the above)" (Skett et al, 1996, p. 11). 686 reports were identified, a rate of 138.6 reports per 100 prisoners. These consisted of: fighting - 429 (62.5%); assault on staff - 51 (7.4%); assault on inmate - 119 (17.3%); threats against staff - 67 (10.2%); threats against inmate - 10 (1.5%); offends against good order/attempts etc. - 10 (1.5%). In 93.9% of cases the charges were proved. In 152 cases there was minor physical injury, a further eight required medical attention and one required hospitalisation (Skett et al, 1996, p. 11). In four-fifths of cases, the inmate only had one offence and thus "it seems that violence within the institution is widespread throughout the population" (Skett et al, 1996, p. 12). As an indication of the extent to which official records will be an under-estimate of the level of violence, Edgar and O'Donnell found that "less than one in five of those who had been victimised said that they had informed an officer afterwards" (Edgar and O'Donnell, 1997, p. 16).

There is less systematice evidence of the levels of bullying and victimisation in residential care but inspection reports and research with young people gives some indication. The Social Services Inspectorate study of residential care in Northern Ireland found that inspectors "noted across all sectors significant levels of bullying and peer child abuse" (Social Services Inspectorate, undated a, p. 38). Similarly, the Social Services Inspectorate report on the inspection of residential child care services in 11 authorities in England identified "incidents of abuse by one child of another which did not appear to have been investigated in accordance with guidance" (Social Services Inspectorate, undated b, p. 29). One in six of the young people in residential care in the Triseliotis et al study of social work services to teenagers stated that they had been bullied or ill-treated by other residents (Triseliotis et al, 1995, p. 176). Grimshaw and Berridge (1994) found that four per cent of the 67 children in their study of special residential schools had suffered severe bullying and bullying was suspected for a further 11 per cent (Grimshaw and Berridge, 1994, p. 104).

> My brother is lying there and someone else is punching him bad... and a member of staff standing there doing nothing. I said.. you should be sorting this out... she said I am not going to get hurt and I had to threaten her so she would help my brother (Young person in Buchanan et al, 1993, p. 59).

The extent of bullying experienced or witnessed by young people distressed the group facilitators of the Dolphin Project consultation (see also Fletcher, 1993). There was a suggestion that "with the restictions on the discipline procedures available to carers, there may be a tendency for carers to involve young people in controlling others, and this could result in considerable distress to some young people" (Buchanan et al, 1993, p. 75; see also Safe & Sound, 1995). The carers involved in the consultation were not aware of the level of bullying and the distress this caused (Buchanan et al, 1993, p. 72).

The Howard League Commission found that bullying "does occur within secure units but at a much lower level than within the prison system" (Howard League, 1995a, p. 76). In her study of a secure unit in Scotland, Kelly found a highly restrictive regime which "succeeded in controlling the movement of all inmates all of the time". Family visits were always supervised by a member of staff, all mail was read by staff and all phone calls monitored. Such measures were used to "maintain psychological control of the children concerned and to prevent their association with each other, particularly in the form of 'anti-authority cliques'" (Kelly, 1992, pp. 142-143). In this environment, "bullying... seemed limited, and at least within the instituion itself, rarely got beyond verbal threat" (Kelly, 1992, p. 190).

Walford (1989) sets his discussion of bullying in public schools in the context of a past where "although... initiation rites were perhaps the worst examples of ritualised sadism, bullying and violence were an integral part of the public school system," and "within the prefect system bullying was legitimated as part of a wider system of corporal punishment" (Walford, 1989, p. 82; see also Benthall, 1991). About 200 pupils in one public school completed a questionnaire and "in all, more than 10 per cent of the boys mentioned bullying, violence or being teased..." (Walford, 1989, p. 83).[35] Walford suggests that bullying in public schools is no longer "a matter of gross physical abuse, but is a mixture of constant teasing and mild violence" (Walford, 1989, p. 87).

The study of the ChildLine Boarding School Line found that bullying was the most common problem referred to in one-fifth of calls.

> A special difficulty for children in boarding schools is that they cannot escape from those who bully them, by going home after school... Bullying in the dormitories is particularly distressing since it leaves the victims feeling they have no safe place to be. One girl spoke vividly of "the night-time horrors of the dormitories". (La Fontaine and Morris, 1991, p. 18; see also Morgan, 1993; Walford, 1989).

Forty-three percent of the cases of bullying of boys included reports of physical assault. Bullying was "severe, frequent or persistent enough to be reported by pupils as a 'worst thing' about being a boarder by 7% of preparatory school pupils and 4% of both secondary and special school pupils" (Morgan, 1993, p. 44). Morgan suggests that these low percentages should not be grounds for complacency, since they do not reflect the total number of pupils being bullied and hide a wide range of variations between different schools.

Responding to Bullying

When an institution creates an atmosphere in which young people feel valued and safe, there is less likelihood of violence and bullying; where unhelpful stereotypes exist, violence and intimidation may regularly occur (Browne and Falshaw, 1996). Work carried out by the staff at the Glenthorne Youth Treatment Centre involved: for the bully - assessing factors that elicit bullying behaviour in the individual; developing specific social skills and anger management; and, demonstrating support for the victim and developing the individual's understanding and empathy for others; for the victim -assessing factors in the individual that elicit bullying by others; developing specific social skills; showing support for the recognition of the victim's experience; and, demonstrating work is being carried out with the bully; for the institution - assessing methods of staff management and control of young people with challenging behaviour; and, reducing the use of threats, intimidation and humiliation by staff in managing young people and promoting reward systems to control behaviour (Browne and Falshaw, 1996, pp. 126-127).

The Prison service sets out five main elements to an anti-bullying strategy: measuring the problem; changing the climate; improving supervision and detection; supporting the victim; and challenging the bully. While individual establishments are expected to develop their own strategies, their implementation is very uneven and most prisons "do little more than segregate bullies and place victims in "vulnerable units" (Howard League, 1995a, p. 40). The Commission describes the attempt at Lancaster Farms Young Offender Institution and Remand Centre to tackle bullying.

35 The questionnaire did not ask direct questions about bullying or violence but asked about "the most important personal problems" caused by life at the school and "the things you most dislike" (Walford, 1989, pp. 84-85).

> The strategy includes rewarding positive behaviour, encouraging victims to come forward, addressing anti-social and offending behaviour and developing an active anti-bullying committee... The anti-bullying policy forms a key part of the induction programme including a one hour group work session on bullying... all prisoners are asked to sign an agreement not to take part in any bullying, not to help others to bully and to share information which may help to prevent bullying. Anyone who refuses to sign the agreement is prevented from earning any privileges, including home leave (Howard League, 1995a, p. 42).

In interviews with 92 prison staff, Edgar and O'Donnell found that just over half believed that the prevention of bullying was a priority for the Prison Service, there was wide variation in the extent to which staff were aware of both national and local anti-bullying strategies, and there was little consensus about how best to prevent victimisation (Edgar and O'Donnell, 1997, pp. 16-17). The authors stress that:

> Improved communication; training for staff in responding to victimisation, support for victims, and situational crime prevention all have the potential to reduce victimisation. Important as these elements are, they must be integrated in a comprehensive policy which links anti-victimisation initiatives to other programmes within the establishment and which clearly sets out the priority to be given to preventing victimisation. These coordinated strategies have become known as the 'whole prison approach'. (Edgar and O'Donnell, 1997, p. 19).

Tattum (1995) outlines the development of an anti-bullying programme in the YOI/RC wing of Cardiff prison which houses young men aged 15-21. A range of strategies involving crisis-management, intervention and prevention are used. Crisis management entails isolation of the victim for his own safety but also isolation of the bully and challenge of his violent behaviour. Intervention strategies include:

> ... the Listener Scheme, which uses trained and trusted inmates to advise and counsel other inmates. The Helpline, which is the official Wing post box into which inmates can post notes to a trusted officer to tell about bullying cases. Other elements are increased time out cells, educational and recreational programmes, and increased contact with family and friends (Tattum, 1995, p. 19; see also Cooke, 1991; Davies, 1994).

Preventative approaches, which aim to create a humane and trusting climate, include a week-long Induction Programme and a well developed Personal Officer Scheme. Over the first two years of the programme, serious attempts of suicide fell from 23 attempts in 1992 to 8 attempts in 1994 and there was an 80% reduction in acts of self harm (Tattum, 1995, p. 19).

Staff vigilance is the most potent deterrent against bullying so that children and young people who bully will know that it will be dealt with, and the victims of bullying will also have confidence. There needs to be open discussion about bullying and a clear statement of its unacceptability. In confronting the bully or bullies in relation to specific incidents it is important to:

- Be absolutely certain about the known facts
- Confront the "bully" with the allegations
- Make it clear that the behaviour is unacceptable
- See each "bully" separately if appropriate
- Be specific about sanctions if bullying does not stop
- Follow up to check that behaviour has ceased

(Support Force for Residential Child Care, 1996, p. 65)

La Fontaine and Morris recommend that boarding schools should consider promoting 'whole school' policies on bullying (La Fontaine and Morris, 1991, p. 55; see Sharp and Smith, 1993; Tattum, 1993, for discussion of 'whole school' policies on bullying).

Sexual Abuse by Young People

There is increasing evidence of the problem of the sexual abuse of children by other residents. White, writing in the mid-1980s, decried the lack of attention, in terms of research, information and reports, that this subject gets apart from in the aftermath of scandals such as Kincora.

> Generally, speaking, there are now guidelines affecting the type and degree of corporal punishment, discipline or restraint in the residential care of adolescents. There do not seem to be guidelines of a similar nature for sexual contact and relationships (White, 1987, p. 64)

Parkin argues that there is an ambiguity in terms of residential establishments. On the one hand they are 'homes': ambiguous, 'intermediate zones' where the domestic is part of the welfare bureaucracy. On the other hand, she argues that they have much in common with 'total institutions' in that they are concerned with the surveillance and control of their residents.

> In the ambiguous intermediate zone the question of why issues of sexuality and sexual exploitation fail to reach formal decision-making processes could be seen as a mobilization of bias. This operates when essentially male-dominated decision-making processes protect oppressive men's sexuality, condoned and accepted in both the public and private realms. (Parkin, 1989, p. 122)

Fisher and Vine describe the situation in one English local authority. Their research showed that 26 children who had been placed in residential establishments as victims of sexual abuse were re-abused while in care by other residents. They conclude that the authority is:

> ... unique only insofar as it has had the foresight to recognise and deal with the problem. The problem exists in all areas if one wishes to see it (Fisher and Holloway-Vine, 1990, p. 3).

In the United States, Spencer and Knudsen's study gave information on the perpetrators of sexual abuse in different out-of-home care settings.

> ... child perpetrators were involved in 6 per cent of the foster home cases; 70 per cent (88/126) of residential home cases; 50 percent (21/42) of state institution cases; and 67 percent (10/15) of hospital cases. Abuse by another resident also may indicate lack of supervision, but except for foster homes, other children or residents were more likely than custodial staff to be the perpetrators of sexual abuse (Spencer and Knudsen, 1992, p. 488).

The report on the ChildLine Boarding School Line found that there were 20 cases (13% of all sexual abuse cases) where children were abused by other children. In 15 of the cases the victims were boys and in all but three cases the abusers were boys (La Fontaine and Morris, 1991, p. 23). Morgan found that a very small number of pupils "wrote about sexual abuse by other pupils... or identified particular areas of the school or particular toilet blocks which were used for such activities" (Morgan, 1993, p. 45). Grimshaw and Berridge asked the child and four staff members in their study to assess current emotional and behavioural problems. Sexual exploitation (taking advantage of a partner) was identified most frequently by deputy heads (care); for a quarter (26.1%) of the children. Teaching staff identified this least frequently; for 14.1% of the children, and nine of the children (14.5%) self assessed this as a current problem (Grimshaw and Berridge, 1994, pp. 106-107).

King (1992) reviews the evidence on sexual assault in prison settings but states that although "sexual assault is acknowledged to occur in prisons, surprisingly little research has been undertaken to delineate the nature and extent of the problem" (King, 1992, p. 67) and there is no specific mention of young people in penal institutions. Dumond, however, cites one research study in the USA which indicates that just under 10% of residents in juvenile institutions in Southeastern USA reported sexual victimization and another which found that "sexual assault was five times more likely among youth in prison than in training school" (Dumond, 1992, p. 137; see also Cotton and Groth, 1984).

Kelly (1995) gives an example of a 14 year old boy who had experienced 28 different residential placements in the 11 years he had been in care and had been abused three times by different known juvenile abusers. As a former inspector of children's homes, Kelly found several instances of homes accommodating convicted or known juvenile abusers and sexually abused children. However, Kelly also found that the 95 per cent of staff interviewed during inspections were unaware of the Children Act guidelines that it is inappropriate to place a sexually abused child in a home accommodating children who are themselves abusers. Utting (1991) suggests as a principle that "victims of abuse should be separated from children who are perpetrators of abuse" (Utting, 1991, p. 34) and this "has implications for placement decisions and requires authorities to make available an adequate range of facilities" (Utting, 1991, p. 35).

The Centre for Residential Child Care make the important point, however, that while placing young people who have been sexually abused and sexually abusing young people in the same establishment should be avoided, it can never be entirely prevented.

> The reason is that some young people do not reveal their history of sexual abuse or sexually abusing behaviour until after they have been placed, and some individuals have histories of having been abused sexually as well as of abusing others in this way. In the second place, some young people who have been sexually abused display such overtly sexualised behaviour as a result of their own abuse, that it can be perceived as, or actually becomes sexually abusive towards others, without that necessarily being their clear intention (Centre for Residential Child Care, 1995, p. 2; see also NCH, 1992, p. 34).

In an early paper, McNeil and Morse discuss the management of sexual behaviour in residential settings. They describe the range of behaviour as including "sexual language and gestures, "playing the dozens"[36], group and individual masturbation, homosexuality, exhibitionism, attempts to promote heterosexual experience and some standard and not-so-standard perversions" (McNeil and Morse, 1964, p. 116). They describe the management of sexuality as following a general set of principles. Sexual language is not "reacted to with shock or surprise but it is not encouraged by any staff member" and "although the fact of sexuality is not disapproved, it is classified as a private activity and the source and nature of public views of sex are explained" (McNeil and Morse, 1964, p. 116; see also Lambert, 1976). Children are supplied with sexual information whenever it is requested and the request is deemed legitimate. McNeil and Morse see the problems of controlling sexual behaviour as arising primarily from the "fusion of sex and aggression" (McNeil and Morse, 1964, p. 119).

> The fusion of sexuality with issues of power, domination, and aggression undoubtedly reflects in most of these youngsters the extent to which they felt dominated, controlled, and sometimes abused in relation to early caretakers (Crenshaw, 1988, pp. 67-68)

McNeil and Morse highlight a number of issues in the adult response to sexuality. They warn against the generalized suppression of sexual behaviour or the denial of its existence. Along with understanding the individual child, group dynamics need to be taken into account in the decision to intercede and the technique of intervention, and the handling of sexual incidents must address both the individual and the group. They stress the importance of sex education and supervision of the day-to-day interaction of staff and children (McNeil and Morse, 1964, pp. 121-122).

Hargrave (1991) provides a descriptive analysis of critical sexual incidents reported by 95 workers in three residential agencies. Workshops on developmental sexuality were held in the agencies

36 "Sexual language may evolve into "playing the dozens" as an exercise in verbal sexual proficiency, it may take the form of peer sexual invitation, or it may find its outlet in an exhibitionistic display of sexuality on the part of the child" (McNeil and Morse, 1964, p. 117).

and each staff member provided a written description "of the most difficult sexual incident that he or she had managed in his or her career in residential treatment" (Hargrave, 1991, p. 415). These were subsequently reviewed by two independent judges. The incidents were categorised as: heterosexual incidents, 16 (16.8%); homosexual incidents , 26 (27.4%); staff approached by child or adolescent, 23 (24.2%); singular sexuality, 12 (12.6%); deviant sexuality, 12 (12.6%); miscellaneous, 6 (6.3%).

> An overview of these results suggests that the pattern of incidents clearly follows the expected course of sexual development, with higher rates of heterosexual incidents in adolescent treatment environments and higher rates of homosexual incidents in child settings (Hargrave, 1991, p. 416).

Hargrave argues that the data support the need for training in child and adolescent sexual development; therapeutic management of sexual behaviour of children in group settings; and agency policy and procedures in such incidents (Hargrave, 1991, p. 416).

Carrey and Adams (1992) carried out an analysis of the patterns of sexual acting out in the psychiatric inpatient ward of the Pierre Janet hospital, Quebec, over a one year period. Sexual acting-out was defined as discrete episodes involving at least two children that consisted of "either sexual intercourse, oral-genital contact, digital penetration, or touching of the other child's genitalia" (Carrey and Adams, 1992, p. 19). Twelve children (out of 32 admissions) were involved in seven episodes, committing a total of 32 acts. Six of the children were involved in more than one episode.

> ... the type of sexual activity included anal penetration (2), oral-genital contact (2), attempted sexual intercourse (1), and fondling (2)... coercion may have been a factor in ... two episodes (Carrey and Adams, 1992, p. 20).

Although numbers are small, the study found that "children with past histories of sexual abuse, foster care, learning disabilities, and lack of parental involvement were more likely to sexually act-out" (Carrey and Adams, 1992, p. 23). Carrey and Adams found that an educational approach was the single most important intervention in dealing with sexual acting-out. Information was provided on physical and sexual development and appropriate sexual behaviour.[37]

> Instruction about sexuality is embedded in the overall context of interpersonal relationships linked with tenderness, intimacy, and respect for the other person. Most of these children have linked sexuality with sadistic, aggressive domination or humiliation of the other person (Carrey and Adams, 1992, p. 21).

Although advocating caution about the use of behavioural approaches, time-out, negative reinforcement (e.g. giving children a reward each time they do not engage in the undesirable behaviour), role playing, and use of contracts, were used.

Staff reactions to sexual acting-out "included feelings of anger, betrayal and impotence" and "there were many differences of opinion about what reparative or punitive consequences should follow the acting-out" (Carrey and Adams, 1992, p. 22).

> One partial solution as to what kind of consequence the child should receive depended on whether the acting-out was the result of previous sexual abuse, delinquent acting-out, or age-appropriate sexual exploration (Carrey and Adams, 1992, p. 22).

In one case, sexual acting-out "was so out of control that instead of further contamination of the milieu, the treatment team decided to discontinue treatment and refer the child to a more structured setting" (Carrey and Adams, 1992, p. 23).

37 The issues covered depended on the age of the children, for example, the "preschoolers are not taught about sexuality per se but about respect for their own bodies and the bodies of others and the privacy that can be expected" (Carrey and Adams, 1992, p. 21)

White (1987) suggests that:

> ... the management of sexual drives, approaches, fantasies, is perhaps the most pressing practical task for staff and clients (White, 1987, p. 53).

He goes on to emphasise the degree to which this affects relationships between staff and young people.

> "What is not perhaps realised by those who have not experienced the group care situation first hand is how much of daily living and planning revolves around the issue of sexual behaviour, taboos and fears. Any member of staff at any time is worried about being alone with a child" (White, 1987, p. 53)

Crenshaw (1988) suggests that one of the most difficult judgements for residential workers is the extent to which sexual behaviour is reflective of a developmentally normal process (such as curiosity about sex or experimentation and sex play of a relatively innocent form) and "to what degree is it reflective of developmental disturbance, characterized by excessiveness, compulsiveness, confusion with aggression, and fusion with drives for power and domination, and intertwined with attempts to manipulate, control, and/or dominate peers" (Crenshaw, 1988, p. 58).

Similarly, the Centre for Residential Child Care (1995) stress that not all sexual behaviour between young people is sexually abusive:

> It is natural for young people to experiment with one another, and to exhibit sexual curiosity (Centre for Residential Child Care, 1995, p. 9).

But "the other side of the coin is that **young people <u>do</u> abuse sexually**" and "just as it is a mistake to see all sexual behaviour as abusive, so there is also a danger in seeing everything as "experimentation"" (Centre for Residential Child Care, 1995, p. 9; see also NCH, 1992, p. 25).

The Centre for Residential Child Care identifies six main reasons why sexual abuse induces such anxiety among residential staff: some young people can talk and act in ways which may be experienced as so sexually explicit, provocative and even seductive that residential workers feel very uncomfortable and awkward in knowing how to respond to it; listening to a young person describing the details of sexual abuse they have experienced can be very hard to take, such that residential workers may understandably want to avoid the subject when the young person raises it; residential workers can at times feel very vulnerable, fearing that it may be alleged they have also sexually abused the young person; residential workers can feel very isolated with the responsibility of trying to provide safe care; in any group of people, there are likely to be adults who have themselves been sexually abused and residential staff are no exception; and the uncertainty around knowing what has happened and whether it was sexual abuse can provoke anxiety (Centre for Residential Child Care, 1995, pp. 3-4; see also NCH, 1992, p. 17).

Westcott and Clement (1992) found that approximately one-third of the peer abusers in their study had a previous known history of abuse (Westcott and Clement, 1992, p. 14). NCH (1992) suggests that in many residential establishments, abusive histories are not openly acknowledged and the "young people are allowed to develop a 'cover story'". This can interfere with treatment of the abusive behaviour. Openness about what a child has done can raise fears of 'scapegoating', of being ousted by their peer group, or violence. On the other hand, many carers feel that openness is necessary so that other young people can protect themselves against abuse (NCH, 1992, p. 16). The report concludes that if a young person needs to develop a 'cover story', the placement is an inappropriate one (NCH, 1992, p. 34). The report recommends that:

> ... there is a need within the Continuum of Care for the establishment of more specialist residential treatment facilities for children and young people who have abused other children, who are assessed as being in need of this type of intervention (NCH, 1992, p. 34).

In relation to foster care:

> The Committee recommends that such placements should never be made if there are younger, or developmentally less advanced children or young people in the foster placement (NCH, 1992, p. 36).

Foster carers, furthermore, must have received specialist training in this area of work, although the Committee stated that "there appears to be little, or no specific formal training available for staff or foster carers who are working, or seeking to work in this field" (NCH, 1992, p. 39) Foster carers must also have easy access to support.

Kelly reports that there is often no departmental guidance to residential staff; placement decisions were usually made without consideration of the need to activate child protection procedures; social workers and residential key workers of abused and vulnerable children in many homes were not party to the placement decision; they were not given relevant information about the abuser's history; information was inadequate and often delayed; risk assessments were not done and there was no ongoing monitoring of risk (Kelly, 1995, p. 26).

> Despite a succession of public inquiry reports raising the need for training, it is sobering to think that the vast majority of qualified and unqualified children's home staff have received little or no training in the assessment of risk, in disclosure work or in the treatment of sexually abused and abusing children and young people (Kelly, 1995, p. 27).

Skinner also stresses that where young people who have been abused and young people known to have abused others have to be placed in the same residential unity, there must be careful assessment of the risks, agreed protection plans and appropriate levels of surveillance. Work will also require to be undertaken to enable the young person to accept responsibility for the behaviour and learn more appropriate ways of relating to others. This has implications for agencies' placement policies, staffing levels, training and supervision and requires access to external expert consultancy (Skinner, 1992, p. 34; see also Centre for Residential Child Care, 1995). Doran and Brannan (1996) also highlight the need to "assess vulnerability in young people prior to placement" but argue that the "current shrinking local authority provision and climate of public opinion favouring punishment of young people, particularly adolescent boys, militated against good practice in relation to vulnerability issues" (Doran and Brannan, 1996, p. 165).

The Centre for Residential Child Care stress the importance of a culture of anti-oppressive practice, "devaluing people on the basis of gender, race, disability or any other difference between them is unacceptable, be it between staff and staff, staff and young people, or between young people themselves" (Centre for Residential Child Care, 1995, p. 9). It is absolutely necessary for staff to model good, respectful, balanced relationships and young people must be "helped to develop self-respect, and the skills to be clear and firm about what they want and do not want, without becoming aggressive and devaluing to other people in the process" (Centre for Residential Child Care, 1995, p. 9).

> It's... important to challenge openly behaviour and attitudes which they or other people may display which diminish others or misuse power(Centre for Residential Child Care, 1995, p. 14).

There must be honesty about what goes on and who knows and "healthy and open attitudes to sex, which assist young people to develop their own sexuality at their own pace, as they mature, are vital" (Centre for Residential Child Care, 1995, p. 9).

> ... it is not difficult to include information about what is considered acceptable behaviour in sexual terms. This can include issues such as touching, privacy, sexual language, pornography etc. By being specific, you give permission to young people to say "no" to advances by other young people or adults, and you also give a clear message to

potentially abusive individuals that their behaviour will not be acceptable or accepted (although they themselves are and will be accepted). (Centre for Residential Child Care, 1995, p. 16; see also Crenshaw, 1988).

Individual care plans and contracts need to include the issue of acceptable and unacceptable forms of behaviour and contact, including sexual ones, between the young person and staff and other residents (Centre for Residential Child Care, 1995, p. 17).

> The Committee also affirm the importance of children and young people in residential care having a programme of preventative education, and an environment which allows for discussion and openness about sexual matters... In residential care, the atmosphere and attitudes of staff play a crucial educative function, and gender issues such as how the young people are treated and the way in which relationships between female and male staff are dealt with should not be played down (NCH, 1992, p. 26).

O'Mahoney (1989) calls for written policies to be available in social services departments and in residential establishments about sexual relationships for young people in care which will address questions such as what boundaries need to be drawn and what exactly constitutes a sexual relationship. Guidelines need to address relationships between consenting peers of the same age and distinctions need to be made between adolescent experimentation and continuing sexual relationships. The effects of heterosexual or homosexual relationships on the rest of the residential unit need to be addressed and staff "have to know what limitations are placed on a young person's sexual development because he or she is in residential care, who is responsible for their implementation and what supports there will be when conflict arises" (O'Mahoney, 1989, p. 32; see also Crenshaw, 1988; Harrell and Orem, 1980).

Fostering the Sexually Abused Child

The difficulties and problems involved in fostering children who have been sexually abused have been discussed by Macaskill (1991); Roberts (1986, 1989, and 1993) and Batty (1991). Of particular relevance to this review is the incidence of sexualised behaviour. Macaskill's study showed that there was clear evidence of sexualised behaviour in 80 per cent of the 80 cases (Macaskill, 1991, p. 71).

> Sexual overtures from abused children included a range of behaviour from touching the foster or adoptive parents' genital areas, through to demands for sexual intercourse (Macaskill, 1991, p 73).

In over half the placements, some type of sexual activity was directed towards another child in the family (Macaskill, 1991, p. 86). Roberts also discusses this. She writes:

> The most immediate problem for many foster families is that the sexually abused child will teach other children in the home sexual play. Very young children may be particularly vulnerable to being interfered with. At the other extreme, older children in the home may be invited and provoked into a sexual relationship which they do not understand (Roberts, 1986, p. 10).

What effect this behaviour has on the further likelihood of sexual abuse in foster care? A study in the US found that younger children who were sexually abused in foster homes were likely to have been previously sexually abused although this was not as likely for older victims (McFadden and Ryan, 1991, p. 224). Russell suggests that perpetrators of sexual abuse may be able to identify and exploit children who have already been sexually abused and "MacFarlane reports that approximately 25 per cent of the children in one study who were in treatment were revictimized by someone else during the treatment period (personal communication, 1982)" (Russell, 1984, p. 267). In linking inappropriate sexual behaviour to the possibilities of further sexual abuse, however, care must be take not to repeat the argument of the 'seductive child'. Responsibility for the abuse must remain firmly with the perpetrator. Morris and Wheatley (1995) also highlight the particular vulnerability of children who have previously been sexually abused to abuse in foster care (Morris and Wheatley, 1995, p. 59).

It was noted above that stress could be a factor in the sexual abuse of children, and Macaskill points out that fostering for children who have been sexually abused is itself extremely stressful.

> Abused children invaded family life, unsettling established roles and relationships and sapping away the energies of those caring for them. Foster and adoptive parents were especially vulnerable as their tolerance level was often stretched to its ultimate level. Several admitted that it was virtually impossible to estimate in advance how heavy the personal toll would be of caring for an abused child. (Mackaskill, 1991, p. 69).

Benedict et al (1996) compared the child health characteristics before and during the foster care experience in a sample of foster children who were the victims of substantiated maltreatment in foster care with those of a group of children in foster care who were not maltreated. Significantly more children overall with substantiated maltreatment reports during foster care had physical health, developmental, behaviour and mental health problems reported than did the children not reported as maltreated in foster care (Benedict et al, 1996, p. 565).

> This population of foster children, both maltreated and nonmaltreated, had a multitude of health, development and school problems... maltreatment while in foster care was associated with probable exacerbation of existing problems or precipitation of new problems in this foster child sample, particularly for the children who were sexually abused (Benedict et al, 1996, p. 567)

McFadden and Ryan (1991) comment that much of abuse in foster care happens "not in inadequate families but in families stressed by the rigors of fostering, especially sequential overloading" (McFadden and Ryan, 1991, p. 215). They go on to stress the importance of regular reviews which would assess levels of stress in the foster home. This also raises important issues about the need for additional supports and resources to foster carers who are caring for children and young people who are severely troubled and exhibiting disturbed behaviour. The call for foster care to be incorporated into the formal economy as a professional, salaried service (Maclean, 1989; Rhodes, 1993; Robinson, 1991; see also Cavanagh, 1992) has recently led to the establishment of such a service in some departments.

Suicide, Self -Harm and Deaths in Care

Suicide and self-harm of young people living away from home is of continuing concern. Most attention has been paid to this in penal institutions. During 1993-94, "at least 12% of young people in Young Offender Institutions (YOIs) were recorded (907 incidents) as having deliberately harmed themselves" (Howard League, 1995b, p. 2). The suicides in 1990-91 of Philip Knight, Jeffrey Horler and Craig Walsh, all 15 year old boys in prison (Howard League, 1995b), through to the deaths of Kelly Holland and Arlene Elliott, 17 year old girls in Cornton Vale have highlighted the vulnerability of young people incarcerated in prison (Galloway, 1997)[38].

A study of suicide attempts and self harm in a representative sample of 16 prison establishments in England between July 1991 and June 1992 identified 305 incidents involving 248 prisoners (Liebling and Krarup, 1994, p. 39; Liebling, 1995, p. 175)[39]. The study found that 43 per cent of the prisoners were under 21 whereas 17 per cent of the average daily prison population in 1991 and 31 per cent of annual receptions into custody were under 21 (Liebling, 1995, p. 176)[40]. The youngest person was 14 years old (Liebling and Krarup, 1994, p. 40).

The Howard League Commission found widespread self-harm throughout the prison system. The majority of those who self-harm are young and includes two thirds of all female prisoners (Howard League, 1995a, p. 57). While some young people have serious behavioural and psychological

38 These were followed by the deaths of four young women aged between 19 and 26 in Cornton Vale (Galloway, 1997)

39 However, Liebling also writes that the "data recieved were not a complete sample: regular checking... suggested that the data were unevenly incomplete for particular establishments and/or at particular times during the year" (Liebling, 1995, pp. 175-176)

40 The figure for the percentage of prisoners aged under 21 is different in the two papers, Liebling and Krarup give the figure as 52% (Liebling and Krarup, 1994, p. 40)

problems which the Prison Service cannot address or have deep-seated personal problems which cannot be resolved while they are in prison, most self-harm and suicide attempts are a response to pressures within the prison system and bullying (Howard League, 1995a, p. 60). Liebling studied suicidal behaviour in four young offenders institutions. A group of 50 prisoners who had attempted suicide were interviewed as well as a randomly selected control group (Liebling, 1992; 1993). Those who had attempted suicide had fewer qualifications from schools (most had difficulty in reading and writing). They were more likely: to have been involved in violence at school and have been the victims of bullying; to have been in local authority care; to have received psychiatric treatment and to report major alcohol and drug problems; and to have injured themselves before coming into custody. The suicide attempt group were also more likely to have spent time on remand; described themselves as more isolated in prison; and were far more likely to report difficulties with other inmates (Liebling, 1992, pp. 14-15; 1993, pp. 392-394).

> The most significant point to emerge from the responses to questions about the experience of imprisonment was the consistency with which the subject group were (and felt) worse off than their fellow inmates in terms of the availability and desirability of work, education, PE, and other methods of occupation.. They did not see as many opportunities for themselves in prison, nor did they seem able to make constructive use of their time. The combination of practical constraints and their own lethargy left them helpless and resourceless in the face of hours of unfilled time. Inmates in the subject group appeared to be less able to occupy themselves constructively when locked in their cells. They felt more bored, did less, got more bored as the sentence went on, and yet spent more time there. If there is a vulnerability factor not yet explored in prison suicide research, this must be one of the most significant (Liebling, 1993, p. 394).

Liebling argues that a "new understanding of risk should be based on the notion of vulnerability to suicide" and may be "reframed in terms of inmates' coping ability" (Liebling, 1993, p. 403). She differentiates between three groups of prison suicides: the psychiatrically ill, life/long sentence prisoners, and 'poor copers'. The 'poor copers' have a lower age profile, "constitute the most numerous group of prison suicides and... the significance of the immediate prison situation may be most acute in these cases" (Liebling, 1995, p.182; see also Power and Spencer, 1987).

In relation to residential care, the Dolphin Project consultation with 45 young people looked after in three local authorities found that just under one-fifth (18%) "made unsolicited statements saying they had undertaken acts with the intention of ending their life" (Buchanan et al, 1993, p. 81). The report also presents figures from unpublished research that 20% of 11-17 year olds presenting at accident and emergency departments were 'looked after' young people and that "75% of the repeaters, that is those who had been seen previously as a result of an act of deliberate self harm were in residential care" (Buchanan et al, 1993, p. 81). Kendrick (1995) discusses the breakdown of residential placements and found that self-destructive behaviour such as self-mutilation or suicide attempts were involved in a small number of cases and three of the thirteen secure care placements in the study were because of self-destructive behaviour (Kendrick, 1995, p. 80).

The Howard League Commission found that there were issues of self-harm in secure accommodation although "there was very little evidence of self-harm as a response to bullying" and it "is widely believed that much of the self-harming seen in secure units is related to a past history of abuse" (Howard League, 1995a, p. 79). The main response to self-harm involved providing constant observation, counselling and referral to specialist agencies but the Commission was concerned about the lack of proper training for staff. The review of secure care in Scotland presents information on 74 young people in secure care on a date in 1994[41]. 62 of the 74 young people (83%) were considered to be a risk to themselves - 15 of the 16 girls and 47 of the 58 boys (Social Work Services Inspectorate, 1996, p. 20). The review of secure care also looked at cases of children who had died in care since 1989 and examined information on young people aged 11 or over whose deaths were not from natural causes[42]. The causes of death included drug overdoses, solvent- and drug-related deaths, road traffic accidents where the child had taken a risk (for example by being a passenger in a stolen car), hangings and murder.

41 This date is not specified.

42 The review does not give figures for deaths of children in care or for those who had not died from natural causes.

Preventing Suicides and Self-Harm

In response to the sharp increase in the numbers of prison suicides in the 1980s, the "Prison Service with the support of the Samaritans decided on a fundamental change of direction" (Biggar and Neal, 1996, p. 209). In 1991, it established the Suicide Awareness Support Unit and the Samaritans appointed a full-time Prison Liaison and Development Officer. The death of Phillip Knight in Swansea Prison led to the development, with the involvment of community representatives and prisoners themselves, of the Listener Scheme where prisoners were supported and trained by the Samaritans "to befriend other prisoners not so fortunate or skilled at coping with prison life" (Davies, 1994, p. 126; see also Biggar and Neal, 1996).

> The prisoners called themselves **Listeners**, for that is what they were called on to do. Like their Samaritan colleagues in the community, the Listeners were to shoulder the burden of others (Davies, 1992, p. 19).

The young offender wing, however, was not represented on the Listener Scheme because "it proved impossible to select a suitable candidate from this age group... and all four Listeners situated on 'normal' location were regularly called to the young offender unit to respond to individual cries for help" (Davies, 1994, p. 127).

In the first 12 months there was a 50 per cent reduction in the incidence of serious self-harm and there were no deaths. While a number of other changes have taken place alongside the Listener Scheme, "it is widely acknowledged that the scheme has played an important part in the changes that have occurred at Swansea" (Davies, 1994, p. 128). Davies also stresses that the Listener scheme has brought about a change in the climate in the prison, chipping "away at traditional assumptions of **them** and **us**" and promoting prisoner involvement:

> Listeners are actively involved in planning, implementing and decision-making in key areas of a prisoner's life. Give prisoners responsibility and they are likely to respond constructively, humanely and professionally (Davies, 1992, p. 21)[43].

Liebling argues that the recognition of significance of the environment in self-harm and suicides means that:

> ... prevention strategies may take on a broader and more supportive approach... For many prisoners, support may be offered in the form of contact, activity and time spent listening (by staff, prisoners, or others...). Many of the more immediate 'solutions' to suicide risk may be located on wings rather than in health care centres. Multi-disciplinary teams able to co-ordinate health care, probation, psychology, and regime-based provision for those at rist are well placed to make the necessary connections between 'suicide awareness' and other related policy areas such as sentence planning, throughcare, incentives, and 'positive regimes'... (Liebling, 1995, pp. 181-182).

The Support Force for Children's Residential Care stress that it is important for staff not to view self-harming behaviour as an indication of a failing placement but rather "in terms of work in progress" (Support Force for Children's Residential Care, 1996, p. 81).

> For the majority of children and young people demonstrating these behaviours, it is likely that they will have low confidence, poor self esteem, and few interests. A pro-active approach by residential staff will ensure that these problems are faced in a systematic and planned way that avoids a jollying-along approach (Support Force for Children's Residential Care, 1996, p. 81).

Appropriate referral to the general practitioner, in the first instance, and to a consultant is essential.

43 Samaritan branches are now involved in all prisons and young offender institutions in England and Wales and by 1996 there were 83 Prisoner-Befriending Schemes (Biggar and Neal, 1996).

Alcohol and Drug Abuse

Heads of secure units in Scotland "said that half of the young people in secure accommodation were having problems with drug, alcohol or substance abuse" (Social Work Services Inspectorate, 1996, p. 39). However, only one unit had a written policy on the management of problems associated with alcohol, drug and substance abuse, and only three units "reported that their staff were trained to identify and cope with the unpredictable or disruptive behaviour which results from being drunk or using drugs or solvents" (Social Work Services Inspectorate, 1996, p. 39).

> Children in care find alcohol and other dangerous substances particularly attractive and are at risk of harming themselves and others, including the risk of death. (Social Work Services Inspectorate, 1996, p. 39).

Since 1993, two young people in secure care have died as a direct result of drug, alcohol or substance abuse; one of them was on home leave (Social Work Services Inspectorate, 1996, p. 40). The review recommended that:

> All care and education staff in secure units should receive training in how to deal with drug, alcohol and substance abuse...
> Each unit's quality development plan should include a section on drug, alcohol and substance abuse which sets out targets for action and a timetable
> (Social Work Services Inspectorate, 1996, p. 41).

Grimshaw and Berridge found that "solvent abuse was alleged in a maximum of nine per cent of cases (by care staff) but children and teachers both put it as low as three per cent.... alcohol abuse was alleged in a maximum of 24 per cent of cases (by care staff) but teachers perceived it in six per cent, slightly lower than children" (Grimshaw and Berridge, 1994, p. 106).

In their study in a young offender establishment, Skett et al found that three-quarters (49) of the 65 prisoners admitted using drugs and all respondents "agreed that drugs were readily available inside, especially cannabis" (Skett et al, 1996, p. 9). Over one-third (37%) of the total sample admitted to using cannabis at least once a day and 11% admitted to taking amphetamines every day. The authors comment on the specific issue of "bullying and taxing (particularly in a young offender institute), related to the possession, concealment and exchange of drugs and currencies (Skett et al, 1996, p. 9).

The Support Force for Children's Residential Care consider that residential staff will need information about preventing drug and solvent abuse and to be able to recognise the signs and symptoms. They will need counselling skills but also access to specialist counselling services. Drug-related issues should be discussed with children and young people, working towards preventing experimentation. A "heavy approach, with grim and dire warnings of the dangers of drugs and solvents" may not have the desired effect as it may glamorise them. They should be aware of their responsibilities as a role model and also be constantly vigilant (Support Force for Children's Residential Care, 1996, p 103).

Control, Sanctions and Physical Restraint

Setting Limits, Defining Boundaries

> Setting limits, and defining boundaries are important aspects of proactive residential care. These activities should be carried out as positively as possible (Support Force for Children's Residential Care, 1996, p. 52).

Inconsistency in responding to children and young people in residential care, because of a failure to set clear boundaries, can have very damaging implications. However, this does not mean that the more rules and regulations there are, the better it will be for the children and young people and "residential units/homes should have only those rules and limits that are absolutely necessary for reasonably smooth day-to-day operation" (Support Force for Children's Residential Care, 1996, p.52). It is important the children and young people know who is setting the limits and why; whether they can have a part to play in deciding the limits; exactly what the limits are; what will happen if they are not adhered to; that the limits will be consistently applied; and who benefits from them and why. Children and young people also need to be prepared in terms of the less obvious boundaries which apply in social situations outwith the residential home (Support Force for Children's Residential Care, 1996, p. 53).

Rewards and Positive Reinforcements

In reinforcing rules, it is important to "make greater use of rewards and positive reinforcements, and only use sanctions and punishments where absolutely essential (Support Force for Children's Residential Care, 1996, p. 58). Members of residential staff can provide positive reinforcements by:

- recognising that something has been attempted or achieved, and acknowledging it. This can apply whether it relates to something practical, personal, or social.
- saying "Thank you" for complying with a request
- saying "Thank you" for any small courtesies, given voluntarily
- giving encouragement in the form of feedback during a task

(Support Force for Children's Residential Care, 1996, p. 59).

Kahan comments that "the most successful rewards in any school or home are those provided by staff who recognise effort and provide genuine praise and support for what a child is doing" (Kahan, 1994, p. 108). Swanson and Richard suggest the following guidelines in giving praise: make eye contact; be sincere; praise the specific behaviour; give praise immediately; gradually increase praise; do not contaminate praise (e.g. by saying "Why didn't you do that before"); and vary the wording so praise does not become repetitious and meaningless (Swanson and Richard, 1988, p. 80).

More tangible rewards may also be needed, particularly for severely damaged children and young people.

> … it is worth remembering that it will be necessary to vary these rewards according to the individual. Even where the behaviour of two children or young people is similar, they may need different rewards in order to motivate them (Support Force for Children's Residential Care, 1996, p. 59).

It is important that any system of rewards is clear to the child or young person and linked explicitly to the specific improvements in behaviour which are expected (Kahan, 1994; see also Swanson and Richard, 1988).

A Positive Ethos

Millham et al (1981) argued that it is the 'ethos' of the establishment which effectively controls:

> … by fashioning a system of mutually held expectations, values and norms of conduct which exercise restraint on members. Control in a community home rests, as it does in a family, in demonstrating that within its walls a child receives more physical care, more love, understanding and encouragement than he is likely to experience outside (Millham et al, 1981, p. 48)[44].

Young people must perceive that they are getting tangible benefits from the experience of residential care.

> Children's short-term instrumental preoccupations mean that they can be controlled by manipulation of rewards and sanctions which are immediate and tangible. Rules should be clear and self-evident, reiterated by staff but open to discussion with the children and holding the possibility of change (Millham et al, 1981, p. 49)

While there is no prescription for creating a positive 'ethos' in a residential establishment and there are many varied ways of establishing a caring and safe 'ethos', the authors suggest that there are five features which seem to be common to all successful establishments:

> …(a) Young people should feel enriched by their residential experience in which they should perceive some caring role.
>
> (b) The pupils see themselves as acquiring clear instrumental skills during their stay in care.
>
> (c) Pursuit by the institution of a set of goals which are matched to the primary rather than to the secondary needs of the children. That is to the needs which necessitated absence from home rather than those brought about by living away. The aims are reiterated in a wide variety of ways and permeate the whole control process.
>
> (d) Effective institutions demonstrate some consensus amongst staff, pupils and parents about what these goals should be and how they should be achieved. To maintain this consensus, leadership should be clear and consistent. Staff should be reminded of the strengths of residential care as well as warned against its weaknesses.
>
> (e) The institution should make efforts to fragment the informal world of children by a variety of structural features. This may be by creating small group situations, by appointing senior children to positions of responsibility or by close staff/pupil relationships (Millham et al, 1981, p. 52).

The Influence of the Organisation on Staff Attitudes

Krause (1974) studied the relationship between staff attitudes on authoritarianism, dogmatism and coercion and the type of institution in which they were employed and the position held in the institution and found that there was a clear association.

44 Agnew also stresses the influence of a negative school ethos and dominant `male' values on increased aggressive behaviour and bullying (Agnew, 1989).

Child care workers, regardless of their education, age or experience in the institution, selected alternatives for handling problems on the basis of the type of institution in which they were employed. For example, regardless of age and background characteristics, child care workers in Intensive Treatment programs selected mainly normative handling alternatives, while child care workers in Group Care programs selected mainly coercive handling alternatives (Krause, 1974, p. 28).

While it was originally assumed that individuals who scored high on authoritarianism and dogmatism would favour more coercive handling techniques, this was not supported by the findings. This suggests that "specific attitudes regarding compliance orientations developed as a result of socialization experiences in the institution and were not determined by basic attitudes" (Krause, 1974, p. 29; see also Baldwin, 1990) and the author stresses the importance of staff training, supervision and communication in influencing the attitudinal climate of the institution.

Rindfleisch and Baros-Van Hull also studied direct care workers' attitudes toward the use of physical force with children and the findings were somewhat different to those of Krause (Rindfleisch and Baros-Van Hull, 1982). One hundred direct care givers in 15 children's homes in Ohio completed a self-administered questionnaire to examine the relationship between a number of social factors and attitudes toward the use of physical force.

Five factors were found to be uniquely associated with willingness to use force:

1. Amount of resentment toward the children;
2. Management of routines of everyday life in an organization-centered way;
3. Seldom or never participating in decision making in the facility
4. Size of the community in which the direct care giver was reared; and
5. Age of the care giver.

(Rindfleisch and Baros-Van Hull, 1982, p. 120)

The authors suggest that the higher levels of willingness to use force by older carers "can be interpreted as an effect of their having come to maturity at an earlier period, when use of force was widely supported in the society as a normal means of care giving" (Rindfleisch and Baros-Van Hull, 1982, p. 121). However, it can be seen that two of the factors are organisational and the authors suggest that increasing carers' participation in decision making and individualising children's care will lower the amount of force likely to be used. They also suggest that, based on the findings about resentment toward the children, care giving may "flow less from generosity and concern with the needs of children, but more on the basis of the care giver's feelings of equity and inequity resulting from the exchange between him/herself and the children (Rindfleisch and Baros-Van Hull, 1982, p. 121). They link this to burnout which is characterised by hostility toward clients and agency, apathy, detachment of oneself from client problems and duties on the job, negativism, lack of attentiveness, increased absenteeism, cynicism, and little motivation to perform well on the job (Rindfleisch and Baros-Van Hull, 1982, p. 122). The authors again stress the importance of selection and training procedures in establishments.

Averting Crises

Katz (1988) stresses the importance of identifying the situations, events or experiences that may underlie or trigger crisis-related episodes and of helping children and young people to develop skills in handling such situations that might otherwise develop into crises (Katz, 1988, p. 48). Certain general situations are seen as placing some children at greater risk of out-of-control behaviour: transition periods; perceived competitive situations; home visits or family visits; perceived change in a relationship with a team member; stressful situations ; or a decrease in the level of supervision (Katz, 1988, pp. 34-35). When triggering events have been identified, children can be helped to become more aware of them and to anticipate and plan for situations that they find particularly troubling. Children can also be helped to recognise emotional warning signs and to learn and use more effective responses to emotionally difficult situations (Katz, 1988, pp. 42-47).

Sanctions

> Ill-considered and inappropriate discipline can increase the psychological damage already experienced by children in residential care and where knowledge exists, alternative rule of thumb methods should have no place (Millham et al, 1981, p. 1).

> ... effectively controlled institutions and successful staff are characterised by the sparing use of sanctions (Millham et al, 1981, p. 48).

Sanctions must be clearly defined and, wherever possible, be both immediate and consistent. Equally, they must be achievable as it is pointless to make threats which cannot be carried out. Again, sanctions and punishments must be appropriate to each child and young person and must be relevant to the problem, although there may be a tension between consistency of sanctions and responding to the individual child. Kahan (1994) states that it is likely to be better to deal with each event as seems most appropriate at the time so that the child can understand the connection between the 'offence' and the sanction and each day can be seen as a new start (Kahan, 1994, p. 108). A punishment for an individual should not affect the rest of the group. Sanctions in the form of withdrawal of privileges are suggested to be the most effective (Kahan, 1994, p. 109) and the Support Force for Children's Residential Care suggest that a range of sanctions might include: reproof; reprimand[45]; reparation; and loss of privileges (Support Force for Children's Residential Care, 1996, p. 61; see also Swanson and Richard, 1988).

> Our authority will come from being true to ourselves, expressing concern and disapproval in a personal and authentic way. In order for our disapproval to mean something to another person, on its own and without a complicated and impersonal system of sanctions to back it up, we have to build relationships on mutual affection, respect, trust, acceptance and commitment (Burton, 1993, p. 69; see also Harrell and Orem, 1980).

The Use of Sanctions

Skinner (1992) lists the range of measures used in residential establishments: restricted leisure activities (82% of establishments); early to bed (74%); physical restraint (67%); control of pocket money (62%); extra tasks (46%); isolation (20%); withholding of normal clothing (11%); grounding/staying in unit boundaries (6%); reduction in family contact (5%); loss of home visits (4%); reparation for damage (4%) (Skinner, 1992, p. 64; see also Harvey, 1992).

The draft guidelines on care sanctions and restraints (Skinner, 1992) lists controls which are not permitted..

1. *No young person regardless of age should be subjected to any form of physical punishment, or the threat of physical punishment. No young person should be hit or smacked* (Skinner, 1992, p. 98).

Millham et al (1981) argue that corporal punishment is inappropriate for a number of reasons. Firstly, "difficult children and adolescents can be and are controlled by means other than corporal punishment" (Millham et al, 1981, p. 37). They also argued that those establishments which made use of corporal punishment tended to be ineffective when measured by other criteria such as rates of absconding and other disruptive behaviour. Finally, they argue that there is evidence that corporal punishment is generally applied to those children who are least likely to be affected in a positive way by it (Millham et al, 1981, p. 38).

2. *No young person should be deprived of any meal, nor should normal planned menus be modified or altered for the purposes of punishment* (Skinner, 1992, p. 98)

3. *No young person should be deprived of contact with any professional e.g. field social worker, lawyer, doctor* (Skinner, 1992, p. 98).

45 Swanson and Richard suggest that "soft reprimands, ones that only the child can hear, are more effective in reducing disruptive behavior..." and although "soft reprimands initially require more work, they usually "pay off" in terms of the child's showing more positive behavior and the staff's having to reprimand less" (Swanson and Richard, 1988, p. 84).

Isolation was at the very core of the 'pindown' regime in Staffordshire and also involved restricting access to fieldworkers and other professionals. Children and young people in Leicestershire children's homes were similarly deprived of contacts with professionals (Levy and Kahan, 1991; Kirkwood, 1993).

> 4. *Depriving a young person of contact with parents or adults with whom they have a significant relationship should never be used as a sanction; this includes, for instance, cancelling home leave* (Skinner, 1992, p. 98).

Millham et al (1981) also identified limiting access to parents, friends and relatives as an inappropriate sanction and although they suggested that denial of home leave was only considered appropriate in situations where serious offences had occurred as a direct result of being on leave.

> Any opportunity to keep family and other relationships going or to foster new ones should..., be sought by the residential institution and by the child's field social worker. This curtailment of family and neighbourhood contacts for short-term control ends might be effective but will make ongoing relationships more difficult (Millham et al, 1981, p. 44).

> 5. *Withdrawal of communication or positive engagement ("being sent to Coventry") should not be used* (Skinner, 1992, p. 98)

Again, this was central to the regime of 'pindown' in Staffordshire with extremely damaging results (Levy and Kanhan, 1991).

> 6 *No young person should be sent to bed early. This can be a more frightening and lonely experience than may be evident from the young person's behaviour. It is effectively unsupervised exclusion from the group and therefore carries potential dangers. Young people may be disallowed from staying up late to watch T.V. etc.)* (Skinner, 1992, p. 98)

> 7. *Withholding or use of medication, or medical or dental treatment, should not be used as a sanction* (Skinner, 1992, p. 98)

Millham et al considered that the use of drugs was not appropriate for the control of children since: "... a need to sedate young people often reflects a failure to establish relationships within the home and arises out of other problems in the institution such as staff shortages or inexperience" (Millham et al, 1981, p. 47). Moss et al (1990) identified the use and abuse of sedation to be a widespread practice, particularly in adolescent psychiatric units (Moss et al, 1990, pp 6-7). Complaints about the methods used in St Charles Youth Treatment Centre included the injection of sedative drugs against the young person's will and by force and these complaints were upheld by an independent inquiry (Howard League, 1995a, pp. 88-89).

> 8. *Humiliation in any form should not be used* (Skinner, 1992, p. 98)

Millham et al (1981) also considered that the threat of transfer or threat of removal to another residential setting was also considered to be unacceptable.

> As a threat, it is widely used and, sadly, transfer itself is frequently employed to rid the institution of difficult children. Unfortunately, it creates a problem child out of one that is initially merely irritating and testing-out (Millham et al, 1981, p. 41).

Millham et al (1981) suggest that group punishment "is effective in checking a general drift of indiscipline - a growing casualness on the part of the children which is highlighted by some obvious deficiency" (Millham et al, 1981, p. 42). However, the use of group punishments to get an individual to own up to a misdemeanour was not thought to be warranted.

The use of public disapproval was considered to be appropriate only "when it is an integrated part of an institution's philosophy and related to its implemented goals" (Millham et al, 1981, p. 44). In other situations, "such sanctions can crystallise a 'we and them' polarity" (Millham et al, 1981, p. 45). In a similar vein, the authors:

> ... would discourage the hostile identification of children in other ways such as forcing them to wear unusual clothes or to eat alone. Keeping boys in pyjamas to discourage their absconding behaviour still seems a popular control device in some institutions and can last for several days (Millham et al, 1981, p. 45)

The 'pindown' experience in Staffordshire showed the degree to which inappropriate sanctions can become routinised, not just in terms of controlling severely disturbed and violent young people, but as a knee-jerk response to any child who is perceived as not conforming to the rules.

Skinner (1992) stresses that for all staff the development of skills in setting clear limits for acceptable behaviour, and the use of appropriate sanctions and controls is essential. Induction training should include training on the establishment's approach within the context of agency policy and guidelines and should emphasise the importance of consistency in the staff team's approach. It should also cover how staff can raise concerns about inappropriate sanctions and controls used by other staff.

Restraint and Holding

> **Seán**
> *"I was physically assaulted by residential workers when they were trying to 'restrain' me. This happened all the time. They'd 'restrain' you to make sure you went along with their instructions. Physical assaults were just a routine part of the home's discipline procedure"* (Safe & Sound, 1995, p. 6)

> . . . residential staff should not take action to restrain a child or young person except as a very last resort (Support Force for Children's Residential Care, 1996, p. 89).

80 per cent of the young people in the NAYPIC survey complained of forcible restraint which they felt was unnecessary.

> Most young people felt that staff went far further than was necessary. They also felt restraints were used for petty reasons, like one girl who told us four male staff had restrained her for running in a corridor (Moss et al, 1990, p. 6).

The Howard League Commission found that the use of physical restraint in secure units varies considerably and "some units still appear to use it virtually every day while in others, it is very rare" (Howard League, 1995a, p. 81). Grimshaw and Berridge, in their study of residential schools, gave a number of examples where physical restraint was used "where the circumstances included children's attempts to move out of a supervised area or to refuse compliance with the routine" (Grimshaw and Berridge, 1994, p. 94).

> In these cases there is room for doubt about the extent to which these actions were in keeping with the spirit of the guidance and regulations issued under the Children Act 1989 . . . (Grimshaw and Berridge, 1994, p. 94).

Leadbetter (1996) suggests that the issue of physical restraint has remained a taboo subject in many agencies.

> The historical tendency has been to "individualise" the question of the management of challenging behaviour. To frame it simply as a matter of individual staff competence with risk viewed as simply "part of the job". This perspective has effectively de-emphasised

> the role and responsibilities of the agency and focused the responsibility for risk assessment and intervention on the individual staff member, who inevitably remains in the frame when things go wrong (Leadbetter, 1996, p. 36; see also Ross, 1994).

The failure to produce practical guidance and training, he suggests, is likely to drive practice underground and to reinforce the high levels of stress experienced by staff who deal regularly with challenging and difficult behaviour.

Lindsay (1996) stresses that while the most important parts of a policy involving physical restraint are those which "relate to avoiding, de-escalating and debriefing after incidents involving violence", physical restraint is sometimes necessary and has to be a part of the policy. Policy also needs to be linked extremely closely to training and management. Unless policy is absolutely clear and specific:

> . . . staff will lack confidence, being unsure what the agency wants them to do in difficult situations . . .
> . . . Young people will be unclear about how difficult behaviour of any sort will be responded to . . .
> . . . Restraint techniques will be used which are inappropriate and/or hidden
> . . . Restraint may not occur when it should do . . .
> (Lindsay, 1996, p. 8)

Lindsay suggests that the criteria for selection of a method of physical restraint should be considered from the perspectives of: young people; staff; managers/agency; and general issues. From the perspective of young people, the method must take account of: dignity (avoiding humiliation and 'loss of face'); effectiveness (must work, so young people feel it will restore control rapidly); safety (must minimise risk of injury); pain (must not deliberately use pain); clarity (must be easy to understand so young people know in advance what will happen if restraint is used); release (can be safely and gradually released as the young person regains control); 'onlookers' (avoids danger to other young people in the vicinity) (Lindsay, 1996, p. 9).

From the perspective of staff, it must take account of: dignity (allowing staff to feel comfortable in its use); effectiveness (must work so staff can predict results in any situation); safety (must minimise the risk of injury); learning (must be relatively easy to learn); simple (must be easy to apply in a range of situations; confidence (must result in staff feeling more confidence in handling these situations (Lindsay, 1996, p. 9).

From the managers' and agency viewpoint, it must be: acceptable (to staff and young people); accountable (specific enough to allow monitoring); learning (must be easy enough to teach rapidly and get thorough coverage of staff); practical (must be possible to do with the number of staff available (Lindsay, 1996, p. 10).

In general, the method must take account of: size/age (must be appropriate to the size and age of children and young people; gender (must be appropriate for use with different genders); cultural/religious issues (appropriate to different cultures and religions of children and young people); abuse (must take account of children and young people who have been abused); physical factors (account must be taken of disabilities and medical issues); environment (must be possible within the envisaged environment (Lindsay, 1996, p. 10).

In discussing technical aspects of physical restraint, Leadbetter (1996) comments that "in the absence of regulation, the decision about which method of physical restraint is acceptable within any care sector agency rests on the judgement of responsible managers and politicians" (Leadbetter, 1996, p. 34). However, rigorous published research on the safety of different approaches is not available. Stark (1996) found that "there was no information available to allow comparison of injury rates to clients and staff using different restraint techniques" (Stark, 1996, p. 29). Following allegations that at least 6 children had suffered broken bones during restraint at

Aycliffe, the methods in operation were prohibited. However, The Howard League Commission found evidence that arm and wrist locks were still being used by staff (Howard League, 1995a, p. 83).

Leadbetter states that there are basically four approaches which have been used as the basis of a restraint system:

- The immobilisation of the subject by the use of weight or strength
- The restriction of movement of the long bones by some form of hold or lock
- Maintaining the subject in an off balanced position
- The use of pain compliance

(Leadbetter, 1996, p. 40)

Leadbetter poses four key questions which must be asked of any technique or system: are the techniques being taught effective?; do they contain specific foreseeable risks?; are the techniques ethical?; are they appropriate to the specific setting? (Leadbetter, 1996, p. 41).

In relation to the issue of effectiveness, Leadbetter stresses that any approach must offer a realistic chance of success since a situation will be escalated and prolonged if an approach is not successful. It is essential that restraint systems offer a selection and hierarchy of responses which can be matched to situations of escalating behaviour. Similarly, the ability to easily and progressively relax techniques is crucial (see also Kahan, 1994, pp. 130-131). Leadbetter suggests that a number of technical factors will influence the question of effectiveness: an effective technique will minimise the subject's freedom of movement since the more limbs which are unrestrained, the greater the risk of injury to all parties; the grips used must be secure which invariably requires two points of contact with the grasped limb, the grip closed and the hands opposed; and probably with a very resistant subject floor restraints offer a greater degree of security but it is absolutely essential that if a restraint involves a descent to the floor that the restrainer is able to control their own balance since uncontrolled descents are a significant source of potential injury (Leadbetter, 1996, pp. 42-43).

In terms of the safety of a technique, Leadbetter cautions that no system can offer an unequivocal guarantee of safety since there are too many variables involved. Stark (1996) identifies the main issues in relation to injuries associated with restraint techniques. Restraint methods should offer protection to the head, neck, airway and abdomen since damage could lead to severe injury or death. Other potential injuries include injury to a long bone (e.g. arm or thigh) such as a spiral fracture resulting from the long bone being twisted further than anatomically possible; joint injuries to bones, tendons or ligaments resulting from moving the joint further than it usually moves or forcing it in a direction other than its normal movement. Small joints (such as those in the wrist or hand) are vulnerable to injury because large pressures can be exerted at one point (Stark, 1996, p 31-32).

Leadbetter lists commonly reported sources of injury as including: involvement of excessive staff numbers; failure to co-ordinate the intervention of staff; failure to give explicit protection to the head of the restrained person; the application of weight or pressure to the back or abdomen; failure to control descents; wrist injury. He stresses that the safety of both staff and young people require equal consideration (Leadbetter, 1996, p. 43). It is essential that all residential staff are appropriately trained. Leadbetter emphasises that there is clear evidence that staff competence will decrease over time, highlighting the need for periodic update training (Leadbetter 1996. p. 44).

Ethical issues about restraint techniques probably require the most difficult judgement since some techniques, even if effective, will be inappropriate in relation to specific children and young people because of differences such as age, gender, health, disability, or previous experience of physical or sexual abuse. Staff must be aware of a child or young person's: history (e.g. physical or sexual abuse);

fears or phobias; size and maturity; state of health; state of mind (whether they are under the influence of alcohol, drugs, solvents, etc.) (Support Force for Children's Residential Care, 1996, p. 90).

Some techniques may also be more likely to compromise the dignity of the young people and careful consideration needs to be given to the use of certain techniques, including:

- All Techniques which involve 'flooring'.
- Techniques which involve holding the trunk such as Bear Hugs.
- Techniques which involve 'straddling' a young person on the ground.
- Techniques which involve pain compliance such as wrist locks
- Techniques which push a young persons face into the floor

(Leadbetter, 1996, p. 45).

Finally, Leadbetter discusses the question of whether approaches work for a specific care setting. He identifies a number of issues for consideration. The age, needs, size and potential risks of specific resident groups must be taken into account. The composition of the staff group and the number of staff on duty at any one time is also an important consideration. The physical layout of the building is crucial and the environment in which incidents occur (for example, confined spaces such as corridors or rooms where there are hard floors) will determine the practicality and safety of particular techniques (Leadbetter, 1996, pp. 45-46).

In the prison service, training on physical "control and restraint" (C & R) methods "is a key part in the nine weeks basic training received by every prison officer. This reflects the emphasis on security and physical control implicit in the concept of imprisonment" (Howard League, 1995a, p. 43). A number of prisoners complained of excessive force being used during restraint and the Commission concluded:

> . . . it appears to be no accident that restraint is used less routinely in the institutions with better developed anti-bullying policies... In any event, it is a matter of some concern that prison staff routinely resort themselves to potentially dangerous restraint measures when it is not required as a matter of urgency to protect someone from serious injury (Howard League, 1995a, p. 44).

Creating A Safe and Secure Environment

> The establishment of an environment in which young people feel safe and secure is the first priority. This entails the establishment of routines within the unit and definitions of acceptable behaviour which are understood by everyone - both staff and young people. Security is provided for children and young people through continuity of care and experience in an environment which is predictable and consistent. Physical and emotional security are the basis for healthy growth and development and residential care must provide this before anything else can be achieved (Skinner, 1992, p. 62)

Mercer (1982) stressed that most approaches to institutional abuse at the time he wrote, emphasised reporting, investigation and correction of incidents and that this must be:

> . . . followed up by more comprehensive thinking about the problems of residential facilities, about measures to prevent abuse, and finally about positive, rather than negative, constructs for improving the quality of care in residential facilities (Mercer, 1982, p. 128)

Daly and Dowd stress that a harm-free environment is not only free from abuse and neglect "but also promotes children's rights and offers children the opportunity to receive care and treatment that promote spiritual, emotional, intellectual, and physical growth" (Daly and Dowd, 1992, p. 489). The Support Force for Children's Residential Care highlight the importance of creating an "aware culture" which includes "the elements necessary for a positive care environment, and the shared awareness that staff need to have, to reduce the possibility of children and young people being abused" (Support Force for Children's Residential Care, 1996, p. 83). However, the Social Services Inspectorate was concerned that child protection within the homes and the potential which exists for abuse were not as high on the agenda of staff as one might have expected (Social Services Inspectorate, undated b, p.,28).

The Support Force for Children's Residential Care identified a number of areas to reduce the risk of abuse. Exclusiveness and secrecy in relationships between young people and adults should be challenged. Taking children and young people home should be generally discouraged but if it is to happen it should be an integral part of the care plan and closely monitored. Trips and outings should be spread across the staff group and there should be careful monitoring if a member of staff is closely linked to a particular young person or group of young people or frequently comes in while off-duty or volunteers for extra duties. There should be clear guidelines about appropriate privacy boundaries in relation to personal care and hygiene activities and access to bedrooms. No pornographic or erotic materials should be held on the premises and children and young people should always be appropriately dressed in photographs. Staff need to be aware of what constitutes normal sexual development patterns and when these are being breached. There needs to be awareness of the impact of sexual abuse on children and young people. The establishment needs to operate with an anti-oppressive environment; where sex can be talked about as part of health development; and where children and young people can express their concerns (Support Force for Residential Child Care, 1996, pp 84-86).

> An atmosphere of open communication is essential for the prevention of child sexual abuse since, almost by definition, sexual abuse demands a closed, secretive environment... Residents need to feel that staff will work hard to understand their communication and that staff will help youngsters distinguish what is real from what is imagined without being afraid to hear what is real (Suskind, 1986, pp. 26-27).

McGrath stresses the individual responsibility of the child care worker to protect a positive climate for children and young people in their care. As a professional, the child care worker needs to maintain a professional attitude in a "concrete, shift-by-shift way" (McGrath, 1986, p. 63).

> Read at least one article a week related to your clients. Explore new ideas, introduce and force discussion at team meetings on professional techniques when faced with problems which children and young people bring with them for your care. Make constant reference to child care practice as a professional act, in the day-to-day routine. Stated another way don't overpersonalize (McGrath, 1986, p. 63).

The child care worker should inform him/herself about the law, rules and procedures. He or she should consult with, involve, and challenge managers and policy-makers both in specific situations and in day-to-day routine. Other team members should be trusted to share "an essentially positive and healthy respect for clients" (see also Baldwin, 1990).

> Develop and nurture your liking for clients as persons. Guard very concretely and practically against the erosion of your own positive regard, liking and enjoyment of children or young people in care, for their complexity and their difficulty (McGrath, 1986, p. 64).

The child care worker must examine and reflect on the mistakes in their practice and "own" the behaviours, not for the purpose of feeling guilty and bad, but to identify the lines of alternative ways of handling things, to pinpoint the missing elements of support, either structural or situational, which led to the error, with a view to building a more solid foundation for improved child care practice tomorrow or the next shift" (McGrath, 1986, p. 64).

In the face of abuse, "approach fellow workers individually and privately and share your concerns" (McGrath, 1986, p. 63), when situations go too far:

> . . . confront, bluntly and directly. Pay the price of your refusal to accept "that's just the way things are here." With the support of other members of the team, this price is often less costly and less painful, in the long run, than the price of compromise (McGrath, 1986, p. 64).

Harrell and Orem argue that there are "three possible "breaks" in the circle of silence surrounding the child, and thus three forces with potential to stop institutional maltreatment or prevent it from happening" (Harrell and Orem, 1980, p. 38). These are: *the child* - self-reporting, ombudman, advocacy; *the staff* - selection, training, support; *the community* - involvement, review.

Listening to Children

> But probably the best lesson to be learned from Castle Hill is that the pupils themselves first brought forward the information which led to action. Those disclosures made to parents at home, and the follow-up by the police and social worker team, proved more significant than the many investigations and inspections, cursory or otherwise, which took place at the school (Fielding, 1991, p. iii).

However, this has to be set against the need to believe such disclosures since, as was noted above, Brannan et al highlighted that parents and professionals were unable initially "to accept and comprehend the sheer volume and extent of the abuse" (Brannan et al, 1993, p. 273). Young people themselves, have expressed a reluctance to talk to anyone about their difficulties because they believe that: adults are unable to understand their experiences and concerns; adults make little effort to listen and impose their own views; adults trivialise issues or over-react (Butler and Williamson, 1994; see also Buchanan et al, 1993; La Fontaine and Morris, 1991).

Complaints Procedures

> **Girl, 16**
> *. . . one member of staff used to walk in on me when I was undressing without knocking. I just felt there was a lack of privacy in the home. I complained to B... but he didn't do anything about it.*
> (Social Services Inspectorate, undated a, p. 66)

> Complaining is rarely easy. Most people prefer to avoid conflict and, although complaints procedures are - at least in part - intended to depersonalise conflict, they will never completely do away with the stress involved in challenging others. There are real emotional costs to any potential confrontation with an individual or organisation (Simons, 1995, p. 4; see also Lindsay, 1992).

Complaints procedures have two main purposes: resolving individual or group complaints on particular matters; and improving services (Gulbenkian, 1993, p. 102).

Warner (1992) conducted a survey which showed that almost all local authorities "have arrangements whereby children can make complaints outside the line management of the home. In over 80% of cases this can be done privately (eg., by the use of Freephone facilities, tear-off slips to the Director of Social Services), or by direct access to the head of the independent inspection unit or Children's Rights Officer." (Warner, 1992, p. 103). However, in inspections of residential child care services in 11 authorities in England between November 1992 and March 1993, the Social Services Inspectorate found that in seven of the authorities "children's ability to complain was significantly limited by a lack of user friendly information" (Social Services Inspectorate, undated b, p. 22). Both children and residential staff were dissatisfied with the complaints procedures in that "some were unclear about the outcome of complaints, whilst others were not confident that their views would be taken seriously or that they would be supported during investigations" (Social Services Inspectorate, undated b, p. 22).

> Children in care have shown extreme reluctance in complaining, doubting, with some justification, that anyone will believe them and fearing, with equal justification, victimisation and reprisals if they complain against those who can exercise so much power and control over their lives (Lindsay, 1992, p. 437; see also Moss, 1990).

Triseliotis et al found that:

> Almost two thirds of residents in children's homes had been given information about how to make a complaint but in residential schools the proportion was only a third. The advice was usually to report the matter to a member of staff or the social worker. The practice of giving information about how to pursue a complaint outwith the unit was largely confined to two agencies (Triseliotis et al, 1995, p. 181).

In one agency, young people were routinely given written information on admission to care which "included a prepaid post-card addressed to the district manager which could be used to initiate a complaint and most young people were aware of how it could be used" (Triseliotis et al, 1995, p. 181). Significantly, Triseliotis et al found that awareness of complaints procedures was less common among those in foster care than in residential care (Triseliotis et al, 1995, p. 278; see also Fletcher, 1993). Lindsay highlights the issue of children and young peoples' lack of knowledge of complaints procedures and it "is incontrovertibly the case that no child "being looked after" will be able to use a complaints procedure which s/he does not even know exists" (Lindsay, 1992, p. 434).

In Northern Ireland, each child should receive an information booklet which explains their rights and responsibilities and outlines how to make a complaint. Inspectors "noted that some children had not received their booklets" and where a booklet was provided "often this occurred some time after admission" (Social Services Inspectorate, undated a, p. 43). A significant number of parents said that they did not know how to make a complaint. Some children were concerned that there might be recriminations or disapproval by staff if they complained and Inspectors considered that "the absence of an independent investigation system for the handling of serious complaints may result in children perceiving that their views are not taken seriously" (Social Services Inspectorate, undated a, p. 44). The Social Services Inspectorate Report also pointed out that some of the procedures which apply to children in children's homes "do not extend to those living with foster carers or home-on-trial"(Social Services Inspectorate, undated a, p. 72) and that "all children in care should be covered by a uniform complaints and child protection procedures". (Social Services Inspectorate, undated a, p. 72).

The Children Act 1989 requires all authorities and agencies providing care for children and young people to have a complaints procedure. The procedure must include an arrangement for an "independent person" to oversee the investigation, and to ensure that the complaint is dealt with thoroughly and fairly (Support Force for Children's Residential Care, 1996, p. 108; see also Gulbenkian, 1993). In Scotland, the National Health Service and Community Care Act 1990 made complaints procedures statutory for all client groups (Black, 1992).

Lindsay questions the effectiveness of the independent element of the complaints procedure as set out in the Children Act.

> Potentially, there is nothing independent about the Children Act 1989 provision for complaints procedures. The spirit of "independence" is too easily compromised by close or former association or by the appointment of "independent persons" who might not reasonably be expected to have much understanding of matters relating to the care system (Lindsay, 1992, p. 439).

He also expresses concern about the way in which there "has been a tendency for social work managers to rule that "*serious allegations*" fall outside the remit of complaints procedures" (Lindsay, 1992, p. 437). He therefore stresses the need for children and young people to have unrestricted access to independent advice and advocacy (see below).

There needs to be a culture "which makes it easy for children to complain, and welcomes complaints for the positive contribution they can make to the development of services" (Gulbenkian, 1993, p. 102). *Working Together* stresses that "it is essential that children and staff are encouraged to report their concerns to the appropriate persons in the local area" (Home Office, 1991, p. 34).

> An essential part of effective management arrangements for children's homes are robust and accessible complaints procedures that provide for the thorough and speedy investigation of:
>
> - Complaints and allegations by children against staff and other children
> - Concerns by staff about the behaviour of other staff or superiors towards children
>
> (Warner, 1992, p. 102)

Reacting positively to complaints will: help children and young people to make complaints and criticisms in an acceptable way; enable complaints to be dealt with as close to the user of the service as possible; make it possible to deal with the majority of issues raised on a day-to-day basis within the home; give opportunities for complaints to be raised about matters outside the residential unit - e.g. school or family; make children and young people aware that they have rights; help them raise complaints about difficult issues and matters that might have appeared alright to them within the context of their experience but which are not generally acceptable in society; and reduce the number of complaints that have to be dealt with formally (Gulbenkian, 1993, p. 110).

Rindfleisch (1988b) describes a demonstration project in Ohio to test the effectiveness of alternative approaches to detecting and reporting possible maltreatment. The case finding methods tested were an advocate within the line of authority; a complaint box accessible to staff and residents, an advocate outside the line of authority and a hot line accessible to residents and staff. The hot line and advocate outside the line of authority generated the most investigations, however, the use of the hot line as a case-finding mechanism was not well received by child protective agencies. The internal advocate outside the line of authority, however, was accepted by both residential facilities and child protective agencies (Rindfleisch, 1988b, p. 60).

Access to Telephones and Telephone Helplines

> Easy access to a telephone where they can speak privately and publicity about telephone hotlines should be available to all children resident in homes and schools. (Home Office, 1991, p. 35).

The provision of an easily accessible and private telephone in schools and residential homes may be the first step in providing children with a means to talk to someone about abuse they are suffering (Westcott and Clement, 1992, p. 19; see also Utting, 1991; Skinner, 1992). The Social Services Inspectorate found that five out of 11 authorities had equipped all the children's homes visited with pay phones, four had some and two had none. However, there were instances of telephones kept in locked rooms (Social Services Inspectorate, undated b, p. 19). Triseliotis et al also noted that lack of privacy in residential establishments "extended to telephones where often it was not possible to have a private conversation with a parent or friend" (Triseliotis et al, 1995, p. 180; see also La Fontaine and Morris, 1991). In the Who Cares? Trust/ National Consumer Council survey, 36% of young people in residential care and 29% of those in foster care said they could not use a phone in private when they needed help (Fletcher, 1993, p. 71).

Childline was established in 1986 "to listen to, comfort and protect children in trouble or danger" and by 31st March 1994, the agency had counselled 383,952 children (Morris and Wheatley, 1994, p. 7).

> Our counsellors aim to listen attentively to what children say; to encourage them to explore their feelings, to think through how difficulties might be tackled; to consider how they want to proceed and the consequences of taking particular courses of action. We try, wherever appropriate, to help them identify an adult they trust, in whom they could confide their problems and concerns (Morris and Wheatley, 1994, p. 8).

When Childline first reviewed the use made by children in care of the helpline, "we found them to be among the most troubled and unhappy children to whom we have talked, and among the most isolated and alone" (Morris and Wheatley, 1994, p. 12). Following this review a special line for children in care was established in 1992. While the Childline study described above focuses on the 676 children counselled in the first six months of the special line, 508 children in care were counselled in the subsequent year and another 1,711 children who called the main ChildLine number identified themselves as currently or previously in care (Morris and Wheatley, 1994, pp. 18-19).

> We began Childline for Children in Care to contribute to the wellbeing of children in care... If only one thing is taken from this document, it should be the absolute necessity for us all to combine in finding ways which enable children to be heard (Morris and Wheatley, 1994, p.19).

Morgan (1993) describes the Oxfordshire pupils' telephone helpline run by the social services inspection unit which was welcomed by many pupils and although "as yet too new to evaluate in practice,... it is certainly being used by pupils to raise their welfare concerns" (Morgan, 1993, p. 52).

> Information about confidential telephone help-lines, the identification of trusted people who agree to offer support and advice, contact with other children in care, confidential medical advice (and encouragement to use it) all encourage children to identify and use the protective strategies they find most helpful (Boushel, 1994, p. 38).

Child Care Reviews

The importance of including children and young people in decision making and planning has long been recognised and Sinclair highlights that "the right of children to participate is closely linked to their rights to protection" (Sinclair, 1996, p. 91). Child care review meetings are important in involving children and young people in decision-making and research in both Scotland and England has shown that children and young people are routinely invited to attend review meetings and planning meetings (Kendrick and Mapstone, 1991, 1992; Sinclair and Grimshaw, 1995). However, it must be recognised that the formal and bureaucratic nature of such meetings and the large numbers of professionals who may attend them can inhibit children and young people from fully participating and they will not always be appropriate for younger children. Gulbenkian (1993) call for the extension of formal review arrangements involving the children themselves to "all children being accommodated in institutions and quasi-institutional settings thoughout the UK" (Gulbenkian, 1993, p. 170).

Internal programme audit

Daly and Dowd (1992) argue that there should be an internal programme audit, a system to detect abuse or neglect. They describe a system where each child is periodically interviewed confidentially and asked whether any adult or youth has ever treated him or her improperly . Over 500 interviews take place annually, revealing an average of 18 claims of inappropriate adult activity. All allegations of inappropriate practices are investigated by a person knowledgeable about the program but independent of its day-to-day administration (Daly and Dowd, 1992).

Consultation

As well as listening to individual children, the importance of consulting more generally with children and young people about the standard and provision of services has been highlighted by Buchanan et al (1993) and Freeman et al (1996). Freeman et al describe a consultation exercise carried out in Strathclyde Social Work Department in "the preparation of a plan for the development of child care services" (Freeman et al, 1996, p. 229). In the first stage of the consultation, 150 young people in residential care or attending intermediate treatment groups took part in group discussions in order to "elicit young people's views on the child care services in general, not just their own children's home or intermediate treatment unit" (Freeman et al, 1996, p. 229). The second stage took the form of a three day residential event.

> Consultation sessions were interspersed with football and gymnastic sessions, and with other group activities designed to help the group communicate, as well as for fun. The methods used in the residential consultation sessions included group discussions, workshops where groups worked on presentation of sketches and role plays on selected themes, and the use of questionnaires. Group leaders wrote reports on the activities of their groups, group discussions were recorded and the group presentations were videotaped (Freeman et al, 1996, p. 231).

Consultation with the young people continued through the analysis and report-writing stage and four young people "took a report to the [Social Work] committee and spent an hour discussing it with Regional Councillors who endorsed specific recommendations" (Freeman et al, 1996, p. 237).

Such consultation of children and young people and their families needs to be high on the agenda in developing the new, statutory local authority Children's Services Plans (Kendrick et al, 1996; Sutton, 1995).

> Many people complain that the idea and practice of children's rights has distracted attention away from the real issues in residential care - control and discipline, resources, staff cutbacks and low morale. In reality what children's rights often does is turn our minds and actions on young people and away from staff and the organisation: *young people become the most important part of residential services*. This new way of thinking - where young people are at the forefront of everything we do - means continually questioning our attitudes, practice and behaviour (Willow, 1996, p. 108).

Children's Rights Officers and Child Advocates

> Children's rights officers in social work departments can provide a useful background for children's rights and promote good practice in residential child care. They also provide an appropriate way of handling the vast majority of complaints and concerns (Skinner, 1992).

Since the first children's rights officer was appointed by Leicestershire County Council in 1987, an increasing number of local authorities have established such posts. While some local authorities have located children's rights services in social services or social work departments, many "have entered into partnership with voluntary child care organisations to establish some independence for them" (Willow, 1996, p. 31).

> The purpose of children's rights services are, generally, to provide independent advocacy, support and representation to young people who are looked after in various settings. Most children's rights and advocacy officers have regular and frequent contact with young people and offer advice and information to help resolve difficulties (Willow, 1996, p. 31).

Other specialist posts include Birmingham's Young Person's Forum Co-ordinator who has "a key role in advocating on behalf of young people who are looked after both regionally and nationally" and posts "for the investigation of complaints and allegations of abuse in residential and foster care" (Willow, 1996, p. 32). In 1993, in line with its policy that children should not be incarcerated in penal institutions, the Howard League established the Troubleshooter Project which has sought to "provide an independent body to log, monitor and intervene in cases where 15 year olds have been remanded or sentenced into prison custody." The project has three direct objectives: *Rescue* - to remove 15 year olds from custody as quickly as possible; *Research* - to monitor the cases of 15 year olds remanded or sentenced into penal custody; *Advocacy* - to provide advocacy services to young people while they remain in prison custody (Howard League, 1995b, p. 3).

> An independent advocate may make all the difference to a young person in prison. Even real fears which are voiced by a young person in custody may not be take as seriously by the prison authorities when it is only the young person who is voicing those fears... Other concerns which the Howard League brought to the attention of youth justice teams included incidents of self harm, assaults on a young person and the relocation of a young person to the segregation unit (Howard League, 1995b, pp. 28-29).

In the United States, draft federal standards "indicate that every institution should have a formal child advocacy program to represent residents' interests" and every child "should have an identifiable advocate" (Harrell and Orem, 1980, p. 45).

Children's Commissioners

In 1981, Norway established the Ombudsman for Children through national legislation "in recognition that children needed an independent spokesperson, a national defender, and a public conscience arouser on their behalf" (Flekkoy, 1989, p. 114). The Ombudsman for Children deals with individual cases through "information and persuasion" and dealt with some 4,500 cases in its first six years involving: children in institutions, child welfare and child abuse; child care and public leisure facilities; school problems; cultural and consumer questions; family circumstances (divorce, conflicts with neighbours, family economy, housing and labour, etc.); and physical conditions, urban and rural planning (Flekkoy, 1989, pp. 116-117). The Ombudsman for Children is also influential in creating public debate and raising public awareness about children's issues, and in the legislative process. The Swedish Children's Ombudsman is employed by a voluntary organisation, Radda Barnen (Save the Children) and thus works outside the state administration (Ronstrom, 1989, p. 123)[46]. The Swedish Ombudsman works to: mould public opinion and disseminate information on the needs and rights of children; conduct research; provide education and training; and offers a telephone advisory service for individual cases (Ronstrom, 1989, pp. 124-126).

In 1984, the Jerusalem Children's Council was established to "function as an informed advocate and lobby on behalf of the children of Jerusalem" (Rauche-Elnekave, 1989, p. 103) and in 1986 a children's ombudsman was appointed under the auspices of the Council to: receive complaints concerning children; to discover weaknesses in legislation and in provision of welfare and education services; and to provide information to the public about the needs and rights of children (Rauche-Elnekave, 1989, p. 103). New Zealand established a Commissioner for Children in 1989, funded by and having administrative links with the Department of Social Welfare; and Costa Rica appointed the Defensor de la Infancia in 1987 and gave the initiative full legal status in 1990 (Ludbrook, 1994, p. 7; see also Rosenbaum and Newell, 1991).

In Australia, while there have been calls for a Children's Commission at national and state level, only South Australia has set up a government agency authorised to speak and act on behalf of children, The Children's Interests Bureau "has a wide brief to make comment and safeguard children's rights" (Boss et al, 1995, p.xxv). Its mandate includes: increasing public awareness of children's rights and children's welfare; research, evaluation and monitoring of the policies of the statutory state welfare authority; and providing independent advocacy for children at risk and/or in state care (Harvey, 1993).

The National Commission into the Prevention of Child abuse suggests that priority be given to establishing the role of Children's Commissioner. The main responsibilities of the Commissioner would be:

> ...to promote the welfare of children throughout the geographically defined area of his/her responsibilities.
> ... to give advice on and keep under review the working of legislation affecting children and... to draw up and submit to the Secretary of State proposals for amending legislation affecting children.
> ... periodically report on the degree of compliance achieved with the UN Convention
> ...establish advisory groups of children and young people to provide input on a range of different policy areas.
> ...conduct research or assist... any other research into children's issues which appeared necessary or expedient.
> ...publish an annual report to Parliament which would provide regularly updated information about children...
> ...issue codes of practice containing practical advice relating to the conduct of services, statutory or voluntary, for or affecting children...
> ...make a regular review of complaints procedures involving children and used by public authorities.
> ...to report on the extent to which recommendations of child abuse inquiries, past or present, have been or are being implemented.
> (Williams of Mostyn, 1996, pp. 60-61).

46 The Finnish ombudsman for children also functions outside the state administration and"is the legal arm of the Mannerheim League foir Child Welfare, a private advocacy group" (Rauche-Elnekave, 1989, p. 105).

The National Commission also considered that the Children's Commissioner could promote a Charter for Children "bringing together all issues concerned with children for which public services are responsible" (Williams of Mostyn, 1996, p. 61; see also Rosenbaum and Newell, 1991; Gulbenkian, 1993)

Children and Young People's Organisations

Willow stresses the importance of the the collective action of young people in the development of rights and entitlements of young people (Willow, 1995; see also Lindsay, 1992). In 1975, the National Children's Bureau's *Who Cares?* conference brought together 100 young people and led to the *Who Cares? Young People's Working Group* and the production of the first national publication of the views of young people in care (Page and Clark, 1977). In 1979, the National Association of Young People in Care (NAYPIC) was formed. Its aims were to:

- promote the views and opinions of young people in care and those who had left care;
- offer advice and assistance to young people in care and ex-care;
- educate the public and child care professionals on matters relating to young people in care

(Willow, 1996, p. 26).

We saw above that NAYPIC produced one of the first studies of abuse in the care system (Moss et al, 1990). NAYPIC continued to campaign for improvements in the care of children and young people until 1994. The Who Cares? magazine developed from a local magazine into a national publication with a distribution of over 30,000 and the Who Cares? Trust also provides a telephone linkline for young people in residential and foster care. In Scotand, Who Cares? Scotland and in Wales, Voices from Care also provide support, advice and a campaigning voice for young people in care. Black and in Care has been influential in raising awareness of the rights and needs of black young people (Willow, 1996). Safe & Sound has been formed by a group of young people who were abused in care to provide a support and advice service and to work with professionals to develop safe child care services (Safe & Sound, 1995).

Staff Recruitment, Selection and Assessment

> Systems of staff selection which are properly organised, and properly conducted, are essential to building any good staff team. The vulnerability of many of the young people in residential child care, and the dependency they must have on the staff to whose care they are entrusted, are such that very particular care in staff selection should always be taken (Skinner, 1992, p. 69).

Many of the inquiry reports dealing with abuse in residential care have highlighted inadequacies in recruitment practice. Williams and McCreadie (1992) in the Inquiry into Ty Mawr Community Home wrote:

> We were deeply disturbed to establish that recruitment of care staff sometimes occurred simply on a visit to the job centre. Appointments were made by County Council members. We regard this as unsatisfactory (Williams and McCreadie, 1992, pp 11-12).

Levy and Kahan (1992) state that:

> The problems in Staffordshire social services department which led to the Inquiry were in no small measure due to poor staffing policies and practices... They included restrictive advertising, inadequate staff selection procedures, low staffing ratios, dependence on untrained staff, over use of volunteers and casual staff, lack of training, lack of supervision, absence of career structures for residential staff and inadequate budget support (Levy and Kahan, 1992, p. 161).

In Staffordshire Social Services Department, posts tended to be filled from within the department and while Levy and Kahan acknowledge that this gave a level of stability in the organisation they considered that it led to a resistance to innovative thinking. Selection procedures were also considered to be lax and a number of witnesses to the Inquiry "commented critically on the interviewing process which they believed was often merely a formality" and they "were also aware of the inevitability of references being drawn from the internal sources..." (Levy and Kahan, 1992, p. 161). The Inquiry also identified a readiness to appoint unqualified staff even to posts requiring a qualified person (Levy and Kahan, 1992, p. 161).

The Social Services Inspectorate study of small unregistered children's homes raised a number of concerns about staffing (Social Services Inspectorate, 1995). Social services departments reported that some homes were recruiting people, often students, who had little or no experience and without relevant qualifications. They were often employed on part-time or short-term contracts leading to high staff turn-over and lack of stability for the young people in their care. There were examples of staff employed "after only cursory recruitment checks and provided with only minimal, if any, basic training for the job" (Social Services Inspectorate, 1995, p. 11). There was also a lack of clarity about police checks for staff in small private homes.

> There were some examples quoted of very unsuitable, unsatisfactory people moving into this area of provision. There were some who had a history of financial misdealing ... There were others against whom allegations of both physical and sexual abuse had been made prior to them setting up small homes, and some of these have subsequently been convicted and sentenced. In all the cases given as examples, however, local authority checks had not been sufficiently robust to prevent them from placing children in the care of these people (Social Services Inspectorate, 1995, p. 11).

The Social Services Inspectorate report on the inspection of residential child care services in 11 authorities in England found that 27% of staff had not been subject to a police check and suggested that this might be explained by staff being in post before the requirement for police checks came into force. In addition the local authorities were not able to supply information on 13% of the staff and only two authorities were able to supply the information for all staff (Social Services Inspectorate, undated b, p. 74)[47]. The Department of Health Consultancy list had been checked for less than half the staff and this information was not available for a quarter of staff. The report also found that there was no consistent approach to the range of selection methods used (Social Services Inspectorate, undated b, p. 75).

Following the trial and conviction of Frank Beck for numerous sexual and other offences in a local authority children's home, an enquiry was established to look specifically at selection and recruitment methods for staff working in children's homes (Warner, 1992). Following the publication of *Choosing with Care*, the Support Force for Children's Residential Care (SFCRC) was established "to offer advice to individual authorities on the quality of care and management with particular reference to the appointment, selection, personnel management, support, development and training of residential care staff" (Support Force for Children's Residential Care, 1995a, p. 3).

Defining the Post

> At present many staff enter employment in children's homes with no very clear idea about the purpose of their job and what they are supposed to achieve (Warner, 1992, p. 30)

Warner (1992) considers that the first step in improving employers' practices in the recruitment of staff is to use clear, up-to-date statements of the purpose and functions of children's homes as the basis for job descriptions for heads of homes and care staff (Warner, 1992, p. 30). Alongside the job description, a person specification should be drawn up which will provide a set of criteria against which to measure the suitability of candidates. This should be produced for each vacancy and should consider the skills, personal attributes, experience and qualifications needed for the particular post (Warner, 1992, pp. 31-32; see also Support Force for Children's Residential Care, 1995a, pp. 7-9).

47 There is a typographical error in relation to the figure of 27%. Initially, the report states "27% were identified as having been the subject of police checks". Later, it states "Given the need now to have police checks on staff, it is surprising that 27% of the staff overall had not been checked". I have assumed that the latter is the accurate statement.

Advertising Posts

> A feature of children's homes where disturbing episodes have occurred has often been a reluctance to fill vacancies from a wide field of competition (Warner, 1992, p. 33).

The Inquiry stresses the importance of openness and competition in advertising posts, and employers should advertise posts externally to the home in all cases and, apart from situations where an employer faces redundancies, externally to the employing authority; nationally in the case of posts for head of home (Warner, 1992, p. 34). SFCRC state the aims of advertising as:

> to draw a strong response of potentially suitable candidates in order to have a range of people from whom to choose;
>
> to give unsuitable candidates the information they need in order to decide not to apply;
>
> to present an image of the agency, local authority, department or service with a view to future recruitment.
>
> (Support Force for Children's Residential Care, 1995a, p. 18)

Selecting Staff

> Most appointments are made on the basis of an application form and a formal interview. In many cases the interviews are conducted in panels of four or more people, which is hardly a forum for exploring aspects of personality (Warner, 1992, p. 43)

Selection procedures need to aim at all stages to collect as much relevant information about a candidate as possible so that decisions on the most appropriate candidate can be made on an informed basis. The interview on its own is not a good predictor of further job performance (Warner, 1992, p. 43). Kahan (1994) reiterated concern at the widespread use of the panel interview as the main method of selection since its "limitations and unreliability as a method are now so well established that managers need to explore the use of more penetrating and work-specific methods" (Kahan, 1994, pp. 289-290; see also Bowles, 1995).

Application forms for posts in children's homes should be specifically designed for the posts and collect relevant, core information, as defined by the job description and person specification. Written exercises can be designed to test clarity of thought and expression and the results of written exercises should be used in the selection process (Warner, 1992, p. 47). SFCRC see written exercises, in addition to testing literacy skills, as indicating the candidate's ability to: understand instruction; think clearly and pick out key issues; analyse problems; organise material logically; apply professional knowledge; communicate; and demonstrate self awareness (Support Force for Children's Residential Care, 1995a, p. 33).

All short-listed candidates should be required to visit the home in advance of the interview and meet with staff and young people (Warner, 1992, p. 48).

> The visit is used to gather information about the candidates' reactions to the home, the staff they meet and the children and young people, and their reaction to the candidates. It is also used to provide information for the candidate (Support Force for Children's Residential Care, 1995, p. 33)

Lindsay and Rayner (1993) describe an initiative by The Children's Society and Cleveland's children's rights service to involve young people in the recruitment process. Five young people were involved in interviewing groups of candidates to "assess each candidate's ability to communicate with and relate to young people" (Lindsay and Rayner, 1993, p. 24). A common 'fault' identified by the young people was a failure by candidates to see young people as individuals and not simply as problems to be dealt with.

> The young people… felt they had been listened to and treated as responsible people, an experience which they commonly contrasted with their interactions with social services. In particular, they prized highly the principle of being given a say in who looks after them. They brought experience and insights to the interviewing process which could not have been matched within any conventional interviewing panel. They provided the employing agency with a critical opportunity to observe how well the candidates actually interacted and communicated with young people (Lindsay and Rayner, 1993, p. 25).

The SFCRC state that there are strong arguments for involving children and young people in the selection of staff and "that they have a stake in the outcome of the interviews and a right to be involved" (Support Force for Children's Residential Care, 1995a, p. 18). However, the SFCRC stresses that the process has to be handled carefully if it is to be effective. Children and young people should be properly briefed and trained and it should be made clear that they are not involved in the actual decision-making.

Group exercises can simulate the environment of the children's home although the Inquiry stresses that they need to be carefully planned and assessors need to be thoroughly trained (Warner, 1992, p. 49).

> Residential child care workers have to be good team members, presenting a consistent approach to the children and young people they care for, being complementary to other team members in terms of their skills and the roles they play, standing in for each other and providing support. These aspects of the work are dynamic, and therefore perhaps best seen in a dynamic situation, such as a group exercise (Support Force for Children's Residential Care, 1995a, p. 40).

Aptitude Tests and Personality Profiling

While the Warner Inquiry received conflicting views on psychometric tests, it concluded that:

> …providing the appropriate level of tests are used for particular jobs and are administered and interpreted by qualified people, they are valuable in assisting the selection of staff for children's homes. In particular they have three main roles:
>
> - To provide information about the possession of certain skills and competencies important in the person specification.
> - To assess personality against the profile sought in the person specification
> - To provide information about the personality characteristics or abilities that need to be probed further at interview
>
> (Warner, 1992, p. 50).

Aptitude tests can provide a measure of more or less specific skills such as numeracy, comprehension and reasoning ability though they must be related to the specific requirements of the job description and person specification (Warner, 1992, p. 51).

Personality tests, although they should not be seen as a stand-alone method of selection, should be used to help determine the extent to which a candidate fits a person specification (Warner, 1992, pp. 52-53). Discussing methods of nurse selection, Bowles reviews the use of personality tests designed to assess factors such as: adaptation to stress; levels of autonomy; interpersonal skills; self-actualisation; and predisposition to caring (Bowles, 1995, pp. 28-29).

A number of screening tools have been devised to aid in the selection of workers with children and young people but it must be stressed that caution needs to used in considering these tools. McCormack and Selvaggio (1989) present details of an interview screening device designed to aid in the identification of sexual offenders, more specifically, the paedophile. The screening device was developed for a youth-oriented community agency which matches a child from a single-parent family with a caring adult volunteer from the community. Based on the work of Lanning (1986), McCormack and Selvaggio identify nine characteristics which could be operationalised into indicators:

> 1. *Indicates a preference for a child of a specific age…*
> 2. *Indicates a preference for a child who has a history of abuse and neglect…*
> 3. *Has himself a history of sexual abuse…*
> 4. *Had little social contact as a teenager…*
> 5. *Experienced frequent moves…*
> 6. *Has been overly active in the community in the affairs of children…*
> 7. *Has friends who are much younger than he…*
> 8. *Refers to children as innocent or pure…*
> 9. *Has many hobbies and interests that are appealing to children…*
>
> (McCormack and Selvaggio, 1989, pp. 39-40).

A tenth characteristic was added based on work undertaken in the agency which "suggests that suspicion should be aroused if the volunteer is undergoing his second or subsequent match with a child" (McCormack and Selvaggio, 1989, p. 40). Questions to measure these characteristics were then incorporated into the 24 page volunteer interview questionnaire. While "devices such as the one presented here should not be used in isolation or used to "prove" that volunteer workers are child molesters" (McCormack and Selvaggio, 1989, p. 42), they can help the caseworker to feel more confident about the decision to reject a volunteer. Follow-up work was being carried out to develop an a scoring mechanism for the screening device and further work was to be carried on the validation of the instrument (McCormack and Selvaggio, 1989, p. 42).

Warner (1992) stresses that personality tests will not identify potential sexual abusers of children and cites the conclusions of a review of the literature:

> At best the available instruments are able to assess some of the psychological characteristics which make people vulnerable to paedophilia but these cannot be said to be determining factors (Wilson and Leslie, 1987, cited in Warner, 1992, p. 53).

Haddock and McQueen (1983) developed a battery of screening tests to identify an employee's potential for child abuse: "Milner's Child Abuse Potential Inventory, the Minnesota Satisfaction Questionnaire, and a General Information Form…" (Haddock and McQueen, 1983, p. 1022). This battery of tests was administered to a sample of 21 identified abusive employees and 21 non-abusive employees of out-of-home care institutions in Southern California.

> …the combined variables of the CAP-I abuse scale, the subscales MSQ-10, MSQ-4, MSQ-2, the employees' number of own children, the monthly alcohol consumption, whether they viewed their parent's discipline as extreme, and [marital status][48] provided a 100% correct classification of non-abusers and 85.7% classification of the abusers (Haddock and McQueen, 1983, p. 1024).

While the authors acknowledge that this is an early attempt to develop an assessment tool to screen staff and that additional validity data is required to take account of gender, age, educational level, job classification and work environment:

> …present use of these instruments is indicated as a preventative measure to understand the extent of the problem in an institution and then to enact steps to reduce stress that affects employees' client care skills (Haddock and McQueen, 1983, p. 1028).

48 In the text, this appears as "mental status", however, in the discussion, the eighth factor is "marital status" and I have therefore amended this quotation.

Ross and Hoeltke (1985) also describe a selection tool for residential child care workers which focuses on "life themes" of highly rated child care workers and uses these themes in selection interviews. Life themes are defined as "recurring patterns of thought, feeling and behavior" (Ross and Hoeltke, 1985, p.47). Highly successful child care workers were identified by agency supervisory and administrative staff and "theme constructs were developed that were believed to identify outstanding child care workers" (Ross and Hoeltke, 1985, p.48). The themes identified were:

> *Mission*... workers with a strong sense of mission are committed to making a significant contribution to young people...[and] have a clear service orientation and purpose related to their work activities.
> *Relationship*... [a] worker with strength in this theme has the ability to develop an approving and mutually favorable relationship with each young person. The child care worker likes young people and expects them to reciprocate...
> *Empathy*... provides the child care worker with feedback about an individual young person's feelings and thoughts...
> *Responsibility*... clear responsibility for his or her work and behavior and is a good model for others...
> *Kinesthic Work Orientation*... tend to be physically active and always involved in their work... sees work and physical activity as positive and personally satisfying.
> *Gestalt*... have a drive toward completeness and closure... However, they do not impose this "urgency for completeness" on others...
> *Activation*... capable of stimulating young people to think, respond, and learn
> *Courage*... have the ability to express their own emotionality in a positive, genuine way... are willing to risk rejection from others because of what they believe.
> *Objectivity*... has the ability to deal with issues fairly and openly... tends to get information from the people affected before making an important decision.
> *Developer*... has the capacity to receive satisfaction from the growth of others in a vicarious manner... gives time, talents, and resources to bring about the greatest change for the good in others...
> (Ross and Hoeltke, 1985, pp. 48-49).

On the basis of these themes, a 50-item structured interview was developed and the "final result was a structured, low-stress interview that assisted the interviewer in gaining an understanding of the talents of the interviewee and the depth of those talents (Ross and Hoeltke, 1985, p. 50). Theme-to-theme correlations indicated that each theme significantly contributed to the total score and that each of the themes represented "a unique core construct of the interview" (Ross and Hoeltke, 1987, p. 177). The instrument was validated against four external criteria: self-ratings, supervisor's ratings, resident children's ratings, and the MOOS Correctional Institutions Environment Scale (Form R), on a sample of 95 child care workers employed in 10 agencies in Iowa (Ross and Hoeltke, 1985, p. 51). The interview score was significantly correlated with all of the criteria in the initial concurrent validity study and with three out of four of the criteria in the repeat measures which took place at 3 and 6 months and "... individuals earning high scores on the interview were also individuals who tended to be noted positively by both the worker's supervisor(s), by residents in individual units, and by themselves" (Ross and Hoeltke, 1985, p. 52). The authors conclude that:

> The achievement of predictive validity has the potential for great impact on group care, principally by decreasing the risk of turnover and institutional child abuse (Ross and Hoeltke, 1985, p. 54).

A follow-up study was carried out with repeats of the measures at 9 months and 19 months. The interview score was significantly correlated with the self rating and the supervisor's rating at 9 months but was not significantly correlated with any of the external criteria at 18 months.

However, Ross and Hoeltke suggest that because of the reduction in the sample size to 30 because of resignations, transfers, firings, and promotion, the lack of predictiveness at the 18 month time period is of limited meaning (Ross and Hoeltke, 1987, p. 177). The study also compared the interview's ability to identify personnel who will remain in place against those who left. Results were statistically significant indicating "that the Child Care Perceiver Interview is able to predict those individuals who are likely to remain with an agency" (Ross and Hoeltke, 1987, p. 179). The impact of demographic characteristics were also investigated and it was found that the interview was independent of age, sex and race.

SFCRC stressed again that while psychometric testing can be a useful part of the recruitment process by providing certain types of information on a systematic validated basis, they should be treated with caution and "it is important to determine which characteristics are being assessed in the candidates before deciding whether psychometric testing is helpful in identifying them" (Support Force for Children's Residential Care, 1995, p. 41). Bowles also stresses that selectors "must first determine the desired qualities for nursing," but "the production of a set of clear-cut selection criteria is likely to be highly problematic" (Bowles, 1995, p. 28).

Interviews

The Warner Inquiry advocates that preliminary interviews should be used:

> ... to ensure shortlisted candidates have a full understanding of the requirements of the job and its difficulties. They can explore candidates' attitudes to control and punishment issues involving children; probe the extent to which they have characters strong enough to resist sexual temptation from children in their care; and whether their sexual interests were likely to cause them to pursue children for purposes of sexual gratification (Warner, 1992, p. 54; see also Support Force for Children's Residential Care, pp. 31-32).

Suskind (1986) suggests that vignettes might be used "to discover how the worker would deal with sexually charged situations and how he responds to and views issues of generational boundaries and adult responsibility" (Suskind, 1986, p. 23).

Final interviews should always contain the line manager for the post, his or her line manager and at least one other person independent from line management but should not involve elected members (Warner, 1992, pp. 59-60), and the Inquiry considers that the panel should consist of a maximum of three people. Employers are also urged to strive to achieve more balance in terms of race and gender in interview panels (Warner, 1992, p. 60). The final interview is used to: check factual information; to test the accuracy and consistency of the application form and curriculum vitae of the candidate with oral evidence; find out the candidate's views about him/herself; assess the candidate's motivation for the work; weigh up the candidate's likely commitment to the job; identify the values that underpin the candidate's work; clarify the candidate's attitudes to key issues; assess skills relating to interviewing and test the candidate's knowledge on a sample of important areas (Support Force for Children's Residential Care, 1995a, p. 43).

References

> The current position on the pursuit and use of references is unsatisfactory, even though potentially useful information from previous employers can be very revealing about candidates. Although employers in all sectors seek references from two or three previous employers, many do not seek or obtain references until after the final interview (Warner, 1992, p. 55)

The Inquiry stressed that information obtained by telephone is often more accurate and revealing and "local authorities should abandon any embargoes on obtaining information about candidates by telephone" (Warner, 1992, p. 56). Candidates should be asked to name all previous employers and should be told that "the new employer reserves the right to approach any previous employer and will specifically ask about disciplinary offences" (Warner, 1992, p. 56; see also Support Force for Children's Residential Care, 1995a, p. 29). References should be provided by people with direct experience of the candidate and should be encouraged to comment frankly on candidates' strengths and weaknesses in relation to job descriptions and personal specifications for the post (Warner, 1992, p. 58).

> ***Appointments should never be made subject to references***
> (Support Force for Children's Residential Care, 1995, p. 29, emphasis in original).

In relation to the nursing profession, the Clothier Report recommended that "in addition to routine references the most recent employer or place of study should be asked to provide at least a record of time taken off on grounds of sickness" (Clothier, 1994, p. 128).

Warner summarises which techniques should be required and which should be optional for heads of home posts and for care workers in the form of a table:

TABLE 4.2

Selection Technique	Heads of Homes	Other Care Staff
Application Form	Required	Required
Written Exercise (as part of application form)	Required	Required
Visit to Home	Required	Required
Group Exercise	Optional	Optional
Aptitude Test	Required	Optional
Personality Profiling	Required	Optional
Preliminary Interview	Required	Required
References	Required	Required
Final Interview	Required	Required

(Warner, 1992, p. 64)

SFCRC gives examples of possible selection exercises programmes. For a basic grade unqualified residential care worker it suggests a one-day programme (with formal interviews on a second day) which includes: explanation of the appointment procedure; presentation by residential services manager and head of home; group discussion of a current child care issue; written exercise; tour round the home; (parallel exercises) i) presentation to panel including an assessor, staff member and young person; ii) question time. For a head of home position it suggests a two-day programme including: information session by divisional manager and residential services manager; psychometric testing; tour round the home; (parallel exercises) i) written exercise; ii) oral exercise; personnel information session; group exercise; formal interviews (Support Force for Children's Residential Care, 1995a, Appendix E, pp. 11-12).

Mitchell (1993) reports on some of the recruitment changes being introduced by social services and social work departments following the Warner Report. Croydon Social Services Department ask candidates for managerial posts to "carry out practical exercises based, where possible, on authentic situations" which could include "a staff performance incident, a budget exercise, or handling a critical incident involving a child" (Mitchell, 1993, p. 28). Staffordshire SSD encourages service user involvement in the selection of all front-line posts and other social services departments were exploring the involvement of users. Oxfordshire SSD uses psychometric tests for managers and has extended them to include heads of homes (Sone, 1992, p. 6) and Kent SSD uses psychometric testing "automatically for posts carrying a salary of £19,500 and above" (Mitchell, 1993, p. 29). Staff interviews could involve "multiple interviews, group interviews, group discussions, and feedback sessions." A number of other departments were exploring the introduction of psychometric testing or extension to lower levels of management (see also Chamberlain, 1992; Healy, 1992).

Police Checks

> Checks on criminal records are widely considered to help protect society against people who may seek to abuse positions of trust. The police, who are responsible for maintaining records, have for many years made arrangements to release details of previous convictions of people in certain categories (The Scottish Office, 1996, p. 1).

In Scotland, police checks are mostly carried out by the Scottish Criminal Record Office (SCRO) although individual police forces have on-line access to the SCRO database. The majority of the checks are requested by statutory organisations in respect of potential employees who will have substantial access to children.

> As a result of the check, the prospective employer is given a list of previous convictions, or is informed that there are no such convictions. For potential employees who will have substantial access to children, the list includes convictions which would normally be "spent" under the Rehabilitation of Offenders Act 1974 (The Scottish Office, 1996, p. 1).

The Scottish Office acknowledges that police checks are not the sole answer to ensuring applicants' suitability as "many people who abuse positions of trust are not known to the police and have no previous convictions" (The Scottish Office, 1996, p. 1). Warner states that while only 4% of all offences committed result in a criminal conviction and police checks will reveal only a small proportion of child abusers, they can act as a deterrent (Warner, 1992, p. 72).

One of the recommendations of the Inquiry was that police checks should be extended to voluntary and private homes (Warner, 1992, p. 76). In December 1992, a Home Office Circular announced the extension of pilot schemes in England and Wales which provided vetting arrangements through the Voluntary Organisations Consultancy Service (VOCS) but the "scheme for police checks is only available to certain national voluntary organisations, although requests from other national organisations to be admitted will be considered" (Gulbenkian Foundation, 1993, p. 140). Private agencies do not at present have access to police records (Support Force for Residential Child Care, 1995, p. 48). The Scottish Office stated that from Autumn 1996 existing arrangements will extend to cover people who are working in voluntary child care organisations (The Scottish Office, 1996, p. 2).

In England and Wales, the police also disclose information which goes beyond the formal particulars of convictions and this "includes police cautions and bind-overs, which have no direct Scottish equivalent, and factual information about individuals which is deemed reliable and could indicate that an individual is unsuitable for the post in question" (The Scottish Office, 1996, pp. 4-5). Warner, commenting on the possible implications of the national computer system in England and Wales, considered that:

> it would seem to us likely that local police forces will continue in future to have sensitive but relevant information that needs to be passed on to employers about applicants for jobs in children's homes. We believe that it would not be in the best interests of children to do anything to jeopardise this flow of information (Warner, 1992, p. 75).

This has not been the practice in Scotland where only information about convictions and cases which have yet to come to court are disclosed but The Scottish Office has requested views about whether "the established Scottish practice of disclosing only conviction information (and details of pending cases) should be continued or whether the practice in England and Wales (of disclosing limited non-conviction information) should be followed in future" (The Scottish Office, 1996, p.5).

Hebenton and Thomas (1994) are critical of the way in which the Warner Report deals with criminal records checks; "Warner devoted some space and time to police checks but the analysis is slim and the chance for a wider public debate went missing (Hebenton and Thomas, 1994, p. 56). While the statement that "the Warner Report lay heavy emphasis on pre-employment screening by means of a criminal record check" (Hebenton and Thomas, 1994, p. 55) could be disputed, the authors do raise important issues. In particular, they discuss the important question of "the "interpretation" of criminal records as a pointer to a person's future behaviour". They point out that decisions are often made on nothing much more than "common sense" and that there is wide variation in interpretation and decision-making from authority to authority and even from section to section within the same authority (Hebenton and Thomas, 1994, 57). In a draft code of practice, The Scottish Office proposes that:

> Organisations and their associates eligible to obtain access to criminal record information on their job applicants, volunteers or existing job holders would be obliged to:-
>
> (a) have a written policy on the employment of ex-offenders, and a written strategy/action plan for implementation of the policy;...
> (c) consider in each case:-
> - whether the conviction is relevant to the employment;
> - the length of time since the offence occurred;
> - whether the applicant had a pattern of convictions;
> - whether the applicant's circumstances had changed since the offence was committed;
>
> before deciding to rule the individual out; possession of a conviction must not be an automatic bar to employment....
> (The Scottish Office, 1996, pp. 8-9)

SFCRC strongly recommends that appointments should not be confirmed until checks have been completed. Where appointments are made subject to checks, "such staff should never be on duty with children unless they are closely supervised by a more senior member of staff" (Support Force for Residential Child Care, 1995a, p. 48).

Other sources may be used for vetting potential employees although there is some confusion in the literature concerning the situation in Scotland.

In England and Wales, the Department of Health maintains a Consultancy Service Index "which lists people who have worked in the child care field and those who have been dismissed or have resigned in circumstances which suggest the welfare or safety of children has been put at risk" and "people who have been, or might have been, notified to the Department by the police following convictions for offences against children or which suggest that the person involved might be a risk to children (Support Force for Children's Residential Care, 1995a, p. 49)[49]. In Northern Ireland, the Department of Health and Social Services maintains a register of people who have left or been dismissed from employment in circumstances which indicate they may pose a threat to children (Social Services Inspectorate, undated a, p. 41). An equivalent list is not kept in Scotland (Cullen, 1996, p. 141).[50]

In England and Wales, the Department for Education maintains a list (List 99) "of people who have been employed in schools who the Secretary of State has considered unsuitable for relevant employment. The names on this list are also included in the Department of Health's Consultancy Service Index" (Support Force for Children's Residential Care, 1995a, p. 49). In Scotland, an equivalent list (List 1R) is maintained by the Scottish Office Education and Industry Department.[51]

49 SFCRC give contact addresses for the Department of Health Consultancy Service Index, the DfEE List 99 and CCETSW.

50 Gulbenkian Foundation (1993) describe such a list maintained by the Social Work Services Group of the Scottish Office but this list had not been in operation for a number of years prior to 1993 (Children's Safeguards Review Team).

51 Cullen states that these lists are held by local authorities (Cullen, 1996, p. 140).

SFCRC also states that superannuation information can be checked against the curriculum vitae provided by the candidate and inconsistencies can be investigated (Support Force for Children's Residential Care, 1995a, p. 50). Finally, SFCRC states that CCETSW has details of "all the staff who obtained preliminary certificates or full professional qualifications issued by itself or CTC[52]" (Support Force for Children's Residential Care, 1995, p. 51) and verification of qualifications can be done through CCETSW's registry.

The National Commission of Inquiry into the Prevention of Child Abuse recommended that a fully integrated and automated system should be established "to record information about all those working in children's services found guilty of, or cautioned or subjected to formal disciplinary action for, any kind of assault against children or other serious misdemeanour which has placed children at risk" (Williams of Mostyn, 1996, p. 51). This would be accessible to employers and voluntary organisations.

The Gulbenkian Foundation (1993) concluded that there has been "little attempt to look comprehensively at how to use recruitment and vetting procedures effectively to seek to safeguard children from ill-treatment and abuse by people working with or for them" (Gulbenkian Foundation, 1993, p. 147). Nunno and Rindfleisch also state that screening strategies have never been formally evaluated but that "our survey found that many child protective professionals were sceptical of their usefulness since the great majority of abusers have not been identified formally by the judicial system, and reliance on police checks gives one a false sense of security" (Nunno and Rindfleisch, 1991, pp. 302-303).

Probation and Induction

Skinner (1992) stresses that there should be a period of probation for new staff and this must be linked to induction and probationary training and assessment. The report recommends that staff who have not previously worked in residential child care should serve a one year probationary period and that their performance should be assessed at level 2 of the Scottish Vocational Qualifications (SVQ) for Staff in Residential and Day Care Services (Skinner, 1992, p. 73). Warner (1992) also recommends a twelve month probationary period but considers that this should be regardless of the background of the person appointed (Warner, 1992, p. 82).

> Regular formal assessment should ensure that at all stages of the probation period the individual is aware of progress and of his or her shortcomings, and advised on how problems are to be tackled (Warner, 1992, p. 82).

Formal assessment should take place initially within six weeks of appointment, a further assessment within six months, and the final assessment at 12 months. Assessment should relate to the person specification and job description and initial progress and shortcomings should be formally identified, recorded and plans made for any necessary action (Support Force for Children's Residential Care, 1995a, p. 61). A written certificate at successful completion of probation should be seen as "a record that the individual has satisfied line management that he or she is competent to work with children in that particular home" (Warner, 1992, p. 83, emphasis in original).

> If the worker's standards do not meet expectations after 12 months, it is then possible to extend probation, to redeploy the person, or, as a last resort, to dismiss them (Support Force for Children's Residential Care, 1995a, p. 61).

The provision of induction training varied widely across different agencies in Scotland (Skinner, 1992, p. 74). The Skinner report recommends that:

> "all residential child care staff should have 2 weeks' induction training. This should be the training target given first priority" (Skinner, 1992, p. 74).

This needs to cover a general introduction to residential child care and in more detail needs to include: "the functions and objectives of the particular home, handling admissions, relationships

52 Central Training Council in Child Care, CCETSW's predecessor prior to 1971.

with young people and children, their parents, other professionals, responding to crises, handling issues of sanctions and control ..." (Skinner, 1992, p. 74).

> ... our discussions with staff suggests that all too often induction of new staff is given a low priority... There are still about a fifth of employers providing no induction at all. This situation is in our view unacceptable and unsafe (Warner, 1992, p. 129).

Induction training must be flexible and personal so the first stage involves an assessment and identification of an individual's gaps in knowledge and experience. New staff must be given information on the home's aims, policies and principles. There will also be a need for information on the type of children looked after and their particular problems; the therapies used; and the aims of the home in terms of outcomes (Warner, 1992, p. 130). The Support Force for Residential Child Care sets out the purpose of the induction programme as:

> to ensure that the new member of staff can work safely, competently and consistently within legal and departmental requirements
>
> to enable the whole residential staff team to understand and be clear about their professional role and place within the organisation
>
> to raise the quality of unit practices and standard of care received by children and young people through consistent practice
>
> to enable new managers to effectively discharge their responsibilities with the best use of resources and achievement of good quality residential care in the minimum time after their commencement in post (Support Force for Residential Child Care, 1995a, p. 58).

Induction training should be seen as part of an integrated staff development programme and should offer a variety of learning approaches (Support Force for Residential Child Care, 1995, pp. 59-60). A model two week induction programme is set out:

> *preparatory stage* - documentation and information sent to the new staff member before s/he starts work;
>
> *first week* - the induction process; role of the unit; care planning as a provider; policies and procedures; administrative systems;
>
> *second week* - corporate context and departmental perspective; role of the worker; child study; observation of direct work and external visits; reflection on learning and identification of future learning ;
>
> *evaluation of progress, follow-up and reinforcement* - close formal supervision and support should explicitly monitor progress in assimilating the requirements of the job and competence level (Support Force for Residential Child Care, 1995a, Appendix a, pp. 42-45).

Foster Care Assessment

Anderson (1982) comments that reviewing the literature:

> ... leads one to conclude that there is a common agreement about the qualities that are needed for good foster parenting, a frustration over how to determine ahead of time whether applicants possess those qualities, and a concern about the time involved in doing the studies. (Anderson, 1982, pp. 37 - 38; see also Shaw, 1989)

Anderson advocates an assessment process which involves: an initial interview to describe the agency and screen out grossly unsuitable applicants; a second interview to complete a questionnaire based on research by Cautley; a third interview to administer a genogram, a social and emotional history that includes detailed information about marriages, relationships, family, and occupation and education; a home visit to meet all members of the applicant family and to assess their emotional system and communication skills; and interviews with referees (Anderson, 1982, pp. 42 - 43).

Anderson does raise the issue that "the process depends heavily on self-reporting and people do not always tell the truth, or the whole truth, about themselves" (Anderson, 1982, p. 45). This issue has been addressed by Ryburn and he argues for a model of assessment in which "the social work role is one of skilled facilitation and the evaluative judgements are those of the consumers" (Ryburn, 1991, p. 25). Shaw also stresses that in assessing "the actual or potential effectiveness of a foster family, it will be more fruitful (if more difficult) to apply a systems perspective than to study the personal characteristics of any one of the participants" (Shaw, 1989, p. 150).

Only one article was identified as focusing specifically on the issue of child sexual abuse in relation to the assessment of foster carers. Barnardo's New Families in Humberside, following an instance of sexual abuse by the foster father with the knowledge of the foster mother, changed their method of assessing foster carers. The assessment process stressed:

> **information giving** (interview with social worker + full day group meeting). Most of the children on referral to the Project were known to have been sexually abused and the likelihood of disclosure was stressed to prospective adopters. The need to investigate and assess as to whether the applicants' family is a safe one is clearly stated (to be open about what the procedures entail, and hopefully to deter potential sexual abusers)
>
> **information collection** (obtaining statutory and personal references, police checks, medicals etc.). With the knowledge and permission of the applicants, all referees are specifically asked whether they have any reason to believe that the applicant(s) would physically or sexually abuse a child. Previously married applicants are asked permission to contact their ex-spouse or a referee who knew them well during the previous marriage.

At this stage, a brief report goes forward to the adoption panel asking for a recommendation for the application to proceed or not.

> **Family and Individual Interviews** (a family form is completed by applicants, individual interviews and a family interview are conducted). The family form includes questions on how they learned the facts of life, previous significant relationships, courtship, adjustments to sex, and present sexual relationships. Individual interviews include questions on whether they feel a child would be 'safe' in their family, and about issues of sexuality, and growing up. The family interview will address issues such as:
>
> - the adults' and children's ability to be open and comfortable about bodily parts
> - power relationships within the family
> - family boundaries
> - 'open' and 'closed' families
> - the family's ability to accept and express feelings
> - family secrets
> - adult understanding of norms and taboos
>
> (Francis, 1991, pp. 72 - 77).

Francis concludes that this paper is "one agency's attempt to address what we believe to be hitherto unexamined areas of work" and that the "fear that we may, despite all of our attempts to assess accurately, approve further abusing families is very real and does not go away" (Francis, 1991, p 78). NFCA also stress the importance of addressing attitudes to sex and sexuality in assessment as these will have direct implications for children placed in foster care. Assessment should provide:

> ... opportunity for discussion of sexual matters and provides a start for looking at sexual relationships both within and outside the family. It also opens discussion on dealing with sexualized behaviour from potential foster children, and gives an opportunity for considering how safe the placement can be for everyone. (NFCA, 1993, p. 8).

Finkelhor, Williams and Burns suggest that in relation to day-care, "many of the most heated public policy debates revolve around whether it is possible to develop procedures that would more effectively exclude potential abusers from day-care operations" (Finkelhor, Williams and Burns, 1988, p. 65). They concluded from their study that perpetrators did not have characteristics which would distinguish them easily from other staff members or other people in general. While a number of abusers had problem histories which may or may not have been related to their abusing, "the number of cases is truly impressive in which perpetrators appeared to be very upstanding individuals who made a good impression on parents and licensers and who had nothing noteworthy in their backgrounds" (Finkelhor, Williams and Burns, 1988, p. 68). They conclude that it is not feasible to screen people for problems in their backgrounds and ferret out child molesters.

There is no reason to believe that the situation would be any different in terms of other forms of care and it is unlikely that selection and assessment will ever be able to effectively screen out all abusers. Macaskill writes:

> Even when social workers may consider that they have undertaken the most thorough assessment and preparation of a substitute family, it is essential for them to recognize the possibility that sexual abuse could still occur within this foster or adoptive family (Macaskill, 1991, pp. 108 - 109, see also Pringle, 1993; Sone, 1992).

In relation to residential care, Utting makes a similar point:

> However good the checks employed in the selection of staff there can be no guarantee that staff will not abuse children placed in their care. Consequently there must be management machinery in place which can detect abuse and be alert to the potential for abuse (Utting, 1991, p. 36).

Support of Carers and Staff

Supervision

Supervision of staff in most children's homes is irregular and some temporary staff were entirely excluded from the supervisory process. In only a minority of homes is supervision a frequent occurrence, properly minuted and afforded clear priority (Social Services Inspectorate, undated a, p. 50). Warner found that formal appraisal systems for heads of homes existed in only 30% of local authorities and in 18% of authorities for care staff (Warner, 1992, p. 94). Supervision took place fortnightly to monthly in nearly all cases although "many employing authorities report that the bulk of supervision in children's homes is 'informal'" (Warner, 1992, p. 95; see also Social Services Inspectorate, undated b) which was taken to mean unplanned, ad hoc and irregular. Warner recommended that

> The Government should require employers to ensure that regular supervision of all staff by line managers takes place at least fortnightly and appropriate remedial or developmental action is agreed, recorded and taken as a result (Warner, 1992, p.96).

Supervision presents an opportunity to raise concerns about particular children or the actions of another member of staff. An annual formal performance appraisal was also recommended (Warner, 1992, p. 97).

> Without regular and effective supervision care workers can become worn down as they find there is nobody with whom they can talk through their own reactions and responses to the behaviour with which they are confronted. Their own anger and frustration can turn in on themselves and the result is burn-out and less effective care for children. Standards can drop and inappropriate staff behaviour can develop unchecked (Warner, 1992, p. 94).

Suskind argues that "supervision that is sensitive to the subtle ways in which staff express their own need for help and their own dependency is most important" (Suskind, 1986, p. 24) and supervisors need to be alert to the signs of burn-out.

Karban and Mills (1995) found, in a small scale study in one local authority, that experienced residential workers identified agency commitment and resources for supervision as one of the most important factors in recruiting suitably qualified and experienced staff to senior worker and manager posts; "the over-riding theme appeared to be an emphasis on the need for supervision for the manager himself and the opportunity to offer support and supervision to the team" (Karban and Mills, 1995, p. 26). The Support Force for Children's Residential Care have produced a practice guide to supervision which highlights the three strands to supervision "getting the work done well - or oversight; staff support; staff development" (Support Force for Children's Residential Care, 1995b, p. 7).

Training

Throughout this review, the importance and necessity of training has been consistently highlighted in the literature; "training of staff in institutions is a major factor in preventing and correcting institution abuse" (Harrell and Orem, 1980, p. 40).

> Training and staff development ensure that practice does not stagnate; and it can prevent poor practice becoming the norm, by encouraging staff to reassess their approaches and procedures. It is the prime means of bringing new ideas and practices into children's homes. Training is essential to good child care practice and ultimately the safety of children (Warner, 1992, p. 113).

Sluyter and Cleland (1979) stress that training should place an emphasis on development of caregiver skills, and suggest that there needs to be ongoing supervision, on-the-job training from a supervisor who is on-call 24 hours a day. They also stress that in-service training needs to include an explanation that both administrative action and possibly court action can and will be taken against any employee guilty of resident abuse - verbal or physical and that failure of employees at any level to record an accident or injury to a resident could lead to discharge (Sluyter and Cleland, 1979). Mills (1995) calls for training for residential staff "to be provided within the overall context of anti-oppressive practice" and with opportunities for "career developments through secondment policies for unqualified staff" (Mills, 1995, p. 62).

The training and support of foster carers has also been stressed as vital. A number of training programmes for foster carers on issues of child sexual abuse have been described in the literature (Blumler et al, 1986; Davis et al, 1987; Devine and Tate, 1991; Sanders and McAllen, 1995; see also, Pine and Jacobs, 1989). NFCA now provide a range of training courses which include: 'Caring for children who involve others in sexual activities'; 'Child protection and foster care'; 'Managing behaviour'; 'Managing stress in foster care'; 'Men in child care'; 'Safe caring: minimising the risk of false allegations'; 'Sex and sexuality' (NFCA, 1996).

Since most sexual abuse in foster families is carried out by foster fathers, it is crucial that they are included in preparation and training about abuse and its effects on the victim. Finkelhor, Williams and Burns, in relation to day-care, stress the importance of:

> ... clear sexual-abuse-deterrence training for family members of day-care operators. Classes, literature, and briefings could be made mandatory for all those in the household, explicitly discussing sexual abuse, in the hope of thereby deterring some possible perpetrators. (Finkelhor, 1988, p. 69).

Macaskill also highlights the importance of preparing other children in the foster family. While most families in the study made some attempt to prepare the other children in a general way, very few prepared them in terms of the issue of sexual abuse and how this might affect them. She found clear evidence that "bringing a sexually abused child into the family placed the other children in a vulnerable situation, especially when they were not adequately forewarned about potential difficulties" (Macaskill, 1991, p. 84). She highlights the need to prepare other children for: sexual overtures from the abused child; disruptive and anti-social behaviour; and inevitable loss of parental attention (Macaskill, 1991, p. 90).

Whistleblowing

> Evidence suggests that a procedure enabling staff to voice their concerns about the actions of other staff in the home or more senior management is essential. Staff have expressed to us their difficulty in making known their views about professional issues arising in homes... We have had our attention drawn to several cases where a member of staff has felt that they had to resign before they could express their concerns about their experiences (Warner, 1992, p. 104).

Staff in all children's homes must be able to raise concerns outside their line management structure in the confidence that genuine complaints will not have repercussions for them in their day to day work or their later careers (Warner, 1992; see also Gulbenkian, 1993).

External Support

Warner stresses the need for support from specialists in other agencies, such as child psychiatrists and educational psychologists:

> The picture to emerge from our visits is that too often staff in children's homes are left to cope with abused, disturbed and violent young people without access to the specialist psychiatric and psychological services that are needed (Warner, 1992, p. 144).

Over half the heads of units in the survey of residential establishments in Scotland felt they needed additional support such as a specialist adviser, consultant or psychologist, and "often such a specialist was required to provide a service both to residents and/or staff, such as an independent counsellor" (Harvey, 1992, pp. 27-28). Warner also highlights the importance of staff care schemes such as stress counselling (Warner, 1992, pp. 154-155). Berry, in 1975, advocated as her main recommendation that all residential workers should have opportunities for support and consultation and "every residential unit requires a special senior supporter who devotes himself (sic) to the staff without being directly responsible for the children... a consultant, counsellor, supervisor or therapist (but not an inspector)" (Berry, 1975, p. 134).

Boushel also stresses the importance of emotional and practical support to foster carers to prevent 'burnout' and stress-related abuse (Boushel, 1994, p. 36).

External Systems

Inspection, Monitoring and Standards

> An important safeguard for children's homes ought to be the new independent inspection and registration arrangements... 'arms-length' unit (i.e., independent of the home's line management) for inspecting their own and private children's homes (Warner, 1992, p. 108).

Standards need to include: statement of purposes and objectives; physical state of repair of building; amenities available; privacy and individualisation; rewards and sanctions used; control procedures used; treatment and care policies; staffing levels; experience, qualifications and training of staff ; frequency and nature of supervision; children's rights and complaints procedures (Warner, 1992, p. 109).

Warner also stresses the importance of monitoring by line managers of homes through the effective collection of information and processes for acting on that information (Warner, 1992, p. 110) However, Social Services Inspectorate "identified considerable weaknesses in the external management and monitoring of residential child care services" (Social Services Inspectorate, undated b, p. 87).

Warner called for a national definition of standards which would provide a more rational framework for registration and inspection and recommended that

> The Government should commission the preparation of a Code of Practice defining the national standards of residential care for different groups of children and young people, that should be followed by all employers and inspection and registration units (Warner, 1992, p. 166).

In 1994, the Social Services Inspectorate published standards for residential care to support inspections of residential child care services (Social Services Inspectorate, 1994). The National Commission of Inquiry into the Prevention of Child Abuse suggest a number of points should be taken into account in the final determination of the future role of the social services inspection: regulation should be extended to cover all situations where children are cared for away from home; there should be an integrated approach to the inspection and regulation of provisions for children away from home, whether they be predominantly education, health, or social care in emphasis; the provision of care for children should not be seen in the same light as other "small businesses"; regulation should not be regarded as unnecessary bureaucracy but as essential to protect children from abuse; training for residential work with children should ensure that staff are equipped to work with children and young people who have often had very damaging experiences (Williams of Mostyn, 1996, pp. 91-92).

Family and Community Involvement

Effective programmes are consumer orientated, a harm free environment is open to the scrutiny of persons outside the treatment environment. Daly and Dowd describe a system which actively seeks consumer input. In each home of eight children, over 75 consumers are canvassed to assess caregiver pleasantness, concern and co-operation, as well as child improvement and development. Kahan (1994) states that effective monitoring of arrangements and activities in an establishment will include regular review meetings of staff; regular written reports reviewing work and matters such as young people's behaviour. These reviews should incorporate feedback from young people as well as others associated with the establishment, particularly local authority inspection units. Kahan (1994) advocates that everyone visiting a residential establishment in an official capacity should be aware of their responsibility to safeguard the welfare of children and young people living there.

> ... it is important that parents, placing agencies and others with an interest in the children have regular access to the home or school to help ensure that children's welfare is properly safeguarded and promoted (Kahan, 1994, p. 187; see also Sullivan et al, 1987)

Parents and informal visitors also need to be told about complaints procedures and how to make their concerns known.

Whitaker stresses the importance of building community supports through linkages to family, neighbourhood, and other caregivers who are potential sources of social support to young people and their families (Whitaker, 1987, p. 89; see also Mercer, 1982). There is:

> … no better antidote to institutional maltreatment exists than the presence of concerned, knowledgeable, and committed citizens asking "naive" questions. (Whitaker, 1987, p. 98).

Similarly, Boushel highlights how a 'rich social network' for children in foster care can provide "potential confidantes, role models, opportunities to develop social skills, and intellectual and social stimulation" (Boushel, 1994, p. 36).

In the United States, federally sponsored projects have "sought to address the isolated nature of institutions by creating oversight criteria and citizens' review committees to examine day-to-day care of children and open the facility to the community (Nunno and Rindfleisch, 1991, p. 303; see also Harrell and Orem, 1980). Silberberg and Silberberg (1982) also advocate the establishment of community review teams, "consisting of consumers and sympathetic service providers would have investigative or appeal functions" (Silberberg and Silberberg, 1982, p. 136; see also Gil and Baxter, 1979; Whitaker, 1987).

Warner warns however, that while external visiting is an important part of the "checks and balances", it is important to remember that children's homes are primarily <u>homes</u> and "children should not be subjected to endless visits from strangers concerned for their welfare" (Warner, 1992, p. 101).

Conclusion

This review has aimed to pull together the research and literature on the nature and extent of abuse and other harm experienced by children and young people living away from home. While it has focused on the negative aspects of abuse and harm, it has also aimed to highlight the measures which can protect children and promote their well-being. Central to the review has been the intention of highlighting the importance that children and young people gain a positive, individualised experience of care.

It is crucial that a holistic and integrated approach to the care and protection of child and young people is adopted. This must take into account their experiences of care on a day-to-day basis and link this to the wider organisational and policy contexts in which care is provided; to the relationships between different professions and agencies; and to the social, economic and legislative processes which underpin the provision of care and the protection of children (Kendrick, 1995; Kendrick et al, 1996). This means that providing a safe and caring environment involves action at all levels; in day-to-day practice; in management and planning; and in politics and policy-making at local and national level. Children in the care of the state have often experienced abuse and neglect in their own home environment, the least they should expect is safety from abuse when in care.

> If a society damns its institutions as reflecting its evil and uncaring self and therefore doesn't provide them with enough resources, it becomes a self-fulfilling prophecy that under-funded institutions will attract individuals who are less well trained and less motivated, less caring and less responsible, and less healthy, thereby providing an increasingly fertile ground for all kinds of abuse (Siskind, 1986, p. 28)
>
> "Who can we trust? Who do we trust? Who should we trust?
> (young person abused in care, Safe & Sound, 1995)

References

Abrahams, C. and Mungall, R. (1992) *Runaways: Exploding the Myth*, London, NCH.

Agathanos, H. (1983) Institutional child abuse in Greece: some preliminary findings, *Child Abuse & Neglect*, Vol 7, pp. 71-74. **(Greece)**

Agnew, S. (1989) Aggressive behaviour in boys: to what extent is it institutionalised?, in Tattum, D.P. and Lane, D.A. (eds) *Bullying in Schools*, Stoke-on-Trent: Trentham Books, pp. 59-72.

Ahmad, B. (1990) *Black Perspectives in Social Work*, London: Venture Press.

Ahmed, S, Cheetham, J., and Small, J.(eds) (1986) *Social Work with Black Children and their Families*, London: Batsford.

Alexander, B. (1996) Response to 'A challenge to residential fundamentalists', *Centrestage, The Newsletter of Scottish Residential Childcare*, Issue 4, p. 4.

Allen, D. (1993) In the wake of Allitt, *Nursing Standard*, Vol 7 No 36, pp. 18-19.

Ammerman, R.T., Van Hasselt, V.B., Hersen, M., McConigle, J.J. & Lubetsky, M.J. (1989) Abuse and neglect in psychiatrically hospitalised multihandicapped children, *Child Abuse & Neglect*, Vol 13 No 3, pp. 335-343. **(USA)**

Anderson, L.M. (1982) A systems theory model for foster home studies, *Child Welfare*, Vol 61 No 1, pp. 37 - 47 **(USA)**

Atten, D.W., and Milner, J.S. (1987) Child abuse potential and work satisfaction in day-care employees, *Child Abuse & Neglect*, Vol 11, pp 117-123. **(USA)**

Audit Commission (1994) *Seen But Not Heard: Co-ordinating Community Child Health and Social Services for Children in Need*, London: HMSO.

Authier, K.J. (1987) The community basis for protecting handicapped children, in Garbarino, J., Brookhouser, P.E. and Authier, K.J. (eds) *Special Children - Special Risks: The Maltreatment of Children with Disabilities*, New York: Aldine de Gruyter, pp. 231-243. **(USA)**

Baldwin, N. (1990) *The Power to Care in Children's Homes*, Aldershot: Avebury.

Barn, R. (1993) *Black Children in the Public Care System*, London: Batsford.

Barrett, D. (1995) *Child prostitution, Highlight*, No 135, National Children's Bureau.

Batty, D. (ed) (1991) *Sexually Abused Children: Making Their Placements Work*, London: British Agencies for Adoption and Fostering.

Bedarf, A.R. (1995) Examining sex offender notification laws, *California Law Review*, Vol 83, pp. 885-939. **(USA)**

Bell, L. and Tooman, P. (1994) Mandatory reporting laws: a critical overview, *International Journal of Law and the Family*, Vol 8, pp. 337-356

Belson, P. (1993) Children in hospital, *Children & Society*, Vol 7 No 2, pp. 196-210.

Benedict, M.L., Zuravin, S. Brandt, D. and Abbey, H. (1994) Types and frequency of child maltreatment by family foster care providers in an urban population, *Child Abuse & Neglect*, Vol 18 No 7, pp. 577-585. **(USA)**

Benedict, M.I., Zuravin, S., Somerfield, M. and Brandt, D. (1996) The reported health and functioning of children maltreated while in family foster care, *Child Abuse & Neglect*, Vol 20 No 7, pp 561-571. **(USA)**

Benthall, J. (1991) Invisible wounds: corporal punishment in British schools as a form of ritual, *Child Abuse & Neglect*, Vol 15, pp. 377-388.

Berridge, D. (1985) Children's Homes, Oxford: Blackwell.

Berridge, D and Brodie, I. (1996) Residential child care in England and Wales: the inquiries and after, in Hill, M. and Aldgate, J. (eds) *Child Welfare Services: Developments in Law, Policy, Practice and Research,* London: Jessica Kingsley.

Berridge, D. and Cleaver, H. (1987) *Foster Home Breakdown*, Oxford: Blackwell.

Berry, J. (1975) *Daily Experience in Residential Life: A Study of Children and Their Care-Givers*, London: Routledge and Kegan Paul.

Besharov, DJ (1984) Child welfare malpractice: suing agencies and caseworkers for harmful practices, *Trial*, March, pp 56 - 64. **(USA)**

Besharov, D. (1987) Reporting out-of-home maltreatment: penalties and protections, *Child Welfare*, Vol 66 No 5, pp. 399-408. **(USA)**

Bibby, P (1996) Definitions and recent history, in Bibby, P. (ed) *Organised Abuse: The Current Debate*, Aldershot: Arena.

Biggar, K. and Neal, D. (1996) Caring for the suicidal in custody: developing a multi-disciplinary approach, *Omega - Journal of Death and Dying*, Vol 33 No 3, pp. 207-213.

Black and In Care (1992) *Black and In Care Annual Report 1991/1992*, London: Black and In Care.

Black, S. (ed) (1992) *Mustn't Grumble: Social Work Complaints Procedures*, Seminar Paper No. 2. Dundee: Social Services Research Group Scottish Branch.

Blatt E.R. (1992) Factors associated with child-abuse and neglect in residential care settings, *Children & Youth Services Review*, Vol 16 No 6, pp 493 - 517 **(USA)**

Blatt, E.R. and Brown S.W. (1986) Environmental influences on incidents of alleged child abuse and neglect in New York state psychiatric facilities: towards an etiology of institutional child maltreatment, *Child Abuse & Neglect*, Vol 10, pp 171 - 180. **(USA)**

Bloom, R.B. (1992) When staff members sexually abuse children in residential care, *Child Welfare*, Vol 71 No 2, pp. 131 - 145 **(USA)**

Blumler, J., Keyte, M., and Wiles, A. (1987) Training foster parents about sexual abuse, *Adoption and Fostering*, Vol 11 No 2, pp. 33-35.

Bolton, F., Laner R., and Gai D. (1981) For better or for worse? foster parents and foster children in an officially reported child maltreatment population, *Child and Youth Services Review*, Vol 3 Nos 1 - 2, pp 37 - 53 **(USA)**

Boss, P., Edwards, S. and Pitman, S. (eds) (1995) *Profile of Young Australians: Facts, Figures and Issues*, Melbourne: Churchill Livingstone. **(Australia)**

Boushel, M. (1994) Keeping safe: strengthening the protective environment of children in foster care, *Adpotion & Fostering*, Vol 18 No 1, pp. 33-39

Bowles, N. (1995) Methods of nurse selection: a review, *Nursing Standard*, vol 9 No 15, pp. 25-29.

Brannan, C., Jones, J.R., and Murch, J.D. (1993a) *Castle Hill Report: Practice Guide*, Shropshire County Council.

Brannan, C., Jones, J.R., and Murch, J.D. (1993b) Lessons from a residential special school enquiry: reflections on the Castle Hill Report, *Child Abuse Review*, Vol 2, pp. 271-275.

Brindle, D. (1997) Eighty are called by abuse tribunal, *The Guardian*, 18 January 1997, p. 6.

Brookhouser, P.E. (1987a) Ensuring the safety of deaf children in residential schools, *Otolaryngology - Head and Neck Surgery*, Vol 99 No 4, pp.361-368 **(USA)**

Brookhouser, P.E. (1987b) Medical issues, in Garbarino, J., Brookhouser, P.E. and Authier, K.J. (eds) *Special Children - Special Risks: The Maltreatment of Children with Disabilities*, New York: Aldine de Gruyter, pp. 161-178. **(USA)**

Brookhouser, P.E., Scanlan, J.M., Knutson, J.F. and Schulte, L.E. (1991) Patterns of physical and sexual abuse of communicatively handicapped children, *Annals of Otology, Rhinology & Laryngology*, Vol 100 No 3, pp. 188-194 **(USA)**

Brookhouser, P.E, Sullivan, P., Scanlan, J.M. and Garbarino, J. (1986) Identifying the sexually abused deaf child: the otolaryngologist's role, *Laryngoscope*, Vol 96 No 2, pp. 152-158 **(USA)**

Browne, K. and Falshaw, L. (1996) Factors related to bullying in secure accommodation, *Child Abuse Review*, Vol 5, pp. 123-127

Buchanan, A., Wheal, A., Walder, D., Macdonald, S. and Coker, R. (1993) *Answering Back: Report by Young People Being Looked After on The Children Act 1989*, Southampton: CEDR, Department of Social Work Studies, University of Southampton

Burton, J. (1993) *The Handbook of Residential Care*, London: Routledge.

Butler, I. and Williamson, H. (1994) *Children Speak: Children, Trauma and Social Work*, Harlow: Longman.

Caesar, G., Parchment, M. and Berridge, D. (1994) *Black Perspectives on Services for Children in Need*, London: National Children's Bureau and Barnardo's

Carbino, R. (1991) Advocacy for foster families in the United States facing child abuse allegations: how social agencies and foster parents are responding to the problem, *Child Welfare*, Vol 79 No 2, pp. 131 - 149. **(USA)**

Carbino, R (1992) Policy and practice for response to foster families when child abuse or neglect is reported, *Child Welfare*, Vol 71 No 6, pp. 497 - 509. **(USA)**

Carrey, N..J. and Adams, L. (1992) How to deal with sexual acting-out on the child psychiatric inpatient ward, *Journal of Psychosocial Nursing*, Vol 30 No 5, pp. 19-23. **(Canada)**

Cavanagh, J. (1992) Children and young people in out-of-home care: treating and preventing individual, programmatic and systems abuse, *Children Australia*, Vol 17 No 2, pp. 17-25. **(Australia)**

Cavara, M. and Ogren, C. (1983) Protocol to investigate child abuse in foster care, *Child Abuse & Neglect*, Vol 7, pp. 287-295. **(USA)**

Centre for Residential Child Care (1995) *Guidance for Residential Workers Caring for Young People who have been Sexually Abused and Those who Abuse Others*, Glasgow: Centre for Residential Child Care.

Chamberlain, L. (1991) On faith or fact? *Community Care*, 8 October 1991.

Cheetham, J. (1986) Introduction, in Ahmed, S, Cheetham, J., and Small, J. (eds) *Social Work with Black Children and their Families*, London: Batsford.

Childright (1995) Child prostitution - protection not prosecution, *Childright*, No 121, pp. 7-8.

Clayden, M. (1992) The aftermath of betrayal, *Community Care*, 15.10.92, pp. 20-22.

Cliffe, D. with Berridge. D. (1991) *Closing Children's Homes: An End to Residential Care?*, London: National Children's Bureau.

Clothier, C. (1994) *The Allitt Inquiry: Independent Inquiry Relating to Deaths and Injuries on the Children's Ward at Grantham and Kesteven General Hospital During the Period February to April 1991*, London: HMSO.

Colton, M. and Vanstone, M. (1996) *Betrayal of Trust: Sexual Abuse by Men who Work with Children... In Their Own Words*, London: Free Association Books.

Conen, M.L. (1995) Sexual abuse by professionals in residential agencies for children and adolescents, *Praxis der Kinderpsychologie und Psychopsychiatrie*, Vol 44 No 4, pp. 134 - 140. **(Germany)**

Connell, A. and Farrington, D.P. (1996) Bullying among incarcerated young offenders: Developing an interview schedule and some preliminary results, *Journal of Adolescence*, Vol 19 No 1, pp. 75-93. **(Canada)**

Connett, D. and Calvett, J. (1997) The school for sex abusers, *The Observer*, 9 March 1997, pp.8-9.

Cooke, D.J. (1991) Violence in prisons: The influence of regime factors; *Howard Journal of Criminal Justice*, Vol 30 No 2, pp. 95-109.

Cotton, D.J. and Groth, A.N. (1984) Sexual assault in correctional institutions: prevention and intervention, in Stuart, I.R. and Greer. J.G. (eds) *Victims of Sexual Aggression: Treatment of Children, Women and Men*, New York: Van Nostrand Reinhold, pp. 127-155. **(USA)**

Craft, A. and Hitching, M. (1989) Keeping safe: sex education and assertiveness skills, in Brown, H. and Craft, A. (eds) *Thinking the Unthinkable: Papers on Sexual Abuse and People with Learning Difficulties*, London: FPA Education Unit.

Crenshaw, D.A. (1988) Responding to sexual acting-out, in C.E. Schaefer and A.J. Swanson (eds) *Children in Residential Care: Critical Issues in Treatment*, New York, Van Nostrand Rheinhold, pp. 50-76 **(USA)**

Crenshaw, W.B., Bartell, P.A. and Lichtenberg, J.W. (1994) Proposed revisions to mandatory reporting laws:an exploratory survey of child protective service agencies, *Child Welfare*, Vol 73 No 1, pp. 15-27 **(USA)**

Crimmens, D. (1994) Residential childcare: the future of comparative European research, *Social Work in Europe*, Vol 1 No 1, pp. 22-26. (reproduced in Caredata)

Cross, M. (1992) Abusive practices and disempowerment of children with physical impairments, *Child Abuse Review*, Vol 1, pp. 194-197.

Crossmaker, M. (1991) Behind locked doors - institutional sexual abuse, *Sexuality and Disability*, Vol 9 No 3, pp. 201-219. **(USA)**

Daly, D.L. and Dowd, T.P. (1992) Characteristics of effective, harm-free environments for children in out-of-home care, *Child Welfare*, Vol 71 No 6, pp. 487-495 **(USA)**

Davies, B. (1992) Suicide awareness: the Listener Scheme at Swansea, in *Perspectives on Prison: A Collection of Views on Prison Life and Running Prisons*, London: HMSO.

Davies, B. (1994) The Swansea Listener Scheme: views from the prison landings, *Howard Journal of Criminal Justice*, Vol 33 No 2, pp. 125-136

Davis, E., Kidd, L. and Pringle, K. (1987) *Child Sexual Abuse Training Programme for Foster Parents with Teenage Placements*, Newcastle upon Tyne: Barnardo's North East Division.

Deisz, R., Doueck, HJ, George, N. and Levine, M. (1996) Reasonable cause - a qualitative study of mandated reporting, *Child Abuse & Neglect*, Vol 20 No 4, pp. 275 - 287. (USA)

Degener, T. (1992) The right to be different: implications for child protection, *Child Abuse Review*, Vol 1, pp. 151-155.

Department of Health (1991) *Patterns & Outcomes in Child Placement: Messages from Current Research and their Implications*, London: HMSO.

Devine, C. and Tate, I. (1991) An introductory training course for foster carers, in Batty, D. (ed) *Sexually Abused Children: Making Their Placements Work*, London: British Agencies for Adoption and Fostering.

DHHS (1980) Proceedings - 1978 *National Conference on Child Abuse and Neglect*, Washington: US Department of Health and Human Services. **(USA)**

Donald, T. and Jureidini, J. (1996) Munchausen Syndrome by Proxy: child abuse in the medical system, *Archive of Pediatric and Adolescent Medicine*, Vol 150, pp. 753-758.

Doran, C. and Brannan, C. (1996) Institutional abuse, in Bibby, P. (ed) *Organised Abuse: The Current Debate*, Aldershot: Arena, pp. 155-166.

Downey, R. (1992) Abuse of power, *Social Work Today*, 17 September 1992, pp. 12-13

Dumond, R.W. (1992) The sexual assault of male inmates in incarcerated settings, *International Journal of the Sociology of Law*, Vol 20, pp. 135-157. **(USA)**

Durkin, R. (1982a) Institutional child abuse from a family systems perspective: a working paper, *Child & Youth Services*, Vol 4, pp 15 - 22 **(USA)**

Durkin, R. (1982b) No one will thank you: first thoughts on reporting institutional abuse, *Child and Youth Services*, Vol 4 Nos 1-2, pp. 109-113. **(USA)**

Earl-Hubbard, M.L. (1996) The child sex offender registration laws: the punishment, liberty deprivation, and unintended results associated with the Scarlet Letter laws of the 1990s, *Northwestern University Law Review*, Vol 90 No 2, pp. 788-862. **(USA)**

Edgar, K. and O'Donnell, I. (1997) Responding to victimisation, *Prison Service Journal*, No 109, pp. 15-19.

Edwards, P. and Miltenberger, R. (1991) Burnout among staff members at community residential facilities for persons with mental retardation, *Mental Retardation*, Vol. 29 No. 3, pp. 125 - 12. **(USA)**

Elliott, M., Browne, K. and Kilcoyne, J. (1995) Child sexual abuse prevention: what offenders tell us, *Child Abuse & Neglect*, Vol 19 No 5, pp. 579-585.

Elvik, S.L, Berkowitz, C.D. Nicholas, E., Lipman, J.L. and Inkelis, S.H. (1990) Sexual abuse in the developmentally disabled: dilemmas of diagnosis, *Child Abuse & Neglect*, Vol 14 No 4, pp. 497 - 502. **(USA)**

Ennew, J. (1986) *The Sexual Exploitation of Children*, Cambridge: Polity Press.

Fielding, N. (1991) Could it ever happen again? *Community Care*, 29.8.91, pp. ii-iii.

Finkelhor, D., Araji, S., Baron, L., Browne, A., Doyle Peters, S. and Wyatt, G.E. (1986) *A Sourcebook on Child Sexual Abuse*, Newbury Park: Sage Publications. **(USA)**

Finkelhor, D., Williams, L.M. and Burns, N. (1988) *Nursery Crimes: Sexual Abuse in Day Care*, Newbury Park: Sage Publications. **(USA)**

Fisher, D. and Holloway-Vine, J. (1990) *Nottingshamshire Young Sex Offenders Group*, information paper.

Flekkoy, M.G. (1989) Child advocacy in Norway: the ombudsman, *Child Welfare*, Vol 58 No 2, pp. 113-122 **(Norway)**

Fletcher, B. (1993) *Not Just a Name: The Views of Young People in Foster and Residential Care*, London: National Consumer Council.

Francis, P. (1991) Child sexual abuse and assessment of substitute families, in Batty, D. (ed) *Sexually Abused Children: Making Their Placements Work*, London: British Agencies For Adoption and Fostering.

Freeman-Longo, R.E. (1996) Feel good legislation: Prevention or calamity, *Child Abuse & Neglect*, Vol 20 No 2, pp. 95 - 101. **(USA)**

Friend, B. (1993) After Allitt, *Nursing Times*, Vol 89 No 21, p. 21.

Galbally, R. (1993) Child abuse and children with disabilities, *Australian and New Zealand Journal of Family Therapy*, Vol 14 No 4, pp. 225-228 **(Australia)**

Gallagher, B., Hughes, B. and Parker, H. (1996) The nature and extent of known cases of organised child sexual abuse in England and Wales, Bibby, P. (ed) *Organised Abuse: The Current Debate*, Aldershot: Arena, pp. 215-230.

Galloway, J. (1997) Forsaken on Romeo Block, *The Guardian Weekend*, February 8 1997, pp. 21-29

Garbarino, J. (1987) The abuse and neglect of special children: An introduction to the issues, in Garbarino, J., Brookhouser, P.E. and Authier, K.J. (eds) *Special Children - Special Risks: The Maltreatment of Children with Disabilities*, New York: Aldine de Gruyter, pp. 3-14. **(USA)**

Garrett, J.R. (1979) Institutional maltreatment of children: an emerging public issue, *Residential and Community Child Care Administration*, Vol 1, pp 57 - 68. **(USA)**

Gazan, H. and Flynn, J. (1986) The role of licensing in child placement and child protection, *Child Welfare*, Vol 65 No 2, pp 129-139. **(USA)**

Geddes, I. (1994) *Bullying and the Independent School*, M.Ed. Thesis, University of Edinburgh

Giovannoni, JM (1995) Reports of child maltreatment from mandated and non-mandated reporters, *Children and Youth Services Review*, Vol 17 No 4, pp. 487 - 501. **(USA)**

Gil, E. (1982) Institutional abuse of children in out-of-home care, *Child & Youth Services*, Vol 4 Nos 1-2, pp. 7-13. **(USA)**

Gil, E. and Baxter, K. (1979) Abuse of children in institutions, *Child Abuse & Neglect*, Vol 3, pp. 693-698 **(USA)**

Gilligan, R. (1996) Irish child care services in the 1990s: The Child Care Act 1991 and other developments, in Hill, M. and Aldgate, J. (eds) *Child Welfare Services: Developments in Law, Policy, Practice and Research*, London: Jessica Kingsley Publishers, pp. 56-74. **(Ireland)**

Glasper,E.A and Whiting, M. (1993) Implications of the Allitt case, *British Journal of Nursing*, Vol 2 No 11, pp. 555-556

Gough, D. (1996) An overview of the literature, in Bibby, P. (ed) *Organised Abuse: The Current Debate*, Aldershot: Arena.

Grimshaw, R. and Berridge, D. (1994) *Educating Disruptive Children: Placement and Progress in Residential Special Schools for Pupils with Emotional and Behavioural Difficulties*, London: National Children's Bureau.

Groze, V. (1990) An exploratory investigation into institutional maltreatment, *Children & Youth Services Review*, Vol 12, pp. 229-241. **(USA)**

Gulbenkian Foundation (1993) *One Scandal Too Many: The Case for Comprehensive Protection For Children in All Settings*, London: Gulbenkian Foundation.

Gustavsson, N.S. and Segal, E.A. (1994) *Critical Issues in Child Welfare*, Thousand Oaks: Sage Publications. **(USA)**

Gwynn, C., Meyer, R., and Schaefer, C. (1988)The influence of the peer culture in residential treatment, in C.E. Schaefer and A.J. Swanson (eds) *Children in Residential Care: Critical Issues in Treatment*, New York: Van Nostrand Rheinhold, pp. 30-49. **(USA)**

Hargrave M.C. (1991) Sexual incidents in residential treatment, *Child & Youth Care Forum*, Vol 20 No 6, pp 413 - 419. **(USA)**

Harrell, S.A. and Orem, R.C. (1980) *Preventing Child Abuse and Neglect: A Guide for Staff in Residential Institutions*, Washington: U.S. Department of Health and Human Services. **(USA)**

Harvey, J. (1992) A postal survey of heads of residential child care units in Scotland, in *The Review of Residential Child Care in Scotland: The Three Supporting Research Studies*, Central Research Unit Papers, Edinburgh: Scottish Office.

Harvey, J. (1993) Advocacy for children and protection of their rights within the public care system: the role of the child advocate within the South Australian Children's Interests Bureau, paper presented to the *Fourth Australasian Conference on Child Abuse and Neglect*, Griffith University, Queensland. **(Australia)**

Healy, P. (1992) Right for the job, *Social Work Today*, 19 November 1992, pp. 19-20

Hicks, C. and Nixon, S. (1991) Unfounded allegations of child abuse in the United Kingdom: a survey of foster parents' reactions to investigative procedures, *Child & Youth Services*, Vol 15 No 2, pp. 249 - 260.

HMSO (1995) *Child Protection: Messages from Research*, London: HMSO.

Home Office (1991) *Working Together Under the Children Act 1989*, London: HMSO

Home Office (1996) *Sentencing and Supervision of Sex Offenders: A Consultation Document*, London: HMSO.

Home Office/Scottish Office (1997) *Sex Offenders: A Ban on Working with Children: A Consultation Paper*, London: HMSO.

Howard League (1995a) *Banged Up, Beaten Up, Cutting Up: Report of the Howard League Commission of Inquiry into Violence in Penal Institutions for Teenagers under 18*, London: Howard League for Penal Reform

Howard League (1995b) *Troubleshooter: A Project to Rescue 15 Year Olds from Prison*, London: Howard League for Penal Reform.

Hudson, J.R. (1996) Response to 'A challenge to residential fundamentalists', *Centrestage, The Newsletter of Scottish Residential Childcare*, Issue 4, p. 4.

Hughes, W.H. (1986) *Report of the Inquiry into Children's Homes and Hostels*, Belfast: HMSO

Hutchison, E. (1993) Mandatory reporting laws: child protective case finding gone awry? *Social Work*, Vol 38 No 1, pp. 56-63 **(USA)**

Ivory, M. (1996) Taking liberties, *Community Care*, 18.7.96, p. 21.

Janus, M.-D., Archambault, F.X, Brown, S.W, and Welsh, L.A. (1995) Physical abuse in Canadian runaway adolescents, *Child Abuse & Neglect*, Vol 19 No 4, pp. 443-447. **(Canada)**

Jerusalem, M.P. (1995) A framework for post-sentence sex offender legislation: perspectives on prevention, registration and the public's "right" to know, *Vanderbilt Law Review*, Vol 48, pp. 219-255. **(USA)**

Jesson, J. (1993) Understanding adolescent female prostitution - A literature review, *British Journal of Social Work*, Vol 23 No 5, pp 517 - 530

Jones, J. (1994) Towards and understanding of power relationships in institutional abuse, *Early Child Development and Care*, Vol 100, pp. 69-76.

Joseph, C. (1995) Scarlet wounding: issues of child prostitution, *The Journal of Psychohistory*, Vol 23 No 1, pp. 2-17. **(USA)**

Kahan, B. (1994) *Growing up in Groups*, London: HMSO

Kalichman, S.C. (1993) *Mandated Reporting of Suspected Child Abuse: Ethics, Law and Policy*, Washington, DC: American Psychological Association. **(USA)**

Kalichman, S.C. and Brosig, C.L. (1992) The effects of statutory requirements on child maltreatment reporting: A comparison of two state laws, *American Journal of Orthopsychiatry*, Vol 62 No 2, pp. 284-296 **(USA)**

Kamerman, S.B. and Kahn, A.J. (1990) Social services for children, youth and families in the United States [Special Issue] *Children and Youth Services Review*, Vol 12. **(USA)**

Karban, K and Mills, S. (1995) Testing the market - The recruitment of qualified and experienced residential child care staff, *Journal of Practice and Staff Development*, Vol 4 No 4, pp. 21-33.

Katz, M. (1988) Crisis intervention in residential care, in C.E. Schaefer & A.J. Swanson (eds) *Children in Residential Care: Critical Issues in Treatment*, New York: Van Nostrand Rheinhold, pp. 30-49. **(USA)**

Kelleher M.E. (1987) Investigating institutional abuse: a post-substantiation model, *Child Welfare*, Vol 66 No 4, pp 343 - 351. **(USA)**

Kelly, B. (1992) *Children Inside: A Study of Secure Provision*, London: Routledge.

Kelly, G. and Pinkerton, J. (1996) The Children (Northern Ireland) Order 1995: Prospects for Progress? in Hill, M. and Aldgate, J. (eds) *Child Welfare Services: Developments in Law, Policy, Practice and Research*, London: Jessica Kingsley Publishers, pp. 40-55

Kelly, L. (1992a) The connections between disability and child abuse: A review of the research evidence, *Child Abuse Review*, Vol 1, pp. 157-167

Kelly, L. (1992b) Can't hear or won't hear? - The evidential experience of children with disabilities, *Child Abuse Review*, Vol 1, pp. 188-190

Kelly, L. and Scott, S. (1993) The current literature about organized abuse of children, *Child Abuse Review*, Vol 2, pp. 281-287.

Kelly, J. (1995) Blissful ignorance, *Community Care*, 22.6.95, pp. 26-27

Kendrick, A. (1994) *Fostering Assessment in the Context of Child Sexual Abuse: A Literature Review*, Dundee: Tayside Region Social Work Department.

Kendrick, A. (1995) *Residential Care in the Integration of Child Care Services*, Central Research Unit Papers, Edinburgh: Scottish Office.

Kendrick, A. and Fraser, A. (1992) The review of residential child care in Scotland: a literature review', in *The Review of Residential Child Care in Scotland: The Three Supporting Research Studies*, Central Research Unit Papers, Edinburgh: Scottish Office.

Kendrick, A.J. and Mapstone, E. (1991) 'Who decides?: child care reviews in two Scottish social work departments', *Children & Society*, Vol 5, No. 2, pp. 165 - 181.

Kendrick, A.J. and Mapstone, E. (1992) *Social Work Department Reviews of Children in Care*, Central Research Unit Papers, Edinburgh: Scottish Office.

Kendrick, A., Simpson, M. and Mapstone, E. (1996) *Getting it Together: Changing Services for Children and Young People in Difficulty*, York: Joseph Rowntree Foundation.

Kennedy, M. (1992) Not the only way to communicate: A challenge to voice in child protection work, *Child Abuse Review*, Vol 1, pp. 169-177.

Kennedy, M. and Kelly, L. (1992) Inclusion not exclusion, *Child Abuse Review*, Vol 1, pp. 147-149

Kempe, C.H., Silverman, F., Steele, B., Droegmueller, W. and Silver, H. (1962) Battered-child Syndrome, *Journal of the American Medical Association*, Vol 181, p. 17-24. **(USA)**

King, M.B. (1992) Male rape in institutional settings, in Mezey, G.C. and King, M.B. (eds) *Male Victims of Sexual Assault*. Oxford: Oxford University Press, pp. 67-74.

Kirkwood, A. (1993) *The Leicestershire Inquiry 1992*, Leicester: Leicestershire County Council.

Knutson, J.F. and Sullivan, P.M. (1993) Communicative disorders as a risk factor in abuse, *Topics in Language Disorders*, Vol 13 No 4, pp.1-14. **(USA)**

Krause, K. (1974) Authoritarianism, dogmatism, and coercion in child caring institutions: a study of staff attitudes. *Child Welfare*, Vol 53, pp. 23-30. **(USA)**

Kufeldt, K. and Nimmo, M (1987) Youth on the street: abuse and neglect in the eighties, *Child Abuse & Neglect*, Vol 11, pp. 531-543 **(Canada)**

La Fontaine, J. (1990) *Child Sexual Abuse*, Polity Press: Cambridge

La Fontaine, J. and Morris, S. (1991) *The Boarding School Line: January - July 1991, A Report from ChildLine to the D.E.S.*, London: ChildLine.

Lambert, P. (1976) Memo to child care workers: notes on the management of sex and stealing, *Child Welfare*, Vol 55 No 5, pp 329-334. **(USA)**

Lambert, R and Millham, S. (1968) *The Hothouse Society: An Exploration of Boarding-School Life through the Boys' and Girls' Own Writings*, London: Weidenfield and Nicholoson.

Lanning, K.V. (1986) *Child Molesters: A Behavioral Analysis*, Washington D.C.: Center for Missing and Exploited Children. **(USA)**

Leadbetter, D. (1996) Technical aspects of physical restraint, *Physical Restraint - Practice, Legal, Medical & Technical Considerations*, Glasgow: Centre for Residential Child Care, pp 33-48

Lee, M. and O'Brien, R. (1995) *The Game's Up: Redefining Child Prostitution*, London: The Children's Society.

Leenders, F. (1995) Malevolent intervention, *Paediatric Nursing*, Vol 7 No 9, pp. 6-7.

Levy, A. and Kahan, B. (1991) *The Pindown Experience and the Protection of Children: The Report of the Staffordshire Child Care Inquiry*, Stafford: Staffordshire County Council.

Lewis, C.L. (1996) The Jacob Wetterling Crimes against Children and Sexually Violent Offender Registration Act: An unconstitutional deprivation of the right to privacy and substantive due process, *Harvard Civil Rights-Civil Liberties Law Review*, Vol 31, pp. 89-118. **(USA)**

Liebling, A. (1992) Suicides in prisons - young offenders, *Prison Service Journal*, Issue 85, pp. 10-19.

Liebling, A. (1993) Suicides in young prisoners: A summary, *Death Studies*, Vol 17 No 5, pp. 381-409

Liebling, A. (1995) Vulnerability and prison suicide, *British Journal of Criminology*, Vol 35 No 2, pp. 173-187.

Liebling, A. and Krarup, H. (1994) Suicide attempts in male prisons, *Home Office Research and Statistics Department Research Bulletin*, No 36, pp. 38-43.

Liddell, M.J. (1990) Black on black: system abuse of adolescents needing care and protection, in Slattery, M. (ed) VICSPAN *Third Annual Conference: Proceedings*, Port Melbourne, Victoria, Victorian Society for the Prevention of Child Abuse and Neglect, pp. 134-143. (Australia)

Lindsay, M. (1991) Complaints procedures and their limitations in the light of the "Pindown" inquiry, *Journal of Social Welfare and Family Law*, pp. 432-441.

Lindsay, M. and Rayner, S. (1993) Balanced judgements, *Community Care*, 1 June 1993, pp. 24-25.

Lindsay, M. (1996) Chapter Two, *Physical Restraint - Practice, Legal, Medical & Technical Considerations*, Glasgow: Centre for Residential Child Care, pp7-11.

Lindsey, D. (1994) Mandated reporting and child abuse fatalities - requirements for a system to protect children, *Social Work Research*, Vol 18 No 1, pp 41 - 54. (USA)

Little, M. (1990) *Young Men in Prison: The Criminal Identity Explored Through the Rules of Behaviour*, Dartmouth: Aldershot.

Long, T. (1992) 'To protect the public and ensure that justice is done': an examination of the Philip Donnelly case, *Journal of Advanced Nursing*, Vol 17 No 1, pp. 5-9.

Lowe, M.I. and Verity, P. (1989) The right to dignity, fairness and compassion, *Foster Care*, March 1989, pp.14-15.

Ludbrook, R. (1994) *Why Australia Needs a Commissioner for Children*, Discussion Paper No 2, Sydney: National Children's and Youth Law Centre. **(Australia)**

Lunn, J. (1994) Implications of the Allitt inquiry, *British Journal of Nursing*, Vol 3 No 5, pp. 201-202

Lyon, C.M. (1996) The impact of legal provisions, England and Wales (with occasional notes on Northern Ireland), in Williams of Mostyn (1996) *Childhood Matters: Report of the National Commission of Inquiry into the Prevention of Child Abuse*, London: The Stationery Office, Appendix 11, pp. 262-333.

Macaskill, C. (1991) *Adopting or Fostering a Sexually Abused Child*, Batsford: London.

MacDonald, A. (1995) Allitt: lest we forget, *Paediatric Nursing*, Vol 7 No 9, pp. 10-11

MacDonald, A. (1996) Responding to the results of the Beverly Allitt inquiry, *Nursing Times*, Vol 10 No 92, pp. 23-25.

Maclean, K. (1989) Towards a fee-paid fostering service, *Adoption and Fostering*, Vol 13 No 3.

Mahoney, K.S. (1995) School personnel and mandated reporting of child maltreatment, *Journal of Law and Education*, Vol 24 No 2, pp. 227-239. **(USA)**

Marchant, R. and Page, M. (1992) Bridging the gap: investigating the abuse of children with multiple disabilities, *Child Abuse Review*, Vol 1, pp. 179-183.

Margolin, L. (1991) Child sexual abuse by non-related caregivers, *Child Abuse and Neglect*, Vol 15 No 3, pp. 213 - 221. **(USA)**

Margolin, L. and Craft, J.L. (1990) Child abuse by adolescent caregivers, *Child Abuse and Neglect*, Vol 14, pp. 365 - 373. **(USA)**

Marrett, M. (1991) Raw deal for black children in care, *Community Care Insight*, pp. vii-viii

Marshall, K. (1996) The National Commission of Inquiry into the Prevention of Child Abuse: Legal provisions, Scotland, in Williams of Mostyn (1996) *Childhood Matters: Report of the National Commission of Inquiry into the Prevention of Child Abuse*, London: The Stationery Office, Appendix 10, pp. 237-261.

Maslach, C. and Jackson, S.E., (1981) *Maslach Burnout Inventory*, California: Consulting Lists Press (USA)

Mattingly, M.A. (1981) Occupational stress for group care personnel, in Ainsworth, F. and Fulcher, L. C. (eds) *Group Care for Children: Concepts and Issues*, London: Tavistock,

Maximé, J.E. (1986) Some psychological models of black self-concept, in Ahmed, S, Cheetham, J., and Small, J.(eds) *Social Work with Black Children and their Families*, London: Batsford, pp. 100-116.

McCormack, A. and Selvaggio, M. (1989) Screening for pedophiles in youth-oriented community agencies, *Social Casework: The Journal of Contemporary Social Work*,Vol. 70 No1, pp. 37-42 **(USA)**

McFadden, E.J. and Ryan, P. (1991) Maltreatment in family foster homes: dynamics and dimensions, *Child & Youth Services*, Vol 15 No 2, pp. 209 - 231. **(USA)**

McGrath T. (1986) Overcoming institutionalized child abuse: creating a positive therapeutic climate, *Journal of Child Care*, Vol 2 pp 59 - 65. **(Canada)**

McHale, J.V. (1992) Whistleblowing in the NHS, *Journal of Social Welfare and Family Law*, pp. 363-371.

McNeil, E.B. and Morse, W.C. (1964) The institutional management of sex in emotionally disturbed children, *American Journal of Orthopsychiatry*, Vol 34, pp 115-124 **(USA)**

Mercer, M. (1982) Closing the barn door: the prevention of institutional abuse through standards, *Child & Youth Services*, Vol 4 Nos 1-2, pp. 127-132. **(USA)**

Millham, S., Bullock, R. Hosie, K. and Haak, M. (1981) *Issues of Control in Residential Child-care*, London: HMSO.

Mills, S. (1995) Creating a safe environment in residential child care, in Stone, K. and Vallender, I. (eds) *Spinning Plates - Practice Teaching and Learning for the Residential Child Care Initiative*, London: CCETSW, pp. 59-63.

Milner, J.S. (1991) Physical child abuse perpetrator screening and evaluation, *Criminal Justice and Behavior*, Vol 18 No 1, pp. 47-63. **(USA)**

Milner, J.S., Gold, R.G., Ayoub, C. and Jacewitz, M.M. (1984) Predictive validity of the child abuse potential inventory, *Journal of Consulting and Clinical Psychology*, Vol 52 No 5, pp. 879-884. **(USA)**

Milner, J.S. and Robertson, K.R. (1985) Development of a random response scale for the child abuse potential inventory, *Journal of Clinical Psychology*, Vol 41 No 5, pp. 639-643. **(USA)**

Mitchell, D. (1993) Natural selection, *Community Care*, 25 November 1993, pp. 28-29.

Molin, R. (1988) Treatment of children in foster care: issues in collaboration, *Child Abuse & Neglect*, Vol 12, pp. 241-250. **(USA)**

Monroe, L.D. and Schellenback, C.J. (1989) Relationship of child abuse potential inventory scores to parental responses: a construct validity study, *Child & Family Behavior Therapy*, Vol 11 No 3/4, pp 39-57. **(USA)**

Morgan, R. (1993) *School Life: Pupils' Views on Boarding*, London: HMSO.

Morris, S. amd Wheatley, H. (1994) *Time to Listen: The Experiences of Young People in Foster and Residential Care*, London: Childline.

Moss, M., Sharpe, S. and Fay, C. (1990) *Abuse in the Care System: A Pilot Study by the National Association of Young People in Care*, London: National Association of Young People in Care (NAYPIC).

Motz, J.K. & Nunno, M.A. (1988) Institutional abuse case review teams, in Bross, D.C., Krugman, R.D., Lenherr, M.R., Rosenberg, D.A. and Schmitt, B.D. (eds) *The New Child Protection Team Handbook*, New York: Garland Publishing, Inc. **(USA)**

NCH (1992) *The Report of the Committee of Inquiry into Children and Young People who Sexually Abuse Other Children*, London: National Children's Home.

NFCA (1993) Assessment, *Making it Work*, London: National Foster Care Association, London.

NFCA (1996) *Foster Care Training: A Guide to NFCA Training Courses in Scotland 1996/97*, Glasgow: NFCA

Nixon, S. and Verity, P. (1996) Allegations against foster families, *Foster Care*, January 1996, pp. 11-14.

Nunno, M. and Motz, J.R. (1988) The development of an effective response to the abuse of children in out-of-home care, *Child Abuse & Neglect*, Vol 12, pp. 521 - 528. **(USA).**

Nunno, M. and Rindfleisch, N. (1991) The abuse of children in out of home care, *Children & Society*, Vol 5 No 4, pp 295 - 305

O'Connor, A. (1996) Mandatory child abuse reporting urged, *Irish Times on the Web*, http://194.125.58.5/irish-times/paper/0418/hom20.html. **(Ireland)**

O'Mahony, B. (1989) Key issues for managing adolescent sexual behaviour in residential establishments, in A. Hollows and H. Armstrong (eds) *Working with Sexually Abused Boys*, London: National Children's Bureau, pp. 31-34

O'Neill, M., Goode, N. and Hopkins, K. (1995) Juvenile prostitutes: the experience of young women in residential care, *Childright*, No 113, pp. 14-16.

O'Neill, M., Green, J., and Mulroy, S. (forthcoming) Young people and prostitution from a youth service perspective, in Barrett, D. (ed) *Child Prostitution*, London, National Children's Bureau.

Overton, J. (1993) Child abuse, corporal punishment, and the question of discipline: the case of Mount Cashel, *Critical Social Policy*, Issue 36, pp. 73-95

Page, R. and Clark, G.A. (eds) (1977) *Who Cares? Young People in Care Speak Out*, London: National Children's Bureau.

Parkin, W. (1989) Private experiences in the public domain: sexuality and residential care organizations, in Hearn, J. (ed) *The Sexuality of Organizations*, London: Sage Publications.

Parliament of Victoria Crime Prevention Committee (1995) *Combating Child Sexual Assault: An Integrated Model*, First Report upon the Inquiry into Sexual Offences against Children and Adults, Melbourne: L.V.North, Government Printer. **(Australia)**

Payne, M. (1995) Understanding going missing - issues for social work and social services, *British Journal of Social Work*, Vol 25 No 3, pp 333 - 348

Pine, B.A. and Jacob, M. (1989) The training of foster parents for work with adolescents, in Aldgate, J., Maluccio, A. and Reeves, C. (eds) *Adolescents in Foster Families*, London: Batsford.

Police Complaints Authority (1993) *Inquiry into Police Investigation of Complaints of Child and Sexual Abuse in Leicestershire Children's Homes: A Summary*, London: Police Complaints Authority.

Poteat, G.M., Cope, J.G., Choate, C. and Grossnickle, W.F. (1989) Wife abuse as it affects work behavior in a center for mentally retarded persons, *Journal of Clinical Psychology*, Vol 45 No 2, pp. 324-330 **(USA)**

Power, K.G. and Spencer, A.P. (1987) Parasuicidal behaviour of detained Scottish young offenders, *International Journal of Offender Therapy and Comparative Criminology*, Vol 31 No 3, pp. 227-35.

Powers, J., Mooney, A. and Nunno, M. (1990) Institutional abuse: a review of the literature, *Journal of Child and Youth Care*, Vol 4 No 6, pp. 81-95. **(USA)**

Powers, J.L., Eckenrode, J. and Jaklitsch, B. (1990) Maltreatment among runaway and homeless youth, *Child Abuse & Neglect*, Vol 14, pp 87-98.

Pringle, K. (1993) Child sexual abuse perpetrated by welfare personnel and the problem of men, *Critical Social Policy*, vol 36, pp. 4 - 19.

Rabb, J. and Rindfleisch, N. (1985) A study to define and assess severity of institutional abuse/neglect, *Child Abuse & Neglect*, Vol 9, pp 285 - 294. **(USA)**

Rauche-Elnekave, R, H. (1989) Advocacy and ombudswork for children: Implications of the Israeli experience, *Child Welfare*, Vol 58 No 2, pp. 101-112. **(Israel)**

Rees, G. (1995) Running away from residential care, in Stone, K. and Vallender, I. (eds) *Spinning Plates - Practice Teaching and Learning for the Residential Child Care Initiative*, London: CCETSW.

Reiniger, A., Robison, E. and McHugh, M. (1995) Mandated training of professionals - a means for improving reporting of suspected child-abuse, *Child Abuse & Neglect*, Vol 19 No 1, pp 63 - 69. **(USA)**

Repper, J. (1995) Munchausen Syndrome by Proxy in health care workers, *Journal of Advanced Nursing*, Vol 21, pp. 299-304.

Rhodes, P. (1993) Charitable vocation or 'proper job'? the role of payment in foster care, *Adoption and Fostering*, Vol 17 No 1, pp. 8 - 13.

Rindfleisch, N. (1988a) Combating institutional abuse, in C.E. Schaefer and A.J. Swanson (eds) *Children in Residential Care: Critical Issues in Treatment*, New York: Van Nostrand Rheinhold, pp. 263-283. **(USA)**

Rindfleisch, N. (1988b) Political obstacles to reporting in residential child care settings, in Manye A. and Wells S. (eds) *Professional Responsibilities in Protecting Children*, New York: Praeger. **(USA)**

Rindfleisch, N. and Baros-Van Hull, J. (1982) Direct care workers' attitudes toward use of physical force with children, *Child & Youth Services*, Vol 4, pp 115 - 125. **(USA)**

Rindfleisch, N. and Bean, G.J. (1988) Willingness to report abuse and neglect in residential facilities, *Child Abuse & Neglect*, Vol 12 No 4, pp 509 - 520. **(USA)**

Rindfleisch, N. and Hicho, D. (1987) Institutional child protection: Issues in program development and implementation, *Child Welfare*, Vol 63, pp 329 - 342. **(USA)**

Rindfleisch, N. and Nunno, M. (1992) Progress and issues in the implementation of the 1984 out-of-home care protection amendment, *Child Abuse & Neglect*, Vol 16, pp 693-708. **(USA)**

Rindfleisch, N. and Rabb, J. (1984a) How much of a problem is resident mistreatment in child welfare institutions, *Child Abuse & Neglect*, Vol 8, pp 33 - 40. **(USA)**

Rindfleisch, N. and Rabb, J. (1984b) Dilemmas in planning for the protection of children and youths in residential facilities, *Child Welfare*, Vol 63, pp 205 - 215. **(USA)**

Roberts, J. (1986) Fostering the sexually abused child, *Adoption and Fostering*, Vol 10 No 1, pp. 8 - 11.

Roberts, J. (1989) Substitute care of abused and neglected children, *Adoption and Fostering*, Vol 13 No 3, pp. 37 - 43.

Roberts, J. (1993) Abused children and foster care - the need for specialist resources, *Child Abuse Review*, Vol 2, pp. 3 - 14

Robertson, K.R. and Milner, J.S. (1985) Convergent and discriminant validity of the child abuse potential inventory, *Journal of Personality Assessment*, Vol 49 No 1, pp. 86-88. **(USA)**

Robin, M. (1982) The abuse of status offenders in private hospitals, *Child & Youth Services*, Vol 4 Nos 1-2, pp. 79-87. **(USA)**

Robinson, J. (1991) Beyond the frontiers of fostering - the employment of a 'professional carer', *Adoption and Fostering*, Vol 15 No 1, pp 47 - 49.

Robitaille, J., Jones, E., Gold, R.G., Robertson, K.R., and Milner, J.S. (1985) Child abuse potential and authoritarianism, *Journal of Clinical Psychology*, Vol 41 No 6, pp. 839-844 **(USA).**

Rogers, R. (1993) Qualified in caring?, *Nursing Standard*, Vol 8 No 22, pp. 21-22.

Ronstrom, A. (1989) Sweden's children's ombudsman:: A spokesperson for children, *Child Welfare*, Vol 58 No 2, pp. 123-128. **(Sweden)**

Rosenbaum, M. and Newell, P. (1991) *Taking Children Seriously: A Proposal for a Children's Rights Commissioner*, London: Calouste Gulbenkian Foundation.

Rosenthal, J., Motz, J., Edmondson, D., and Groze, V. (1991) A descriptive study of abuse and neglect in out-of-home placement, *Child Abuse & Neglect*, Vol 15, pp. 249 - 260. **(USA)**

Ross, A.L. and Hoeltke, G. (1985) A tool for selecting residential child care workers: An initial report, *Child Welfare*, Vol 64 No 1, pp. 46-54. **(USA)**

Ross, A.L. and Hoeltke, G. (1987) An interviewing tool for selection of residential child care workers: a follow-up report, *Child Welfare*, Vol 66 No 2, pp. 175-183. **(USA)**

Ross, S. (1994) Controlling children's "challenging behaviour", *SCOLAG Journal*, August 1994, p. 115-116

Royal College of Nursing (1994) *The Care of Sick Children: A Review of the Guidelines in the Wake of the Allitt Inquiry*, London: Royal College of Nursing.

Royal College of Nursing (1996) Protection of nurses working with children and young people, *Issues in Nursing and Health*, No 39.

Russell, D. (1984) *Sexual Exploitation: Rape, Child Sexual Abuse and Workplace Harassment*, Newbury Park: Sage Publications. **(USA)**

Ryburn, M. (1991) The myth of assessment, *Adoption and Fostering*, Vol 15 No 1, pp. 21 - 26.

Safe & Sound (1995) *So Who Are We Meant to Trust Now? Responding to Abuse in Care: The Experiences of Young People*, London: NSPCC.

Sanders, R.M. and McAllen, A. (1995) Training foster carers of children who have been sexually abused: issues and dilemmas, *Child Abuse Review*, Vol 4, pp. 136-145.

Savells, J. (1983) Child abuse in residential institutions and community programs for intervention and prevention, *Child Abuse & Neglect*, Vol 7, pp. 473-475 **(USA)**

Scottish Office (1996) *On the Record in Scotland: Proposals for Improved Access to Criminal Records*, Edinburgh: The Scottish Office.

Seymour, J. (1990) Family crisis, *Social Work Today*, 6 September 1990, pp. 14 - 15

Sharp, S. and Smith, P.K. (1993) Tackling bullying: The Sheffield Project, in Tattum, D. (ed.) *Understanding and Managing Bullying*, Oxford: Heinemann School Management, pp. 45-56..

Shaughnessy, M.F. (1984) Institutional child abuse, *Children and Youth Services Review*, Vol 6, pp. 311 - 318. **(USA)**

Shaw, M. (1989) Thinking about assessment of foster parents, in Aldgate, J., Maluccio, A. and Reeves, C. (eds) *Adolescents in Foster Families*, London: Batsford.

Silberberg, N.E. and Silberberg, M.C. (1982) Abusing poor children by trying to protect them, *Child & Youth Services*, Vol 4 Nos 1-2, pp. 133-137. **(USA)**

Simms, P. (1995) Measuring equality in residential care, in Stone, K. and Vallender, I. (eds) *Spinning Plates - Practice Teaching and Learning for the Residential Child Care Initiative*, London: CCETSW, pp. 53-58.

Sinason, V. (1989) , Uncovering and responding to sexual abuse in psychotherapeutic settings, in Brown, H. and Craft, A. (eds) *Thinking the Unthinkable: Papers on Sexual Abuse and People with Learning Difficulties*, London: FPA Education Unit, pp. 39-49

Sinclair, R. (1996) Children's and young people's participation in decision-making: the legal framework in social services and education, in Hill, M. and Aldgate, J. (eds) *Child Welfare Services: Developments in Law, Policy, Practice and Research*, London: Jessica Kingsley.

Sinclair, R. and Grimshaw, R. (1995) *Planning and Reviewing under the Children Act: Shaping a Framework for Practice*, London: National Children's Bureau.

Single, T. (1989) Child sexual assault in which the alleged offender is a child care professional, *Australian Social Work*, Vol 42 No 4, pp. 21-28. **(Australia)**

Siskind, A.B. (1986) Issues in institutional child sexual abuse: The abused, the abuser and the system, *Residential Treatment for Children & Youth*, Vol 4 No 2, pp 9-30 **(USA)**

Skett, S., Braham, L. and Samuel, J. (1996) Drugs and violence in a young offender establishment, *Prison Service Journal*, Issue 106, pp. 9-13.

Skinner, A. (1992) *Another Kind of Home: A Review of Residential Child Care*, Edinburgh: The Scottish Office.

Sluyter, G.V. and Cleland, C.C. (1979) Resident abuse: a continuing dilemma, *American Corrective Therapy Journal*, Vol 33, pp. 99-102 **(USA)**

Small, J. (1986) Transracial placements: conflicts and contradictions, in Ahmed, S, Cheetham, J., and Small, J.(eds) *Social Work with Black Children and their Families*, London: Batsford.

Social Services Inspectorate (undated a) *Caring for Children: A Study of Residential Care in Northern Ireland*, Belfast: Department of Health and Social Services.

Social Services Inspectorate (undated b) *Corporate Parents: Inspection of Residential Child Care Services in 11 Local Authorities, November 1992 to March 1993*, London: Social Services Inspectorate.

Social Services Inspectorate (1994) *Standards for Residential Child Care Services: A Handbook for Social Services Managers and Inspectors, Users of Services and their Families*, London: HMSO.

Social Work Services Inspectorate (1996) *A Secure Remedy: a Review of the Role, Availability and Quality of Secure Accommodation for Children in Scotland*, Edinburgh: Social Work Services Inspectorate.

Sone, K. (1992) Fostering abuse, *Community Care*, 13 February 1992, pp. 12 - 14

Spencer, J.W. and Knudsen, D.D. (1992) Out-of-home maltreatment - an analysis of risk in various settings for children, *Children & Youth Services Review*, Vol 14 No 6, pp 485 - 492 **(USA)**

Stark, C. (1996) Medical aspects of physical restraint, *Physical Restraint - Practice, Legal, Medical & Technical Considerations*, Glasgow: Centre for Residential Child Care, pp 29-32.

Stein, M., Rees, G. and Frost, M. (1994) *Running - the Risk; Young People on the Streets of Britain Today*, London: The Children's Society.

Sullivan, P.M.. (1993) Sexual abuse therapy for special children, *Journal of Child Sexual Abuse*, Vol 2 No 2, pp. 117-125 **(USA)**

Sullivan, P.M., Brookhouser, P.E., Knutson, J.F., Scanlan, J.M. and Schulte, L.E. (1991) Patterns of physical and sexual abuse of communicatively handicapped children, *Annals of Otology, Rhinology & Laryngology*, Vol 100 No 3, pp. 188-194 **(USA)**

Sullivan, P.M. and Scanlon, J.M. (1990) Psychotherapy with handicapped sexually abused children, *Developmental Disabilities Bulletin*, Vol 18 No 2, pp. 21-34. **(USA)**

Sullivan, P.M., Vernon, M. and Scanlan, J.M. (1987) Sexual abuse of deaf youth, *American Annals of the Deaf*, Vol 132, pp. 256-262

Support Force for Children's Residential Care (1995a) *Code of Practice for the Employment of Residential Child Care Workers*, London: DoH.

Support Force for Children's Residential Care (1995b) *Staff Supervision in Children's Homes*, London: DoH.

Support Force for Children's Residential Care (1996) *Good Care Matters: Ways of Enhancing Good Practice in Residential Child Care*, London: DoH.

Sussman, A. (1975) Child abuse reporting: a review of the literature, in Sussman, A. and Cohen, S. (eds.) *Reporting Child Abuse and Neglect: Guidelines for Legislation*, Cambridge, MA: Ballinger, pp. 57-115. **(USA)**

Sutton, P. (1995) *Crossing the Boundaries: A Discussion of Children's Services Plans*, London: National Children's Bureau.

Swanson, A.J. and Richard, B.A. (1988) Discipline and child behaviour managment in group care, in C.E. Schaefer and A.J. Swanson (eds) *Children in Residential Care: Critical Issues in Treatment*, New York, Van Nostrand Rheinhold, pp. 77-88. **(USA)**

Swanson, D., (1987) Stress and burnout I: the development of a taxonomy, *Residential Treatment for Children and Youth*, Vol. 4 No. 3, pp. 9 - 30. **(USA)**

Tattum, D. (1993) Short, medium and long-term management strategies, in Tattum, D. (ed.) *Understanding and Managing Bullying*, Oxford: Heinemann School Management, pp. 59-75.

Tattum, D. (1995) Bullying in prisons, *Young Minds Newsletter*, Issue 22, pp. 18-19

Thanki, V. (1994) Ethnic diversity and child protection, *Children & Society*, Vol 8 No 3, pp. 232-244.

Thomas, B.R. (1982) Protecting abused children: helping until it hurts, *Child & Youth Services*, Vol 4 Nos 1-2, pp. 139-154. **(USA)**

Thomas, N. (1995) Allegations of child abuse in local authority care, *Practice*, Vol 7 No 3, pp. 35-44.

Tolfree, D. (1995) *Roofs and Roots: The Care of Separated Children in the Developing World:* Aldershot: Arena

Tomison, A. (1995) New measures for combating child sexual assault, *Family Matters*, No 42, pp. 36-41. **(Australia)**

Tomison, A. (1996) A summary of mandatory reporting across Australia, *Child Abuse Prevention*, Vol 4 No 2, pp. 7-8. **(Australia)**

Triseliotis, J, Borland, M., Hill, M., and Lambert, L. (1995) *Teenagers and Social Work Services*, London: HMSO.

Turnbull, A. (1995) A challenge to residential fundamentalists, *Centrestage, The Newsletter of Scottish Residential Childcare*, Issue 3, p. 4.

Utting, W. (1991) *Children in the Public Care: A Review of Residential Child Care*, London: HMSO.

Verity, P. and Nixon, S. (1995) Allegations against foster families: Survey results, *Foster Care*, October 1995, pp. 13-16

Vinten, G. (ed.) (1994) *Whistleblowing: Subversion or Corporate Citizenship*, London: Paul Chapman Publishing Ltd.

Vizard, E. (1989) Child sexual abuse and mental handicap: A child psychiatrist's perspective, in Brown, H. and Craft, A. (eds) *Thinking the Unthinkable: Papers on Sexual Abuse and People with Learning Difficulties*, London: FPA Education Unit, pp. 18-25.

Walford, G. (1989) Bullying in public schools: myth or reality, in Tattum, D. and Lane, D.A. (1989), *Bullying in Schools*, Stoke-on-Trent: Trentham Books, pp. 81-88.

Waller, B. and Lindsay, M. (1990) The abuse of power, *Community Care*, 21 June 1990, pp. 20 - 22.

Walmsley, S. (1989) The need for safeguards, in Brown, H. and Craft, A. (eds) *Thinking the Unthinkable: Papers on Sexual Abuse and People with Learning Difficulties*, London: FPA Education Unit, pp. 5-16

Walters, D. (1995) Mandatory reporting of child-abuse - Legal, ethical and clinical implications within a Canadian context, *Canadian Psychology*, Vol 36 No 3, pp. 163 - 182. **(Canada)**

Ward, D. (1997) Paedophile 'led a career of abuse', *The Guardian*, 8 March 1997, p. 5.

Wardhaugh, J. and Wilding, P. (1993) Towards an explanation of the corruption of care, *Critical Social Policy*, Issue 37, pp. 4-31)

Warner, N. (1992) *Choosing with Care: The Report of the Committee of Inquiry into the Selection, Development and Management of Staff in Children's Homes*, London: HMSO.

Waterhouse, L, Dobash, R.P. and Carnie, J. (1994) *Child Sexual Abusers*, Central Research Unit Papers, Edinburgh: Scottish Office.

West, R. (1996) Protecting people in residential care, *Can Do - Newsletter of the New South Wales Community Services Commission*, Issue. 8, pp. 1-3. **(Australia)**

Westcott, H. (1991a) *Institutional Abuse of Children - From Research to Policy: A Review*, London: NSPCC.

Westcott, H.L. (1991b) The abuse of disabled children: a review of the literature, *Child: Care, Health and Development*, Vol 17 No 4, pp. 243-258.

Westcott, H. (1993) *Abuse of Children and Adults with Disablities*, London: NSPCC

Westcott, H. and Clement, M. (1992) *NSPCC Experience of Child Abuse in Residential Care and Educational Placements: Results of a Survey*, London: NSPCC.

Weisberg, D. (1985) *Children of the Night*, Boston: Lexington Books. **(USA)**

Whitaker, J.K. (1987) The role of residential institutions, in Garbarino, J., Brookhouser, P.E. and Authier, K.J. (eds) *Special Children - Special Risks: The Maltreatment of Children with Disabilities*, New York: Aldine de Gruyter, pp. 83-100. **(USA)**

White, K., (1987), Residential care of adolescents: residents, carers and sexual issues in Horobin, G. (ed) *Sex, Gender and Care Work*, Research Highlights in Social Work 15, London: Jessica Kingsley.

White, R. (1993) Residential care under review, *Child Abuse Review*, Vol 2, pp. 134-136.

Williams,G. and McCreadie, J. (1992) *Ty Mawr Community Home Inquiry*, Gwent County Council.

Williams of Mostyn (1996) *Childhood Matters: Report of the National Commission of Inquiry into the Prevention of Child Abuse*, London: The Stationery Office.

Willow, C. (1996) *Children's Rights and Participation in Residential Care*, London: National Children's Bureau.

Zellman, G. and Antler, S. (1990) Mandated reporters and CPS: a study in frustration, *Public Welfare*, Vol 48 No 1, pp. 30-37. **(USA)**

Zuckerman, M. Abrams, H.A. and Neuhring, E.M. (1986) Protection and advocacy agencies: National survey of efforts to prevent residential abuse and neglect, *Mental Retardation*, Vol 24, pp 197 - 201. **(USA)**

Zuravin, S.J., Benedict, M. and Somerfield, M. (1993) Child maltreatment in family foster care, *American Journal of Orthopsychiatry*, Vol 63 No 4, pp. 589-596 **(USA)**

Printed in Scotland for The Stationery Office Limited
J26955 , C20, 11/97, CCN 003808.